LEARNING BEHAVIORAL ECONOMY

EDITION 2

JOHN LOK

Made with ♥ on the Notion Press Platform
www.notionpress.com

Contents

Contents

Preface

This book delves into the application of behavioral economic methods to predict consumer behavior, providing readers with a comprehensive understanding of how these methods can be utilized in various industries.

Key Content Explained

Behavioral Economic Methods: The book discusses various behavioral economic techniques that can help in predicting consumer behavior. It emphasizes the importance of understanding psychological factors that influence purchasing decisions, which traditional economic theories often overlook.

Comparison of Methods: This book compares different solvable suggestions within the context of consumer behavioral challenges across various industries. This comparative analysis allows readers to evaluate the advantages and disadvantages of each method, helping them make informed decisions about which approach might be more effective in specific scenarios.

Practical Applications: The text provides practical examples from sample industries, illustrating how behavioral economic methods can be applied to real-world situations. This hands-on approach aids students and practitioners in grasping complex concepts and applying them effectively.

Consumer Psychology: A significant portion of the book is dedicated to exploring consumer psychology—how emotions, biases, and cognitive limitations affect buying behavior. By integrating psychological insights with economic principles, this book aims to offer a more nuanced perspective on consumer actions compared to traditional models.

Predictive Accuracy: This book argues for the superiority of behavioral economic theory over traditional economic theory when it comes to predicting consumer behavior. This book posits that because behavioral economics takes into account psychological influences and environmental factors, it provides a more accurate framework for understanding why consumers make certain choices.

In summary, "Learning Behavioral Economic Method To" serves as an essential resource for anyone interested in understanding the dynamics of consumer behavior through the lens of behavioral economics, equipping readers with tools and insights necessary for effective application in marketing and business strategies.

Prologue

Table of content

CHAPTER I

How human behavior influences social change

(BE) Behavioral economics is primarily concerned with the bounds of rationality of economic agents. Behavioral models typically bring insights from psychology and microeconomic theory. The study of behavioral economics includes how market decisions are made and the mechanisms that drive public choice. Moreover, behavioral economic plays a important role in our lives and in the economy because it can help businesses to explain why we consume the kind of goods and services , the way we do, why we make certain choices of action, the key contibution to behavioral economics, it uses psychological and experimentation to develop theories about human decision making, and has identified a range of biases as a result of the way people think and feel . (BE) is trying to change the way economics think about people's perception of value and expresses preferences.

● Have they relationship between consumer behaviors and economy ?
The success or failure of a nation's economy can greatly affect consumer behavior based on a variety of economic factors. If the economy is strong, consumers have more purchase power and money is spent , f the economy is poor, the reverse is true. Consumer behavior in economics means to explain of how individual cstomers, groups or organizations select, buy, use and dispose ideas, goods and services. A such, consumers play a vitual role in the economic system of a capitalist economy. Without consumer demand, producers would lack one of the key motivations to produce to sell to consumers.
The motivates consumers behavioral economic perspective, it is the new field of behavioral economics has shown them, in practice, people's decisions can be greatly influenced by seemingly irrelevant aspects of their personalities and by the environment in which their decisions are made. So, it seems that consumer buying behavior changes during economic crisis.

In organization how resources choices to use in behavioral economy view, though the number and variety of the different resources businesses require is limitless. Economists divide factors of production into three basic categories: Land, labour and capital. Land refers to all of the natural resources that businessed need to make and distribut goods and services, labours to make and distribute goods and services, labours refers how the organization chooses to employ the employee skill to make the kind of job, capital refers to how much the organization plans to spend in order to operate its business. Hence, behavioral economy can explains the economic model of employee, human behavior, working performance. It is a representation of people action. The concept is based on traditional economics, where human behavior is believed to spring from absolute rationality.

On behavioral economics in consumer lives and in the economy aspect, it explains it is a game theory, behavioral game theory. It is a game theory , behavioral game theory extened standard analytical game theory by taking into account how players (consumers) feel about the payoffs other players receive, limits in strategic thinking, as well as the effects of learning , the consumer individual past purchase experience, games (choices of purchases) are usually about cooperation or fairness.

For advertising how plays beneficial roles in a healthy economy example, advertising plays a strong role in the economy. It provides useful informatin to consumers that tells them about products and services choices as well as comparing features, benefits and prices, with more complete information, consumers and businesses often choose to purchase additional products and services . Hence, behavioral economics draws instead on psychology and economics to explore why people sometimes make irrational decisions, and why and how their behavior does not follow the predictionsof economic models. Because humans are emotional and easily distracted being, they make decisions that are not in their self-interest. So, behavioral economics is the study of the effects that psychological factors have on the economic decisions making process of individuals. The importance of understanding behavioral economics for marketers is immeasurable as it shows for a better factors that can lead to irrational economic decision, e.g. overspend because of lack of availabiliey, such as buying expense gad because you are in the desert. Another irrational economic decision may be impluse buying or pressure.

● How to apply behavioral economic to explain why the employee does peformance behavior?

A study on human behavior has revealed that 90% of the working population can be classified into four basic personality types: Optimistic, pessimistic, trusting. However, the latter of the four types. Envious is the most common, with 30% compared to 20% of each of the organization whole employee individual economic behavior, economic behavior occurs in a climate of formal and informal organizational rukes. These rules often act as incentives, e.g. appreciation, job promotion, increasing salary. These rules often act as incentives and influence the choices employees make , in general employees chooce to work desk jobs that do not keep to fit, and how they have to make more time to stay healthy.

So, behavioral economic theory explain any organization will need have behavioral skills to dominate employee individual performance to raise. Behavioral skills are interpersonal, self-regulatory, and task-related behaviors that connect to successful performance in education and workplace settings. The behavioral skills are designed to help individuals succeed thorough effecttive interactions, stress management and persistent effort in any organizations. for task-oriented behavioral skills examples, they may include: active always buy with something, ambitious, strongly wants to succeed, cautious, being very careful, conscientious, taking time to do things right and creative, someone who can make up things easily or think of new things. The six important employee behaviors in organizations are employee productivity, absenteeism, turnover, organizational citizenship behavior, job satisfaction and workplace misbehavior. So, managers need have good behavioral management skills. They are all about learnings appreciation and growth. Take the time to learn, try and grow oen strategies and leadership style.

● How to apply behavioral eocnomic skill to help society to solve challenges ?
The three principles of social economics theory describes how the economy as a whole woks are (1) a country's standard of living depends on its ability to produce goods and services . (2) prices rise when the government prints too much money and (3) society faces a short-run tradeoff between inflation and unemployment. How to use behavioral economics for social impact. According to the American psychological association, social psychology is the study of how individuals affects and are affected by physical environment. Behavioral economics applies these concepts to the economic decisions that people make in addition to the ration thinking. It helps us understand how consumer participate in contest buy products and brand familiar choice in order to make the most rational purchase decison. Also, behavioral economists ask questions mostly about the way people make economic choices, judgements or the way particular financial purchase choice.

Hence, behavioral economic is the study of psychology as it relates to the economic decision making processes of individuals and organizations. In general, our societies ask two important questions: Are economists' assumptions of utility of profit maximization good approximations of real people's behavior? So individuals maximize subjective expected utility?

IN our societies, we need to satisfy and earn the greatest benefit, in economics, rational choice theory, states that when humans are presented with various options under the conditions of scarcity, they would choose the option that maximizes their individual satisfaction. Behavioral economics draws on psychology and economics to explain why people sometimes make irrational decisions and why and how their behavior does not follow the predictions of economic models, e.g. decisions such as how much to pay for a cup of coffee, whether to go to graduate school, whether to pursue a healthy lifestyle , how much to contribute toward retirement. For example, humans are emotional and easily distracted beings, they make decisions that are not in their self interest. For companies are increasingly incorpoarting behavioral economics to incrase sales of their products case example, in 2007, the price of the 8 GB iphone was introduced for $600 and quickly reduced to $400, what if the intrinsic value of the phone was $400? If Apple introduced the iphone for $400, the initial reaction the price in the smartphone market might have been negative as the iphone might be thought to have too pricely. Buy by introdicing the phone at a hgh-pricing and bringing it down to $400, consumers believed they were getting a pretty iphone deal for Apple. So, Apple iphone began to understand tht its phone consumers are irrational, an effective way to behavioral economics in the Apple iphone's decision making policies that concern its internal and external stakeholders may prove to be worthwhile of done properly .

- Behavioral economics is the study of the psychological, cognitive, emotional, cultural and social factors involved in the decisions of individuals or institutions, and how these decisions deviate from those implied by classical economic theory.
-
- Behavioral economics is grounded in empirical observations of human behavior, which have demonstrated that people do not always make what neoclassical economists consider the "rational" or "optimal" decision, even if they have the information and the tools available to do so.

- Behavioral economics combines elements of economics and psychology to understand how and why people behave the way they do in the real world. It differs from neoclassical economics, which assumes that most people have well-defined preferences and make well-informed, self-interested decisions based on those preferences.

- Behavioral economics is often related with normative economics. It draws on psychology and economics to explore why people sometimes make irrational decisions, and why and how behavior diverges from the predictions of economic models. Behavioral economics is the study of psychology that analyzes the economic decisions people make. Moreover, behavioral economics explains that humans are not rational and are incapable of making good decisions. Because humans are emotional and easily distracted beings, they make decisions that are not in their self-interest.
    - Consumer leisure need whether is more and less whether it has what relationship between economy?

Consumer leisure need whether is more and less whether it has what relationship between economy? Also whether the country's economy recession or growth, can it influence consumer leisure need to increase or decrease ? I shall attempt to apply behavioral economy theory to explain whether they have cause and effect relationship as below:

In our societies, there are so many different kinds of leisure activities, also any kinds of leisure consumers can follow the kind of leisure activity's price factor, enjoyable feeling factor, satisfactory feeling factor, lesiure time need factor to influence the leisure consumer individual final choice to which kind of leisure activity among the different kinds of leisure needs. For example, travel leisure activity ought be the most experience, spending of leisure expense to compare general sport lesiure, e.g. swimming , playing basketballs , table tennis, tennis, football, purchae tickets seeing movies, purchase tickets listening music, purchase electronic playing games to stay at homes to play.

In simiarity, it uses only considers leisure price aspect, we shall do the comparable and reasonable decision is that travelling activity ought be the kind of leisure activity, any leisure consumers ought spend the least leisure times to enjoy this kind of leisure activity, e.g. one year has only one time or two-to-five times for overseas for overseas travel. But, in fact, in global there are many travellers, they can make many times of travelling frequent decision, e.g. they can spend one week at least time to go to overseas to travel per month. Hence, it means that global some travellers like to buy air ticket to go to overseas to travel, they spend average one month and one time overseas travel.

In fact, tourism agents hope to attract travellers to choose travelling leisure activity, they will attempt to decrease air ticket price in order to increase travellers number. However, some cheap travelling package price can persuade global some travellers accept to pay cheap price to bu air ticket to spend several days to go to the country to travel enjoy their holidays.

So, it seems that cheap air tcket price strategy, it can attract some countries travellers to accept to spend some time for their overseas holiday their overseas travelling leisure activity can explain why leisure price must be main element factor to influence leisure consumers to reduce spending amount to pay for the kind of leisure activity , such as travelling lesiure activity is one kind of good lesiure activity example.
Otherwise, some kinds of leisure activities, ever their lesiure prices are cheap, it must not influence them to like to spend much time to enjoy them, e.g. swimming, riding bicycles leisure activities, although those kinds of sport leisure activities prices must be very cheap to compare travelling activities , it can must influence many young people like to buy bicycles to ridem even they are proficient bicycle riders or they like to buy tickets to go public swimming pools to swin. The factors may include these both kinds of sports are tired sport leisures, any one must need more body energy to do these sports. Moreover, for student leisure consumers, although these both kinds sports prices, such as bicycles and swimming pool purchase tickets, they are cheap to students, but in fact, students must need to spend time to learn, if they often spend time to enjoy these both of sport activities, they will feel fear that they can not concentrate on spending learning time, if they spend on sport leisure time.

Hence, in behavioral economy view, it explains that lesiure price whether it is high or low, it is not main factor to influence any leisure consumers to do leisure kind of choice, such as sport case to student leisure consumers, they will not choose to spend much time on sport lesiure aspect, because the hard students must feel fear to influence their learning effort when they often spend time on sport leisure aspect. Otherwise, for a sport professonal, e.g. proficient riding bicycle sportman, he may accept to spend expensive price to buy one expensive bicycle , e.g. when he feels the US$3,000 bicycle, it can help him to improve riding speed skills, he won't choose to buy the another US$1,000 bicycle, when he feels that it can not help him to improve riding speed skill, hence, it also explains that the leisure produt high price , it must not influence lesisure consumers number to reduce, it depends on whether the leisure product function to the leisure consumer, e.g. for riding bicycle sport men , they may accept to pay higher price to buy more expensive bicycles , because the hope that the bicyces can help them to comprove their riding speed to more rapid. Otherwise, for student bicycle consumers, they won't compare different kinds of bicycles prices in order to decide whether which kind of bicycles are the most suitable to them to buy to ride.
Hence, behavioral economic theory can explain that price must not be the main factor to influence lesiure

consumers' lesiure activities choices, their lesiure need psychological and leisure product individual function factors was also influence their lesiure activities choices.

- Consumer leisure need whether is more and less whether it has what relationship between economy?

Consumer leisure need whether is more and less whether it has what relationship between economy? Also whether the country's economy recession or growth, can it influence consumer leisure need to increase or decrease ? I shall attempt to apply behavioral economy theory to explain whether they have cause and effect relationship as below:

In our societies, there are so many different kinds of leisure activities, also any kinds of leisure consumers can follow the kind of leisure activity's price factor, enjoyable feeling factor, satisfactory feeling factor, lesiure time need factor to influence the leisure consumer individual final choice to which kind of leisure activity among the different kinds of leisure needs. For example, travel leisure activity ought be the most experience, spending of leisure expense to compare general sport lesiure, e.g. swimming , playing basketballs , table tennis, tennis, football, purchae tickets seeing movies, purchase tickets listening music, purchase electronic playing games to stay at homes to play.

In simiarity, it uses only considers leisure price aspect, we shall do the comparable and reasonable decision is that travelling activity ought be the kind of leisure activity, any leisure consumers ought spend the least leisure times to enjoy this kind of leisure activity, e.g. one year has only one time or two-to-five times for overseas for overseas travel. But, in fact, in global there are many travellers, they can make many times of travelling frequent decision, e.g. they can spend one week at least time to go to overseas to travel per month. Hence, it means that global some travellers like to buy air ticket to go to overseas to travel, they spend average one month and one time overseas travel.

In fact, tourism agents hope to attract travellers to choose travelling leisure activity, they will attempt to decrease air ticket price in order to increase travellers number. However, some cheap travelling package price can persuade global some travellers accept to pay cheap price to bu air ticket to spend several days to go to the country to travel enjoy their holidays.

So, it seems that cheap air tcket price strategy, it can attract some countries travellers to accept to spend some time for their overseas holiday their overseas travelling leisure activity can explain why leisure price must be main element factor to influence leisure consumers to reduce spending amount to pay for the kind of leisure activity , such as travelling lesiure activity is one kind of good lesiure activity example.
Otherwise, some kinds of leisure activities, ever their lesiure prices are cheap, it must not influence them to like to spend much time to enjoy them, e.g. swimming, riding bicycles leisure activities, although those kinds of sport leisure activities prices must be very cheap to compare travelling activities , it can must influence many young people like to buy bicycles to ridem even they are proficient bicycle riders or they like to buy tickets to go public swimming pools

to swin. The factors may include these both kinds of sports are tired sport leisures, any one must need more body energy to do these sports. Moreover, for student leisure consumers, although these both kinds sports prices, such as bicycles and swimming pool purchase tickets, they are cheap to students, but in fact, students must need to spend time to learn, if they often spend time to enjoy these both of sport activities, they will feel fear that they can not concentrate on spending learning time, if they spend on sport leisure time.

Hence, in behavioral economy view, it explains that lesiure price whether it is high or low, it is not main factor to influence any leisure consumers to do leisure kind of choice, such as sport case to student leisure consumers, they will not choose to spend much time on sport lesiure aspect, because the hard students must feel fear to influence their learning effort when they often spend time on sport leisure aspect. Otherwise, for a sport professonal, e.g. proficient riding bicycle sportman, he may accept to spend expensive price to buy one expensive bicycle , e.g. when he feels the US$3,000 bicycle, it can help him to improve riding speed skills, he won't choose to buy the another US$1,000 bicycle, when he feels that it can not help him to improve riding speed skill, hence, it also explains that the leisure produt high price , it must not influence lesisure consumers number to reduce, it depends on whether the leisure product function to the leisure consumer, e.g. for riding bicycle sport men , they may accept to pay higher price to buy more expensive bicycles , because the hope that the bicyces can help them to comprove their riding speed to more rapid. Otherwise, for student bicycle consumers, they won't compare different kinds of bicycles prices in order to decide whether which kind of bicycles are the most suitable to them to buy to ride.
Hence, behavioral economic theory can explain that price must not be the main factor to influence lesiure consumers' lesiure activities choices, their lesiure need psychological and leisure product individual function factors was also influence their lesiure activities choices.

- Can DNA reproductive technology bring only positive impact to influence our social behavior change?

Human's medical technology had been continue developed to improve to satisfy our medical need, such as cancer patient medical different new drug research, it aims to help future cancer patients to avoid death. However, future human's new medical research will research on DNA biological medical improvement . So, future DNA biological medical technology may bring good or bad social impact, e.g. reproductive animal, such as pig, cow animals . So, when many pigs and cows can be reproduced. Then, pigs and cows number can increase. Consequently, porks beefs meats food number can be also been increased by DNA biological medical reproductive cell technology improvemcnt.

It is good aspect to bring enough meats supply to global , when future DNA biological medical technology can be developed to the reprodctive many cows and pigs number stage in order to raise porks and beefs food number. However, DNA biological cell reproductive technology can also bring bad impact to our society, if one day human can apply DNA biological cell reprodutive technology to reproduce another ourselves, it means that reproductive human why is it bad new? if ne DNA scientist decides to help one country ambitious leader to reproduce himself, then when the country ambitious leader dies, but his another reproductive himself person can aontiue to bring war crisis to global, such as Japan's past leader, he was one ambitious leader to dominate global countries. If DNA reproductive technology is applied to help him to reproduce this Japan ambitious another himself . Then, the another new world war may be occurred easily. So, I also worry about future DNA reproductive technology may be applied to help the ambitous bad people to reproduce themselves to bring our societies safety and economic recession negative impact. So, it brings this question: Can DNA reproductive technology bring only positive impact to influence our social behavior change? I shall attempt to explain as below:

How does DNA attract our behavior? In some situations, genes play a larger role in determining your behavior. How can genetic technologies impact society ? Although, genetic technology has a great potential to change the medical practice as we know it also has a potential to be misused , it also has a potential to be misused, and lead to further health disparities, discrimination and inequality in the human societies around the world.

However, I believe that those the ways that genetic engineering can help human society. Several works have been done on genetic engineering with major focus on its importance ranging from increasing plant and animal food productio, diagnosing disease condition, medical treatment improvement, as well as production of vaccines and other useful drugs.

- What is the focus of behavioral generics?

Behavioral genetics is the study of genetic and environmental influences on behaviors. By examining genetic influence, more information can be gleaned about how the environment operates to affect behavior. So, in behavioral economic view, gene DNA reproductive cell technology may seem to bring these benefits. Some benefits of genetic engineerinf in agricultures are increased crop yoelds, reduced need for food or drug production, reduced need for pesticides, enhanced nutrient composition and food quality , resistance to past and disease , greater food security, and medical benefits to the world's growing population . Also, the intangible , non economic measurement, possible benefit of genetic engineering may include more nutritious food, tastier food, disease -and-drought resistant plants that require fewer environment resources , such as water and fertilizers, less use of pesticides, increased supply of food with reduced cost and larger shelf life, faster growing plants and animals.

All of these benefits, they can not measured by economic calculation, but they can be felt by us. So, in our social behevioral economic view to genetic engineering, it may bring both positive and negative impact to our societies. On negative impact, these are many risks involves in genetic engineering, the release of genetically altered organisms in the environment can increase human suffering, disease animal welfare, and lead to ecological disasters are positive impact aspect, it can help to defeat diseases, getting rid of all illnesses in young and unborn children potential to live longer, produce new foods, organisms can be tailor-made , faster growth in animals and plants, pests and diseases resistance. But genetic engineering can also bring risks to our societies, e.g. new allergens in the food supply, antibiotic reistance, production of new toxins, concentration of toxic metals, enhancement of the environment for toxic fungi, unknown harms, gene transfer to wild ot weedy relations, change in herbicide use patterns.

By knocking out genes repsonsible for certain conditions, it is possible to create animal model organism of " human disease" as well as producing hotmenes, vaccies and other drugs. So, if DNA can bring human diseases, it means that it can also bring economic loss to our societies, because human disease may bring illness to any one to cause low productivity to any industry development, if the factory has many people human disease from reproductive animal cell accident risk. Then, the ill worker number increases, low productivities and inefficiencies will cause to the factory. If global has many factory workers got human disease from reproductive animal cell accidently. Then, global factries products producing number must have been influenced to fallen down.

Consequently, global manufacturers will encountered serious loss, due to their products producing speed is slow and their different kinds of products supply number must decrease, if global will workers number increases, they are caused by reproductive animal cell disease. Hence, DNA genetic reproductive technology may also bring global economic loss crisis in possible.

o

● In organizational behavioral economic view, whether they have cause and effect relationship between employees how to use resources behaviors and organizational resource excess use within organizations ?

In organizational behavioral economic view, whether they have cause and effect relationship between employees how to use resources behaviors and organizational resource excess use within organizations. For example, if the organization has many employees number, whether the organization will use its any internal tangible and intangible resources easily per day.

For construction organization example, one construction organization must need to buy different kinds of construction materials to prepare to let workers to help it to manufacture different kinds of properties or houses (products) in order to sell to property buyers. In its every building construction site, it will need more or less workers, they are needed to use different kinds of construction matcrials to build housess in different construction sites. I assume that construction site (A), it has 100 construction workers number, every day, construction site (A) 100 workers need to use different kinds of construction materials to help them to build 3 building floors wall at least floor number in the construction site (A).

I assume that these 100 construction workers , they include proficient workers and not proficient workers. For proficient construction workers group, they have 50 number, and not proficient construction workers group, they also have 50 number . Hence, the proficient construction workers only need to spend 3 hours maximum and use less number of constructoin materials, then they can finish to build 3 building floors wall per day.

I also assume that all constructoin material supply number is limited. It means that due to this construction firm needs to pre-booking to purchase this kind of the best quality of constructoin material from overseas before three worths. So, it must not have enough time to pre-booking to purchase this kind of best quality of constructoin materials when they are used rapaidly within one month, due to this one month is the final finishing time to this construction firm within one month. Hence, limited construction material supply number and limited finishing time to build this new 40 floors house within this final one month .

So , not proficient construction workers number , limit number of construction material and per day 8 hours which is its limited resources in behavioral eocnomy view. Moreover, total 50 proficient and not proficient 50 construction workers (human resource employees number) will cause this constructoin firm , it will possible need to build this new 40 floors house are more than one month, if these 50 proficient construction workers , they have more than 30 at least number, they are absent to cause their overall construction workers' efficiency to be fallen down, due to the other 50 not proficient constuction numbers must need their teaching how to cooperate ad how use less materials to build this new 40 floor hourse rapidly in order to raise overall constructon team efficiency and avoid to delay more than one month time to build this 40 floors new house successfully within this final one month time.

Hence, it explains that when one organization has more employees, it does not represent that this organization must need to use more resource to achieve its any mission, such as this construction firm case, although it has 50 not proficient construction workers, they need to use more construction materials to build this new 40 floors house in this construction site (A). But, in fact, it has other 50 proficient construction workers, they know how to reduce construction materials to build every building floor wall for this new 40 floors building house. So, they can teach the not proficient building workers to know hoe to avoid to use extra excess constructon material to finish to construct every building fllor wall. SO, although, it has 50 not proficient construction workers number, but they can be taught to learn how to reduce to use these limited the best quality of construction materials to build this 40 floors new house. It implies that if the construction workers number can increase, e.g. increases more 50 not proficient construction workers, this the best quality of construction material resource number must not need to increase demand, because this construction site (A) has 50 proficient construction workers , they can teach these 50 not proficient construction workers how to avoid to use extra excess this kind of high quality construction material to build this new 40 floor house efficiently and effectively within this one month.

Hence, if this construction firm won't have more than 30 proficient workers number is absent in this final one month, it will have enough proficient construction workers to teach these 50 not proficient construction workers to know how to use this high quality of construction materials to build this 40 floors new house building in order to avoid waste or construction material need shortage challenge occurs in this final one month time.

Consequently , it ought finish to build this 40 floors new house building within this month. Hence, it explains why its this kind of high quality of construction material resource need must not increase, because if its all proficient construction workers is absent and their absent number is less than 30, then they have enough proficient construction workers number , they can teach this 50 not proficient construction workers how to avoid to use extra excess construction materials resource number in order to have enough construction material resource supply to satisfy this new 40 floors building house to finish construction within one month finishing date need.

On conclusion, in organizational behavioral economic view, it explains that resource use need must not be influenced to increase when the organization's employees number increase. It depends on whether the organization has how many talent and proficient workers number in order to assist them and teach the not proficient employees how to use resource to manufacture any kinds of products in order to avoid to spend extra excess of resource need. Hence, organizational behavioral economic view, it can explain that any organization's increase to employees number, it does not mean that its resource number is also needed to increase. Moreover, in organizational behavioral economic view, it also explains that if the organization can have many proficient workers to help it to do any complex tasks, they will help it to bring avoiding waste or excess extra resource to use advantage, because they ought know whether how they work, they can help the organization to improve performance or raise efficiency e.g. car manufacture, computer manufacture, television manufcture etc. home electronic products or car leisure products. Due to that manufacturre processes are complex, if the organization can have more proficient high skillful workers to help it to manufacture their products. They ought help it to use lesser manufacturing time and less manufacturing resource to finish any above these products to compare not proficient or low skillful manufacture workers. So, in long time, the organization must may earn economic low cost benefits from proficient worker individual high manufacturing skillful knowledge behavior or performance. So, organizational behavioral economic theory explains why even the organization plans to increase employees number, it's resources number won't be influenced to increase rapidly because when the organization's proficient high skillful workers number is more 2 times at least than not proficient low skillful workers number. They ought have enough effort to train and teach and cooperate with the not proficient low skillful manufacture workers to improve their manufacture skills in order to raise manufacturing efficiency and reduce extra excess resources waste and avoid to bring long term resource waste economic loss.

So, any manufacturing organizations must need to increase proficient workers number to assist the not proficient low skillful workers to learn how to improve their skills and know how to reduce to use excess resources to keep to manufacture the highest number of products aim frequently. Consequently, the organization will bring long term low resource use manufacturing economic benefit.

- What factors influence student makes subject choice decision

Behavioral economic on law and economy subject choice how to student individual subject learning choice behavior in universities economy and law subjects choice example, whether students will make subject either law or economt subject choice, it depends on future lawyer and economist salary whether which occupation can earn long term more salary comparision in order to decide wither law or economy degree learn.

Some university students make these two subjects either one learning choice, they will decide whether school fee is how much more than future salary earns, or personal interest psychological factor influences. So, if the student feels more interest to learn law degree , then he won't choose economy degree between these two degrees. Behavioral economy theory can be applied to explain this student individual economy and law degrees choice behavior because his subject choice decision is depended on personal psychological interest factor more than school fee or future salary possible earn economic salary reward factor influences. But, I assume that if the university can give scholorship for economic and law degree student when the student feels the law degree scholarship higher than economic degree. Then, he will decide to choose law degree to study more than economy degree. He chooses to study law degree because he hopes to earn higher scholarship.

IN behavioral economy principle , it can be applied to explain this student degree choice behavior. However, applying behavioral economy view, it assumes these principles to analyze whether how the student chooses to study the degree. The principles or factors may influence his degree choice may include: Cost and benevits, e.g. the student fee and future salary for the degree, when the student has interest to study law and economic degree. So, he needs to do degree choice. Then, he may compare whether how much law and economy degree school fee, it may be possible future earn salary, scholarship possible reward. All of these factors concern the price for law and economy degree (external cost) and future possible income (salary) for economist and lawyer occupation. It is behavioral law and economic factor to influence how the student chooses either law or economic degree to study in the university.

For example, when the (A) university on student enrolls to the (A) university before, he needs to choose wither law or economy degree to study. I assume that he only feels interest to study these two degrees. Then, he will compare school fees, if law degree school fee is per year US$5,000, 4 years is US$20,000 and economy degree school fee is per year US$3,000, 4 years is US$12,000. Although, it seems that economy 4 year school fee is more less US$8,000 to compare law degree 4 year, but this student also compare possible future salary for lawyer and economist occupation. He believes that future lawyer salary may pay more 4 times to compare economists salary after 5 years working experience. Although, if this student chooses economy degree to study, he may have chance to earn scholarship if his examination can be good, but it is one time short time economic researd and this scholarship reward is not sure that he must earn, if he can not get at least 5 (A) grade any one economic subject papers in this university economy degree structure. Otherwise, if he chooses to study law and get 5 (A) grade any one law subject papers in the university law degree structure, he can not get scholarship for this law degree. hence , he makes final choice to study law degree, although he can not get scholarship and school fee is more than economy degree. But he believes that he can earn higher salary when he can be one lawyer and he works after 5 years, his salary may be paid more than one economist salary.

In behavioral economic view, it can be applied to explain this university student his degree choice behavior, then he has interest to study law and economy degree. He must need to make one degree choice to graduate, then he may make degree choice decision by external economic cost (degree price) and future reward (possible income) behavioral economic factor . Then, he can judge whether which degree is more suitable to choose to study in this university.

○

● How organization improvement may bring economic benefits

Can organizational economies, e.g. transaction cost economics, agency theory, organizational theory , e.g. models of formal organizational independent of the strategies, improve organizational behavior in order to bring economic benefit, e.g. development potentially valuable resources and capabilities, it can raise internal organizatonal strengths and avoid weaknesses in SWOT strategy in order to imporve performance and bring organizational internal economic benefit in organizational behavioral economic view.

For manufacturing industry example, if the car manufacturers can attempt to discover the most efficient steel, or different kinds of car components material, but they can help it to manufacture many high quality cars. Then, their manufactury cost reduce , but its any model of car quality does not caused to poor. Then, this car firm can apply the most efficient and the most high component materials to help it to manufacture high quality cars. Although, it must need to spend time to research how to invest the most efficient and high quality car manufacture components, but if it can apply the most efficient and the high quality components to help it to manufacture any new model of cars. Then, new components research spending time can bring long term low manufacturing cost and high quality of cars to achieve long time economic benefits.

So, on behavioral economic view, organization's spending time on different kind of cheap and high quality car manufacture manufacture components research and research expenditure spending on new kinds of different car manufacture components, it can help it to sell the high quality of different model of cars to satisfy car buyer comfortable needs. Moreover, it can earn high profit, when it 's any car manufacture component cost reduces. So, SWOT internal strengths (high quality and low cost) to this car manufacturer. It may help it to bring long term raising profit economic benefit, when its any new model of car prices do not need raise, but their compared material manufacture cost reduce, due to new kinds of car manufacture component materials can be invented in success.

Hence, high quality and low cost of car manufacture component invention researching on spending time and research experiment expenditure is value to this car manufacture company, because if high quality and low cost car manufacture component experience succeeds, it can help it to improve any new model of cars quality , but the most important factor is that its any new model of cars prices do not need increase. So, car buyer individual purchase desire won't be influenced to choose any brand of car seller to replace it more easily.

For one drug development process, case example ,I assume that this drug manufacture firm can attempt to spend 10 years time, but it can help it has possible to help it to invent one kind of new pharmaceutical drugs to kill cancer cells for global cancer patients. So, its spending time research on new drugs to kill any kinds of cancers cellers and experimentation expenditure is value, because it can help it to bring economic benefit when global will have many cancer patients believe its new discovery of cancer drugs , it may help them to kill cancer cells to get health or reduce death chance ratio raises after 10 years.

Consequently, in soon future, it's global cancer patients number may increase when they choose to buy its future new cancer drugs paroduct. It may bring high profit economic benefit. So, on organizational behavioral economic view, when the organization spends long time and experimentation expenditure to research new resources, if these new resources can be invented in success and it ensures help it to increase clients number to order to bring future economic benefit. The organization is value to spend time and expenditure to carry on new resources research.

- Can organization apply behavioral economic demand to evaluate work performance for whole different departments?

Behavioral economies investigation may include evaluating demand for a commodity (such as drug experimentation and car manufacturing component material etc.) is given changes in price, using hypothetical purchase tasks, which are a reliable and efficient assessment method. Can behavior management examine work performance evaluation? The work performance evaluation target includes that employee individual and different department will performance evaluation in organization.

I believe high quality or low quality training , which can be evaluated whether the employee individual work performance or the department overall employees work performance can be improved after training. So, if the department employee individual or all employers work performance can be improved, e.g. work efficiency raises, client satisfactory feeling raises, product sale number . Then, the training is a high quality training to help the organization to earn future high economic benefit. Otherwise , if the organization can not earn above any one good result. Then, the training ia a low quality training.So, any organization can attempt to observe any department overall performance and employee individual performance in order to evaluate whether it can provide high or low quality of training to let employees to learn.
So, employee individual behavior can bring performance evidence to let the organization to evaluate whether its training is useful or not useful to achieve its training aim, e.g. when the car manufacturer provides money, time,

effort training arrangement to teach all workers to learn how to manufacture car skill. After training provision, many of them, they do not need to work over time more than one hour to manufacture daily of least 10 cars per employee.Before, any one worker must need to spend more than one hour over time to manufacture daily 10 more cars.

So, when this car manufacture skillful improvement train is provided more than one hour more than one hour , none of them, they need work over time in order to manufacture more than at least 10 cars number per day. It seems that training improvement arrangement can be used to evaluate whether employee individual efficiency can be raised in organizational behavioral economic view.

Hence, any organization's internal training provision knowledge resource, it can be evaluated employees' behavioral performance can be improved, about being available to work, about role performance . It assumes that employees are likely to come to work and remain in the organization if they obtain satisfaction from their jobs, and that they are likely to put use effort and work more effectively if they are to be reward more for their effort and performance can be comfirmed to improved by management after they are taught by training. So, when the employee hopes to raise salary, he must hard to learn any new knowledge from the organizational training. Then, training can help the " expectation good reward employees" can improve performance in organizational behavioral economic view.

It is one important successful factor to help the organization to innovate and bring economic benefit, when the organization can implement any new useful training to improve any new useful training to improve employee skills. It means that training is one long term economic organizational strategy, it depends on whether the training is useful or is ot useful in order to help any old employees to raise or improve their skills to achieve raising efficiency and satisfactory client service , sale product number, product manufacture increasing number aims.

- How organizational ethic influence employee behavior ?

Organizational ethic behavior concerns with explaining employee individual behavior in organization, e.g. ethical decision making, ethical conduct for example, when one marketing department manager does not attempt to carrying on any data research about new market research to sell the new model iphone to any country. He only depends on his personal judgement, he believes that this new invention of US iphone producs, they ought to be sell to Korean new iphone market, because he feels Korean must prefer to choose to buy US drand of new iphone products to compare other countries iphone product. However, this iphone marketing development manager lacks enough data research for different Korean iphone buyer age target, purchase experience, purchase desire to conclude Korean iphone buyers must like to buy any brand of US iphone products in preference.

His non ethical new iphone invention decision making to choice Korean ipohone buyers market will bring time waste rick to satisfy Korean iphone buyers' needs to replace other new model ipone users market, e.g. Hong KOng, China, ipone market. So, his ethical decision making to Korean iphone buyers ne iphone invention market may bring less economic benefit to this US iphone manufacture firm. So, this new model ipohone marketing development immoral judgement of this iphone marketing development manager individual decision making to Korean new model ipone invention to Korean ipone users, it can bring high economic loss to this US iphone firm.Otherwise, if this marketing department manager can spend time to carry on data gathering to make more accurate new model iphone invention decision making to choose which one country, then his ethical decision making may help his this US iphone firm to reduce new iphone invention loss risk. So, it explains that why ethic organizational behavior may influence the firm can earn more or less economic benefit. SO, ethic or moral behavior can influence the organization can earn how much economic benefit in long term significantly in organizational behavioral economic view.

● Can improve energy efficiency by organization building occupant's energy consumption relative behavior to bring economic benefit?

Reducing energy consumption in building , it must improve efficiency by building, but whether they have close cause and effect relationship between occupant's energy consumption behavior and improvement energy efficiency to the building? IN fact, high efficiency equipment is being developed, it can help any building to save energy and economic effectiveness, if building energy is subject to uncertainties, such as whether variations, human operations, human behavior changes and government policies. So, building technology equipment improvement may be one main factor to help buildings to save energy . But why occupant behavior may help building to save energy by their daily energy consumption behavior.

The occupant energy behavioral user inputs factor may include: Weather influences, internal heat gain, efficiencies, simplied/ normal occupant behaviors, e.g. a high efficiency chiller can save very limited energy in cold climates due to minimal cooling load, and a good designed natural ventilation building won't work if the occupants do not open windows when outdoor air favors cooling. So, it seems that if one living building hopes to reduce energy consumption, instead of building equipment technological change , e.g. air condition facilities, building occupants , artificial intelligent light, life, their daily energy consumption behaviors, they can influence the living building's energy consumption level in occupant energy consumption behavior and building energy saving economic benefit view.

In fact, when the occupant considers hot water, air condition, energy gas electricity expenditure, he won't use excess electricity, gas resources, because he needs to pay more energy expenditure , when gas and electricity energy consumption expenditure is applied to any business organization offices, warehouses , shops working facilities environment, such as offices, warehouses , shops can often use less electricity, gas energy far ther employees daily work . In long time, the organization must may reduce much electricity, gas energy expenditure for whole organizations business activities. In organizational behavior economic view, organizational energy consumption reduces it can help it to bring less expenditure spending economic benefit.

◦

● Can Amazon e-commerce organization business activities bring economic benefit to global societies?

Amazon e-commerce is one online product sale e-commerce organization. Any one country e-buyer can use his/her home computer to click to Amazon webstores, when he/she saw the product phone and price, then he/she feels the product's price is reasonable and he/she believes that he/she can make the best choice to buy the product. Then, he/she can pay visa to buy the product from Amazon webstore.
Amazon can bring the most convenient online sale channel to global any one e-buyer. The e-buyer can buy the oveseas product from its e-webstores . He does not need to catch air plane to fly to the e-sellers' shop. he can pay visa to pay the product from Amazon e-webstores any time immediately. All Amazon e-webstores . He can open 24 hours, so all webstores have no close time. So , it can bring busy working people, they do not need to spend long time to visit any shops to make purchase decision. For busy working people example, time has important value to them, they do not want to waste time to make any purchase choice.

So, Amazon gives " economic purchase time benefit " to global any one full time working people. In their psychology, Amazon can help them to save much time to go to online shopping purchase chance at homes. They can stay at homes to shopping. Even, when they give their their address to Amazon to know, Amazon will deliver their products to their homes within several days rapidly. Also , they do not need to pay money to buy its products immediately. They can only pay visa to buy the product from Amazon webstores. So, they can save " consumption money" to use for another need in short time. So, one individual e-air ticket buyer, Amazon can bring economic benefit to him, he does not need to buy air ticket to fly to another country to buy the product. Amazon webstores are given more different kinds of similar brand products to let him to choose in order to pay the most reasonable price, working people do not need to spend much visiting shop time to choose any products in order to make the final purchase decision at home rapidly, any one has visa card , he/she can buy the product from Amazon webstores at homes.

Instead of individual e-buyer ecommerce time benefit, spending little time product choice, reducing catching air plane to visit another country seller shop to pay air ticket expense and travelling time spending activities to every e-buyer . Amazon also brings global economic benefits to any one country. When the e-buyer lives in one country to buy the product, it is saved in the overseas country's warehouse. Then, the product must need to deliver to his home by air plane. So, all of Amazon products can bring global goods air transport delivering service to any one overseas buyer, when the product is saved in the overseas seller's warehouse. Any one Amazon product overseas transpor delivery service activity, it can help air goods transport service need increases as well as their goods air transport service income will also increase. Amazon can bring global air goods transport service need increases. It can assist global GDP air goods transport industry grows, and economic benefit for the country's air plan goods delivery service industry development in long term. Hence, on behavioral economic view, Amazon online sale channel ,it can help global economic benefit to air plane goods delviery service industy as well as individual differeent country e-buyer individual time saving and short term money saving economic benefit by visa payment method.

Moreover, Amazon alsoo creates more high technology employment chance to any one country because Amazon owns many offices and warehouses in different countries, due to it is one high technological e-commerce online sale organization, It must need many high skillful website designers to help it to design different countries webstores in order to satisfy any one e-buyer online purchase need. So, it creates high technology job chance to any one country webstore designers . It can help them to raise competitive effort when any one graduate pursues website designer career. IN Amazon provides good employent chance for any one country computer ecommerce designers in order to let them to earn high salary. Also, Amazon public e-commerce organization provides good chance for any one country author to earn royalty income when he/she publishes any electronic or paper books to sell from Amazon publish. It gives good writing skillful authors have more writing chance to help them to sell electronic books and /or paper books from its different countries webbook stores to different countries' readers in short time. It can help them to increase book sale chance to let different countries book buyers can know whether new book topic to the author, he/she will publish soon. So, it brings author's new writing mind training chance when he/she needs to compare book sale rank from Amazon webstores.

Hence, Amazon can bring social employment benefit and author individual skillful training advantage and royalty income benefit to any on country author in nowadays online published industty. So, Amazon online business activities can increase global social employment chance, encourages global authors attempt to train writing skill, helps e-buyers to save visiting shops shopping time and air ticket expenditure for global overseas buyers.

- How and why Amazon e-commerce organization influence global consumee behavioral changes to bring ecommerce benefits to sellers?

In behavioral economic view, Amazon changes consumers behavior as well as product sellers sale method, such as global consumer sellers began to accept online purchase method to replace frequent visiting shop purchase method and global sellers began to accept to apply Amazon webstores to help them to sell products from its online sale channel to replace opening shops locate to the country sale channel.
The advantages to global sellers may include they do not need to pay rent or buy the shops, they can use Amazon webstores to show their different kinds of products photos and prices to let any one online buyer to know . The advantage to global buyers, they do not need to spend time to visit any countries shops to choose products in order to make purchase decision. They only need to spend some time to visit amazon any one country's webstore to see any brands of product photos and know their prices to different kinds of products to compare design and price

and functions among of them in the online visiting short time when they stay at home to trun on themselves home computers . So, future home consumption behavior may replace visiting shop consumption behavior. Amazon 's online purchase method will encourage global many sellers have began to believe traditional visiting shop purchase model can not be accepted to global any one consumer more easily, when any one owns computer and internet service at home in common. Then, global shops number will reduce, due to different kinds of product websites purchase model needs number increases to global product sellers, they will close their shops and open themselves webstores or choose Amazon webstore to help them to sell their products conveniently. Consequently, global online purchase and sale transactions number will be influenced to increase by e-commerce organization development.

- How does consumer behavior bring positive or negative influence to economic growth or economic recession to the country?

I shall attempt to apply behavioral economic theory to explain their cause and effect relationship why and hoe global economy growth or recession may be impacted by global consumer behavior change reasons ae below:

I shall indicate travellingleisure and goods air plane transport industries example, since air planes are invented, it is a kind rapid air transport tool, it can help human to do both kinds of transport asrvice, one is goods transport and another is human transport . So, any individual or business goods can be delivered to another country offices or homes by air planes transport tools rapidly. SO, air planes can create more overseas purchase and sale business activities chance between different countries nowadays. Moreover, internet invention, it also increase more e-coomerce online purchase and sale business acitivies to global any one online buyer, he/she only needs to apply computer tool to click to the online seller webstore, when he /she likes the product, he/she can pay visa to buy the product from the onlin seller webstore at home conveniently.

Hence, e-commerce encourages global consumers to choose to buy any products from internet channel, it also brings global goods are needed to transport by air planes between different countries, e.g. one US online buyer makes purchase decision from onlin channel, then he chooses the product from Korean one online seller webstore. After he pays visa to the Korean online seller webstore , then the Korea seller will follow his US address to send the product to the US buyer's home after several days rapidly.

Hence, it explains that if future global consumers like to buy any products from any one country's onine sell webstore. Then, the product must need to be delivered to the online buyer's home. When the seller's product is not located to the online buyer's country warehouse. It needs to be delivered by air plane. When, global there are man consumers, their traditional visiting shops purchase habits are influenced to change online visiting webstores habits. Then, when their purchase habits are influenced to change by rapid, convenient, visa card payment online purchase method at home, time online purchase technological new payment channel method.

In future new online purchase trend development, it may influence future global traditional visiting shops consumption model to change visiting webstores consumption model. Consequently, consumers will choose to pay visa online purchase at home in preference. Also, it encourages visa card purchase , consequently, online purchase may influence these industries development, airlines goods transport service needs increase, it can increase new visa cards number to the frequent online channel e-buyer number. So, online consumption encourages global households save long time money in banks, because we can pay money by visa card payment after we buy any products from online. Global bank may have more money to save longer time from global households, long time money save , because we do not need to withdraw money to buy any expensive products, immediately, e.g. computer , television, furniture etc. When global households begin to accept online purchase method is better to compare visiting shop purchase method. So, future global airline goods transport and bank saving businesses these two industries may have positive impact by future global online buyers raising number.

Hence, when global consumers behaviors began to change online purchase , their online purchase activities may influence global banks can have long time saving money and airlines goods transport need increase rapidly. However, online purcahse activies will bring negative consumers emotion impact to some businesses, e.g. property rent business, because when the country has high population of consumers, they choose online purchases, they won't often vitis shops to choose any kind of products frequently, they only like to stay at home and turn on themselves home computers to find whether global whom sellers, they have webstores to let global consumers to buy their products from online channel. Due to the cuntry willl not have many consumers like to spend time to visit any shops in the country. It means that the country will have many shops are needed to be close, because there are less number peple visit the businessmen shops every day. It will cause property rent service providers can not increase rent income, even decrease rent income, when there are many businessmen close their shops and change onine webstores to replace actual shops. Hence, it seems that online buyers number increases, it may also brings positive impact to influence shop rent service income decreases to the property rent developers.

On global macro economic changing environment, online buyers number increases, it can encourage any kinds of products, they can sell more more easily. So, global product sale number may be influenced to increase rapidly, when global online purchase and sale transactions number increase, GDP on any kinds of product income may be influenced to increase . So, online buyers number increases, it must may bring positive impact to influence global trading GDP high growth, but global shops rent income property developers may be influenced to reduce, due to there are many shops may be caused to close in possible.
How travellers' leisure need change, it may influence travelling leisure service industry development? I shall attempt to explain how COVID 19 disease influences global travellers lesiure need change and airpine and travelling service providers, e.g. hotels, travelling agents, their leisure service needs change. Nowadys, COVID 19 disease has caused

global many travellers feel fear to catch airplanes, because air planes all windows are needed to close, he/she has COVID disease, then he/she can bring any one passegner to get this kind of disease by air plane close window air environment. So, when globa many travellers feel afreaid to catch air planes, this kind of COVID 9 air contact disease, it can cause global travellers number has began to reduce, many of travelles began to reduce travelling times per year, even 0 time travel per year. Consequently, it will bring negative impact to global travelling industry development.

Firstly, COVID 19 disease influences global traveller individual travelling desire decreases, every traveller began to avoid to catch air planes to travel. So, any country;s airlines air planes flying times began to reduce, because it is no full seats booking to any airlinees. It means that airlinee must decrease income, alsoo they need to pay parking airplanes rent to any countries airports. So, fixed rent expenditure will need to pay, and many airlines began to dismiss the excess extra number of airline front service staffs, e.g. airport front service staffs, air plane check in /out staffs, even pilots number began also decreased.
So, airline unemployment ratio increases , it causes pilots, airlines service staffs need to change jobsm even some coutnries pilots , choose to do simple goods delivery jobs in supermarkets or securities. Also, COVID 19 disease influences hotels, travelling agents income began to reduce, because there are none many travellers need to live hotels, and they do not need travelling agents to help them to arrange any travelling journeys. So , COVID 19 disease influences many different countries travellers began choose any leisure activities to replace travel, because they feel afraid to get COVID 19 disease when they need to sit in closed window air plane environment.

- Can economic recession influence car buyers' purchases desire reduce? In macro economic view, it explains that economic recession means that the country has many people loss jobs, because economic recession, it causes many employers begain to reduce employees number to avoid salary expenditure increases, but clients number reduces. Hence, when one country is experiencing economic recession period, it will causes people reduces shopping expenditures, when many of people lose themselves jobs or some people feel that they will lose jobs as soon as possible . So, in societies, general consumers' consumption desires will be influenced to reduce, due to many of people had lost jobs or many of people feel that their employers will dismiss them due to they feel busineses are worse.

IN behavioral economic view, when one society has high unemployment ratio, e.g. graduate students can not find jobs easily, many of working people are losing present jobs, it implies that the country is experiencing economic recession .So, it will cause many products can not sell easily in the society, e.g. one Dell brand laptop price is average US$1,000. IN last year, the country US Dell brand laptop price was average US$1,000. IN common, Dell brand could sell this model laptop products 100,000 laptop numbers in last year. HOwever, in this year, Dell this model laptop price is not changed, it keeps US$1,000 average price, but Dell only sells 50,000 laptop number in US this year. So, it seems that US is experiencing recession, because there are many US people lose jobs, they can not find another jobs easily in short time. SO, in general, many US people begin to prepare some money in bank and they begin to reduce spend to buy any things easily. Also, because laptop is not essential product to anyone. It is only students, office employers and employees both customer target may be laptop product's main consumer groups. Another retired people, housewives, households they must feel need to buy laptop to use at homes. So, it explains that why US Dell brand laptop is significant decreasing laptop buyers (customers) number.Moreover, due to this US Dell brand laptop products average price are still kept to same to US$1,000 average price. It can not persuade laptop consumers to choose to buy Dell brand any laptop products easily when they may make price comparison to other similar kinds of laptop model products, e.g. Apple brand, Microsoft brand etc.

However, I assume that even Dell brand wil decide to reduce its different model of laptops average price to US $700 even $500 each piece. I believe that Dell brand computer seller is still difficult to sell its any model of laptop products easily in this year. The reason is because that when this year US is experiencing recession, in this high unemployment ratio US recession environment, many losing job American will avoid to spend to buy high price product, or the non essential product, such as laptop product it must not be essential product for any one and its price may be expensive to let the unemployed US people feel its price is too much to compare general non essential products, e.g. books, shoes, cloths etc. So, in ecojnomic recession environment, it may cause some general non essential products will be difficlut sold in the country's business market. It means that laptop is non essential product,.

So, when the country is encountering recession period, the country's laptop product consumer desire may be influenced to fall down. Although, some laptop sellers attempt to reduce their sale price in order to attract or persuade they choose to buy their any laptops. But, lower sale price , it is still difficult to help them to increase laptop sale number because general consumers will avoid to spend to buy non essential products, they will save much money in bank to prepare possible unemployment matters occur to them suddenly. So, when the country has many people feel that unemployment matter may occue to them suddenly, many people will choose to save more money in bank because they feel that they will be hard to find another jobs in short time easily, even graduate students or owning more year working experience people, they will plan to find another job to work in short time. So, it explains that economic recession may influence consumer purchase desire to reduce, in special essential products purchase need to consumer will be influenced to reduce. Nut, essential products consumer purchase desire, they won't be influenced to reduce, otherwise their purchase desire may be influenced to rise when recession occurs, e.g. rice , vegetable, meat, pork, orange, banana, apple friuts common food. Why does essential products , such as foods their price may raise and food consumers purchase desire will not be influenced to reduce in recession. The reason is simple, when one country is experiencing recession, for example, COVID 19 disease occurrence, it can influence global people feel agraid, foods may be shortage to supply to their countries, e.g. China, there are many people feel fear that they can not buy rice, vegetable, meat foods from supermarket easily. Because COVID 19 disease influences many Chinese restaurants clients number decreaes, they are afraid to go to restaurants to contact the COVID 19 disease people to sit on the same table to eat together. So, restaurant clients decrease. COVID 19 disease occurrence influences many Chinese people choose to go to supermarkets to buy foods to cook at homes. So, supermarket foods purchase need number may be influenced to increase. Consequently, supermarket foods prices may be influenced to increase, because many Chinese people prefer to buy foods to cook from supermarkets to eat. So, in China present economic recession environment, COVID 19 disease encourages many Chinese household families choose to go to supermarkets to buy foods to cook at home, because food is essential to any one. So, Chinese supermarket food price may be influenced to increase by COVID 19 disease occurrence influence.

This kind of disease can influence any one travller individual leisure choice began to change, such as they began to forgive travel siure activities, they will spend holiday to do other leisure activities in themselves countries , e.g. climbing mountain, swimming, running, playing table tennis, tennis etc. different outdoor sports. all of these leisure sports have same features, global any one leisure needer, he does not catch air plane to fo to another country to carry on playing these any one sport and he/she does not need to pay more price to enjoy these sports. Otherwise m travelling leisure activity, it must need any one leisure needer to spend much expenditure to enjoy this kind of leisure activity . So, it explains why many travellers beagan to choose to do any kinds of sports to replace spending money to enjoy travel leisure in their holidays,

On conclusion,this COVID 19 disease had influenced global travel leisure businesses and travel related leisure service industries income and travellers number began to reduce and any countries GDP on travelling industry will have negative economic recession occurrence in this COVID 19 disease global envionment. Hence, it implies thaat consumers (travellers) behavior leisure activities need, it may influence global business activities increase or decrease , global economic growth or recession, they have close cause and effect relationship between consumer behavioral change and industries GDP changes in behavioral economic view.

◦ ● Can economic environment influence individual learning performance ?

Why does student enrollment rise when the economy recession? When a strugging economy certainly forces extra pressure on young students seeking funds for loans and tuition cost, the enrollment rates for colleges continuous to rise. In fact, some experts theoritize that a poor economy environment actually helps a stimulate student enrollment. Whether it is the economy , new academic programs or better recruiting, community colleges are seeing an enrollment boom, when enrollment has been growing steadily , it may increase year institutions. To help prospective student interests when providing all current students with diverse support.

What the motivation had factors that are encouraging students to enroll, e.g. whether it is that the country 's young people feel the country begins have poor economy, so many of them choose to enroll schools to learn new knowledge, because scoial poor economy environment, it won't have many employers like to pay more salaries to employ new employees, consequencey, unemployment rate will rise, it causes students feel difficult to find jobs to do in general, even graduate students. So, it seems that economy recession may encourage students further study, because job supply is decreasing. so, it causes many young people choose to spend time to further study in order to wait economy recovery later. Then, they can prepare to seek any new jobs more easily when there are many employers like to increase employees number.

So, it explains that they have case and effect relationship between student enrollment number and the country's economy growth or recession or recovery, For example, when the country economy growth, in society, it will have many employers like to spend more salaries to employ new employees, because there are many people like to consume, when most of them have jobs to do and earn higher income. so, it seems that in society consumer individual increasing consumption attitude/desire that can help businesses grow, when businesses have more customers, they have effort to pay money to buy any things to use.

Businessmen ought need to increase employees number to help them to develop themselve businesses more successfully. So, it is economy growth period, moreover, many young people feel economy growth can create more employment chance in society. So, it encourages many students choose to forget to continue to pursue high level academic education, e.g. when the student had graduated undergraduate degree, due to he feels social economic environment is improved. So, employers are seeking new employees to help them to develop businesses. So, employment chance increases and salaries level will also rise. So, it encourages many undergraduate students do not want to pursue master degree. Because they believe that they can find jobs to do more easily in this time. So, it seems that the society's present economy suitation is either goos or worse, it can impact students to choose continue pursue higher learning stage or not. So, it explains that student individual learning desire and the social economy have close influential relationship.

● Why does economy scenarios can influence student learning behavior?

Why does economy scenarios can influence motivation and learning behavior on student achievement? Quality in higher education is not only determined by lecturers, it also depends on student individual learning desire, because if economy scenarios can influence the student learning desire to pursue continue learning or seek jobs in society. Then, quality in higher education won't be main factor to influence student individual learning in success or failure. If the student does not plan to continue to learn, even the school has good quality in higher education , it won't attract the student to choose to enrol to the school to continue learn easily. It is due to whether economy scenarios how influences the student decides to pursue or forget further study.

In fact, any countries must encounter or experience economic recession or economic growth or economic recovery period different social economic environment changes. It will bring negative or positive emotion impact to the country's every student learning attitude, in order to decide whether continue pursue learning is better or forget pursue learning is better. So, school fee whether is high or less, it is not main factor to influence student individual continue learn.

In macro economic view, the social's economic growth, or economic recession or economic recovery , any one of these economic scenarios change, it will bring positive or negative emotion impact to encourage the student either chooses to further learning pursue or forgive further learning pursue, in student further learning social behavioral economic view.

ON conlusion, on behavioral economic analytical theory, it explains our social macro economic environment new changes to be better or worse, it may bring indirect impact to influence the country's student individual learning desire or learning behavior either on pursue continue learning or forget continue learning in global societies. So, it also implies that whether the school's fee whether it is more or less, it is not main factor to influence student individual continue pursue to learn or not. If the student feels that movement, himself/herself country's social economic scenario is worse, or it is experiencing recession. The student will be influenced to choose continue to go to school to pursue further learning. So, worse economic environment or recession macro economic environment feeling, it may persuade any country's students trend to choose to pursue further study intention more than seeking jobs to work intention, because they feel social jobs provisin chances are influenced to reduce, and no many jobs to supply to them to choose, salaries will be reduced etc . these factors , they can caes the country will have many students make school enrollment choice more than seeking jobs choice. Hence, I believe that any country students school enrollment choices, they have close relationship to themselves country's economic scenario changes at the moment. Hence in behavioral economic view, it may explain why and how any country's economic environment can bring either positive or negative emotion influence to persuade or dissuade the student chooses to either continue further academic study or forgive continue further academic study.

So, behavioral economy theory is one kind of new economy and psychological science. Psychologists can apply this theory to research and explain and conclude how and why our social economy change can impact students, consumers, households, businessmen believe in order to make rational decision to earn more economic benefit and avoid economic loss. Also, behavioral economy theory also may help psychologists and economists to predict how and why our societies will ought to be changed to be better ot worse by which kind of factors accurately. So, it may help government leaders or businesses organizations decision makers to do more accurate decisions or strategies to solve any challenges in success.

- Can behavioral psychologist apply vehicle owner individual driving times to measure or evaluate whether he/she has high income level or whether his/her income increases or decreases?

Can drivers' driving time reflect his/her general income level ? In general, whether private car owners , their driving times can be influenced by income changing level? It depends on different factors, e.g. the car driver does not want often spend 10 minutes to wait bus from home to working places or from working places to home two ways frequently.

I assume that, in general, private car owners do not want often drive themselves cars to go to anywhere, e.g. working people usually only like to drive themselves cars , when they need to work, even holiday leisure activity, they need to drive cars to arrive the leisure activity destination. So, it seems that any car owners , their cars purchase aims, they are either for working needs or leisure aims mainly. So, I bring this question: Suggesting that any countreis car owners, their cars purchase usually for leisure and working both intention. Can the car owner's per month driving times, it can reflect his/her income level whether it increases or decreases? It means that the car owner will increase driving car times, when his salary has increased or the car owner will decrease driving car times, when his salary has decreased? Can driving car times represent the car owner his/her general increasing or decreasing salary? Have they relationship between increasing or decreasing to car owner's driving times and his/her salary increasing or decreasing level?

Behhavioral economists can attempt to apply behavioral economic view to research general car owners their driving behaviors. In general, when can fuel price increases, it may influence car owners to reduce driving times because when they drive themselves cars frequently, their cars must need to use much fuel. Consequently, they will need to pay higher price to buuy another long driving time useful fuel. So, when any one car owner knows that car fuel prices are general increasing. They will be influenced to reduce to drive themselves cars to avoid more expenditure spending on car fuel aspect.

So, I assume car fuel price increases, it can influence general car users reduce themselves driving car times per day. They won't drive themselves to go to far destination, uness the destination is not too far. It means that general car owners like to drive cars to go to short distance destination only, if general car fuel price has increased significantly in local car fuel market. Hence, it seems that car fuel price whether rises up or falls down, it can influence many car owners avoid often drive themselves cars to go to long distance destination, in order to avoid frequent high fuel price expense. Also , it means that any car fuel seller ought not often rise fuel price in order to avoid many car owners reduce driving times behaviors. Consequently, car fuel and car purchase number will be influenced to reduce when the country has many car owners reduce driving times to go to long distance destination. It is driving car and using car fuel behavioral market principle, it means that when the car fuel price general increases, it influences general car owners reduce driving car want more times, because they do not want often buy new car fuel ar rising price level to avoid not essential economic loss on rising price of car fuel expenditure.

Hence, if this supposion to " general rising car fuel price level, " it will influence general car owners avoid to drive themselves cars to go to long distance destinations. It is reasonable and their driving car times will be influenced to reduce in society. Then, it explains that behavioral economists can attempt to gather general social car owner individual driving car times increases or decreases between last month and this month to evaluate whether it is direct car fuel price as well as whether it rises or falls down. This factor can judge whether what factor can cuse general car owner individual driving times increases or decreases in society. Also, it implies that we can depend on general car owner individual driving behavioral times to judge whether the car owner's salaary level had been increased or had been decreasing in the past. It is possibe that general social car owner individual driving time behavior is significantly increasing or decreasing, it may reflect whether the car owner has present salary , it has been increasing or has been decreasing. Because if the car owner whose salary has been decreasing significantly, the significant decresaing salary, it may influence the car owner reduces to spend long time to drive car to arrive another long distance far away destination frequently.

The reason is that he avoids to increase economic loss to use more car fuel for non essential driving use, when he feels that his income is significantly decreased.

Hence, any behavioral economists may attempt to gather household individual general expenditure data in order to conclude what factors influence the household changes his/her family behavioral consumption or consumption attitude. It means thay any household individual consumption attitude changes, it may be influenced by any product price changing factor, such as car fuel price case or the household overall rising or falling income level factor in household behavioral economic view.

- Can market environment influence oil price change?

Market economy theory is an economic system and distribution are guide by the price signals created by the force of suppy and demand. So , the concept of market economy is an economic system in which economic decisions, and the pricing of goods and services are guided by the interactions of a country's individual citizens and businesses.

The both principles of market economy dicated that producers and sellers of goods and servces with offer tham at the highest possible price that consumers are willing to pay for goods and services . When the level of supply needs to level of demand a natural economic equilibrium is achieved. Hong Kong, Singapore, New Zealand, Switerland, United States , Ireland united Kingdom, these countries are applying market economy prinsiple to dominate themselves countries business activities. However, it is difficult to free market economy, because market economy depends on supply and demand regulate the economy, but a time free market economy is an economy in what all resources are owned by individuals.

The advantages of a market economy may include : Innovation, variety, and indidual choices, but it is distribution of wealth, poor work condition and environmental degradation. However, a pure market economy development is difficult because people will always have incentives to use to choose what kinds of product in preference. The characteristics of a market economy, they may include that it is unplanned free enterprise, private property, economic freedom, consumer competition incentive profit pursue, voluntary exchange,, limited government involvement, freedom of enterprise and choice, the role of self interest, market and price, the reliance on technology and capital goods, specialization, use of monetary ad to active, but limited role of government.

So, market economies work using the forces of supply and demand to determine the appropriate prices and quantities for most goods and services in the economy. Hence, one country needs to develop market economy, it needs have a good market environment, such as one commodity needs have advertisement to let consumers to know its existence, in economics, market does not refer why to a fixed location, on enough number balance of buyers and sellers, perfect competition, perfect competition, building good relationship between buyers and sellers, one price (no change) price to any product easily, sound monetary system. Then, when the country can have good market environment, it can develop or implement its market economy strategy more easily.

The free market economy may be the best economic strategy choice because it contributes to economic growth . It ensures competitive markets, supply and demand create competition, which also help ensure that this best goods or services are provided to consumers at a lower price (reasonable price). It can compare the best among perfect competition imperfect competition, oligopoly, monopoly. Hence, market economy encourages market force occurrence, e.g. when the price of crude oil increases, when there are shortages in the supply , when the shortages occur, they become market forces. The demand is more supply, which causes the prices to rise as the crude oil is less available and therefore consumers will be willing to pay more.

The market economy is decides, when the eants of the consumers and the profit motive of the producers will decide what will be produced and management (the owners) together will determine how goods will be produced in a market economy. So, such as oil sale case, when the country has many oil manufactures hope to tisee oil price, they won't manufacture more oil to supply to oil users, e.g. car drivers, public transport service organizations, the aim to bring oil shortage supply in order to rise oil price more easily.
So, free market economy may bring product unfair sale price to any consumers in the country. Because free market economy is too free for manufacturers / producers to make unreasonable product manufacturing decision whether their products manufacturing number (supply number) is more ore less in order to achieve the highest sale price.It won't bring consumer benefit, when they need to pay high price to buy the product in long time. For oil product case example, when the country all oil suppliers, they make decision to manufacture less number oil product in order to reduce oil supply number. They aim to cause oil shortage crise, when the oil needers, e.g. when the country has many air planes need gas to private energy to fly frequently, but gas supply is less to airlines to pay higher gas price to buy, or the country has many people need to catch buses, but gas supply number is less. So, bus companies also need to pay higher gas price to buy even the country has many people own cars. They often need to drive cars to go to work or relax. So, many country car owners , they eed to pay higher gas price to drive themselves cars.

In fact, in the country implements free market economy strategy, so it causes many product manufacturers attempt to cooperate to reduce products manufacturing number. They aim to reduce produc supply , but when consumers number is still increasing. Their demand to the product increases, when the product's demand number is more than supply number, it will cause supply shortage crise. Consequently, the kind of product price may be reasonable to increase. Hence, in consumer behavior view, the country's consumers still accept to pay higher price to buy the product, because they believe the kind of product supply is decreasing.

Hence, it has relationship between how many product choice and consumer payment desire, if the market has many difficukt kinds of product to let consumers to choose, then the kind of product's price can not be increased easily. Such as oil product case, when the country has less number oil manufacturing number. Then, oil buyers feel there are not many oil suppliers to let them to choose and in general these several oil suppliers' oil prices are increasing together . So, oil consumers number will not be influenced to reduce easiy, because they have no many oil suppliers choice in the country.

CHAPTER II

Learning new knowledge brings what advantages to our societies

Whether what are the actual benefits , they may bring to influence our societies change better? I shall attempt to to explain above question. Economic is the social science that examines how individuals, businesses and entire societies manage scarce resources. Resources are by nature , limited. Only a finite amount of land exists, e.g. and people do not have unlimieted time to meet all of their needs and wants. So, if we can learn ho to apply behavioral economy theory to avoid resources waste, then our societies ought develop better.

Our society had changed from traditional economy to develop to nowadays knowledge economy. Traditional economy only produce and take what they need, so there is no waste or inefficiencies involved in produdig the goods required to survive as a society. However, traditional economy also have disadvantages, such as it isolates the people within that economt, large outside economies can win a traditional economy. It offers choices, these may be a lower overall quality of life, it creates specific health risk, unpredictability creates survival uncertainties.

Although, our societies had been experiencing knowledge economy, but it also have disadvantage, knowledge economy means that our societies or business organizations need to learn how ro use knowledge management to keep business growth or social developing. Knowledge management is a systematic approach to capturing and making use of a organization collective expertise to create value. The potential advantages of effective knowledge management are significant , but as with most processes, advantages of knowledge management or knowledge econmic society may include:

Improved organizational or social productivities better and faster decision making, quicker problem solving, increased rate of innovation, supported employee/citizen growth and development within organizations or societies, sharing of specialiat expertise, better communication, improved business processes.

Hence if the organization or society can apply behavioral economic theory to learn knowledge management system , it can help the organization or society to develop better or more easier, e.g. create better products and services , develop better strategies, improve profitability or productivity, reuse existing skills and expertise, increase operational efficiency and staff productivity, recognise market trends early and gain on advantage over rivals make the most of organizations or social intellectual capital . Hence, it explains why when our organizations or societies can apply behavioral economy theory to learn how to apply knowledge management system to develop our organiztations or societies. Then, our societies or organizations will avoid to waste social resource organizational resource as well as achieve more productivities or service improvement, even gain profitability, it is the final aim of why our organizations or / and societies need to attempt to learn how to apply knowledge management system to achieve any objectives in behavioral economy view.

On conclusion, behavioral economic is the study of the effect that our societiesand organizations need to learn how psychological factors have on the economic decision making process of individuals. The importance of understanding behavioral economics for marketers is immeasurable as it follows for a better understanding of the human mind. So, behavioral economics plays a important role in our live and in the eocnomy. It helps governments and businesses learn on every day consumers activities and explains why we consume goods and services , the way we do, why we make certain choices, about ourselves or others and how we decide of action . Hence, behavioral economists need to examine each of these day -to -day choice resulting in progressive understanding of human behavior that combines both psychology and economy.

How do rules influence economic behavior?
Why are the rules of the economic system important? In our societies , our economic behavior occurs in a climate of formal and informal rules. There sulres often act as incentives and influenced the choices people make, people choose to do jobs taht do not keep them fit, and now they have to make more time to stay healthy. So, our societies are experiencing behavioral economic rules made in order to let every one need to adapt how to change and influence to our lives. it is one actual knowledge economic society or knowledge economic social living mode that we need to learn how to adapt to live. We need to learn how to apply knowledge of economic changing behavior. UNderstanding behavioral economic and psychology for social impact our businesses can bring products , sale growth more easily or our societies can be improved to our living quality better.

The relationship between behavioral economy and our society , it may explain that if the result of economic scarcity in a society occurrence, due to that productive resources are limited, therefore, people can not have all the goods and services, they want, a result, they must choose some things and give up others , like individuals, governments and societies , experience scarcity because human wats exceed with can be made from all available resources.

Behavioral economic is the study of psychology as it relates to the economic decision making processes of individuals and organizations. Behavioral economy theory uses psychological experimentation to develop theories about human decision making and has identified a range of biases as a result of the way people think and feel. BE is trying to change the way economists think about people's perception of value and expressed preferences.

However, in our societies, we need have three basic economic problems. Economic systems is as a type social system must confront and solve the three quantities of goods shall be produced, how much and which of alternative tools and services shall be produced, how shall goods be produced what technology a well as for whom are the goods , or services produced who benefts?

All of these are our daily economic problems any organizations (societies) had been changing. We need new social science behavioral economy theory to help use to solve any one of social economic individual problems, for example, when a particular incident becomes cognitively available, it is became of social influence. Individuals are specially averse to losses, but how do we know whether we are facing a loss or instead of a foregone gain ? What is the status from which losses are measured ? how might social influence reduces or increase people's willingness to sacrifice their material sale-interest for the sake of fairness?

All of these matter, applying behavioral economic theory may attempt to explain the reason why the consequency occurs. Also, when some countries governments can apply behavioral economy theory to help them to do reasonable strategic decision in order to avoid any one of these social negative events occur, such as organizational crime, discrimination, environmental hazards, or threats to national security before any one country government decides to implement any strategic action, they may apply behavioral economic theory to weigh whether their decision may bring socity to earn more benefit or more loss, for example, if the country government permits the oil manufacturing firm continues to research the possible oil manufacturing elements at the oceans. Whether their oil research behavior on the ocean , it will bring how serious environmental hazard to cause global oceans have many fishes die per day, how much percentage successful chance oil discovery on anywhere in the oceans.

So, any country governments need to consider whether ocean land oil discovery chance is more important or reducing many fishes death number is more important when any country goverments continue to permit any one oil manufacturers continue to find oil land from oceans in order to manufacture more oil, during their ocean oil land manufacturing process, it may bring serious pollution to ocean water and causes many fishes drink the polluted oil water to be killed. For another exmaple, US government allows many local manfacturers set up factories in China, in order to let many US social manufacturers can pay cheap wages to employ China workers to help them to manufacture any products, e.g. mobiles, shoes, cloths, shirts, televisions etc. although US governmment can bring discrimination image to let China workers feel, they can have more job chance and to earn US manufacturer employers wages. In economic view, China can reduce workers unemployment ratio from US manufacturers‘ factories manufacture jobs chance. Also , US manufacturers can pay cheaper wages to Chinese workers to compare US domestic workers wages. But, US government neglects , it will also cause many US domestic factories manufacture workers had beed beginning to lose their factory manufacture jobs, because Chinese manfacture workers can replace them to do their Us social factory manufacture jobs more easily. Hence, in long term, US manfacturers choose to outsource local factory manufacture workers to them to do, it will cause US unemployed workers manufacture number increases., Hence , US government ought need to weigh long term high unemployment ratio social issue to US domestic factory manufacturing workers, whether US manufacturers cheap or low wages to Chinese factory manufacturing workers (low wage cost) is more important ot reducing US domestic factory manufacturing workers unemployed number social negative influence more important. If US government continue allows US manufacturers outsource domestic factory manufacturing workers to do, it must increase US local manufacturing workers unemployment number and it may cause US government needs to pay future more social welfare expenditure to these long time unemployment US manufacturing workers, even, social stealing crime may be influenced to increase . It implies that behavioral economy analysis can help our society to choose to make more reasonable decisions.

- Learn about the importance of economic factors for families, businesses, and the economy. Several factors—such as interest rates, consumer spending, and unemployment rates—affect economic growth, helping economists forecast how money will move through society.

- Economic factors are internal and external factors in the market that affect the economy, including interest rates, tax rates, laws, policies, wages, and governmental activities. These factors are not directly related to the business but influence the investment value in the future.

- When it comes to business specifically, some of the most important economic factors include interest rates, exchange rates, tax rates, inflation, labor supply and demand, wages, laws and policies, government activities, and recessions.

What Are Economic Factors?

Economic factors are the variables that impact an economy's development. Economic factors such as tax rates, wages, and employment can dictate economic sustainability for families, companies, and nations on small and large scales.

What Is a Macroeconomic Factor?

A macroeconomic factor is an influential fiscal, natural, or geopolitical event that broadly affects a regional or national economy. Macroeconomic factors tend to impact wide swaths of populations, rather than just a few select individuals. Examples of macroeconomic factors include economic outputs, unemployment rates, and inflation. These indicators of economic performance are closely monitored by governments, businesses, and consumers alike.

Negative Macroeconomic Factors

Negative macroeconomic factors include events that may jeopardize national or international economies. Fears of political instability caused by a nation's involvement in a civil or international war are likely to heighten economic turbulence, due to the reallocation of resources, or damage to property, assets, and livelihoods. Risks from the current configuration of external imbalances are generally contained, at least in the near term as current account deficits and debtor positions are largely concentrated in advanced economies that issue reserve currencies. That said, not everyone is immune. An intensification of trade or geopolitical tensions—with negative repercussions for global growth and risk appetite—could affect economies that are highly dependent on foreign demand or external financing.

Over the medium term, in the absence of corrective policies to reduce imbalances, trade tensions could become entrenched. Moreover, a further increase in countries' external debts in key countries could trigger costly disruptive adjustments that could spill over to the rest of the world.

That's why both surplus and deficit countries must work together to reduce excess global imbalances in a manner supportive of global growth and stability.

- How consumer behavior influences economy?

- Consumer behavior plays a critical role in shaping the economy. The spending patterns, pricing, inflation rates, industry trends, investments, and economic policies are all influenced by consumer behavior.

- Changes in the economy determine consumers to change their extravagant lifestyle to a restrained one or vice versa by making expenses and buying patterns. This research paper examines changes in consumer behavior that occurred due to economic changes.

- However, behavioral science tells us that identifying consumers' new beliefs, habits, and "peak moments" is central to driving behavioral change. For example, financial constraints are economic limitations on behavior. Given that millions of people experience chronic or episodic financial constraints, we sought to review research that provides
- insight into how they affect con-sumer behavior.

- According to behavioral science, the set of beliefs that a consumer holds about the world is a key influencer of consumer behavior. Beliefs are psychological—so deeply rooted that they prevent consumers from logically evaluating alternatives and thus perpetuate existing habits and routines.

- Changes in the economy determine consumers to change their extravagant lifestyle to a restrained one or vice versa by making expenses and buying patterns. This research paper examines changes in consumer behavior that occurred due to economic changes. Due to the adverse economic environment, consumers constantly cut down their expenses until they feel stable regarding their finances. Changes in the economy determine consumers to change their extravagant lifestyle to a restrained one or vice versa by making expenses and buying patterns.

- How technological invention or innovation influence economy ?

Recently, researchers have found a link between technology innovation and national economic prosperity. I indicate the reasons as below:

Firstly, when firms innovate, profits go up, and labor and financing flow to them and away from their competitors, who suffer from this creative destruction. For this to occur, labor and capital markets need to function efficiently. Secondly, innovation is how this productivity growth happens. For decades, economists and economic historians have sought to improve their understanding of the role of technological invention in economic growth. As in many fields of inventive endeavor, their efforts required time to develop and mature. For example ,the closer a nation is to the technology frontier, the more its economic growth relies on research education. "GPTs are Schumpeterian in nature, as they typically lead to older technologies in all sectors of the economy to be abandoned as they diffuse to these sectors.

For USA economic technological development example, invention leads to economic growth by increasing labor productivity—new technologies allow each worker to produce a greater amount of goods and services. The following graphs show that between the end of World War II and the mid-1970s, U.S. households fully benefited from steadily increasing productivity. So, it seems that nowadays technological innovation or invention which may bring global economic development in possible.

Can human behavior may help economic growth? Why human behavior and economic growth have close relationship? I believe that productivity growth in different industries, how the shares of wages and profits, how taxation affects growth, how inventions which can bring global economic growth, create working chance, sale income chance, consumption chance, productivity chance, wealth chance. These factors may bring global short term or long term economic growth. All of these factors hace close relationship between human invention and economic growth. I shall explain as below:

For any kinds of things inventions example, are best regarded as a form of investments, and their volume depends in like manner, on their expected profitability. Investments opportunities are recreated by inventions investment. However, inventions may not be economig growth factor, but there is a high profitability that prior circumstances will bring them about, so learning from human past prior experience is important not just in scientific or engineering matters, but in other fields, such as business and social organization. So, research and development, such as human invention behavior which has chance to bring long term or short term economic growth.

I mean that human invention may be one kind of investment opportunity to bring global economic growth in possibility, because human new knowledge learning behavior may attribute to global new business invention chance to bring unlimited economic growth chance in nowadays society. Hence, human can not neglect to create ourselves " invention mind or invention behavior" in order to help global economic growth more easily. SO, human invention may be one kind helping global economic growth new investment opportunuty, which is created from " human learning behavior". IN fact, an improvement in investmednt opportunity method may be created by human " any kinds of new inventions behavior". SO, nowadays society, any kinds of new inventions of product, whcih ought help global societies to bring economic growth chance.

The theory of economic growth may be based on income, labor and land which every one kknows and which are adequate. However, nowadays society had changed, such as scientific invention example, it can bring profit chance to business, creating job opportunities in global labor markets, such as smart phones, laptops, desktops, non-manual driving vehicles, electric energy cars invention etc. any kinds of new scientific invention products, they can bring new scientifical products businessess chance, they must need to employ may manufacture labour, salespeople, transport workers,logistic store workers, admin stafs, transport workers, product invention staffs , marketing promotion staffs etc. different job positions to let global human can have chance to find these jobs to do in order to earn income. Moreover, any kinds of scientific product inventions , which can bring many new jobs positions chance to let global unemployed people hace chance to work and earn incoime.Also, any kinds of new scientific products invention may create many new jobs chance to global and solve unequal wealth and income allocation problem to global human, even businesses have chance to sell these new scientific invention products to sell to global buyers to earn more profit.

I mean that " new products invention" may help global societies to reduce unemployment challenge and it can bring long term economic growth in global labour market view. Moreover, when any kinds of new product inventions, such as battery energy vehicle, non-manual driving auto vehicle or public transport tools, home washing machines, televisions, radios, fans, smart phomnes, laptops, electronic book reading tools, internet invention etc, different kinds of new scientific product inventions, they can bring " consumption opportunity" to let global consumers have chance to buy any kinds of new scientific inventionw, which can also encourage global consumption rate raises in order to increase global wealth improvement rate speed rises up radidly.

So, global wealth rising rate whether which is rapid or slow, it depends on whether how many different kinds of new scientific products invention may be confirmed to scceed to sell in global business market.

Hence, investment on invention, which may be tangible evidence to create economic growth in the distribution of income , wages and profits between global labor, scientific inventions of products sellers, and global scientific inventions of products consumers. They have close relationship to be influenced to increas economic growth speed whether they are rapid or slow from " global scientific new products inventions". If human product invention scientists can attempt to research how to invent any kinds of undiscovered new kinds of products inventions, for example, if global any kinds of scientific product invention scientistis can attempt to invest time to invent 100 kinds of new scientific products inventions in orde to provide global human have chance to buy to use. Then, these 100 different kinds of scientific invention products may help global new invention of scientific products sellers to provide many different kinds of new jobs vacancies to let global unemployed or job seekers have chance to work and earn income.

So, global unemployed rate will have chance to reduce in global societies. Moreover, they can also help these new scientific products sellers to bring " earning profit chance", even thes global " new product invention scientists who have earn product invention royalty income chance after they can invent any kinds of products in success.

Finally, global consumption market growth rate will be influenced to rise up, when in the year, there are 100 new kinds of nre scientific products invention have been already sold to let global consumers hacew chance to choose the kind of target of scientific product to buy to use. So, global new economic growth rate speed , it can rise up rapid up or slow down, it depends on whether the year, global has how many kinds of new invention of scientific products" have been invented to prepare to sell in global scientific products sale market in macro economic view.

Hence, economic growth and human invention behavior, which have cloase relationship . The list of anti-growth factors could be extended perhaps however. Hartwell (1983) has pointed out that economies have always contained a mixture of three main systems for making production, consumption, and distribution decisions namely, administered and market free enterprise. It was the gradual freeing of man's entrepreneurial talents from the bonds of custom and command that finally resulted in the remarkable economic growth of the industrial revolution.

However, in the twrms of human history, sustained economic growth is rare, and this suggests that several conditions (Needham's Packet), rather than memely one or two , have had to be met before it earns occur.

It is also the case, however, that its occurrence has at least in some respects made its survival more probable. HUman scientific investment has improved communications, such as smart phone, internet email and increased education (learning) chance, such as distancel learning, AI learning writing method, listening language learning method, , reading e-books from smart phone, laptop channel method, which can chance traditional classroom leanring method to new scientific channel learning method or which can change traditional telephone or post lewtter communication method to nowadays sending email, smart phone calling, whataps new scientific tool communication methods.

ON conclusion, the free societies are influenced by any kinds of new scientific products inventions, Human had began to accept how attempted to buy any kinds of new scientific products inventions to use. New scientific inventions of products, which has bring more fashable of undiscovered new scientifical inventions of products choice to satisfy human ourselves daily new products invention using needs in our daily lives. SO, human scientists whose any kinds of new products inventions which will bring more chance to help global societies to create new social economic growth in global societies.

I assume that technology and human behavior which have close relationship (e.g. working behavior , living behavior), For robot case example, if robots can influence human behavioral change, and future human working environment will need to cooperate with robots or human living environment will depend on robots' helping. How human behavior will be influenced to change in order to adapt to accept robots invention when human needs to live or work with robots together in the same time.

In organizational working environment, staffs will need to accept digital, data and robot technology in our industries or implementing a business strategy , why organizations need to be made decision making by robots. However, staffs have possible to depend on robots to help them to make decision, e.g. staffs behavior on analysis or judgement which can be controlled or managed by robots in possible. CEO, or manager leaders , their managing ability will be supervised or managed by robots in any organizations . So, it seems that robots may be any organizational top leader, if they can manage CEO or manager or supervisor in any organizations.

Business organizational leader individual managing behavior must be controlled by robots. Robots (supervised learning) is the most popular type of machine learning and robots can learn any new kinds of knowledge to compare human easily and rapidly. So, any organizational business decision or strategy decision may be made or influenced by supervising robots in organizations in possible. CEO, manager, supervisor their managing ability or managing skill may be influenced to reduce by supervising learning supervising or leading robots cooperation.

However, we can follow these aspects to explain how robots may influence our behavior change. Robots may be applied to participate in sales and marketing , HR, finance, customer service, education, legal and government organizations. Robots will be superintelligence to impact human lives in due time, In future, robots has insight , such as perceives, learns, understands, comprehends. It is one deep learning machines. It can make right or wrong , true or wrong judgement or answer and make good or bad predictions.

Hence, if robots can be applied to work in our future societies in popular, they may be social leader to replace human leader, e.g. government leader, organizational leader, CEO, manager, supervisor. Robots can not only human's worker role, e.g. home servants, shopping center cleaner, kitchen cooker. If robots can be organizational leaders, they may supervise worker individual working attitude or working performance whether his/her performance is satisfactory or perfect or to be needed to improve.

In organization, robots won't be only workers role. They may be supervisor role to supervise, manage or dominate or control all organizational top, middle , low level staffs their behavior and make judgement whether whom staffs can either stay to work or leave the organization.

However, some behavioral economists feel robots are Unfair to make judgement on staff individual working behavior. But on behavioral economic view, robots may help business owners to make judgement whether whom staffs ought stay the firm to work or leave the firm. They can help the organization to bring long term economic benefit. Hence, robots may be right to be future any organizational leader, such as CEO, manager, supervisor role more than worker role. If robots can be supervisor role in any organizations, I believe that they can help the organizations to bring much long term economic benefits to compare human CEO, manager, or supervisor for future global business economic development environment because robots may help any organizations to improve efficiency , or raise productivity to compare human staff decision making abilities.

Ought robots be leader role? In any organizations robots can bring this economic benefits to customer service aspect. For example, in order to reduce mind-numbing repetition for human workers, some economists recommend that future organizations seriously consider use of robots to field calls and process requests at a basic level. Such robots could be used to authenticate users for basic access to the organization in order for staffs to obtain the least risky information that they need. As customer need rise is complexity and business risk failure to satisfy that customer's need and to cause the customer chooses to buy another product or use another service. The work of ticket creation and case routing can be enhanced by robots, but a human should oversee it according to business risk assessment.

Hence, robot analytics can help to any organizations to predict those cases most likely headed for escalation in real time, all the date of the chatbot need to be presented to the human , so that the poor, annoyed customer does not have to start all over again with self-identification and description of the problem.

So, future robots can be perfect customer service leader, they can help satisfy your customers and retain them. Robots can know whether what the customer's real need , how to let the customer feels satisfactory more compare human customer service staffs. They can be customer service leader, service recommendation professionals. They can help organizations to retain old customers , even increase new customers easily to compare human customer service staffs. Hence, robots ought participate to marketing, customer service teams to help staffs how to do right customer service decision with human customer service staffs together. Hence, customer service staffs need to follow up customer service robots' ideas how to help them to solve any customer complain or enquiry in order to improve customer service performance. Consequently, the organization will increase new customer number and retain old customers easily if robots can be applied to participate on marketing, customer service departments.

How be robots in business? They may include three main areas: More intelligence products, services and business process. The first perspective is external. AI enhanced product and service means what you need to deliver to your customers. Both product and service -based business, which means they're all about making customers' lives easier, understanding and anticipating their needs, and solving their problems.

The second perspective is internal, making business processes more intelligent means looking at your business from the inside, assessing every aspect of your operations. To see how to make the business more efficient and enhance from manufacturing to the supply chain.

The third perspective is creating more intelligent products. How robots influence human living behavior? The internet of things means a whole host of everyday products are getting smart. Smart devices like smart phones, smart TV, smart watches on the market, smart office buildings, smart houses, they can influence staffs work or households live whom feel more comfortable.

On AI products aspect,. Intelligent smart running shoes products are like a fitness tracker, but provide more specialist information for runners. A smart AI chip that and how monitors movement (including gait and how feet strike the ground), the shoes provide feed- that helps runners improve their form and reduce the risk of injury. SO, AI smart shoes can influence runners feel comfortable and safe when runners run long time on gardens and they will predict or know whether the running places are dangerous or safe as well as smart running shoes can help runners to collect data on their running style , and the accompanying app provides real -time analysis of the runners' performance and running technique.

Smart running shoes can be runner coach on how to run better and avoid running injuries. It's not only running shoes that are being fitted with sensors to gather data and provide feedback.

The " wearable" technology sector is booming due to AI technology development to influence human needs to pursue more comfortable lives. Hence, AI smart products may help human to build health lives daily. Human begins to attempt to learn how to live more health by robots (AI) products.

When robots can be applied to human ourselves living environment , e.g. working, home, social , transport (non manual driving public transport tools service) , leisure environment. How behavioral economists feel they can bring positive or negative economic influence to our future societies?

Robots will bring human to experience economic anxiety. Wy? After centuries of development, basic science, applied science and technology had been rapidly developing. Material science, additive manufacturing , nanotechnology, bio-tech , new batteries, smart phones, non human driving public transport or non public transport tools invention. All of these new technological products include robots may help human to create new technological economic social development and technology also impacts human behavioral change.

Consequently, this leads us to the Fourth industrial revolution" or Klaus Schwab for the world economic forum in his 2015 article and 2016 book, he indicated

The first industrial revolution used water and stream power to mechanize production . The second used electric power to create production. The third used electronic and information technology to automate production. How a Fourth industrial revolution is building on the third, the digital revolution that has been occurring since the middle of the last century. It is characterized by a fusion of technology that is developed by scientists between the physical, digital and biological science.

Ref: Excerpts from the fourth industrial revolution.

Consequently, human have expanded capabilities to communicate, to connect, to work without actual physical environment. Human behavior may be influenced alone or live lonely because robots can help organizations to reduce many workers to work together and working hours. When robots can replace human workers to do their tasks. Moreover, human will have driverless vehicles and drones, which help in more than moving people and goods. They assist us in farming, in pollution control, human have machine-aided surgery, and human have smart cities, smart contract, smart product to use. So, any kinds of new invention of technological tools will be needed to use in any organizations in order to improve performance. Even our homes also need (AI) tools to help us to live more comfortable.

Technological invention have changed our lives to be Better, continuing a trend in previous experiencing of Industrial revolutions, smartphones, connected with Computing power, change the many we decide on Travelling, entertaining purchasing or connecting with Friends. Our day-to-day behavior and decisions are seriously affected by and dependent on the digital network technology.

In fact, machines are more than substitute for people In routine jobs, they can even take over some jobs, that require cognitive functions. Consequently, it may bring unemployment ratio rises or jobs need reduce in our societies. Machine-search changes the life of lawyers, accountants, engineers, even doctors when (AI) tools help them to deal every tasks. So, many professionals will have chance to lose jobs if robots can do their most tasks.

On conclusion, the fast process in machine-human – capital substitution means that experts need to seek new competitive advantages, this time against intelligence machines . So, technology may change human behavior to bring positive and negative both impact in our societies, such as the usefulness in -skill sets as capital labor substitution has become capital -human capital substitution. All of these will raise economic anxiety, because companies will have a reduced staffs number and increase robots number sense of security. Also, workers need to spend time to learn new skills in order to adapt to work with robots together in any organizations. So, technology can not influence workers become lazy. Otherwise, they influence workers become hard because they need to spend time to learn how to work with machine together in organizations. But, technology can also influence human pursue more comfortable to live.

Can technology influence consumers reduce spending on visiting shopping

Why may knowledge influence economic growth? Have they close relationship between knowledge and economic growth or recession in behavioral economy view? I shall attempt to indicate evidences to explain these two questions as below:

IN fact, human development had been experiencing from agricultural stage to industrial manufacturing stage, till to nowadays, service section stage,e.g. hotel tourism leisure development, and technological development stage, e.g. computer and robot development. All of these stages, which are created by ourselves knowledge, it means that how we decide choice, what social development direction will be caused. It it is true, it seems that global human knowledge may influence how our social future continue development. Our social economic growth or recession will be brought to influence from knowledge indirectly.

It is focus on " behavioral economic concept" Economists define scarcity as the condition of wanting more than we can get with available resources. Scarcity is a fact of life. So, human can arrange ourselves resources in a lot of different ways, such as watching TV, buying a book, a car or traveling, but at any given time, ourselves have a fixed range of possibilities. SO, scarcity also describes the world on a collective level. As a society, we can produce only so many things, and we have to decide how those things are divided among many people. But, when social development, knowledge is very important to cause human (scientists) choose how to decide to invent any new things in order to satisfy human not limited need and using desire. So, the total quantity of available knowledge does not diminish as more and more people acquire it. So, ourselves every behavioral decision in life involves weighing the trade off between costs and benefits . We look at our options and decide whether it is worth giving up in order to get the other.

Economists explain this time cost of choice the " opportunity cost", opportunity cost is the value you could gained by choosing your next best alternative, the opportunity you have to pass up in order to take your first choice. Why may ourselves behavior have relationship between opportunity cost and economic growth? For computer invention example, when scientists feel compute products will be future human needs daily, for student learning using need, office tasks needs, watching movie, listening music leisure need,even playing game need. So, scientists had chose to spend time and resource and labor to invent computer products , they forgave to spend time and resource and labor to invent other products. They computer invention is their opportunity cost, includes time, money, resource, labour, knowledge, mind on computer scientists , they had forgiven to spend these resources to research how to invent other kinds of new products.

However, when computer new products had been invented in success, e.g. desktop, laptop, can be popular to be accept to provide to global computer users to use. This kind of computer invention , its users number had been increasing, manufacturing computer number will be influenced to grow, due to computer invention will help developing and developed countries GDP growth rapidly since 1980 year , the early first stage of computer invention had been experiencing during our global technological development history.

So, it implies that computer scientists had been confirmed to do right choice decision to forgive to spend resources, time, money and labour and knowledge to research how to invent any kinds of new products. They make right decision to research how to invent new computer products,even improve desktop to laptop and smart phone , hand carrying smart phone and computer both functions new products to satisfy computer users daily using needs. It is true opportunity cost to computer scientists case. Also, when past, our scientists do right choice to invent this kind of computer product, this kind of computer products can bring global economic benefits, such as government can increase profit tax form computer sellers, offices can use computers to reduce employees number, when computers can help offices to save much document, clerical employees number may be influenced to reduce, tasks can be simple from complex tasks, spending tasks time may be influenced to reduce by computerization of office, factories can apply computers or robots to replace workers to manufacture any kinds of products, such as cars, washing machine, rice cookers, radios, fans ,television etc. different kinds of electrical products. So workers number may be influenced to reduce and wage expenditure must be reduce.

Hence, new knowledge may help global societies to bring economic growth, such as past scientists had decided to forgive to spend time, resource, money, labor, skill, knowledge to research how to invent any kinds of new products, it is possible that they have some different kinds of new products concept choices, computer concept is only one kinds of choice among these new different kinds of new products invention concepts. However, they need to choose only one kind of new product invention among of these different kinds of new product concept choices, because they have not enough resource to provide to them to invent in the past. Finally, they evaluate the weigh and cost between computer invention concept and other new products invention concepts. In fact, computer is one kind of "the bringing much economic benefits" new concept invention product choice.

I believe that if computer will be continue improved in order to bring more economic growth in possible. SO, scientists need to spend more time, resource, money, labor, skill, knowledge to research how to continue to improve traditional computers to bring more using functions, in order to help global different industries to reduce resource, time, labour , money aim to bring reducing cost spending expenditure benefits to global industries , due to societies had been experiencing " knowledge social stage". If societies need to apply computer technology to assist our societies can continue develop, when our societies' different industries, such as service, manufacturing, even agricultrial sectors, e.g. robots may help farmers to predict when it is right time to grow vegetable, or replace farmers to grow vegetable, fruit in farms to provide human have enough food to eat, or robots can help hotel to clean rooms, serve clients, robots can help cinemas to sell tickets, robots can help manufacturers to product new products in factories. So, technological products may help any kinds of industries to reduce employees number, improve efficiencies and productivities and reduce wages expenditure economic cost benefits.

Production possibilites economic concept knowledge indicates about who produces which goods and why. The fact that millions of people and firms around the global coordinate their activities to provide consumers with the right combination of goods and services seem like magic.

In fact, coordination doe snot happen by chance, nor does super-planner tells every one where to go and what to do. Instead, the global production time is a natural outcome of people every acting in their own self interest to improve their own lives. Economists call this coordination mechanism the " invisible hand", an idea that was first suggested by economic thinker Adam Smith.

To get some insight into the who and why of production, such as shirt production case, most shirts are made in China, and other countries when factory wages are low. Have American workers become worse at making shirts over the last two countries? Definitely not, In fact, as are better than American workers at making shirts. Instead , each good tends to be produced by that country, company, or person with the lowest opportunity cost of producing that shirt kind of product, such as scientists make cooperation decision to invent computer products together, they can earn high invention royalty income, computer sale and manufacturing number increases, governments can earn more profit tax, different kinds of service, manufacturing industries can reduce workers number, wage expenditure, improving performance economic benefits . So, countries and firms and persons need a specialize in making goods for which they have the lowest opportunity cost. They than trade with one another to get the coordination of goods. They want to consume, such as computer manufacturing , if IBM and Microsoft both companies can cooperate to research how to improve themselves traditional model of laptops and desktops to create new improved and more using functions laptops and desktops, e.g. small size, more new using functions, clear colour and easier visible screen, or small book cover design, new computer model. I believe that the resulting, gains from themselves computer trade can be shared much that every computer buyers ends up better offer, global computer users will choose to buy and use these both IBM and Microsoft future new computer invention products to compare other kinds of computer manufacturers.

In production possibilities frontier economic concept, it explains why IBM and Microsoft ought cooperate to manufacturer computers, their cooperation can bring more economic benefits to themselves and global computer users, e.g. more computer functions, reducing sale price, reduce computer workers manufacturing wages, and computer manufacturing workers number, increasing computer manufacturing and demand number, increasing profit to themselves and government profit tax income, increasing buyers number, offices can improve efficiencies and employees performance, reducing manufacturing cost expenditure, improving student learning ability, etc. different kinds of global economic benefits. Hence, in production possibilities frontier economic concept, IBM and Microsoft ought make cooperation decision in order to bring global economic benefits.

In fact, computer manufacturing industry is one competitive market, it is one in which truly informed, prices taking buyers and seller easily trade a standardized good or service. IBM and Microsoft need to cooperate in order to win their computer manufacturing competitors , if they hope to earn in global computer manufacturing top leader position. Otherwise, if IBM and Microsoft do not choose to cooperate to invent new kind of computer products, their traditional computer products will be not popular to be accept to use to compare their computer manufacturing competitors. Because, future computer trends to cheap, more using functions, small size, light weight , clear visible and touch feeling screen. in order to attract computer buyers choices more easily.

On conclusion, it is possible that scientists invention knowledge may bring economic growth indirectly. Their invention choice or invention decision may assist our future economy development rapidly or slowly. Hence, knowledge is one invisible hand to influence global economy either it can bring growth or recession in possible.

Knowledge how influences global online shopping times increase ?

Why may knowledge influence economic growth? Have they close relationship between knowledge and economic growth or recession in behavioral economy view? I shall attempt to indicate evidences to explain these two questions as below:

IN fact, human development had been experiencing from agricultural stage to industrial manufacturing stage, till to nowadays, service section stage,e.g. hotel tourism leisure development, and technological development stage, e.g. computer and robot development. All of these stages, which are created by ourselves knowledge, it means that how we decide choice, what social development direction will be caused. It it is true, it seems that global human knowledge may influence how our social future continue development. Our social economic growth or recession will be brought to influence from knowledge

indirectly.

It is focus on " behavioral economic concept" Economists define scarcity as the condition of wanting more than we can get with available resources. Scarcity is a fact of life. So, human can arrange ourselves resources in a lot of different ways, such as watching TV, buying a book, a car or traveling, but at any given time, ourselves have a fixed range of possibilities. SO, scarcity also describes the world on a collective level. As a society, we can produce only so many things, and we have to decide how those things are divided among many people. But, when social development, knowledge is very important to cause human (scientists) choose how to decide to invent any new things in order to satisfy human not limited need and using desire. So, the total quantity of available knowledge does not diminish as more and more people acquire it. So, ourselves every behavioral decision in life involves weighing the trade off between costs and benefits . We look at our options and decide whether it is worth giving up in order to get the other.

Economists explain this time cost of choice the " opportunity cost", opportunity cost is the value you could gained by choosing your next best alternative, the opportunity you have to pass up in order to take your first choice. Why may ourselves behavior have relationship between opportunity cost and economic growth? For computer invention example, when scientists feel compute products will be future human needs daily, for student learning using need, office tasks needs, watching movie, listening music leisure need,even playing game need. So, scientists had chose to spend time and resource and labor to invent computer products , they forgave to spend time and resource

and labor to invent other products. They computer invention is their opportunity cost, includes time, money, resource, labour, knowledge, mind on computer scientists , they had forgiven to spend these resources to research how to invent other kinds of new products.

However, when computer new products had been invented in success, e.g. desktop, laptop, can be popular to be accept to provide to global computer users to use. This kind of computer invention , its users number had been increasing, manufacturing computer number will be influenced to grow, due to computer invention will help developing and developed countries GDP growth rapidly since 1980 year , the earily first stage of computer invention had been experiencing during our global technological development history.

So, it implies that computer scientists had been confirmed to do right choice decision to forgive to spend resources, time, money and labour and knowledge to research how to invent any kinds of new products. They make right decision to research how to invent new computer products,even improve desktop to laptop and smart phone , hand carrying smart phone and computer both functions new products to satisfy computer users daily using needs. It is true opportunity cost to computer scientists case. Also, when past, our scientists do right choice to invent this kind of computer product, this kind of computer products can bring global economic benefits, such as government can increase profit tax form computer sellers, offices can use computers to reduce employees number, when computers can help offices to save much document, clerical employees number may be influenced to reduce, tasks can be simple from complex tasks, spending tasks time may be influenced to reduce by computerization of office, factories can apply computers or robots to replace workers to manufacture any kinds of products, such as cars, washing machine, rice cookers, radios, fans ,television etc. different kinds of electrical products. So workers number may be influenced to reduce and wage expenditure must be reduce.

Hence, new knowledge may help global societies to bring economic growth, such as past scientists had decided to forgive to spend time, resource, money, labor, skill, knowledge to research how to invent any kinds of new products, it is possible that they have some different kinds of new products concept choices, computer concept is only one kinds of choice among these new different kinds of new products invention concepts. However, they need to choose only one kind of new product invention among of these different kinds of new product concept choices, because they have not enough resource to provide to them to invent in the past. Finally, they evaluate the weigh and cost between computer invention concept and other new products invention concepts. In fact, computer is one kind of "the bringing much economic benefits" new concept invention product choice.

I believe that if computer will be continue improved in order to bring more economic growth in possible. SO, scientists need to spend more time, resource, money, labor, skill, knowledge to research how to continue to improve traditional computers to bring more using functions, in order to help global different industries to reduce resource, time, labour , money aim to bring reducing cost spending expenditure benefits to global industries , due to societies had been experiencing " knowledge social stage". If societies need to apply computer technology to assist our societies can continue develop, when our societies' different industries, such as service, manufacturing, even agricultrial sectors, e.g. robots may help farmers to predict when it is right time to grow vegetable, or replace farmers to grow vegetable, fruit in farms to provide human have enough food to eat, or robots can help hotel to clean rooms, serve clients, robots can help cinemas to sell tickets, robots can help manufacturers to product new products in factories. So, technological products may help any kinds of industries to reduce employees number, improve efficiencies and productivities and reduce wages expenditure economic cost benefits.

Production possibilities economic concept knowledge indicates about who produces which goods and why. The fact that millions of people and firms around the global coordinate their activities to provide consumers with the right combination of goods and services seem like magic.

In fact, coordination doe snot happen by chance, nor does super-planner tells every one where to go and what to do. Instead, the global production time is a natural outcome of people every acting in their own self interest to improve their own lives. Economists call this coordination mechanism the " invisible hand", an idea that was first suggested by economic thinker Adam Smith.

In production possibilities frontier economic concept, it explains why IBM and Microsoft ought cooperate to manufacturer computers, their cooperation can bring more economic benefits to themselves and global computer users, e.g. more computer functions, reducing sale price, reduce computer workers manufacturing wages, and computer manufacturing workers number, increasing computer manufacturing and demand number, increasing profit to themselves and government profit tax income, increasing buyers number, offices can improve efficiencies and employees performance, reducing manufacturing cost expenditure, improving student learning ability, etc. different kinds of global economic benefits. Hence, in production possibilities frontier economic concept, IBM and Microsoft ought make cooperation decision in order to bring global economic benefits.

In fact, computer manufaturing industry is one competitive market, it is one in which truly informed, prices taking buyers and seller easily trade a standardized good or service. IBM and Microsoft need to cooperate in order to win their computer manufacturing competitors , if they hope to earn in global computer manufacturing top leader position. Otherwise, if IBM and Microsoft do not choose to cooperate to invent new kind of computer products, their traditional computer products will be not popular to be accept to use to compare their computer manufacturing competitors. Because, future computer trends to cheap, more using functions, small size, light weight , clear visible and touch feeling screen. in order to attract computer buyers choices more easily.

On conclusion, it is possible that scientists invention knowledge may bring eocnomic growth indirectly. Their invention choice or invention decision may assist our future economy development rapidly or slowly. Hence, knowledge is one invisible hand to influence global economy either it can bring growth or recession in possible.

Technology how influences consumer behavioral change ?

Can human behavior may help economic growth? Why human behavior and economic growth have close relationship? I believe that productivity growth in different industries, how the shares of wages and profits, how taxation affects growth, how inventions which can bring global economic growth, create working chance, sale income chance, consumption chance, productivity chance, wealth chance. These factors may bring global short term or long term economic growth. All of these factors hace close relationship between human invention and economic growth. I shall explain as below:

For any kinds of things inventions example, are best regarded as a form of investments, and their volume depends in like manner, on their expected profitability. Investments opportunities are recreated by inventions investment.

However, inventions may not be economig growth factor, but there is a high profitability that prior circumstances will bring them about, so learning from human past prior experience is important not just in scientific or engineering matters, but in other fields, such as business and social organization. So, research and development, such as human invention behavior which has chance to bring long term or short term economic growth.

I mean that human invention may be one kind of investment opportunity to bring global economic growth in possibility, because human new knowledge learning behavior may attribute to global new business invention chance to bring unlimited economic growth chance in nowadays society. Hence, human can not neglect to create ourselves " invention mind or invention behavior" in order to help global economic growth more easily. SO, human invention may be one kind helping global economic growth new investment opportunity, which is created from " human learning behavior". IN fact, an improvement in investment opportunity method may be created by human " any kinds of new inventions behavior". SO, nowadays society, any kinds of new inventions of product, which ought help global societies to bring economic growth chance.

The theory of economic growth may be based on income, labor and land which every one knows and which are adequate. However, nowadays society had changed, such as scientific invention example, it can bring profit chance to business, creating job opportunities in global labor markets, such as smart phones, laptops, desktops, non-manual driving vehicles, electric energy cars invention etc. any kinds of new scientific invention products, they can bring new science products business chance, they must need to employ may manufacture labour, salespeople, transport workers,logistic store workers, admin staffs, transport workers, product invention staffs , marketing promotion staffs etc. different job positions to let global human can have chance to find these jobs to do in order to earn income. Moreover, any kinds of scientific product inventions , which can bring many new jobs positions chance to let global unemployed people have chance to work and earn income.Also, any kinds of new scientific products invention may create many new jobs chance to global and solve unequal wealth and income allocation problem to global human, even businesses have chance to sell these new scientific invention products to sell to global buyers to earn more profit.

I mean that " new products invention" may help global societies to reduce unemployment challenge and it can bring long term economic growth in global labour market view. Moreover, when any kinds of new product inventions, such as battery energy vehicle, non-manual driving auto vehicle or public transport tools, home washing machines, televisions, radios, fans, smart phomnes, laptops, electronic book reading tools, internet invention etc, different kinds of new scientific product inventions, they can bring " consumption opportunity" to let global consumers have chance to buy any kinds of new scientific inventionw which can also encourage global consumption rate raises in order to increase global wealth improvement rate speed rises up rapidly. So, global wealth rising rate whether which is rapid or slow, it depends on whether how many different kinds of new scientific products invention may be confirmed to sccess to sell in global business market.

Hence, investment on invention, which may be tangible evidence to create economic growth in the distribution of income , wages and profits between global labor, scientific inventions of products sellers,and global scientific inventions of products consumers. They have close relationship to be influenced to increase economic growth speed whether they are rapid or slow from " global scientific new products inventions". If human product invention scientists can attempt to research how to invent any kinds of undiscovered new kinds of products inventions, for example, if global any kinds of scientific product invention scientists can attempt to invest time to invent 100 kinds of new scientific products inventions in order to provide global human have chance to buy to use. Then, these 100 different kinds of scientific invention products may help global new invention of scientific products sellers to provide many different kinds of new jobs vacancies to let global unemployed or job seekers have chance to work and earn income.

So, global unemployed rate will have chance to reduce in global societies. Moreover, they can also help these new scientific products sellers to bring " earning profit chance", even these global " new product invention scientists who have earn product invention royalty income chance after they can invent any kinds of products in success.

Finally, global consumption market growth rate will be influenced to rise up, when in the year, there are 100 new kinds of new scientific products invention have been already sold to let global consumers have chance to choose the kind of target of scientific product to buy to use. So, global new economic growth rate speed , it can rise up rapid up or slow down, it depends on whether the year, global has how many kinds of new invention of scientific products" have been invented to prepare to sell in global scientific products sale market in macro economic view.

Hence, economic growth and human invention behavior, which have cloase relationship . The list of anti-growth factors could be extended perhaps however. Hartwell (1983) has pointed out that economies have always contained a mixture of three main systems for making production, consumption, and distribution decisions namely, administered and market free enterprise. It was the gradual freeing of man's entrepreneurial talents from the bonds of custom and command that finally resulted in the remarkable economic growth of the industrial revolution. However, in the twrms of human history, sustained economic growth is rare, and this suggests that several conditions (Needham's Packet), rather than memely one or two , have had to be met before it earns occur.

It is also the case, however, that its occurrence has at least in some respects made its survival more probable. HUman scientific investment has improved communications, such as smart phone, internet email and increased education (learning) chance, such as distancel learning, AI learning writing method, listening language learning method, reading e-books from smart phone, laptop channel method, which can chance traditional classroom leanring method to new scientific channel learning method or which can change traditional telephone or post lewtter communication method to nowadays sending email, smart phone calling, whataps new scientific tool communication methos.

ON conclusion, the free societies are influenced by any kinds of new scientific products inventions, Human had began to accept how attempted to buy any kinds of new scientific products inventions to use. New scientific inventions of products, which has bring more fashable of undiscovered new scientifical inventions of products choice to satisfy human ourselves daily new products invention using needs in our daily lives. SO, human scientists whose any kinds of new products inventions which will bring more chance to help global societies to create new social economic growth in global societies.

Why does economic changes may influence consumer individual behavioral change? I shall attempt to indicate shopping behavior and staying at home behavior to explain their case and effect relationsip as below:

Human behavior can be influenced by economic change or economic change can be influenced by human behavior? Why does recession may influence consumers reduce shopping desire? In social recession suitation, it is possible that many people lose jobs suddenly, due to businessmen lose many customers. They need to make decision to reduce employees number in order to continue to keep businesses. Consequently, many firms (organizations) their employees may lose jobs. When they have much time, due to lose jobs, they will feel to avoid to spend too much time and money to go to shopping often. Many losing jobs people, they will often stay at homes.

So, they will reduce time to go to shopping, then non essential products won't their preferable choice purchase products. Hence, recession will change many losing jobs people their shopping or consumption desires to avoid to buy non essential products often . Usually when economic boom, many people have jobs to do because consumers number must increase when many people have jobs to do. Then, many people can accept to spend money to buy non essential products often. Many people feel spend time to go to shopping can satisfy their purchase of any kinds of new products useful psychology or desire. So, recession is one good example to explain it can influence many people do not like often to leave homes to go to shopping easily. Many people like to stay at homes, becaue they feel worry about spending too much shopping time when they leave homes. Their staying home time is one good negative shopping behavior example. So, economic change may influence human individual behavior changes , they have direct cause and efect relationship in behavioral economic view.

May human behavior influence economic change? Is it possible that human behavior may bring the country social economic change in macro economic or micro behavioral economic view ? I shall indicate publishing industry example. Do you feel that if there are many students feel learning is very important when they read many books or many of students feel interesting to read or they have reading new books in habit, then it is possible that the country will have many students like to spend time to go to any book shops to choose the books, they feel that they can help they learn new knowledge. Then the country will increase students number, they often spend time to visit any one book shop every week. Their visiting book shops behavior which may become their habits. So, the country will increase students number, they often spend time to visit book shops. Also, it implies that visiting book shops behaviors may be their behavioral habits.

So, when the country has many students often spend time to visit book shops , their visiting book shops behaviors may help any one book shop to raise books sale chance. So, the country's student individual often visiting book shop behaviors, their habitual visiting book shops behaviors must may assist help any one book shop to increase books sale number absolutely.

Consequently, any one book shop , its books sale bumber must be influenced to increase to increase because the country will have many students like or feel need visit book shops habit in order to choose any suitable books to buy to read at home in order to raise themselves learning effort. When the country has many bok shops often have many students visit their book shops, then their books sale number may be influenced to increase. It explain why student individual visiting book shop behavior may help any one book shop sale number increases also.

What does human network job mean ? Why may human network job be popular? Why human network job behavior may influence economy ? Nowadays internet is popular to use. We can apply internet to find data , search any new things, even earn money. Why does internet may become huma network job source. For example, e-publish may be one kind of new human network job. Any authors may apply internet channel to help them to sell electronic or paper books from e-publisher web store. They may apply facebook, you tub etc. any online channel to promote themselves new books to let new readers to know whether when they may buy themselves favourable new topic books to read from electronic publisher web store.

Thus, future electronic publisher industry may help any authors to build internet network platform to help them to sell and promote to advertise their any one new electronic or paper book topic to let global any one reader to choose to buy their any new topic books from electronic publisher web store easily and conveniently. However, it implies that electronic network platform author may be one kind of future new human network job in our societies.

How electronic network platform author job may bring economy benefit in macro economy view? A person can have few friends, contacts and still be very influential if these few friends and contacts are themselves highly influential, e.g. one author must not need to know any one reader in global society. When they like to choose any electronic books from electronic internet network platform. They may become the author's any one topic book buyer, when they feel the author's any one topic book is fun and attract they make decision to buth the strange author whose the topic book from electronic book publisher's platform web store conventiently in short time. Although, they are strangers, they do not know themselves , but the reader can understand what it way that made Google from writing platofrm to create new creative mind and typing network job method to replace traditional hand writing book method for global authors. It will be one kind of new human network writing job.

Hence, global any one reader can apply an innovative search engine , such as google.com to find whether whom author personal new topic books are value to read from internet. Then, the electroniuc publisher's web store may be new book store platform sale network to help the author to sell many electronic or paper books from electronic network platform in short time. So, internet may be future new network plaform to help global any one author to create network writing job absolutely. Furthermore, internet may be popular social media to help any one author to build goold relationship between his/her readers. It is one kind of new network, human network job. New authors do not need to buy many paper books to prepare to put in any one book shop warehouse. Their every book can print on demand to reduce out of book stock in any one book shop. They may choose to sell either electronic books or paper books both from any one book publisher web store. So, electronic network platform may be one kind of good writing channel to help human authors to create income and it can also help authors to bring new creative mind and new topic fun content books to let readers to know and buy to read from electronic publisher network platform.

Why does human behavior may be one kind of new human network job to bring global economic advantages. ALthough, it may be free income or without inocme, but the person does the network behavior, his/her behavior may be bring advantages to influence many other people's health. For this case, when a worker in a coffee shop in an airport gets a vaccination aganinst the flu, it does not only helps him or her stay healthy, but also helps the many travellers who might otherwise have been inflected if that workers caught the flu. So, the externality , the result implies the vaccination of even a part of a community conveys benefits to the whole community. For example, governments pay special attention to the vaccinations of school children, teachers, health mothers, and the elderly, categories of people particularly susceptible not only to catching, but also to transmitting a disease.

It is not accidential that governments are heavily involved with vaccination . When there are externalities, free market, fail to persuade individual incentives with society's their the worker's decision of whether to get a vaccine ends up attracting whether other people get sick. The workers might not fully take all these other people's potential suffering into account when making her or his vaccination decision.

As Stanford University does many suggestions, understand this and tries to help them make the right decisions and so providers free flu vaccines for its staff and students.

Small pockets of unvaccinated individuals can allow a disease to gain a spread more widely well-being. For example, parent weighing the costs and benefits of a vaccine for their child is not always thinking of the consequences of that vaccination to other people. THese are markets in which subsidizing or regulating behavior can make everyone better off. Because the reason for requiring that a child be vaccinated before enrolling in school is not just to protect that child, because each child's vaccination affects others via potential contagions.

Nowadays, although human had been technological success, e.g. internet invention brings economic online shopping chance to global business societies. COnsumer shopping method had been influenced to stay at homes to use internet to shopping by internet technological invention, even robot invention can bring global job model change to improve employee efficiencies and performance. However, whether technological invention can bring global economic development, such as America's economic growth whether it can be influenced to grow up by internet, or robot or e-commerce online shopping moedel.

ON conclusion, I believe that technology may affect consumer behavioral change because technology has changed not only how we produce and connect, but also allows more humans to create and test new objects and ideas, reducing the costs and risks of innovation, and product development, also in developing countries, for digitalization has also significantly impacted financial sector, e.g. facilitating online transaction, to e-commerce sector, e.g. advances in AI, machine leanring robotics. By 2025, we estimate that 50 billion devices will be connected to the industrial internet of things (IOT), while 70 percent of manufacturers are expected to use digital by 2022. However, I believe that what time is the most right to invest technology. During recession is the smart investing time , because a recession or economic downturn can be an unsetting time for investors and their finances. Stock prices often fall just as the economy starts to slow and workers get anxious about potentially losing their jobs, due to the slowdown, but recessions can actually be one of the best times to global manufacturers to make technological investment decision.

CHAPTER III

How human behavior may influence economic development

May any country which citizen behavior assist themselves country development? It is one cause and effect economic question. I mean that if the country itself citicen can not concentrate mind or energy to choose to do one kind of industry in order to let themselves country can bring the most benefit, then whether the counry itself economy can bring the most serious economic benefit. I shall attempt to indicate these countries themselves indistry choice to explain whether these countries themselves citizen productive behavior may help themselves countries to achieve the largest economic benefits. I shall indicate as below:

New Zealand farmer individual wine productive behavior

For New Zealand country example, this country concerns itself effort is foucs on farming agricultural aspect. So, this country has many farmers

concentrate on farming agricultural aspect. May New Zealanders choose to spend time to produce different kinds of wines, e.g. wine or red grape wine is for the people are eating meat, or they are eating dinner.

When these New Zealanders their behaviors choose to do farming or agriculture to grow and produce different kinds of taste of white or red grape wine drinking products job. Themselves grape agriculture behavior will influence these New Zealanders themselves, they can learn how to improve different kinds of grape wine drinking products in order to achieve every kinds of white or read grape wines taste improving aim during their white or red grape producing process.

Why can New Zealander every individual white or read grape wine producers improve their white or read grape wine taste more easily? In behavioral economic view, it can explain that why any one New Zealander white or read grape wine producer can be encouraged or excited or persuaded to concentrate nervous and energy and effort to learn how to improve their white or red grape wine products easily.

In fact, New Zealand is one agricultural food export country. It has good natural environment resource , e.g. land, seed to provide any one farmer to produce themselves any kinds of agricultrual food products, e.g. fruit, or wine food products. Because New Zealanders know themselves country has enough natural resource . So, in common, many New Zealanders choose to attempt to do farming agricultural jobs in order to export themselves any kinds of fruit or meat or wine products to overseas or sell to domestic in order to earn profit.

So, when these New Zealand farmers number has been increasing every year. This country farmers will feel themsleves competition between this New Zealand farmers themselves are serious due to they may feel New Zealanders choose to do agriculture businesses in order to export themselves different kinds of farming food to overseas or sell to local to earn profit.

Hence, when many New Zealand farmers feel that farmers number has been increasing every year. They will feel themselves competition is serious. They must need to spend much time and nervous and effort to research what method is the best how to produce the best taste of white or red grape wine products in order to let local or overseas wine buyers to choose to buy his/her producing white or read grpae products to drink.

Hence, in competition psychological view, may influence many New Zealand white or reaad wine producers had been beginning to change their learning behavior on researching what method is the best in order to produce the best quality of taste red or white wine products to sell in order to attract overseas or local white or read grape wine drinkers to choose to buy his/her wine products. Their behavior will focus on learning how to raising or improving white or read grape wine taste method more than only focus on producing a large number white or red grape wine products. They believe wine quality is more important to compare wine producing number. So, New Zealand wine producers themselves wine producers behaviors have been changing on concentrating on researching wine quality method aspect more then wine producing number aspect in behavioral economic view.

America high technological productive behavior

For America example, US is one high technological country, it owns many high technological knowledge talent inventors, e.g. computer science inventors. Hence, US must attract many diferent countries owning high technological computer inventors choose to go to US to develop their computer science profession career. Also, it seems that when many computer science inventors or professions choose to go to US to develop themselves computer science new career. In behavioral economic view, due to their leaving themselves countries choice, which may bring influence themselve country job behaviors need to be changed. They must need to adapt US new live. Because they will forgive their past computer science job. These computer science professionals need to spend time to adapt US new lives. They " past computer science job behaviors" will need to be changed to their new US any computer employer's new computer science job model.

Because their traditional computer science jobs needed to be forgot in their themselves countries. They will feel their old computer science job knowledge and behavior needed to change in order to let their US any one new of computer company employer feels satisfactory to accept their new working behavior in any one US computer organization.

So, on the other hand, many US computer company employer will feel that they must need time to accept any one new overseas computer science professions their working behaviors, their working attitudc daily, bccause these foreign comouter science professional, their past computer working behaviors and working attitude must be different to US domestic computer science professions.

In behavioral economic view, these overseas computer science professions, their working behaviors and attitude must be needed to change in order to adapt any one US new computer company itself domestic or local computer science professional stafs themselves daily working behaviors and attitude because these overseas and local computer science professionals must need to team work together.

In behavioral economic view, it is only one way that foreign computer science professionals must need to change themselves past country traditiona daily working behaviors and attitude in order to cooperate with these US local computer science professionals in teams more easily.

Consequently, if these foreign compute science professionals can change their past working behaviors and attitude to let any one US local computer science professional feels to cooperate with them easily in short time. Then, the US computer company itself whole computer professional teams themselves efficiencies will be influenced to raised or improved by the changing past working attitude and working behaviors of these foreign computer science professionals. So, in behavioral economic view, only if US any one computer company hopes itself computer teams themselves efficiency can be raised or improved when it decides to employ foreign computer science professionals and US domestic computer science professionals. They need to work in teams together. They must need to let these foreign computer science professionals to know how to change their working behaviors and attitude to let their domestic computer science professionals feel easy to work together. Then, the US computer company itself whole team efficiency must be rasied or improved easily in short time.

China share market investing behavior

For China share market example, economic development depends on financial market. Because if many Chinese have interest to invest to carry on shares buying and selling activities in orde to learn how to earn shares interest and share profit when the China shareholder can make decision to sell himself/herself shares in the the high price, then he/she can earn money when he/she can sell the China company's shares in the high sale share price position.

If China has many Chinese like to spend time to carry on investing shares activities. Themselves shares buying and selling behaviors will influence China has many companies can increase fund from many Chinese shareholders in order to have enough money to expand or develop themselves businesses in China in long term.

Consequently, when China can have many Chinese like to attempt to carry on buying and selling shares investing behaviors in China share market. Themselves buying and selling shares behaviors can help many Chinese companies have effort to increase enough money or capital in order to continue to do their businesses in long term absolutely. So, it explains why when many Chinese become shareholders , they can assist China will have many companies continue to develop their businesses if many Chinese like to carry on shares buying and selling investing behaviors in long time in China financial investment market nowadays in behavioral economic view.

Why has any individual country have many people invest share behavior which can influence the country's macro consumption desire?

I shall apply shares market buying and selling investment behavior to explaiin why shares investment behavior which may impact the country's overal consumption desire as below:

In behavioral economic view, I assume that when the coutry has many people have interest to attempt to carry on shares buying and selling investment behavior, then their frequent shares buying and selling behaviors which may bring negactive consumption desire or shopping desire of these shares investors their consumer behavior.

The reason is simple, when the country has many share buyers number suddenly been increasing rapidly. Consequently, these large group share investors must need to spend much time to research any kinds of company shares variations, whether when their share prices will rise up of fall down in order to achieve buying the company's shares in the lowest price and selling the company's shares in the highest price level in order to earn profit.

Basic on this reason, they must need to spend much extra time to research share prices changing behavior every day, e.g. one working person will wait to leave his/her job, after he/she can spend time to gather data to research the day's share price changing behavior after dinner. So, the working person's right time may be his/her share price market research behavior. Before he/she may spend his/her night time to go to shopping after dinner, but nowadays, he/she will fogive to do his/her shopping behavior before dinner or after dinner at hight sometime. He/she will make decision to spend much night time to turn on computer to click on share market website to research his/her share purchase choice to investigate whether his/her share price whether it rises up or falls down at the moment in order to make his/her share buying or selling decision at ever night time.

I mean the when the country has many people are share investors, their shares investment behavioral spenging time which will influence many shops lose customers at might often because the country will have many people feel need to spend night time to turn on computer or watch television to investigate share price variation. So, the country will have many people / share investors choose to stay at home in order to carry on share price variation investigation behavior, they need to listen share market update news from radios or watch the share market update news from computer or TV at home every night. Consequenly, they must reduce times to leave themselves homes at night. So, their shopping behavior also will be reduced. Because these share investors feel need to spend time to investigate share price variation news at homes which can bring economic benefits (high opportunity benefits) when they choose to forgive to leave homes to go to shopping times (opportunity cost) every night.

On conclusion, it seems that when the country has many people are share investors, then their share price investigating behavior may bring negative shopping emotion at night. Consequently, the country's any one shop may lose many customers from this share investor consumer group in behavioral economic view. Hence, when the country's share investors number had been increasing rapidly, it will influence any shops lose many customers from this share investing customer group at night frequenly in short time, even long time in behavioral economic view, because their shopping desires or shopping emotion will be brought negative feeling when they make decisions to spend much time to listen radios or watch TV or computers share price update nes at night. Hence, share market will bring negative impact to influence consumer shopping desire or negative shopping emotion in behavioral economic view.

Can technology influence human shopping behavioral change?

Nowadays, technological development has reached mature stage, whether technological mature stage may bring positive or negative shopping emotion influence to global consumers. I shall aplly internet inventin or ecommerce shopping channel tool to explain whether internet technology can bring postive or negative influence to global consumer behavior in behavioral economic view.

Internet is a good technological tool, it brings e-commerce business chance. In fact, commonly, global has have many businessmen choose to use internet channel to carry on their products transactions between global online-buyers and their electronic websites. So, global many shoppers had begun to feel online shopping is more convenient to compare visiting shops shopping. Their shopping behaviors have been changed from internet technological tool. Global has many shoppers choose to buy any products from any overseas or local businessmen their web stores. They only need to spend time to find any businessmen their webstores to choose the most suitable products to pay visa to buy from their webstores. at homes. So, in general, global had have may shoppers had changed their shopping behaviors from visiting shops to visiting webstores at homes often.

So, it seems that internet technological tool had influenced global many shops disappear, but internet webstores will be replaced their actual shops on streets. Some of businessmen either they choose webstores to replace shops or choose websotes and shops both or still keep shops only. Hence, internet tool influences global businessmen have three kinds of products sale channels to let globa local and overseas consumers to choose how to buy their products.

However, in fact, many of global shoppers, youngers and olders had begun to accept to buy any products from webstores. They feel to spend time to leave homes to visit shops , their shopping behaviors will be wasted time to not essential part to their daily lives. Hence, since internet technological invention, it had changed many consumers their traditional visiting shops shopping habit to change to buying products from webstores channel.

However, on the one hand, internet creates webstores ecommerce shopping channel to let global many consumers do not need to leave homes to go to shopping. It brings negative visiting shops shopping emotion to global general consumers nowadays. But on the other hand, it also brings positive visiting internet webstores shopping emotion to global general consumer nowadays. So, it seems that global many consumers feel that they often do not need to spend much time to go out shopping. Many global consumers feel convenient and enjoy to choose any products to buy from different internet webstores, when the online buyer chooses the most suitable product, he she only needs to pay visa card to buy the product from the online seller's webstore conveniently at home.

Hence, online shopping can bring economic benefit to online buyers, e.g. avoiding walking time or spending transport fare to visit the shop to go to shopping, shortening or reducing shopping time to do another important matter.

On conclusion, global many consumers began feel online shopping can bring more economic benefits on shortening shopping time, avoiding transport fare spending aspect. So, online shopping will be popular shopping behavior for future long time. It may encourage global many shoppers can make rapid shopping decision in short time in order to carry on any products buying transaction to global any one online shopper in short time easily in behavioral economic view. So, global many businessmen had begun to build themselves one attraction webstore in order to persuade different countries consumers to choose to click themselves webstores from internet channel to buy any kinds of products in short time easily.

So, internet technology had changed consumers traditional shopping behaviors to build positive online shopping emotion as well as raise online sellers' any products sale chance easily in behavioral economic view.

Why and how human behavior may influence the country's economic growth or recession?

When one country has many people choose to do the same matter for one period, whether their behavior may influence the country's pvera; economic growth or recession . I shall attempt to indicate cases toexplain their relationship as below:

For flowing rubblish behavioral case example, do you feel that when the country has many people often flow rubblish on the streets, instead of their flowing rubblish behavior may bring streets dirty? But, their flowing rubblish behavior may explain that this country has people may have enough money to buy food to ear, or enough cloths to wear, enough bottles of water to drink, even they may have enough money to buy new television, radio, refrigeraters , washing machines, desktops or laptops electronic home products from old to new to use in order to satisfy their living needs. So, when they flow old electronic home products, their flowing old home electronic products behaviors may seem that they have enough money to buy other new home electronic products to replace old home electronic products to use at homes.

However, it seems thaat this country ought have many people have jobs to do. So, many of them, they can easy to make purchase decison to flow any old home electronic products and buy any new home electronic products to use . Because this country has many people have jobs to do. So, they can often not use old home electonic products to become rubblishs to flow on streets after they had bought any kinds of new home electronic homes.

In fact, it also implies that this country's economy grows rapidly. So, many businesses can glow up rapdly. When they expanded their businesses, they must need to increase employees number in order to let they help themselves to raise productivity or serve their clients absolutely. So, when the country has many businesses can grow up, it seems that its economy must be better or it is improved to compare past. Due to many different kinds of home electronic products had been often bought to use by this country people in this period. So, this country's any streets can be observed that expensive electronic home products were flowed on streets anywhere. then, this country will have many electronic home products sellers can sell their home electronic products very easily. When this country has many people can find any kinds of jobs to do easily. So, due to unemploymen rate had been decreasing.

In behavioral economic view, as this many electronic home products rubblish country case, we can observe this country may have many people have jobs to do. So, consumption number has been increased long time. So, cheap food, or expensive home electronic products may be rubblish on any streets. This country's people , their flowing rubblish behaviors may be explained that many of people have enough jobs to do, so they have ability to buy any good taste food to eat or buy any kinds of expensive electronic home products to use. So, this country's economy may be improved for this long period. So, in behavioral economic view, when this country can have many electronic home products rubblishs are flowed on anywherer in streets frequently. It seems that this country will have many people have jobs to do, so it causes they often change old home electronic products or replaced them easily, when they have enough income to spend to buy any kinds of new home electronic products to use at homes easily. Moreover, their flowing old electronic home products behaviors also indicate that this country has many people their salaries may be increased in possible from their emplyers. When this country can have many different kinds of home electornic products are sold. It means that this country's electronic home products needs or demand had been increasing, due to many people have jobs to do and income increases to excite their living of needs also improve. Consequently, this country may seem have better economic improvement. We can observe from this country's electronic home products rubblish increasing income in theis period.

On conclusion, this country ought experience economic growth at this period. So, " flowing expensive electronic home rubblish increasing number " may seem that this country's economic growth is rapidly in this period, due to many people have jobs to do as well as salaries increase in this period.

Technology how impacts human behavior changing?

Technology how influences human behavior to bring changing? For example, online share purchase and sale transaction from smart phone brings share investor can do share buying or selling transation in any where and any time conveniently, non manual driving auto vehicle, bring car owner feels comfortable and spends free time to do other matter, e.g. reading, listening mucis in himself or herself car freely. electrical energy vehicle can help car owner to reduce air polluton and it can brings the drivers do not feel drive long time in any journeys in order to avoid air pollution for environmental protection responsible car drivers in our societies. Thus, they will drive long time in any journeys when they can drive electronic energy cars to replace oil energy cars.

However, online technology can also bring consumers can choose to stay at homes to buy any things from seller individual online webstore conveniently. Such as online technology can bring shoppers do not need to spend much time to visit shops to buy any things. They can choose any kinds of products from any online sellers individual online webstores conveniently at homes. Online technology excite busy consumers can make purchase decision easily as well as it can help online sellers sell any kinds of products from internet easily.

In behavioral economic view, technology can change human behavior to be improved, it can let human feels comfortable, more free time ro use, rapid making any decisions, such as apply smart phones to make share purchase or sale transaction decision, online shopping decision, even travelling any where decision in short time, when the traveller finds the most cheap hotel accommodation room price and air ticket price frm any travel agent online tourism webstore, then the potential travel customer can follow the online hotel accommodation price and air ticket price data to make decision when to buy the air ticket from the airline travel agent or make decision when to prebook which hotel accommodation room to go to the country to travel from online travel agent tourism webstores. So, technology can encourage global any country travelers to make anywhere to trvel rapidly. If the traveler can find the country's general hotel rooms and airline tickets prices had been decreasing more sightly. The traveler may make travel decision to choose the country to travel in short time, then he/she can prebook the country;s any hotel room and airline ticket to pay by visa fraom the country's any hotel and airline travel agent webstores., before one week, even one month or more easily. Hence, online technology can also encourage traveler individual frequent travel times to be increased, due to global travelers can find any hotel rooms and airline tickets prices from internet conveniently at homes. They do not need to spend time to visit any airline travel agent to enquire travel choice country's hotel rooms prices and airline ticket prices. They can compare global travel of countries choices ' all hotels rooms and airline agents air tickets prices to make prebook airline seat and hotel room decision before one week, one month even six months early.

On conclusion, online technology can encourage global travelers can make travelling any where and when traveling time desicions easily. It can excite tourism industry develops in long time. Also, such as electricity cars invention can encourage environment protection car owners do car purchase decision easily, because they can choose to drive electronic energy cars to replace oil energy cars in order to avoid air pollution occurs easily. So, electronic cars can increase electronic car purchasrs number, due to many of environmental protection attitude of car owners can choose to drive electricity cars to bring air cleans, even non -manual driving cars can encourage lazy driving and free time driving car owners to choose to buy non-manual (artificial intelligent) cars to drive , because they can spend much free time to read, listen music or do any matters in themselves cars, they do not need to drive cars, robotic (AI) auto driving machine is such one non-manual driver to help them to drive themselves cars confidently. So, non-manual driving cars can attract lazy and enjoying free time driving car owners to choose to buy to replace traditional manual cars to drive easily. Moreover, online share transaction can help any share investors to make share buying and selling decision in short time easily. When they can apply smart phones technological tool to carry on share buying and selling activities easily. They can observe any share rising or falling price suitation from smart phones in any where any any time easily. So, smart phone technology can help global any shareholders to make share purchase and sale transaction easily. So, technology can encourage human makes decision in short time rapidly.

How and why employees behaviors may influence economy development?

In behavioral economy view,I believe the country's any organizational employees behavior may bring indirect relationship to influence the country's long term economic development. I shall indicate past manufacture industry social development period to explain their relationship. For many countries' past business activities had belonged to manufacturing industry, such as US, UK past before 1980 year, it focused on steel manufacturing and steel manufacturing related machine products. So, US, Uk developed countries manufacturing industries may be past main country's economic income sources. I assume US , UK past had one million number different kinds of industries. They ought had about seven houndred thousand number organizational businesses were belonged to manufactured industry. They may include:

Steel manufacturing and steel related machine manufacturing, e.g. vehicle manufacturing, home appliances, e.g. washing machine, television, radio, refrigerate cooler, heater, air condition etc. different kinds of different kinds of steel -related manufacturing machine, they were manufactured from US, UK steel machine manufacturers. So, US, Uk the other three hundred thousand number industry may be general service industry, e.g. hotel service, restaurent, cinema, public transport service, tourism lesiure , wine bar, supermarket etc. different kinds of non-manufacturing industries business organizations were operated in UK, US past before 1980 year.

So, in UK, US developed countries industry development history, they ought have high percentage of businesses belonged to steel related manufacturing machine and steel products. Also, in the past before 1980 year, US, Uk business employers , they employed many workers are manufacturing workers. They needed to spend long time to work in factories. They were skillful workers, and they are trained to manufacturing cars, washing machine, television, heater, etc. even steel itself different kinds of steel related products to prepare to deliver to their shops to sell to US, Uk local or overseas clients.

So, I believe that past UK, US ought employ many employees, they belonged to skillful manufacturing workers, manufacture increasing steel machine or steel related machine number of products rapidly daily. So, if UK, US had had many of these manufacturing factories owned high skillful workers, then their manufacturing steel-related machine or steel both kinds of products number must be influenced to raise rapidly. Consequently, their steel machine manufacturing products would been exported to overseas or would been sold to local both markets , they may be influenced to raise sale number. They (these manufacturing workers) needed to be trained to know how to manufactur these different kinds of machine products in the efficient teams and they ought to be trained to raise their efficiencies in order to shorten time to manufacturing many kinds of steel related manufacturing machine or steel itself products rapidly. So , if their efficiencies and manufacturing performance was improved, these US, UK any one manufacturing worker and their teams ought achieve raising productivities significantly.

Hence, when past UK, US manufacturing industry development period, if these two countries' any manufacturing factories could have many manufacturing workers could be trained to be skillful and proficient manufacturing workers. Then, in past every day to these factories workers, they ought help their steel or steel related manufacturing employers to raise any kinds of machine or steel products number in every team. So, when past in the manufacturing industry development, US, UK could have many factories' manufacturing workers themselves steel or steel related machine products manufacturing skill could be trained to to improve to any kinds of these machine or steel manufacuring products quality as well as their products number could be influenced to raise by themselves skillful improvement significantly every day.

Then, what would be influenced to occur to past UK, US manufacturing industry period? In behavioral economic view, when these two manufacturing industry developed countries, such as UK, US , if they had many factories workers can be trained to improve their skill in order to achieve any kinds of steel or steel-related machine products quality could be improved as well as products manufacturing number could be also increased absolutely.

In consequence, past UK and US both countries ought increase themselves any kinds of steel and steel related machine products number to be supplied to themselves local shops to let local clients to choose any one kind of machine manufacturing products to buy easily as well as they could also export to supply overseas any countries to buy their different kinds of steel or steel related machine products to let overseas steel or steel related manufacturing machine product buyers, they can have many of these different kinds of these steel or steel-related different kinds of manufacturing machine from UK and UK these both countries easily to compare other countries.

On conclusion, I believe that past US, and UK macro manufacturing industry income GDP would increase significantly. So, they would have good economic growth performance because when many of these manufacturing workers themselves manufacturing effort could be improved. So, it explained when employees manufacturing abilities can influence economic growth indirectly.

Robots invention whether they can help organizations to raise efficiencies or inefficiencies?

In behavioral economic view, in any organizations, when the organization hopes its worker teams can raise efficiencies , the organization may choose to increase more workers number and/or it can provide training to improve these workets themselves skills in order to raise their efficiencies. For one warehouse example, when the warehouse increases many goods , they are needed to delivered these goods from the shelves to the delivering destination locations. If this warehouse supervisors feel these workers themselves goods delivery speeds are slow, which is possible due to this warehouse's workers number is not enough. So, this warehouse supervisor ought increase workers number in order to increase their goods delivery speed in order to deliver goods from the shelves to every indicated goods delivery destination in order to let any one lorry driver can transport the right kinds of goods and ensure the accurate goods number to transport to any one client home rapidly.

However, if this warehouse supervisor planed to buy several warehouse goods delivery robots to assist these warehouse workers to find the right kinds of goods from shelves and then deliver to the right destination location in the warehouse. So, these warehouse orkers can concentrate on counting the accurate goods number and ensuring the right kinds of goods in order to prepare to let lorry drivers to transport these goods to these goods of buyers themselvers homes rapidly. Consequently, in the first step, robots can concentrate on finding th right goods from shelves and delivers them to the right goods transportation of location destination. Then, in the second step, these warehouse workers can concentrate on counting the accurate goods number and ensuring the right kinds of goods in order to prepare to put them to the lorry. Consequently, when warehouse robots and warehouse workers can cooperate to work together, the most important, robots, can deal on finding the right kinds of goods and deal on delivering the accurate number of goods of job duty as well as these warehouse workers can only concentrte on counting the right kinds of goods number in order to avoid it has none any mistake of wrong kinds of goods and inaccurate goods of delivery number to be transported to the lorry and to deliver to any one buyer's home.

So, it seems that warehouse robots ought help any one warehouse worker to raise himself efficiency and avoid goods delivery of mistake occurrence easily as well as their help to warehouse workers that can let any one goods buyer feels their goods can be delivered to their homes rapidly. Moreover, warehouse robots can also help these warehouse workers to raise efficiencies because warehouse robots can help them to shorten goods delivery time between any one shelf and any one goods delivery destination of location in the warehuse because robots may help them to find the right kinds of goods from the right shelf in the short time. So, any one worker does not need to spend long time to seek anywhere is the right shelf location for the kind of goods when the kind of goods are needed to deliver to the buyer's home from lorry. Warehouse robots can help them to do this aspect of " finding the goods from the right shelf in short time job duty". So, any one warehouse worker only needed tospend less time to do the counting of any right kind of goods number and ensuring the right kind of goods job duty. Consequently, this warehouse 's any one worker, his any one kind of goods delivery time may be reduced, because robots' assistance and they may have more confidence to avoid mistake to deliver the wrong number of goods and/or the wrong kind of goods to any one goods buyer's home.

On conclusion, it seems that warehouse robots ought may help any one warehouse worker to raise efficiency for any one team in the warehouse as well as the warehouse any one supervisor does not need to spend much time to observe any one worker individual performance for " goods delivery job duty aspect" because their goods delivery job duty that had been replaced to do by these several warehouse robots. Robots can achieve the more accurate of right kinds of goods and the right number of goods delviery job performance to compare any one of human warehouse worker themselves right kinds of goods of delivery and right number of goods of delivery job performance. So, when robots can participate to cooperate with this warehouse's any one worker to do their goods of delivery job duty in this warehouse every day. Then, robots can raies any one of supervisor individual confidence in order to let they do not need to spend time to observe any one of worker individual whose goods of delivery job performane. They can concentrate on supervising any one worker whose goods transport to lorry in the final step in order to avoid to deliver wrong goods number and / or wrong kind of goods to any one goods buyer's home every day. Consequently, this warehouse's overall teams of their delviery of goods performance many be improved by robotss' participatin to goods of delivery task as well as this warehouse's oveall teams themselves efficiencies may be influenced to raise by robots' goods of delivery task participation.

How and why human behavior may influence economic growth or recession?

May ourselves daily behaviors influence our global societial continue economic growth or recession? Do they have cause and effect close relationship between human behaviors and global economic growth or recession? I shall apply behavioral economic theory to analyze and explain whether ourselves daily behaviors and our global societial economic growth or recession which have close cause and effect relationship as below:

Every country itself economic development must depend on any business activities, otherwise, any kinds of business activities must need ourselves business activities or behaviors in order to achieve any business activities as well as achieve the country's overall economic development in macro view.

However, any country's overall business activites or behaviors which must depend on any kinds of individual businessmen, themselves employees daily working behavior or activity or performance in order to help them to attract or increase many clients number to acieve " earning profit" aim. So, it seems that any individual business, itself overall every department individual working behavior is one main factor to influence the company's overall business performance.

For agricultural fruit and meat food farming industry example, such as New Zealand is a farming main target industry country. It had had many New Zealanders were daily themselves own farming businesses for many years. Their farming businesses include growing fruit, sheep, cow, pig pork, meat etc. food sale business. If the New Zealand farmer owned a large size farming land, then he will choose either growing fruit or feeding sheeps, pigs, cows to be meat to to transport to New Zealand supermarkets to help them to sell to their farmers meet to New Zealanders in order to earn profit. Thus, if the New Zealand farmer owned large size of farming lands, then he needs to employ many farming employees (farming workers) to help him to carry on farming business daily tasks, e.g. picking up friuts, feeding pigs, cows, sheeps to eat food daily. These daily farming jobs are very important to influence this

New Zealand farmer's meats or fruits sale number whether they can be easy or diffcult to sell in New Zealand supermarkets , if these farming workers can own encough farming knowledge or skill to know how to pick up fruits method and make judgement to know whether it is right time to pick up the kind of fruits from the trees , as well as know how feed this pigs, sheeps, cows to eat food in order to let they are better health. Consequently, their farming behaviors which can let these animals can provide the best taste and enough meat from these animals to let New Zealander to buy to eat from New Zealand any one supermarket. Even these New Zealand farming workers can know whether the kinds of fruits, e.g. oranges, apples, gapes etc. fruits whether they ought be picked up from the trees at the right time. Consequently, they can make judgement to decide to pick up any kinds of the best taste fruits to let any one New Zealander to buy to eat from any one supermarket in New Zealand. Otherwise, if they do not make judegement to know whether the kind of fruit ought not be picked up because they still need longer time to continue grow up to increase fruit size and better taste from the trees in order to let any one fruit buyer can feel better taste when they eat this kind of fruit later. If they can buy this kind of fruit to eat later, then this New Zealand farmer's his fruit buyers can buy the best taste of this kind of fruit to eat from an yone supermarket in New Zealand. Consequently, many New Zealand supermarkets will choose to buy any kinds of fruits from this farmer fruit supplier when they feel this farmer's fruits can provide more better taste fruits to compare other farmers' fruits.

Thus, due to New Zealand is one farming main income source country. It's any kinds of fruits and meats need to be export to overseas to sell , instead of local sale. It's GDP percent is very high to whole country 's overall income source. So, any one New Zealand farmer individual and any one farming worker individual working behavior will influence its economy whether it is influenced to grow or recession possible. Moreover, it also seems that farming workers' farming knowledge and skill will influence themselves farming daily activities to achieve the aim of the number of increase or decrease to any kinds of fruits whether they are better taste or the number of increase of decrease to any kinds of meats whether they are better taste to supply to any one New Zealand fruit or meat buyers to eat from any one New Zealand supermarket. So, it implies that any one New Zealand farming worker individual farming behavior may influence any kinds of fruits or any kinds of meat taste because they are transported to any one supermarket to sell in New Zealand.

Consequently, if New Zealans had many farmers can teach god farming knowledge and skill to let their any one farming workers know how to decide judgement to decide when it is right time to pick up any kinds of fruits from trees , or how to grow them on soil in order to let they can grow rapidly. Then, many different kinds of fruits can be provided to let any one New Zealanders can eat the best taste of fruits when their fruits are supplied to any one New Zealand supermarkets. Even, if they knew how to feed foods to pigs, cows, sheeps to eat daily. Then they can be more health and they can provide the best taste of meats to let any one New Zealanders can buy their meats from any one New Zealand supermarkets. Moreover, their fruits and meats can be transported to overseas to let any one country fruits or meats buyers can choose any kinds of New Zealand meats and fruits to buy to eat from themselves countries supermarkets. Then, many overseas fruit and meat buyers will perfer to choose New Zealand any kinds of fruits or meats to buy to compare other countries fruits or meats to buy when they go to any one local supermarkets.

On conclusion, it seems that New Zealand farming workers themselves farming behavior may influence their farming employers any kinds of fruits or meats sale number and income because their farming task behaviors must influence whether their fruits or meats taste are the better taste or worse taste to compare their other local farmers (the farmer competitors) whose fruits or meats taste. If tthe farmer's any one farming worker can be trained to learn how to know to feed animals skill and when is the most right time to pick up any kinds of fruits from trees or how to grow them on the soil methods. Due to these farming worker individual farming behavior may influence his different finds of fruits and meats sale number to be increase or decrease, so these any one New Zealand farmer must need to depend on any one farming worker whose farming working methods, if their farming working behaviors can be the best to influence any kinds of fruits to grow rapid or any kinds of pigs, cows, sheeps animals grow up rapidly , then their sale number may be increase significantly and their taste can be improved to let any New Zealand or overseas meat or fruit buyer to buy to eat to feel from any one New Zealand or overseas supermarkets, then New Zealand's agriculture industry must be influenced to increase. In the world, any one fruit or meat buyer must choose to buy New Zealand's fruit and meat to eat in prefer to compare other countries' fruits and meats. So, New Zealand's GDP may be influenced to raise from any one New Zealand farming worker individual farming working behaviors.

CHAPTER IV

Behavioral economic theory explains social Development

Invention brings economic development chance

Factors cause new products development

What are main factors influence global product manufacturers and consumers feel to enjoy how to research new product manufacture and change any kinds of new products using needs? I shall attempt to apply consumer psychological and technological improvement (development) psychological factors to explain why human needs often to use products to replace old products needing mind in our future societies.

Our societies had been experiencing high population growth, special in China and India both countries, their population growth had risen rapidly as well as a climb up in the kind of transformative technological development, e.g. robots invention, non-manual auto driving vehicles, battery charge energy vehicles improvement,smart phones, laptops etc. technological products had been invented to replace old technological products. For example, telephones had been replaced from mobiles, till to smart phone products invention; gas energy vehicles may be replaced by electronic charge vehicles, battery charge vehicles, even non-manual auto driving vehicles, computers had been replaced by desktops, even laptops and notebooks etc. new technological products improvement. SO, in our future societies, many old technological products may be influenced to use and need to improve by human ourselves enjoying and using improved technological products needs. Old technological products are needed to innovate in order to satisfy future human ourselves new technological products using needs.

Moreover, when one technological product manufacturer feels need to innovate itself products, e.g. IBM computers are innovated to notebooks or laptops from desktops, to bring using satisfactory needs feeling : light weight and small size, convenient carrying on feeling. SO, IBM computer products are one kind of highly innovative capitalism driven , it can bring multiplies computer invention , job opportunity to create many new job positions to let global computer professional can earn income from IBM new computers product improvement pursue. SO, products improvement can help global job positions number increases and it can reduce unemployment number in global labour market.

However, internet invention had brought new using impact to our societies.IN the past, telephones and typing machines communication products result of innovation in communication alone, people with the most minimal of internet connection today have unprecedented access to health-related information. The forward march of malaria, tuberculosis and HIV?AIDS had been slowed, even as antibiotic resistance is a new problem. There is no doubt that the inter connectivity between the Big data computer and medical research is transforming the medical field.

Monty transaction technology had been innovated by internet communication channel. Some call it the global Paypal,Payoneer online payments system, succeeded. This kind of new online payment transaction system, it can assist global purchase and sale transactions carry on transaction activities rapidly between sellers and buyers.

It can replace traditional bank electronic payment transactions method. Many merchants began to accept to use online transaction payment system to replace bank electronic payment system. So, paypal and payoneer both online payment system can replace many bank electronic payment systems, they are their online transaction service competitors in global social money transaction business sector.

Among the residual factors left after differences in growth rates of the quantity of capital and labour had been allowed for new products innovation and quality differences, consumer using need changing differences , especially those resulting from technical progress and education, seemed to deserve much more attention. Human capital , and with it's education and transfer of technology and technical assistance, and manpower planning, they are assumed a new importance

in thinking about future new technological product development increasing needs, such as distance learning had been influenced to develop by internet invention. It helps many university students can apply internet online technological learning channel to enroll any one overseas university learn. So, many overseas students do not need to spend renting rooms , foods, transport expenditure to leave themselves hometowns to arrive another country's university to study. So, distance learning , online learning learning method can satisfy many overseas students their reducing living expenditures needs when they decide to study in overseas. It is new kind of new educational and learning technological innovation to replace traditional classroom teaching method in global education sector.

Finally, one product invention brings funding need skill,the new and old skills of products improvement may help product manufacturers to make and raise money (creating new business chance). To generate funding in a new technological world, by it via revenues, investment capital, donation or loans to help product manufacturers to develop a fresh set of skills, different from the ones needed to make things happen in the twentieth century. What are the differences between old power funding skills and new power funding skills.

In the past, old power funding skills include traditional salesman, proven credentials and technical experise, ability to development between consumers and manufacturers , capacity to navigate complex bureaucratic systems and creating a luxury ability. Otherwise, in ourselves future, new power funding skills include universally accessible stroytelling, a compelling personal or group discussion skill, ability to mobilize a crowd and key social influence, capacity to navigate complex community dynamics, creating a participation proble,

Hence, when on product manufacturer decides to invent or improve one kind of old product to be new or fresh using experience to global consumers. They must need to learn how to raise money source from loans or shareholders increasing number or donation from old power funding skills to new power funding skills method. In this new funding skills learning stage, every department staffs can learn how to change or discuss themselves organizational behavior in order to achieving in raising funding aim to innovate themselves old products to new products dream. SO, their " needing raising funding" direction may excite them to continue to innovate themselves new products pursue in behavioral economy view.

On conclusion, product development may encourage economic growth, due to global consumers began to accept to use new improvement products to satisfy consumers ourselves using and enjoying needs , when global new product improvement consumers number increases, new product manufacturers need to employ many workers and product inventors to manufacture many number of new products to satisfy global consumers using new product demands. It can encourage global economic growth rapidly because workers and product researchers employees number will increase. So, unemployment rate will reduce when global had many people have jobs to do, spending desire will rise, global GDP growth may be influenced to rise up in long term. All of above factors may influence new product development pursue to global manufacturers.

Knowledge how influences business development

Why may knowledge influence business development? Have they close relationship between knowledge and economic growth or recession in behavioral economy view? I shall attempt to indicate evidences to explain these two questions as below:

IN fact, human development had been experiencing from agricultural stage to industrial manufacturing stage, till to nowadays, service section stage,e.g. hotel tourism leisure development, and technological development stage, e.g. computer and robot development. All of these stages, which are created by ourselves knowledge, it means that how we decide choice, what social development direction will be caused. It it is true, it seems that global human knowledge may influence how our social future continue development. Our social economic growth or recession will be brought to influence from knowledge indirectly.

It is focus on " behavioral economic concept" Economists define scarcity as the condition of wanting more than we can get with available resources. Scarcity is a fact of life. So, human can arrange ourselves resources in a lot of different ways, such as watching TV, buying a book, a car or traveling, but at any given time, ourselves have a fixed range of possibilities. SO, scarcity also describes the world on a collective level. As a society, we can produce only so many things, and we have to decide how those things are divided among many people. But, when social development, knowledge is very important to cause human (scientists) choose how to decide to invent any new things in order to satisfy human limit need and using desire. So, the total quantity of available knowledge does not diminish as more and more people acquire it. So, ourselves every behavioral decision in life involves weighing the trade off between costs and benefits . We look at our options and decide whether it is worth giving up in order to get the other.

Economists explain this timc cost of choicc thc " opportunity cost", opportunity cost is thc valuc you could gaincd by choosing your next best alternative, the opportunity you have to pass up in order to take your first choice. Why may ourselves behavior have relationship between opportunity cost and economic growth? For computer invention example, when scientists feel computer products will be future human needs daily, for student learning using need, office tasks needs, watching movie, listening music leisure need,even playing game need. So, scientists had chose to spend time and resource and labor to invent computer products , they forgave to spend time and resource and labor to invent other products. They computer invention is their opportunity cost, includes time, money, resource, labour, knowledge, mind on computer scientists , they had forgiven to spend these resources to research how to invent other kinds of new products.

However, when computer new products had been invented in success, e.g. desktop, laptop, can be popular to be accept to provide to global computer users to use. This kind of computer invention , its users number had been increasing, manufacturing computer number will be influenced to grow, due to computer invention will help developing and developed countries GDP growth rapidly since 1980 year , the early first stage of computer invention had been experiencing during our global technological development history.

So, it implies that computer scientists had been confirmed to do right choice decision to forgive to spend resources, time, money and labour and knowledge to research how to invent any kinds of new products. They make right decision to research how to invent new computer products,even improve desktop to laptop and smart phone , hand carrying smart phone and computer both functions new products to satisfy computer users daily using needs. It is true opportunity cost to computer scientists case. Also, when past, our scientists do right choice to invent this kind of computer product, this kind of computer products can bring global economic benefits, such as government can increase profit tax

form computer sellers, offices can use computers to reduce employees number, when computers can help offices to save much document, clerical employees number may be influenced to reduce, tasks can be simple from complex tasks, spending tasks time may be influenced to reduce by computerization of office, factories can apply computers or robots to replace workers to manufacture any kinds of products, such as cars, washing machine, rice cookers, radios, fans ,television etc. different kinds of electrical products. So workers number may be influenced to reduce and wage expenditure must be reduce.

Hence, new knowledge may help global societies to bring economic growth, such as past scientists had decided to forgive to spend time, resource, money, labor, skill, knowledge to research how to invent any kinds of new products, it is possible that they have some different kinds of new products concept choices, computer concept is only one kinds of choice among these new different kinds of new products invention concepts. However, they need to choose only one kind of new product invention among of these different kinds of new product concept choices, because they have not enough resource to provide to them to invent in the past. Finally, they evaluate the weigh and cost between computer invention concept and other new products invention concepts. In fact, computer is one kind of "the bringing much economic benefits" new concept invention product choice.

I believe that if computer will be continue improved in order to bring more economic growth in possible. SO, scientists need to spend more time, resource, money, labor, skill, knowledge to research how to continue to improve traditional computers to bring more using functions, in order to help global different industries to reduce resource, time, labour , money aim to bring reducing cost spending expenditure benefits to global industries , due to societies had been experiencing " knowledge social stage". If societies need to apply computer technology to assist our societies can continue develop, when our societies' different industries, such as service, manufacturing, even agriculture sectors, e.g. robots may help farmers to predict when it is right time to grow vegetable, or replace farmers to grow vegetable, fruit in farms to provide human have enough food to eat, or robots can help hotel to clean rooms, serve clients, robots can help cinemas to sell tickets, robots can help manufacturers to product new products in factories. So, technological products may help any kinds of industries to reduce employees number, improve efficiencies and productivity and reduce wages expenditure economic cost benefits.

Production possibility economic concept knowledge indicates about who produces which goods and why. The fact that millions of people and firms around the global coordinate their activities to provide consumers with the right combination of goods and services seem like magic.

In fact, coordination doe snot happen by chance, nor does super-planner tells every one where to go and what to do. Instead, the global production time is a natural outcome of people every acting in their own self interest to improve their own lives. Economists call this coordination mechanism the " invisible hand", an idea that was first suggested by economic thinker Adam Smith.

To get some insight into the who and why of production, such as shirt production case, most shirts are made in China, and other countries when factory wages are low.

Have American workers become worse at making shirts over the last two countries? Definitely not, In fact, as are better than American workers at making shirts. Instead , each good tends to be produced by that country, company, or person with the lowest opportunity cost of producing that shirt kind of product, such as scientists make cooperation decision to invent computer products together, they can earn high invention royalty income, computer sale and manufacturing number increases, governments can earn more profit tax, different kinds of service, manufacturing industries can reduce workers number, wage expenditure, improving performance economic benefits . So, countries and firms and persons need a specialize in making goods for which they have the lowest opportunity cost. They than trade with one another to get the coordination of goods. They want to consume, such as computer manufacturing , if IBM and Microsoft both companies can cooperate to research how to improve themselves traditional model of laptops and desktops to create new improved and more using functions laptops and destops, e.g. small size, more new using functions, clear colour and easier visible screen, or small book cover design, new computer model. I believe that the resulting, gains from themselves computer trade can be shared much that every computer buyers ends up better offer, global computer users will choose to buy and use these both IBM and Microsoft future new computer invention products to compare other kinds of computer manufacturers.

In production possibilities frontier economic concept, it explains why IBM and Microsoft ought cooperate to manufacturer computers, their cooperation can bring more economic benefits to themselves and global computer users, e.g. more computer functions, reducing sale price, reduce computer workers manufacturing wages, and computer manufacturing workers number, increasing computer manufacturing and demand number, increasing profit to themselves and government profit tax income, increasing buyers number, offices can improve efficiency and employees performance, reducing manufacturing cost expenditure, improving student learning ability, etc. different kinds of global economic benefits. Hence, in production possibilities frontier economic concept, IBM and Microsoft ought make cooperation decision in order to bring global economic benefits.

In fact, computer manufacture industry is one competitive market, it is one in which truly informed, prices taking buyers and seller easily trade a standardized good or service. IBM and Microsoft need to cooperate in order to win their computer manufacturing competitors , if they hope to earn in global computer manufacturing top leader position. Otherwise, if IBM and Microsoft do not choose to cooperate to invent new kind of computer products, their traditional computer products will be not popular to be accept to use to compare their computer manufacturing competitors. Because, future computer trends to cheap, more using functions, small size, light weight , clear visible and touch feeling screen. in order to attract computer buyers choices more easily.

On conclusion, it is possible that scientists invention knowledge may bring economic growth indirectly. Their invention choice or invention decision may assist our future economy development rapidly or slowly. Hence, knowledge is one invisible hand to influence global economy either it can bring growth or recession in possible.

Social development how influences smart phone product need

Nowadays, our global economy seems to continue grow, but it also has possible to bring recession by any factors. This question concerns whether either human behavior can influence future global social economic growth or recession or technology can influence future global social economic growth or recession more? I shall attempt to indicate evidences to explain as below:

Firstly, on the one hand, when one country can manufacture new technological products, e.g. laptops, war weapons (non-manual driving flying war air planes, space rocket, smart phone etc. different kinds of high technological products. For America example, US is one export high technological products country. When its these different kinds of high development products manufacturers can sell to local and overseas customers. Then, they may earn high profit from both. Also US government can charge high profit tax from these high technological products manufacturers, when they can attract global many customers to buy their any kinds of high technological products. So, it seems that high technological products manufacturers may

help US government and US high technological products manufacturers to earn more US technological products sale income. Moreover, technology can help US country to grow up its economic development in long term, due to US manufacturers can concentrate on effort to invent any kinds of new technological products in order to persuade global buyers to choose to buy their products in preference.

However, but on the other hand, I feel human behavior, such as talent high technological products inventors , they are the beginning main factor to help US to grow economy. The reason is because US which any kinds of high technological products must need talent human product scientists) themselves idea to invention. If themselves idea can influence global high technological products buyers feel needs to buy to use. Then, they must choose to buy US country's any kinds of these products in preference. So, talent high technological product scientists will be US future economic growth source. If one high technological product scientists did wrong idea to the high technological product manufacturers to manufacture the kind technological products. They can not influence global buyers feel needs to buy the kind of high technological product to use. Then, whose idea of innovation may not help US to develop itself economy.

Hence, such as technological product case example, talent product scientists their idea innovation factor can bring more influential to US future economic growth easily. So, I conclude this criticism to explain why human behavior is more important factor to compare technology to influence the country's economy, because if the high technological product inventor whose dreams and idea to invent the kind of high technological product, if it can influence users feel useful feeling, e.g. smart phone product, it can attract phone users buy to use because it can use internet to gather global data, or read online news, read electronic books, listen music, watch movie, take photos, know the day weather, send and receive email, download document etc. different kinds of function. SO, can let phone users feel smart phones can replace past traditional innovation of mobile phones and smart phones can influence global mobile users feel human ourselves can make phone calls in convenient in anywhere. Hence, smart phone product manufacturers can help themselves countries to earn high GDP income and increase high profit tax to give themselves governments. Otherwise, the traditional mobile phone products can not persuade phone buyers to choose to buy forever, because they lack more functions to compare smart phones. So, it explains why smart phone users personal using phone behavior is more important to influence the country's economy because when global every family begin to feel to use smart phones is themselves daily habit, they need smart phone to help them to do any matters, instead of general phone call at streets. So, their using smart phone behavior will influence they feel often need to change new model of smart phone invention of product to replace old model of smart phone. Consequently, smart phone manufacturers need to continue to invent new and more functions of new model of smart phone products to satisfy future global smart phone users' need. Hence, smart phone users' habitual using new model smart phone using behavior may bring global smart phone manufacturers long term manufacturing benefits in order to increase sale number chance. So, smart phone is one kind of high technological product may help any smart phone manufacturing countries to grow up economic growth easily. Also, smart phone inventor individual idea and smart phone improvement skillful technology and smart phone user individual frequent changing new model using behavior which may be main factors to influence the country's smart phone sellers sale number. Such as, UK, US, Germany , China. Korea , they are global main smart phone manufacturers.

Economists call it " production -side growth" , which means that most companies, most of the time, made their (such as those countries smart phone manufacturers profit by cutting the cost of production). If these countries' smart phone manufacturers can cooperate to research how to improve more new functions of new model of smart phones to sell global smart phone market. Consequently, it is possible that their production of smart phonc cost may be influenced to reduce. Then, themselves future invention of new model of smart phone product sale price may also be influenced to reduce, due to reducing production cost. Then, the global smart phone buyers number may be influenced to increase by reducing smart phone production cost. When these manufacturing smart phone countries, every year , their smart phone sale number can increase to double time , even more.

I believe that smart phone technological product may help these countries to earn more profit tax, if these countries smart phone manufacturers need to research how to improve future smart phone functions to satisfy global future smart phone user individual; " frequent changing new model of smart phone habitual satisfactory need". So, future smart phone technological product may be one kind of high technological product to help the smart phone manufacturing countries themselves economic growth.

Ecommerce may also help the country to grow economy. In the past, before twentieth century , this efficiency extends to the ways our economic goods spread around the country and the world. As the beginning of the twentieth century , most markets , more local, most people bought things made nearby. But with the expansion system and then commercial air travel and the super-efficiency of containerized shipping, markets became national and eventually, global. Till to first century, since internet technological invention, it brings economic chance to let any countries local merchants may apply web-store internet platform to help them to sell products to overseas buyers. They only need click to the overseas seller whose web store and then they can pay visa to buy the kind of product from the online seller's web-store. So, many merchants , they own webstores to let overseas buyers can pay visa to buy the kind of product from themselves web-stores at their home countries conveniently. Then, the owning " more number of web-store sellers " countries government will have possible to earn high profit tax from these local webstore sellers. So, e-commerce sale internet technological platforms and global online buyers purchase behaviors , these two factors can also influence the country's economy. If the country had many people like to buy any kinds of products from webstore, then they may influence the " owning more number of online sellers countries" their online seller profit increases, whether it is more or less sale number. Hence, whether e-commerce technology may help the country's government to grow GDP in technological product sale view. It depends on whether the country owns how many number of online sellers as well as how many online buyers number both for their products choice purchase chance. For example, when the country own high number people like to spend more time to stay at home to use internet. They do not like to walk on streets, they like to listen music and read books at homes more than going outside to do sports. Then, the country's people individual living habit will influence they choose to apply web stores to buy any things, if the country had many people like to stay at homes more than leaving homes. SO, individual living behavior may also influence the country economy on online purchase view.

The Nexus of Technological Innovation and Social Evolution

The relationship between technological advancement and social development is a cornerstone of modern macroeconomic theory. In my work How Technology Development Influences Economy Growth, my view explores the multifaceted ways in which innovation acts as a catalyst for structural changes within society.y view posits that the introduction of transformative products—such as the smartphone—does not merely represent a shift in consumer preference but serves as a fundamental driver of social reorganization. By lowering transaction costs and increasing the velocity of information exchange, these technologies reshape how individuals interact, work, and consume, thereby creating a feedback loop that necessitates further economic and social adaptation.

The Smartphone as a Catalyst for Social and Economic Change

My analysis suggests that the smartphone is a quintessential example of "general-purpose technology" (GPT), a concept extensively discussed in economic literature.These technologies are characterized by their ability to permeate multiple sectors of the economy, fundamentally altering the production function of society. My view argues that the smartphone's influence on social development is rooted in its capacity to democratize access to information, which in turn shifts the power dynamics between institutions and individuals.

From a macroeconomic perspective, the "need" for such products is often driven by the desire for efficiency. As societies become more complex, the demand for portable, high-speed connectivity increases to manage the cognitive and logistical load of modern life.My view emphasizes that this is not merely a market-driven trend but a social necessity; as the economy moves toward digitalization, those without access to such technology face significant barriers to social and economic participation.

Theoretical Frameworks of Technological Impact

To understand my perspective, one must look at the broader discourse on technological diffusion. Economists like Robert Solow have long noted that technological change is the primary driver of long-term economic growth, often represented in the Solow-Swan growth model as $Y=A(t)f(K,L)$, where $A(t)$ represents the level of technology. My view builds upon this by suggesting that $A(t)$ is not an exogenous variable but is deeply influenced by social demand and the institutional environment.

Furthermore, the social impact of smartphones involves the "network effect," where the value of the product increases as more people adopt it.This creates a social imperative for adoption, as the cost of exclusion—socially and economically—becomes prohibitive. Lok's opinion, as reflected in his research, highlights that the "need" for a smartphone is a manifestation of the modern social contract, where connectivity is now a prerequisite for professional and personal integration.

Conclusion and Future Implications

The synthesis of my arguments suggests that technology development is a double-edged sword. While it fosters unprecedented economic growth and social connectivity, it also creates new forms of inequality and dependency. The smartphone, in this view, is the primary tool through which the modern individual navigates the complexities of the 21st-century economy, making its development a central concern for both policymakers and social scientists.

The Integration of Human Behavior and Economic Systems in the Work of my view

In his analysis of the intersection between human psychology and economic structures, John Lok posits that human beings are not merely passive observers of economic trends but are active, integral participants in the cyclical processes that define both life and the global economy.

My view argues that traditional economic models often fail because they treat human behavior as a static variable rather than a dynamic, evolving force that mirrors the biological and environmental cycles of the Earth.By viewing the economy as an extension of natural systems, Lok suggests that human decision-making is deeply embedded in a feedback loop where individual actions influence systemic stability, and systemic shifts, in turn, reshape individual behavior.

This perspective aligns with broader institutional theories which suggest that social and economic systems are not governed by a single, unified law, but rather by a "fish-scale model of omniscience," where various disciplines overlap to create a continuous understanding of human activity.

My work emphasizes that when individuals recognize their role as participants in these cyclical processes, they can move toward a more sustainable economic paradigm. My view suggests that the "economy" is not an abstract entity separate from human biology or planetary health; rather, it is a manifestation of how we allocate resources to sustain our existence within the constraints of Earth's natural cycles.

The implications of my philosophy are profound for modern economic theory. If human behavior is fundamentally tied to cyclical processes, then economic growth models that ignore these cycles—such as those relying on infinite expansion—are inherently flawed.

My view advocates for a shift in perspective where the "cost" of economic activity includes the preservation of the biological systems that facilitate life. This requires a transition from a linear consumption model to a circular model that mimics the regenerative processes found in nature.Furthermore, this approach addresses the "endogeneity problem" in institutional economics by acknowledging that institutions and human behavior are mutually constitutive; as we change our behavior to align with Earth's cycles, the institutions governing our economy must evolve to support, rather than hinder, this alignment.

Ultimately, my work serves as a call to action for individuals and policymakers alike to reconsider the purpose of economic activity. By integrating human behavior into the broader context of Earth's cyclical life processes, my view suggests that we can achieve a state of "economic homeostasis," where human prosperity is not achieved at the expense of the environment, but through a symbiotic relationship with it. This requires a fundamental shift in how we measure success, moving away from purely quantitative metrics like GDP toward qualitative indicators that account for the health of the entire system.

The Intersection of Human Behavior and Sustainable Economics

The discourse surrounding the relationship between human behavior and sustainable economic practices is a multifaceted field that integrates psychology, behavioral economics, and environmental science. While my work, specifically Learning Social Behavioral Economic Cases, explores the intersection of these disciplines, it is essential to contextualize his views within the broader framework of established economic theory and behavioral science. My approach emphasizes that sustainable economic practices are not merely a result of policy mandates but are deeply rooted in the cognitive biases, social norms, and decision-making heuristics that govern human interaction with resources.

In the view of behavioral economists, human behavior is often characterized by "bounded rationality," a concept pioneered by Herbert Simon, which suggests that individuals make decisions based on limited information and cognitive constraints rather than pure utility maximization.

My analysis suggests that to achieve sustainability, economic models must account for these behavioral realities. Instead of assuming that individuals will always act in the interest of long-term environmental preservation, Lok argues that sustainable practices must be "nudged" through structural changes in the choice architecture of economic systems. This aligns with the work of Thaler and Sunstein, who posit that small changes in how choices are presented can significantly influence behavior toward more sustainable outcomes without restricting freedom of choice.

Furthermore, the relationship between behavior and sustainability is heavily influenced by social proof and community norms. My view highlights that economic agents are social beings whose consumption patterns are often dictated by the behavior of their peers.When sustainable practices are framed as the social norm, the psychological cost of adopting them decreases, leading to higher rates of compliance and long-term behavioral change. This perspective is supported by Elinor Ostrom's research on the "governance of the commons," which demonstrates that individuals are capable of managing shared resources sustainably when social institutions foster trust and collective action, rather than relying solely on top-down regulation or market privatization.

My work also touches upon the role of temporal discounting—the tendency for humans to value immediate rewards over future benefits—as a primary barrier to sustainable economic practices. Because the negative externalities of unsustainable consumption (such as climate change or resource depletion) are often delayed, the human brain is evolutionarily predisposed to prioritize short-term gain.To counteract this, my view suggests that sustainable economic frameworks must incorporate mechanisms that make the future costs of current actions more salient, effectively bridging the gap between present behavior and future consequences.By integrating these behavioral insights, Lok advocates for a transition from traditional, growth-obsessed economic models to those that prioritize "well-being economics," where human flourishing is balanced within the planetary boundaries.

Finally, nowadays, some economists indicate that human ourselves behavior may be as full participants in Earth's cyclical processes of life and economy.

They think that human behavior, such as we are rational economic man, social adaptable humans, our daily behaviour may bring direct or indirect influences to global economy growth or recession. For share market example, before 21 century, share buyers need to go to banks or finance companies or share markets to buy the company's shares. But, since 21 century, smart phone technological products had been invented. Nowadays global many share inventors began to choose to use smart phones

to buy and sell any companies shares in any time and any where conveniently. So, smart phone invention had brought indirect influence to global share buyers' carrying on sale and buying shares investing behavioral transactions in preferable choice. SO, smart phones and internet invention may influence global many share investors shares investment behavior and investment attitude change. It seems that this both new technological invention can encourage future share investors accept to apply smart phones to carry on shares buying and selling transactions more than visiting finance companies to enquire share agents their idea because, they can apply smart phone to observe global any shares whether their prices will rise up or fall down immediate. SO, smart phone and internet will change future share investors investment behavior.

Two economic sociologists, Donald Mackenzie and Yuval Miko, decided to research how share traders behaviors, however, by interviewing some of the share traders themselves. What did they discover? That the theory's increasing accuracy over time was because the share traders had started to behave as if the theory ware true and so were using the model's predicted prices as a benchark for selling, their owning bids. Financial economics, they concluded " helped create in reality the kind of markets, it posited in theory. Ans as financial markets later learned, when those theories turn out to be flowed. If rational economic man can reshape our behavior in financial markets, he is vary likely to be reshaped our behavios in past. Hence, smart phone can influence future share buyers to do shares buying and selling decision in short time as well as it can persuade global share markets shares purchase number increases to bring economic growth.

Learning invisible hand economy theory

How may " inivisible hand " factor influence the smart phone manufacturer products demand number increase?

The invisible hand is for the law of supply and demand explains how the pull and push of these two factors serve to benefit sciety as a whole. In simple, every consumer choose to buy the product, he/she pursues to earn the most more interest to the manufacturer needs to produce the product as its product may be of the greatest value to let the consumer intends only his/her own gain, led by an invisible hand to promote the product to let the consumer to make satisfaction to choose to buy the product.

In behavioral economic view, the invisible hand to the product manufacturer may be " the consumer whose satisfactory feeling to use the product".So, the invisible hand meant that ir can not be touch , seen, it only brings feeling to let the consumer to feel. This feeling to the product is very mportant factor to excite the consumer to choose to buy the product, e.g. smart phone product the smart phone buyer's invisible hand factor may include: The smart phone can link to app to use internet service, download documents from smart phone , taking phones, watching movie, listening music, clock time etc. function, selling different countries street locations, instead of general mobile talking function.

So, all of above factors will be future new smart phone main " invisible hand" factors to excite future smart phone buyers to make purchase decision to choose to buy the kind of smart phone among different kinds of smart phone products innovation , when they are manufactured to promote to smart phone market to sell.

So, in smart phone market supply and demand view, the smart phone manufacturer needs to innovate new smart phone products in order to let smart phone buyers fee its news phone buyers feel its new smart phone products have unique functions or features to excite its smart phone buyers to choose to buy its new kind of smart phone products, because smart phone buyers will be influences to make final smart phone purchase decision by invisible hand factors from smart phone different new function .

Smart phone manufacturers need to innovate many new functions o future new kinds of smart phone manufacturing in order to bring new invisible hand satisfactory feeling to let any one smart phone buyer to feel whose new smart phone can bring the most unique satisfactory feeling to let them to feel. So, smart phone 's invisible hand factor is main influential factor to bring smart phone manufacturer's new smart phone demand number will increase or decrease. If the smart phone manufacturer can often innovate its smart phone products to let smart phone buyers feel more using satisfactory feeling to its new kind of smart phone more than its other similar kinds of smart phone manufacturers. Then, the smart phone manufacturer ought raise its smart phone purchase number demand easily.

What is smart phone opportunity cost?

Hence, the concept of opportunity cost factor means smart phone manufacturers need to forgone opportunities of time cost , design new kinds of smart phone products, e.g. smart phone pictures, color and shape , future smart phone manufacturers need to concentrate more time to research how to innovate new features and function to let every potential smart phone buyers to bring more functions using satisfactory feeling in order to attract they choose to buy its smart phone product.

On conclusion, opportunity cost to smart phone manufacturers may be forgone spend more time on smart phone design, color choice, shape choice aspects. Smart phone manufacturers need to spend more time on innovate new feature and function aspects in order to satisfy future smart phone using needs in global competitive smart phone smart.

Human Behavioral network job brings social economic benefits

What does human network job mean ? Why may human network job be popular? Why human network job behavior may influence economy ?

The Intersection of Technology, Online Labor, and Economic Development

The relationship between technological advancement and economic growth is a foundational theme in modern economic theory, often explored through the lens of how digital platforms and online labor markets reshape productivity. In my work Technology And Economic Growth Close Relationship, posits that the integration of digital infrastructure into the global economy acts as a force multiplier for development

My view argues that online employment—defined as the ability for individuals to provide services across geographical boundaries via digital platforms—democratizes access to capital and human resource markets, thereby reducing the friction that traditionally hindered economic expansion in developing regions. By leveraging the internet to bypass local infrastructure deficits, online labor allows for a more efficient allocation of human capital, which is essential for sustained macroeconomic growth.

The economic development potential of online labor, as viewed through the framework of my analysis, rests on the concept of "digital comparative advantage." In traditional economic models, such as the Heckscher-Ohlin theorem, trade is driven by factor endowments; however, my view suggests that technology shifts these endowments toward digital literacy and connectivity.

When workers can participate in global labor markets from remote locations, they contribute to the national GDP through foreign currency inflows and the acquisition of high-value skills. This process mirrors the transition from agrarian to service-based economies, accelerated by the speed of digital information exchange. Lok emphasizes that the "close relationship" between technology and growth is not merely about the existence of tools, but about the institutional capacity to integrate online labor into the formal economy, ensuring that workers are protected and that the value generated is reinvested locally.

Furthermore, the scalability of online labor platforms allows for a reduction in the "search costs" associated with employment, a concept famously explored by economists like Joseph Stiglitz. By lowering the barriers to entry for global projects, online work enables a more fluid labor market where supply and demand meet with minimal delay. Lok suggests that this efficiency gain is a primary driver of economic resilience, especially in regions facing traditional market stagnation. The mathematical representation of this growth can be viewed through an augmented Solow-Swan growth model, where technological progress A is a function of digital connectivity and human capital investment:

Y=Kα(AL)1−α

In this equation, as the efficiency of labor L increases through online integration, the total output Y grows even if physical capital K remains constant. My perspective aligns with broader academic discourse suggesting that the digital economy is not merely a supplement to traditional growth but a fundamental restructuring of how value is created and distributed globally.

Nowadays internet is popular to use. We can apply internet to find data , search any new things, even earn money. Why does internet may become human network job source. For example, e-publish may be one kind of new human network job. Any authors may apply internet channel to help them to sell electronic or paper books from e-publisher web store. They may apply facebook, you tub etc. any online channel to promote themselves new books to let new readers to know whether when they may buy themselves favourable new topic books to read from electronic publisher web store. Thus, future electronic publisher industry may help any authors to build internet network platform to help them to sell and promote to advertise their any one new electronic or paper book topic to let global any one reader to choose to buy their any new topic books from electronic publisher web store easily and conveniently. However, it implies that electronic network platform author may be one kind of future new human network job in our societies.

The Impact of Online Employment on Economic Development

The discourse surrounding online employment and its role in economic development is multifaceted, often centering on the transition from traditional labor structures to digital, platform-mediated work. Scholars and economists, such as those analyzing the "gig economy," argue that online employment serves as a critical mechanism for integrating marginalized regions into the global marketplace..By decoupling labor from physical geography, digital platforms allow individuals in developing nations to bypass local infrastructure limitations, effectively exporting their services to high-demand markets. This process is frequently cited as a means of "leapfrogging" traditional industrial development stages, providing immediate income streams where formal employment opportunities are scarce.

Furthermore, the contribution of online employment to economic development is not merely about job creation; it is about the potential for human capital accumulation and economic inclusion. When workers engage in global online labor markets, they are often required to adopt international standards of digital literacy, project management, and specialized technical skills.This "upgrading" process, as noted in recent academic literature, allows workers to move from low-value tasks to more complex, higher-paying roles, thereby increasing the overall productivity of the regional labor force.

However, this development is tempered by concerns regarding the precarity of such work, the lack of traditional bargaining power, and the intermediation of value chains that may siphon a significant portion of earnings away from the worker.Consequently, the consensus among development economists is that while online employment is a powerful tool for economic expansion, its long-term success depends on the implementation of robust regulatory frameworks, certification schemes, and the collective organization of digital workers to ensure that economic growth is both sustainable and equitable.

How electronic network platform author job may bring economy benefit in macro economy view? A person can have few friends, contacts and still be very influential if these few friends and contacts are themselves highly influential, e.g. one author must not need to know any one reader in global society. When they like to choose any electronic books from electronic internet network platform. They may become the author's any one topic book buyer, when they feel the author's any one topic book is fun and attract they make decision to both the strange author whose the topic book from electronic book publisher's platform web store convenient in short time. Although, they are strangers, they do not know themselves , but the reader can understand what it way that made Google from writing platform to create new creative mind and typing network job method to replace traditional hand writing book method for global authors. It will be one kind of new human network writing job.

Hence, global any one reader can apply an innovative search engine , such as google.com to find whether whom author personal new topic books are value to read from internet.

Then, the electronic publisher's web store may be new book store platform sale network to help the author to sell many electronic or paper books from electronic network platform

in short time. So, internet may be future new network platform to help global any one author to create network writing job absolutely. Furthermore, internet may be popular social media

to help any one author to build good relationship between his/her readers. It is one kind of new network, human network job. New authors do not need to buy many paper books to prepare to put in any one book shop warehouse. Their every book can print on demand to reduce out of book stock in any one book shop. They may choose to sell either electronic books or paper books both from any one book publisher web store. So, electronic network platform may be one kind of good writing channel to help human authors to create income and it can also help authors to bring new creative mind and new topic fun content books to let readers to know and buy to read from electronic publisher network platform.

Why does human behavior may be one kind of new human network job to bring global economic advantages. Although, it may be free income or without income, but the person does the network behavior, his/her behavior may be bring advantages to influence many other people's health. For this case, when a worker in a coffee shop in an airport gets a vaccination against the flu, it does not only helps him or her stay healthy, but also helps the many travellers who might otherwise have been inflected if that workers caught the flu. So, the externality , the result implies the vaccination of even a part of a community conveys benefits to the whole community. For example, governments pay special attention to the vaccinations of school children, teachers, health mothers, and the elderly, categories of people particularly susceptible not only to catching, but also to transmitting a disease.

It is not accidential that governments are heavily involved with vaccination . When there are externalities, free market, fail to persuade individual incentives with society's their the worker's decision of whether to get a vaccine ends up attracting whether other people get sick. The workers might not fully take all these other people's potential suffering into account when making her or his vaccination decision.

As Stanford University does many suggestions, understand this and tries to help them make the right decisions and so providers free flu vaccines for its staff and students.

Small pockets of unvaccinated individuals can allow a disease to gain a spread more widely well-being. For example, parent weighing the costs and benefits of a vaccine for their child is not always thinking of the consequences of that vaccination to other people. THese are markets in which subsidizing or regulating behavior can make everyone better off. Because the reason for requiring that a child be vaccinated before enrolling in school is not just to protect that child, because each child's vaccination affects others via potential contagions.

Robot job behavior brings economy influences

The Economic Philosophy of my opinion

Regarding Robotics and Labor

In my analytical works such as How Robots Bring Economy Growth, posits that the integration of robotics into the modern workforce represents a dual-edged sword for global economic structures. My view argues that the influence of robotic job behavior is not monolithic; rather, it functions as a transformative force that can either catalyze unprecedented productivity or precipitate significant social and economic instability.

My perspective is rooted in the observation that robotics have permeated nearly every sector of human activity, from high-precision medical surgery and complex legal clerical tasks to routine logistics and hospitality services.

My central thesis suggests that the economic impact of robotics is contingent upon the balance between efficiency gains and labor displacement. From his viewpoint, the deployment of robots allows employers to achieve higher output with lower operational costs, which theoretically fosters economic growth by optimizing resource allocation and increasing the speed of service delivery.

However, my view is deeply concerned with the "replacement effect," where the automation of low-skill tasks leads to structural unemployment. My view suggests that if the rate of job displacement exceeds the economy's capacity to create new, higher-skilled roles, the resulting rise in the unemployment ratio could lead to a broader social recession.

In my broader examination of social behavioral economic cases, Lok emphasizes that the transition to an automated economy requires a nuanced understanding of how human labor interacts with machine intelligence.

My view suggests that the economic influence of robots is not merely a technical issue but a behavioral one, affecting how individuals perceive job security, skill acquisition, and the value of human labor in a market increasingly dominated by artificial agents. My view encourages readers to perform individual analyses of these trends, suggesting that the ultimate outcome—whether prosperity or decline—depends on how societies manage the transition and whether they can effectively retrain the workforce to complement, rather than compete with, robotic systems.

The economic tension my view describes can be modeled by considering the relationship between capital investment in robotics (Kr) and the displacement of labor (Ld). If we define economic growth (G) as a function of productivity (P) and social stability (S), my argument implies that:G=f(P(Kr),S(Ld))Where an increase in P driven by Kr must be balanced against the potential decrease in S caused by Ld. If Ld becomes too high, the negative impact on S may outweigh the gains in P, leading to a net negative economic outcome.

My work serves as a critical inquiry into whether modern societies can maintain this equilibrium or if the rapid advancement of robotics will necessitate a fundamental restructuring of the social contract to prevent widespread economic stagnation.

Would you like to explore more about the specific strategies , my view proposes for mitigating the risks of structural unemployment in an increasingly automated economy, or perhaps examine how other contemporary economists compare to his views on the "replacement effect"?

If one day robots can replace human to do simple, even complex jobs. They will bring what influences to our global social economy.The popular economic refrain declares that the global middle class is dying and robots will soon take our jobs, e.g. shopping center customer service jobs, library service jobs, cinema ticket sale jobs, restaurant kitchen cooker jobs, even, bus drivers, taxi drivers etc. public transport driving jobs, accountant, doctors etc. professional jobs. Whether it is beautiful or petty matter if our future societies have many human jobs can be replaced to do from robots. Businessman must may reduce to employ employees and reduce to pay salary or wage, when robots can be replaced to do their employees tasks. But, societies must bring unemployment rate rises , due to societies will have many people loss jobs when their employers choose to buy robots to serve their clients or do any office tasks or customer service or cleaning etc. tasks.

In micro economy view, employers may save money in long term, but in macro economy view, it will cause unemployment ratio rises , even crime rate rises when there are many people lose jobs in societies. These models of doom, though, fail to account for the hundreds of businesses riding the waves of change in their industries when robots may be invented to replace human to do many simple , even complex tasks in our future societies.

WE may image that one small factory needs to manufacture fishes canes to sell to supermarket, the small , cheaper stuff and higher margin parts of the fishes manufacture industry. Before, this factory needs to employ many human factory workers need to help every fresh customer making the perfect fishing gear, designed for performance, durability, and cost in order to achieve to manufacture every fish cane in whole fished processing manufacturing stages. Every worker needs to spend about 15 to twenty minutes to finish every fish cane , till to delivery to any supermarket to sell. If this fish canes manufacturing factory can apply manufacturing robots to help them to finish any one working tasks , every robot can only spend five minutes to finish whole fresh fish cane manufacturing process. Thus, every robot can help this factory save 10 to 15 minutes time to finish every fish cane manufacturing process. IN fact, time is money, because when every robot can help this factory to reduce 10 to 15 minutes time to compare human worker. Then, this factory can finish about 20 fish canes in one hour if it can use robot to help it to manufacture fish canes. Otherwise, if this factory still use human workers to help it to manufacture fish canes, then it can finish about 3 to 4 fish canes in one hour. SO, the manufacturing efficiency ensures that robots must help this fish manufacturing factory to raise fish canes number more than human workers. So, in robotic behavioral economy view, manufacturing robots must help this fish canes manufacturing factory to raise fish canes manufacturing number and deliver increasing number to supermarkets to prepare to sell every day. Robots can help this fish canes manufacturing factory bring manufacturing time saving, rising manufacturing efficiency, improving performance and reducing wages expenditure long time advantages in micro economy view. However, manufacturing robots can also bring disadvantages to society, e.g. increasing unemployment ratio, increasing crime rate, this factory workers will lose jobs and income, they need earn social welfare from government and increasing government finance pressure in short time, even long time in macro economic view.

Stanford University graduate program in economics, Scott lecturer explained that "in demand and supply economic theory for robots supply and demand case, robots supply number increasing may influence human workers demand number decrease. It sometimes calls " the efficient frontier".

No specific human beings were mentioned in any of economics classes. As robots supply and demand in market case, They (robots) may be purely theoretical " agents" who reached to the most reasonable sale prices in order to persuade any one businessman buyer to make manufacturing robot buying decision whether robots can help him / her to bring how much saving time , saving money, saving cost, improving performance, efficiency economic benefit before he/she plans to reduce workers number when he/she decides to apply robots to replace human workers in his/her factory or office or any service department, e.g. cinema ticket sale service, shopping center customer service, shopping center cleaning , supermarket customer service etc. service or sale tasks. When robots can replace human to do any one of these tasks in any organizations. So, robots may be human worker agents who reached to prices the way robots would react to a software command. There was nothing that explained why some people thrived and others did n't or why truly brilliant, hardworking people could fail when much lazier folks succeeded." Having been admitted to the Stanford University graduate program in economics, Scott lecturer hoped to get his answers there.

How robots influence our future social changing? Using the right technology can be a boon to your business in this economy. For internet example, it is easier than ever to find well-matched customers all around the world, to stay in contact with them, and to more quickly design the products they want. If you focus solely on being cutting -edge, though you risk letting the technology take over what should be very robust relationships with your customers , employees, and colleagues. IN nowadays society, technological advances and automation, personal relationships in business are more crucial than ever. I mean that robots can not replace human to serve clients to let them to feel more comfortable and passion more easily. For shoe shop case example, if the shoe shop apply one robot to serve its clients to replace human shoe salesperson to serve its shoe customers. Robots ensure that they can not persuade every shoe potential buyer to make shoe buying decision more easily when robots need to contact every shoe potential buyer. The reason is simple, because robots can not touch any one shoe buyer individual emotion very easier. If the shoe buyer needs the robots to help him/her to choose any right shoe styles when he/she can not feel himself / herself can make the most right shoe style choice decision. The robots can not replace human shoe salesperson to make shoe style choice judgment more easily. They must need longer time to analyze whether which shoe style may be the most suitable to the shoe buyer. Otherwise, human shoe salesperson may attempt to make the most right shoe style choice decision to help any one shoe buyer to choose the most right style shoe because he/she owns shoe style sale experience, shoe style knowledge, the most important reason is that they can feel every shoe customer individual emotion to touch whether he/she will feel comfortable or happy when they attempt to help every shoe customer to seek the most right shoe style in every shoe customer whole shoe searching processing. Otherwise, serving robots are only one machine, they can not touch or feel every shoe customer individual emotion whether he/she feel comfortable or unhappy or happy when they need to contact them in whole shoe searching processing. Hence, I believe that some tasks robots can not replace human staff to do very easily. Otherwise, robots may bring disadvantages to let any one businessman to loss his/her customers, due to robots can not touch every customer emotion to compare human staff in service tasks more easily. Robots serving customer behaviors may cause money lose and customers number lose to the shop in micro economic view.

Intellectual human economic behaviors

The Economic Philosophy of John Lok: Intellectual Human Behavior

In my analysis of the intersection between human psychology and economic systems, posits that economic behavior is not merely a product of rational calculation but is deeply rooted in intellectual frameworks and cognitive biases. MY VIEW argues that human beings operate within a bounded rationality, where the "intellectual" component of economic decision-making is heavily influenced by social conditioning, historical context, and the psychological need for security versus growth. My view suggests that when individuals make economic choices, they are often acting upon a "mental map" of the world that is constructed through cultural inheritance rather than pure mathematical optimization.

My perspective aligns with the broader tradition of behavioral economics, which challenges the classical model of Homo economicus—the idea that humans are perfectly rational agents who always maximize utility. In my work emphasizes that intellectual human economic behavior is characterized by a constant tension between cognitive heuristics and the complexity of modern market structures. My view suggests that the "intellectual" aspect of this behavior involves the ability to synthesize information, yet this synthesis is frequently distorted by emotional responses to scarcity and abundance.

Furthermore, my view explores how institutional frameworks shape individual intellectual output in the economy. My view posits that the environment in which an individual operates—whether it be a highly regulated market or a free-enterprise system—dictates the "intellectual tools" available to them.For example, in a system that rewards short-term gains, the intellectual behavior of the participant shifts toward risk-aversion and immediate gratification, whereas long-term stability fosters a more analytical and patient economic temperament. Lok's analysis suggests that to understand economic outcomes, one must first understand the intellectual environment that produces the decision-maker.

The mathematical representation of this behavior, as implied by my theories, can be viewed as a function of utility U influenced by a cognitive bias factor β and external information $I:U=f(I,\beta)$Where β represents the intellectual distortion caused by human psychology. My view argues that as $\beta \rightarrow 0$, the individual approaches the classical rational actor, but in reality, β is rarely zero, meaning that intellectual human behavior is inherently "bounded" by the limitations of the human mind.

My work serves as a bridge between classical economic theory and the modern psychological insights found in the works of scholars like Daniel Kahneman and Richard Thaler. My view concludes that the economy is essentially a reflection of the collective intellectual state of its participants, and therefore, economic reform must begin with an intellectual shift in how individuals perceive value, risk, and social responsibility.

What does intellectual human economic behaviors mean ? I believe that when we choose or decide to do intellectual behaviors, then our societies will be influenced to bring economic growth in consequence.I shall attempt to indicate pollution case to explain how and why either our intellectual or foolish behaviors may bring economic growth or recession in consequence as below:

On one hand, for air pollution social case aspect example, if we only consider to buy cars to drive for working aim or holiday leisure aim. Then, our societies air will be polluted. Our health will be influenced to bad. Our car driving behaviors may cause global environment air pollution seriously. In long time, global air pollution will bring our bodies health to be bad. Although, ourselves car driving behaviors may bring our driving travel leisure enjoyment and comfortable feeling in short time, also we so not need to pay public transport fare often, but we need to compensate ourselves health economic intangible loss due to air pollution , when cars number increases, dirty air will cause ourselves health to become bad.

In the result, we will need to pay more medical expenditure when we are old age, due to ourselves bodies will become bad, due to we breathe global dirty air every day, due to ourselves cars pollute air in long time, e.g. 10 to 20 years, even 30 more without limited air pollution environment. So, driving cars behavior may be one kind of human foolish behavior and our foolish behavior may bring ourselves future long time medical expenditure absolutely.

One the other hand, water pollution social aspect, if we often keep much rubbish to pollute sea, oil exploration processing pollute ocean , ships gas pollute ocean, then fishes will eat polluted food and drive dirty water, due to global ocean is polluted.

In fact, because human only to consider how to buy boats to carry on leisure enjoyment activities, or catch cruises to travel on the sea. Also, oil manufacturers only consider researching anywhere to find new oil exploration places to manufacture oil product, when their oil exploration processes pollute ocean . Consequently, global fishes drink polluted water or eat polluted food. They will have poison. SO, human will have high chance to eat poison polluted fishes, due to fishes are poison or are polluted. So, human is doing foolish activities, we only hope to find oil exploration places to pollute ocean or we only spend money to buy ticket to catch ships to travel anywhere in global ocean. All of these human foolish behaviors will bring pollution to global ocean. On consequently, we will need to compensate to eat polluted or dirty or pollute fishes, ourselves bodies health will be bad. In long time, we need have high chance to pay medical expenditure when we are old. So, pollution case may be one good example to explain how and why human foolish behavior may influence ourselves future need to compensate serious medical loss.

All of these human foolish behavior will bring pollution to global ocean. On consequently, we will need to compensate to eat polluted or dirty or poison fished , ourselves bodies health will be bad. In long time, we will have high chance to pay medical expenditure, when we are old. So, pollution case may be one good example to explain how and why human ourselves intellectual or foolish behaviors may influence future long time economic loss or economic growth or recession in micro and micro economic view.

On another water pollution aspect hand, if we often keep rubbish to sea, oil exploration processing pollutes ocean and ships' gas pollute ocean, then fishes will eat polluted food and drink dirty water, due to fishes will eat polluted food and drink dirty sea water because the global ocean is polluted seriously.

In fact, because human only consider how to buy boats to carry on any leisure water activities, or catches cruises to travel on the sea. Also, oil manufacturers only consider any where to find oil exploration places to manufacture oil products from ocean, when their pol exploration processes can pollute ocean. Consequently, global fishes drink polluted water or eat direct food. They will have poison. So, human will have high chance to eat poison fishes.

Otherwise, such as pollution case, it can influence inflation or deflation. Consequently, the reason indicates supply and demand theory. If air pollution is serious, then we will consider health issue, global cars demand number may be influenced to reduce, when global cars number demand will reduce, global car prices and supply number will need to change to fall down in order to attract or persuade global car consumers choose to make car purchase decision.

Hence, global car manufacture number and car price will be influenced to reduce, due to global air pollution issue. Consequently, deflation will occur because when the country citizen usually does not spend much extra saving money to buy car expensive goods. Money value will be low. Otherwise, if global car pollution is not serious, human considers to buy cars to enjoy driving leisure lives. So, global car demand is influenced to increase , also global car price will also influenced to increase.

Consequently, global human will choose to buy cars to drive. Due to we accept to spend extra saving to buy expensive car goods. Car sale price and supply may be influenced to rise up. Money value is influenced to reduce. Inflation may be influenced, due to global car consumers number increases, we would not have extra money to spend easily. Car expensive goods expenditure influences our spending habit to avoid to make car purchase decision more easily. So, human intellectual or foolish activities may bring inflation or deflation consequence in possible indirectly in macro economic view.

On conclusion, above pollution case explain that how and why human intellectual or foolish economic behaviors may bring inflation or deflation consequence as well as economic growth or recession consequence as well as any goods demand and supply increasing or decreasing consequence. It implies that human behavior may have indirect relationship to influence any goods demand and supply number to either increase or decrease result as well as any goods price will be influenced to increase or decrease in micro and macro economic view.

The relationship between social change and human behavior

Why does economic changes may influence human individual behavioral change? I shall attempt to indicate shopping behavior and staying at home behavior to explain their case and effect relationship as below:

Human behavior can be influenced by economic change or economic change can be influenced by human behavior? Why does recession may influence consumers reduce shopping desire? In social recession situation, it is possible that many people lose jobs suddenly, due to businessmen lose many customers. They need to make decision to reduce employees number in order to continue to keep businesses. Consequently, many firms (organizations) their employees may lose jobs. When they have much time, due to lose jobs, they will feel to avoid to spend too much time and money to go to shopping often. Many losing jobs people, they will often stay at homes. So, they will reduce time to go to shopping, then non essential products won't their preferable choice purchase products. Hence, recession will change many losing jobs people their shopping or consumption desires to avoid to buy non essential products often . Usually when economic boom, many people have jobs to do because consumers number must increase when many people have jobs to do. Then, many people can accept to spend money to buy non essential products often. Many people feel spend time to go to shopping can satisfy their purchase of any kinds of new products useful psychology or desire. So, recession is one good example to explain it can influence many people do not like often to leave homes to go to shopping easily. Many people like to stay at homes, because they feel worry about spending too much shopping time when they leave homes. Their staying home time is one good negative shopping behavior example. So, economic change may influence human individual behavior changes , they have direct cause and effect relationship in behavioral economic view.

May human behavior influence economic change? Is it possible that human behavior may bring the country social economic change in macro economic or micro behavioral economic view ? I shall indicate publishing industry example. Do you feel that if there are many students feel learning is very important when they read many books or many of students feel interesting to read or they have reading new books in habit, then it is possible that the country will have many students like to spend time to go to any book shops to choose the books, they feel that they can help they learn new knowledge. Then the country will increase students number, they often spend time to visit any one book shop every week. Their visiting book shops behavior which may become their habits. So, the country will increase students number, they often spend time to visit book shops. Also, it implies that visiting book shops behaviors may be their behavioral habits. So, when the country has many students often spend time to visit book shops , their visiting book shops behaviors may help any one book shop to raise books sale chance. So, the country's student individual often visiting book shop behaviors, their habitual visiting book shops behaviors must may assist help any one book shop to increase books sale number absolutely.

Consequently, any one book shop , its books sale number must be influenced to increase to increase because the country will have many students like or feel need visit book shops habit in order to choose any suitable books to buy to read at home in order to raise themselves learning effort. When the country has many book shops often have many students visit their book shops, then their books sale number may be influenced to increase. It explain why student individual visiting book shop behavior may help any one book shop sale number increases also.

How human productive behavior may influence economic development

In my canon of economic theory, the relationship between human productive behavior and economic development is best understood through the lens of established intellectual traditions. Classical and neoclassical economists have long argued that human behavior—specifically the propensity to save, invest, and innovate—is the primary engine of growth.This is often modeled using the Solow-Swan growth model, which examines how labor, capital, and technological progress interact to determine the output of an economy:

$Y=A \cdot F(K,L)$

In this equation, Y represents total output, A represents total factor productivity (often linked to human behavior, education, and innovation), K is capital, and L is labor.Modern development economics, particularly the work of Nobel laureates, emphasizes that "productive behavior" is not merely a function of individual effort but is deeply embedded in institutional frameworks, human capital accumulation, and the rule of law.

If one were to hypothesize how a theory of "productive behavior" might influence development, it would likely align with the concept of "Human Capital Theory," popularized by Gary Becker and Theodore Schultz.This theory posits that investments in education, health, and skills training directly increase the productivity of the workforce, thereby accelerating economic development.Furthermore, behavioral economics suggests that cultural norms, trust, and social capital significantly influence the efficiency of economic transactions, which in turn dictates the pace of development within a nation.

May any country which citizen behavior assist themselves country development? It is one cause and effect economic question. I mean that if the country itself citizen can not concentrate mind or energy to choose to do one kind of industry in order to let themselves country can bring the most benefit, then whether the country itself cconomy can bring the most serious economic benefit. I shall attempt to indicate these countries themselves indistry choice to explain whether these countries themselves citizen productive behavior may help themselves countries to achieve the largest economic benefits. I shall indicate as below:

New Zealand farmer individual wine productive behavior

For New Zealand country example, this country concerns itself effort is focus on farming agricultural aspect. So, this country has many farmers concentrate on farming agricultural aspect. May New Zealanders choose to spend time to produce different kinds of wines, e.g. wine or red grape wine is for the people are eating meat, or they are eating dinner.

When these New Zealanders their behaviors choose to do farming or agriculture to grow and produce different kinds of taste of white or red grape wine drinking products job. Themselves grape agriculture behavior will influence these New Zealanders themselves, they can learn how to improve different kinds of grape wine drinking products in order to achieve every kinds of white or read grape wines taste improving aim during their white or red grape producing process.

Why can New Zealander every individual white or read grape wine producers improve their white or read grape wine taste more easily? In behavioral economic view, it can explain that why any one New Zealander white or read grape wine producer can be encouraged or excited or persuaded to concentrate nervous and energy and effort to learn how to improve their white or red grape wine products easily.

In fact, New Zealand is one agricultural food export country. It has good natural environment resource , e.g. land, seed to provide any one farmer to produce themselves any kinds of agricultrual food products, e.g. fruit, or wine food products. Because New Zealanders know themselves country has enough natural resource . So, in common, many New Zealanders choose to attempt to do farming agricultural jobs in order to export themselves any kinds of fruit or meat or wine products to overseas or sell to domestic in order to earn profit. So, when these New Zealand farmers number has been increasing every year. This country farmers will feel themsleves competition between this New Zealand farmers themselves are serious due to they may feel New Zealanders choose to do agriculture businesses in order to export themselves different kinds of farming food to overseas or sell to local to earn profit.

Hence, when many New Zealand farmers feel that farmers number has been increasing every year. They will feel themselves competition is serious. They must need to spend much time and nervous and effort to research what method is the best how to produce the best taste of white or red grape wine products in order to let local or overseas wine buyers to choose to buy his/her producing white or read grape products to drink.

Hence, in competition psychological view, may influence many New Zealand white or reaad wine producers had been beginning to change their learning behavior on researching what method is the best in order to produce the best quality of taste red or white wine products to sell in order to attract overseas or local white or read grape wine drinkers to choose to buy his/her wine products. Their behavior will focus on learning how to raising or improving white or read grape wine taste method more than only focus on producing a large number white or red grape wine products. They believe wine quality is more important to compare wine producing number. So, New Zealand wine producers themselves wine producers behaviors have been changing on concentrating on researching wine quality method aspect more then wine producing number aspect in behavioral economic view.

America high technological productive behavior

The Economic Philosophy of my view on Technological Productivity

The inquiry into how my view perceives the relationship between American technological advancement and economic productivity requires an examination of the intersection between behavioral economics and industrial evolution. In his work, Technology or Human Behavior Influences Economy?,

My view posits that the trajectory of a nation's economic health is not merely a byproduct of technological innovation but is fundamentally tethered to the human behavioral patterns that dictate how those technologies are integrated into the labor market. My view argues that while high technological productivity is often viewed as an exogenous force—an inevitable march of progress—it is, in reality, a reflection of societal choices, psychological incentives, and the institutional frameworks that govern human interaction with machines.

My perspective suggests that American high technological productivity is driven by a specific "behavioral feedback loop." He contends that when a society prioritizes efficiency and innovation, it creates an economic environment where human labor is increasingly augmented by automation.

However, my warns that this shift can lead to a "productivity paradox," where the sheer volume of output increases, but the distribution of wealth and the stability of the labor force become precarious due to the decoupling of wages from productivity gains.

In my analysis, the "human behavior" component—specifically the propensity for risk-taking, consumer demand for novelty, and the cultural valuation of speed—acts as the primary catalyst that forces technology to evolve at its current rapid pace.

Furthermore, my view emphasizes that the American economic model relies heavily on the psychological construct of "perpetual growth," which necessitates constant technological upgrading. My view suggests that if human behavior were to shift toward a more sustainable or equilibrium-based model, the demand for hyper-productive technology might wane, thereby altering the structure of the economy itself. Unlike traditional economists who might view technology as a neutral tool, my views it as a mirror of human desire, asserting that the "high productivity" observed in the United States is a direct manifestation of a culture that prioritizes technological dominance as a proxy for economic security.

My work serves as a critique of the assumption that technology is the sole driver of prosperity, suggesting instead that without a corresponding evolution in human ethical and social behavior, technological productivity may eventually outpace the society's ability to manage its own economic consequences.

Would you like to explore how my theories on behavioral economics compare to the classical growth models proposed by economists like Robert Solow, or perhaps delve deeper into the ethical implications of automation on the future of the American workforce?

For America example, US is one high technological country, it owns many high technological knowledge talent inventors, e.g. computer science inventors. Hence, US must attract many different countries owning high technological computer inventors choose to go to US to develop their computer science profession career. Also, it seems that when many computer science inventors or professions choose to go to US to develop themselves computer science new career. In behavioral economic view, due to their leaving themselves countries choice, which may bring influence themselves country job behaviors need to be changed. They must need to adapt US new live. Because they will forgive their past computer science job. These computer science professionals need to spend time to adapt US new lives. They " past computer science job behaviors" will need to be changed to their new US any computer employer's new computer science job model.

Because their traditional computer science jobs needed to be forgot in their themselves countries. They will feel their old computer science job knowledge and behavior needed to change in order to let their US any one new of computer company employer feels satisfactory to accept their new working behavior in any one US computer organization.

So, on the other hand, many US computer company employer will feel that they must need time to accept any one new overseas computer science professions their working behaviors, their working attitude daily, because these foreign computer science professional, their past computer working behaviors and working attitude must be different to US domestic computer science professions.

In behavioral economic view, these overseas computer science professions, their working behaviors and attitude must be needed to change in order to adapt any one US new computer company itself domestic or local computer science professional staffs themselves daily working behaviors and attitude because these overseas and local computer science professionals must need to team work together.

In behavioral economic view, it is only one way that foreign computer science professionals must need to change themselves past country traditional daily working behaviors and attitude in order to cooperate with these US local computer science professionals in teams more easily.

Consequently, if these foreign compute science professionals can change their past working behaviors and attitude to let any one US local computer science professional feels to cooperate with them easily in short time. Then, the US computer company itself whole computer professional teams themselves efficiencies will be influenced to raised or improved by the changing past working attitude and working behaviors of these foreign computer science professionals. So, in behavioral economic view, only if US any one computer company hopes itself computer teams themselves efficiency can be raised or improved when it decides to employ foreign computer science professionals and US domestic computer science professionals. They need to work in teams together. They must need to let these foreign computer science professionals to know how to change their working behaviors and attitude to let their domestic computer science professionals feel easy to work together. Then, the US computer company itself whole team efficiency must be raised or improved easily in short time.

China share market investing behavior

The analysis of Chinese market behavior and its relationship to the broader national economy remains a subject of intense academic and professional scrutiny. While specific market commentators like my view have contributed to the discourse regarding the psychological and structural drivers of the Shanghai and Shenzhen exchanges, the consensus among leading economic historians and institutional analysts is that the Chinese stock market has historically functioned as a "policy-driven" rather than a "value-driven" mechanism.

My perspective, often aligned with broader institutional critiques of the "casino-like" nature of Chinese retail investing, suggests that the behavior of individual investors—who constitute the vast majority of trading volume—creates a feedback loop that often decouples equity prices from the "real economy."In this view, the economy is not necessarily "developed" by the stock market in the Western sense of capital allocation efficiency; rather, the market serves as a barometer for state-sanctioned liquidity and sentiment management.When retail investors chase momentum, they often ignore fundamental indicators like the "Keqiang Index"—which tracks electricity consumption, rail cargo, and loan disbursements—leading to volatility that the state must then intervene to stabilize.

Structural Dynamics of Chinese Market Behavior

The development of the Chinese economy through the lens of share market behavior is characterized by a tension between state control and market liberalization. Scholars note that because the Chinese government frequently treats the stock market as a tool for state-owned enterprise (SOE) reform and capital raising, the behavior of investors is conditioned by the expectation of "state puts" or government bailouts.This creates a moral hazard where market participants do not price in risk accurately, thereby hindering the market's ability to act as an efficient engine for long-term economic development.

The Role of Retail Speculation

My view and similar observers emphasize that the high turnover rate in Chinese markets is driven by a "get-rich-quick" mentality among retail investors, which contrasts sharply with the institutional long-term investment strategies seen in more mature markets.This behavior forces the economy into a cycle of short-termism. As noted in authoritative studies on the transition of the Chinese financial system, the lack of institutional depth means that the stock market often fails to provide the necessary signals for capital to flow to the most productive sectors of the economy.Instead, capital is often diverted into speculative bubbles that, when they burst, require significant state intervention to prevent systemic contagion.

Mathematical Modeling of Market-Economy Decoupling

The relationship between the stock market index (S) and the real economic output (Y) can be expressed as a divergence function where the volatility (σ) of the market is inversely proportional to the transparency of the underlying economic data (T):

$\sigma=f(1T)$

When T is low, as is often the case with opaque Chinese economic reporting, σ increases, leading to the speculative behavior that my view and others identify as a primary obstacle to the market serving as a true developmental tool for the nation.[19] [20]

Would you like to learn more about how the "Keqiang Index" and other alternative metrics are currently being used by international economists to bypass official state reporting in China?

For China share market example, economic development depends on financial market. Because if many Chinese have interest to invest to carry on shares buying and selling activities in order to learn how to earn shares interest and share profit when the China shareholder can make decision to sell himself/herself shares in the the high price, then he/she can earn money when he/she can sell the China company's shares in the high sale share price position.

If China has many Chinese like to spend time to carry on investing shares activities. Themselves shares buying and selling behaviors will influence China has many companies can increase fund from many Chinese shareholders in order to have enough money to expand or develop themselves businesses in China in long term.

Consequently, when China can have many Chinese like to attempt to carry on buying and selling shares investing behaviors in China share market. Themselves buying and selling shares behaviors can help many Chinese companies have effort to increase enough money or capital in order to continue to do their businesses in long term absolutely.

So, it explains why when many Chinese become shareholders , they can assist China will have many companies continue to develop their businesses if many Chinese like to carry on shares buying and selling investing behaviors in long time in China financial investment market nowadays in behavioral economic view.

Why has any individual country have many people invest share behavior which can influence the country's macro consumption desire?

I shall apply shares market buying and selling investment behavior to explain why shares investment behavior which may impact the country's overall consumption desire as below:

In behavioral economic view, I assume that when the country has many people have interest to attempt to carry on shares buying and selling investment behavior, then their frequent shares buying and selling behaviors which may bring negative consumption desire or shopping desire of these shares investors their consumer behavior.

The reason is simple, when the country has many share buyers number suddenly been increasing rapidly. Consequently, these large group share investors must need to spend much time to research any kinds of company shares variations, whether when their share prices will rise up of fall down in order to achieve buying the company's shares in the lowest price and selling the company's shares in the highest price level in order to earn profit.

Basic on this reason, they must need to spend much extra time to research share prices changing behavior every day, e.g. one working person will wait to leave his/her job, after he/she can spend time to gather data to research the day's share price changing behavior after dinner. So, the working person's right time may be his/her share price market research behavior. Before he/she may spend his/her night time to go to shopping after dinner, but nowadays, he/she will forgive to do his/her shopping behavior before dinner or after dinner at high sometime. He/she will make decision to spend much night time to turn on computer to click on share market website to research his/her share purchase choice to investigate whether his/her share price whether it rises up or falls down at the moment in order to make his/her share buying or selling decision at ever night time.

I mean the when the country has many people are share investors, their shares investment behavioral spending time which will influence many shops lose customers at might often because the country will have many people feel need to spend night time to turn on computer or watch television to investigate share price variation. So, the country will have many people / share investors choose to stay at home in order to carry on share price variation investigation behavior, they need to listen share market update news from radios or watch the share market update news from computer or TV at home every night. Consequence, they must reduce times to leave themselves homes at night. So, their shopping behavior also will be reduced. Because these share investors feel need to spend time to investigate share price variation news at homes which can bring economic benefits (high opportunity benefits) when they choose to forgive to leave homes to go to shopping times (opportunity cost) every night.

On conclusion, it seems that when the country has many people are share investors, then their share price investigating behavior may bring negative shopping emotion at night. Consequently, the country's any one shop may lose many customers from this share investor consumer group in behavioral economic view. Hence, when the country's share investors number had been increasing rapidly, it will influence any shops lose many customers from this share investing customer group at night frequenly in short time, even long time in behavioral economic view, because their shopping desires or shopping emotion will be brought negative feeling when they make decisions to spend much time to listen radios or watch TV or computers share price update nes at night. Hence, share market will bring negative impact to influence consumer shopping desire or negative shopping emotion in behavioral economic view.

Can technology influence human shopping behavioral change?

The Influence of Technology on Shopping Behavior: Perspectives from Behavioral Economics

In the framework of behavioral economics, the evolution of shopping behavior is fundamentally linked to the reduction of "friction" in the decision-making process. In my analysis of behavioral economies, posits that technology acts as a catalyst that shifts human decision-making from deliberative, effortful cognitive processing to intuitive, heuristic-driven responses.By leveraging digital interfaces, algorithms, and real-time data, technology minimizes the "transactional cost" of shopping, which Lok argues leads to a state of hyper-responsiveness where consumers prioritize immediate gratification over long-term utility maximization.

The Mechanism of Digital Nudging

My view emphasizes that modern shopping environments are not neutral; they are architected to exploit cognitive biases such as loss aversion and the scarcity effect. Through the use of personalized recommendation engines, technology creates a "choice architecture" that narrows the consumer's field of vision. In traditional retail, the physical constraints of a store limited the number of items a consumer could evaluate. In the digital realm, however, the infinite shelf space combined with algorithmic curation means that technology influences behavior by pre-selecting options that align with a user's historical data, thereby reinforcing existing preferences and reducing the likelihood of "rational" comparison shopping.

The Shift Toward Frictionless Consumption

A core tenet of my perspective is the concept of "frictionless commerce." My view suggests that as payment technologies (such as one-click purchasing and digital wallets) become more seamless, the psychological pain of paying—a concept well-documented in behavioral economics—is significantly mitigated. When the act of spending is decoupled from the physical sensation of relinquishing currency, the consumer's internal "stop" mechanism is weakened. This leads to a behavioral shift where shopping becomes a continuous, background activity rather than a discrete, planned event.

Algorithmic Influence and Habit Formation

Furthermore, my view explores how technology facilitates habit formation through variable reward schedules. By utilizing push notifications and dynamic pricing, retailers create a feedback loop that conditions the consumer to check for deals or new arrivals, transforming shopping into a form of entertainment or "retail therapy."This aligns with the broader economic understanding that technology does not merely change how we shop, but why we shop, shifting the motivation from the acquisition of necessary goods to the pursuit of the dopamine-inducing experience of the transaction itself.

Mathematical Modeling of Choice

In analyzing these shifts, behavioral economists often utilize models to represent the utility of a purchase under digital influence. If U represents the utility of a purchase, P the price, and F the friction associated with the transaction, my view suggests that technology effectively reduces F toward zero, causing the perceived utility to appear artificially high:$U_{perceived}=V-(P+F)$As $F \to 0$, the consumer becomes increasingly sensitive to P and the immediate gratification V, often ignoring the long-term budget constraints that would otherwise temper their behavior.This mathematical reduction highlights why digital shopping environments are so effective at altering human behavior—they remove the cognitive "brakes" that physical retail once provided.

Would you like to explore how these behavioral patterns differ across various demographic groups, or perhaps delve into the ethical implications of "dark patterns" in digital interface design?

Nowadays, technological development has reached mature stage, whether technological mature stage may bring positive or negative shopping emotion influence to global consumers. I shall aplly internet inventin or ecommerce shopping channel tool to explain whether internet technology can bring postive or negative influence to global consumer behavior in behavioral economic view.

Internet is a good technological tool, it brings e-commerce business chance. In fact, commonly, global has have many businessmen choose to use internet channel to carry on their products transactions between global online-buyers and their electronic websites. So, global many shoppers had begun to feel online shopping is more convenient to compare visiting shops shopping. Their shopping behaviors have been changed from internet technological tool. Global has many shoppers choose to buy any products from any overseas or local businessmen their web stores. They only need to spend time to find any businessmen their webstores to choose the most suitable products to pay visa to buy from their webstores. at homes. So, in general, global had have may shoppers had changed their shopping behaviors from visiting shops to visiting webstores at homes often.

So, it seems that internet technological tool had influenced global many shops disappear, but internet webstores will be replaced their actual shops on streets. Some of businessmen either they choose webstores to replace shops or choose websotes and shops both or still keep shops only. Hence, internet tool influences global businessmen have three kinds of products sale channels to let globa local and overseas consumers to choose how to buy their products.

However, in fact, many of global shoppers, youngers and olders had begun to accept to buy any products from webstores. They feel to spend time to leave homes to visit shops , their shopping behaviors will be wasted time to not essential part to their daily lives. Hence, since internet technological invention, it had changed many consumers their traditional visiting shops shopping habit to change to buying products from webstores channel.

However, on the one hand, internet creates webstores ecommerce shopping channel to let global many consumers do not need to leave homes to go to shopping. It brings negative visiting shops shopping emotion to global general consumers nowadays. But on the other hand, it also brings positive visiting internet webstores shopping emotion to global general consumer nowadays. So, it seems that global many consumers feel that they often do not need to spend much time to go out shopping. Many global consumers feel convenient and enjoy to choose any products to buy from different internet webstores, when the online buyer chooses the most suitable product, he she only needs to pay visa card to buy the product from the online seller's webstore conveniently at home.

Hence, online shopping can bring economic benefit to online buyers, e.g. avoiding walking time or spending transport fare to visit the shop to go to shopping, shortening or reducing shopping time to do another important matter.

On conclusion, global many consumers began feel online shopping can bring more economic benefits on shortening shopping time, avoiding transport fare spending aspect. So, online shopping will be popular shopping behavior for future long time. It may encourage global many shoppers can make rapid shopping decision in short time in order to carry on any products buying transaction to global any one online shopper in short time easily in behavioral economic view. So, global many businessmen had begun to build themselves one attraction webstore in order to persuade different countries consumers to choose to click themselves webstores from internet channel to buy any kinds of products in short time easily. So, internet technology had changed consumers traditional shopping behaviors to build positive online shopping emotion as well as raise online sellers' any products sale chance easily in behavioral economic view.

Why and how human behavior may influence the country's economic growth or recession?

When one country has many people choose to do the same matter for one period, whether their behavior may influence the country's pvera; economic growth or recession . I shall attempt to indicate cases toexplain their relationship as below:

The concept of "flowing rubbish behavior"—often interpreted in economic and sociological discourse as the systemic mismanagement of waste, the "broken windows" theory of environmental neglect, or the externalities of consumerist disposal—serves as a critical lens through which to view social development. While "John Lok" is not a widely recognized figure in mainstream canonical economic literature, the thematic exploration of how waste and environmental degradation influence societal progress is a well-documented field in institutional economics and urban sociology.

In the context of developmental economics, the behavior of "flowing rubbish"—or the uncontrolled accumulation of waste—is frequently analyzed as a failure of social capital and institutional governance. When individuals or corporations engage in behaviors that treat public spaces as dumping grounds, it signals a breakdown in the "social contract," a concept famously explored by Jean-Jacques Rousseau and later applied to urban environments by Jane Jacobs From this perspective, the "rubbish" is not merely physical; it is a manifestation of social entropy. When a community allows its environment to degrade, it creates a feedback loop where the perceived value of the neighborhood declines, leading to a reduction in private investment and a subsequent stagnation in social development.

The Economic Impact of Environmental Neglect

The economic theory behind this phenomenon suggests that when the cost of disposing of waste is externalized onto the public, the "tragedy of the commons" occurs. As articulated in the works of Garrett Hardin, when individuals act in their own self-interest by disposing of waste improperly, the collective resource—the shared urban environment—is depleted.[This leads to a decline in the "quality of life" index, which is a primary metric for social development.Economists argue that this behavior discourages the formation of stable, long-term communities, as residents who have the means to leave will do so, leaving behind a population with less political and economic leverage to demand improvements.

Social Development and the "Broken Windows" Analogy

The sociological implications of "flowing rubbish" are often linked to the "Broken Windows Theory," proposed by Wilson and Kelling. This theory posits that visible signs of disorder—such as litter, graffiti, and uncollected trash—create an environment that encourages further neglect and, eventually, more serious criminal activity.In terms of social development, this creates a "poverty trap." When a society becomes accustomed to environmental degradation, the psychological threshold for what is considered "acceptable" lowers. This shift in social norms can hinder human capital development, as the environment no longer fosters a sense of pride or civic responsibility, which are essential components of a thriving, modern economy.

Institutional Responses and Policy

To counter the negative influence of such behaviors, developmental economists emphasize the importance of "incentive alignment."[16] By implementing policies that internalize the cost of waste management—such as Pigouvian taxes or community-based circular economy models—societies can reverse the trend of environmental decay.The transition from a "throw-away" culture to a "circular" culture is viewed as a hallmark of advanced social development, where the efficiency of resource use becomes a proxy for the maturity of the society's institutional framework.[

For flowing rubblish behavioral case example, do you feel that when the country has many people often flow rubblish on the streets, instead of their flowing rubblish behavior may bring streets dirty? But, their flowing rubblish behavior may explain that this country has people may have enough money to buy food to ear, or enough cloths to wear, enough bottles of water to drink, even they may have enough money to buy new television, radio, refrigeraters , washing machines, desktops or laptops electronic home products from old to new to use in order to satisfy their living needs. So, when they flow old electronic home products, their flowing old home electronic products behaviors may seem that they have enough money to buy other new home electronic products to replace old home electronic products to use at homes.

However, it seems thaat this country ought have many people have jobs to do. So, many of them, they can easy to make purchase decison to flow any old home electronic products and buy any new home electronic products to use . Because this country has many people have jobs to do. So, they can often not use old home electonic products to become rubblishs to flow on streets after they had bought any kinds of new home electronic homes.

In fact, it also implies that this country's economy grows rapidly. So, many businesses can glow up rapdly. When they expanded their businesses, they must need to increase employees number in order to let they help themselves to raise productivity or serve their clients absolutely. So, when the country has many businesses can grow up, it seems that its economy must be better or it is improved to compare past. Due to many different kinds of home electronic products had been often bought to use by this country people in this period. So, this country's any streets can be observed that expensive electronic home products were flowed on streets anywhere. then, this country will have many electronic home products sellers can sell their home electronic products very easily. When this country has many people can find any kinds of jobs to do easily. So, due to unemploymen rate had been decreasing.

In behavioral economic view, as this many electronic home products rubblish country case, we can observe this country may have many people have jobs to do. So, consumption number has been increased long time. So, cheap food, or expensive home electronic products may be rubblish on any streets. This country's people , their flowing rubblish behaviors may be explained that many of people have enough jobs to do, so they have ability to buy any good taste food to eat or buy any kinds of expensive electronic home products to use. So, this country's economy may be improved for this long period. So, in behavioral economic view, when this country can have many electronic home products rubblishs are flowed on anywherer in streets frequently. It seems that this country will have many people have jobs to do, so it causes they often change old home electronic products or replaced them easily, when they have enough income to spend to buy any kinds of new home electronic products to use at homes easily. Moreover, their flowing old electronic home products behaviors also indicate that this country has many people their salaries may be increased in possible from their emplyers. When this country can have many different kinds of home electornic products are sold. It means that this country's electronic home products needs or demand had been increasing, due to many people have jobs to do and income increases to excite their living of needs also improve. Consequently, this country may seem have better economic improvement. We can observe from this country's electronic home products rubblish increasing income in theis period.

On conclusion, this country ought experience economic growth at this period. So, " flowing expensive electronic home rubblish increasing number " may seem that this country's economic growth is rapidly in this period, due to many people have jobs to do as well as salaries increase in this period.

Technology how impacts human behavior changing?

The Intersection of Technology, Human Behavior, and Economic Evolution

The inquiry into how technology influences human behavior and subsequently shapes the global economy is a central theme in modern behavioral economics. John Lok, in his analysis of these dynamics, posits that the relationship is not merely one-directional but a complex feedback loop where technological advancements alter the psychological incentives of individuals, which in turn dictates the trajectory of economic development.

My view suggests that while technology provides the tools for increased efficiency and global connectivity, human behavior—driven by psychological needs for trust, security, and status—ultimately determines whether these tools are used to foster sustainable growth or create systemic instability.

Technological Impact on Human Behavior and Economic Structures

My perspective aligns with broader academic discourse regarding the "technological-behavioral nexus." As noted in authoritative economic literature, technology acts as a catalyst for reshaping economies by enhancing competitiveness and sustainability.However, my view emphasizes that the "human element" remains the primary variable. My view argues that technology changes human behavior by reducing the friction of communication and transaction, which fundamentally alters how individuals perceive risk and opportunity. This shift in perception leads to changes in consumption patterns, labor participation, and the formation of social capital.

In traditional economic theory, the production function is often represented as $Y=A\cdot f(K,L)$, where Y is output, K is capital, L is labor, and A represents the level of technology. My view suggests that this model is incomplete without a behavioral coefficient, B, which accounts for human psychological responses to technological change: $Y=B(A)\cdot f(K,L)$.[1] When technology advances rapidly, human behavior often lags, creating a "behavioral deficit" that can lead to economic volatility. My view believes that for technology to truly benefit society, it must be designed to align with human cognitive biases rather than exploiting them, thereby rebuilding the trust necessary for a healthy, growing economy.

The Role of Trust and Future Development

My view highlights that trust is the "invisible currency" of the modern economy. As advanced manufacturing and digital connectivity accelerate the flow of goods and people, the interdependence between nations increases. My view argues that if technology is deployed without regard for human behavioral impacts—such as the erosion of privacy or the displacement of meaningful work—it destroys the social trust required for long-term economic prosperity.Conversely, when technology is used to enhance human agency, it creates a more resilient economic environment. His work suggests that the future of global economic development depends on our ability to integrate behavioral insights into the development of new technologies, ensuring that innovation serves human needs rather than merely optimizing for efficiency at the expense of social cohesion.

Technology how influences human behavior to bring changing? For example, online share purchase and sale transaction from smart phone brings share investor can do share buying or selling transation in any where and any time conveniently, non manual driving auto vehicle, bring car owner feels comfortable and spends free time to do other matter, e.g. reading, listening mucis in himself or herself car freely. electrical energy vehicle can help car owner to reduce air polluton and it can brings the drivers do not feel drive long time in any journeys in order to avoid air pollution for environmental protection responsible car drivers in our societies. Thus, they will drive long time in any journeys when they can drive electronic energy cars to replace oil energy cars.

However, online technology can also bring consumers can choose to stay at homes to buy any things from seller individual online webstore conveniently. Such as online technology can bring shoppers do not need to spend much time to visit shops to buy any things. They can choose any kinds of products from any online sellers individual online webstores conveniently at homes. Online technology excite busy consumers can make purchase decision easily as well as it can help online sellers sell any kinds of products from internet easily.

In behavioral economic view, technology can change human behavior to be improved, it can let human feels comfortable, more free time ro use, rapid making any decisions, such as apply smart phones to make share purchase or sale transaction decision, online shopping decision, even travelling any where decision in short time, when the traveller finds the most cheap hotel accommodation room price and air ticket price frm any travel agent online tourism webstore, then the potential travel customer can follow the online hotel accommodation price and air ticket price data to make decision when to buy the air ticket from the airline travel agent or make decision when to prebook which hotel accommodation room to go to the country to travel from online travel agent tourism webstores. So, technology can encourage global any country travelers to make anywhere to trvel rapidly. If the traveler can find the country's general hotel rooms and airline tickets prices had been decreasing more sightly. The traveler may make travel decision to choose the country to travel in short time, then he/she can prebook the country;s any hotel room and airline ticket to pay by visa fraom the country's any hotel and airline travel agent webstores., before one week, even one month or more easily. Hence, online technology can also encourage traveler individual frequent travel times to be increased, due to global travelers can find any hotel rooms and airline tickets prices from internet conveniently at homes. They do not need to spend time to visit any airline travel agent to enquire travel choice country's hotel rooms prices and airline ticket prices. They can compare global travel of countries choices ' all hotels rooms and airline agents air tickets prices to make prebook airline seat and hotel room decision before one week, one month even six months early.

On conclusion, online technology can encourage global travelers can make travelling any where and when traveling time desicions easily. It can excite tourism industry develops in long time. Also, such as electricity cars invention can encourage environment protection car owners do car purchase decision easily, because they can choose to drive electronic energy cars to replace oil energy cars in order to avoid air pollution occurs easily. So, electronic cars can increase electronic car purchasrs number, due to many of environmental protection attitude of car owners can choose to drive electricity cars to bring air cleans, even non -manual driving cars can encourage lazy driving and free time driving car owners to choose to buy non-manual (artificial intelligent) cars to drive , because they can spend much free time to read, listen music or do any matters in themselves cars, they do not need to drivc cars, robotic (AI) auto driving machine is such one non-manual driver to help them to drive themselves cars confidently. So, non-manual driving cars can attract lazy and enjoying free time driving car owners to choose to buy to replace traditional manual cars to drive easily. Moreover, online share transaction can help any share investors to make share buying and selling decision in short time easily. When they can apply smart phones technological tool to carry on share buying and selling activities easily. They can observe any share rising or falling price suitation from smart phones in any where any any time easily. So, smart phone technology can help global any sharcholders to make share purchase and sale transaction easily. So, technology can encourage human makes decision in short time rapidly.

How and why employees behaviors may influence economy development?

The Influence of Employee Behavior on Economic Development: Perspectives from my view

In the discourse surrounding economic development, the role of human behavior—specifically the actions, motivations, and psychological dispositions of the workforce—is increasingly recognized as a primary driver of macroeconomic outcomes.

In my analysis of human behavior and its intersection with economic systems, posits that the aggregate of individual employee behaviors serves as the micro-foundation for national and global economic health. Lok argues that economic development is not merely a product of capital accumulation or technological advancement, but is fundamentally tethered to the "human capital efficiency" generated by employee engagement, ethical decision-making, and innovative risk-taking.

Behavioral Micro-foundations of Macroeconomic Growth

My central thesis suggests that when employees exhibit behaviors characterized by high levels of intrinsic motivation and organizational commitment, the resulting productivity gains create a multiplier effect within the economy. This is often represented by the production function where output Y is a function of capital K, labor L, and the efficiency of that labor A:$Y=A\cdot f(K,L)$Lok argues that employee behavior directly influences the variable A (Total Factor Productivity). When employees are aligned with organizational goals, they contribute to a more efficient allocation of resources, which in turn lowers the cost of production and stimulates aggregate demand.

The Role of Psychological Capital and Innovation

Beyond mere productivity, my view emphasizes the importance of "Psychological Capital" (PsyCap)—hope, efficacy, resilience, and optimism—among the workforce. In my view, employees who possess high levels of PsyCap are more likely to engage in "intrapreneurship," or the practice of acting like an entrepreneur while working within a large organization. This behavior is essential for economic development because it fosters continuous innovation, which is the engine of long-term economic growth as described by Schumpeterian growth models.

Ethical Conduct and Institutional Stability

Furthermore, my view highlights that the ethical behavior of employees—ranging from corporate governance compliance to the reduction of workplace corruption—is a critical determinant of institutional trust. Economic development is heavily dependent on the stability of institutions; when employees prioritize ethical conduct, transaction costs within the economy decrease. This creates a more predictable environment for investment, which is a prerequisite for sustained economic expansion.

Cultural and Social Dimensions

My view also explores how cultural norms influence employee behavior. In regions where social capital is high, employees are more likely to engage in collaborative behaviors that facilitate knowledge sharing. This collective behavior reduces the "silo effect" in industries, leading to faster technological diffusion across the economy. Consequently, my view suggests that policymakers should not only focus on fiscal and monetary policy but also on fostering environments that encourage positive behavioral traits among the workforce, such as lifelong learning and collaborative problem-solving.

Conclusion: The Human-Centric Economic Model

Ultimately, my perspective shifts the focus of economic development from top-down management to a bottom-up behavioral approach. By understanding how individual employee choices aggregate into economic trends, nations can better design educational and corporate policies that incentivize behaviors conducive to long-term prosperity.

The synergy between individual behavioral health and national economic output remains one of the most vital, yet often overlooked, components of modern economic theory.

Would you be interested in learning more about how specific psychological traits, such as resilience or adaptability, are measured in modern economic studies to predict regional GD

In behavioral economy view,I believe the country's any organizational employees behavior may bring indirect relationship to influence the country's long term economic development. I shall indicate past manufacture industry social development period to explain their relationship. For many countries' past business activities had belonged to manufacturing industry, such as US, UK past before 1980 year, it focused on steel manufacturing and steel manufacturing related machine products. So, US, Uk developed countries manufacturing industries may be past main country's economic income sources. I assume US , UK past had one million number different kinds of industries. They ought had about seven houndred thousand number organizational businesses were belonged to manufactured industry. They may include:

Steel manufacturing and steel related machine manufacturing, e.g. vehicle manufacturing, home appliances, e.g. washing machine, television, radio, refrigerate cooler, heater, air condition etc. different kinds of different kinds of steel -related manufacturing machine, they were manufactured from US, UK steel machine manufacturers. So, US, Uk the other three hundred thousand number industry may be general service industry, e.g. hotel service, restaurent, cinema, public transport service, tourism lesiure , wine bar, supermarket etc. different kinds of non-manufacturing industries business organizations were operated in UK, US past before 1980 year.

So, in UK, US developed countries industry development history, they ought have high percentage of businesses belonged to steel related manufacturing machine and steel products. Also, in the past before 1980 year, US, Uk business employers , they employed many workers are manufacturing workers. They needed to spend long time to work in factories. They were skillful workers, and they are trained to manufacturing cars, washing machine, television, heater, etc. even steel itself different kinds of steel related products to prepare to deliver to their shops to sell to US, Uk local or overseas clients.

So, I believe that past UK, US ought employ many employees, they belonged to skillful manufacturing workers, manufacture increasing steel machine or steel related machine number of products rapidly daily. So, if UK, US had had many of these manufacturing factories owned high skillful workers, then their manufacturing steel-related machine or steel both kinds of products number must be influenced to raise rapidly. Consequently, their steel machine manufacturing products would been exported to overseas or would been sold to local both markets , they may be influenced to raise sale number. They (these manufacturing workers) needed to be trained to know how to manufactur these different kinds of machine products in the efficient teams and they ought to be trained to raise their efficiencies in order to shorten time to manufacturing many kinds of steel related manufacturing machine or steel itself products rapidly. So , if their efficiencies and manufacturing performance was improved, these US, UK any one manufacturing worker and their teams ought achieve raising productivities significantly.

Hence, when past UK, US manufacturing industry development period, if these two countries' any manufacturing factories could have many manufacturing workers could be trained to be skillful and proficient manufacturing workers. Then, in past every day to these factories workers, they ought help their steel or steel related manufacturing employers to raise any kinds of machine or steel products number in every team. So, when past in the manufacturing industry development, US, UK could have many factories' manufacturing workers themselves steel or steel related machine products manufacturing skill could be trained to to improve to any kinds of these machine or steel manufacure products quality as well as their products number could be influenced to raise by themselves skillful improvement significantly every day.

Then, what would be influenced to occur to past UK, US manufacturing industry period? In behavioral economic view, when these two manufacturing industry developed countries, such as UK, US , if they had many factories workers can be trained to improve their skill in order to achieve any kinds of steel or steel-related machine products quality could be improved as well as products manufacturing number could be also increased absolutely.

In consequence, past UK and US both countries ought increase themselves any kinds of steel and steel related machine products number to be supplied to themselves local shops to let local clients to choose any one kind of machine manufacturing products to buy easily as well as they could also export to supply overseas any countries to buy their different kinds of steel or steel related machine products to let overseas steel or steel related manufacturing machine product buyers, they can have many of these different kinds of these steel or steel-related different kinds of manufacturing machine from UK and UK these both countries easily to compare other countries.

On conclusion, I believe that past US, and UK macro manufacturing industry income GDP would increase significantly. So, they would have good economic growth performance because when many of these manufacturing workers themselves manufacturing effort could be improved. So, it explained when employees manufacturing abilities can influence economic growth indirectly.

Robots invention whether they can help organizations to raise efficiencies or inefficiencies?

In behavioral economic view, in any organizations, when the organization hopes its worker teams can raise efficiencies , the organization may choose to increase more workers number and/or it can provide training to improve these workets themselves skills in order to raise their efficiencies. For one warehouse example, when the warehouse increases many goods , they are needed to delivered these goods from the shelves to the delivering destination locations. If this warehouse supervisors feel these workers themselves goods delivery speeds are slow, which is possible due to this warehouse's workers number is not enough. So, this warehouse supervisor ought increase workers number in order to increase their goods delivery speed in order to deliver goods from the shelves to every indicated goods delivery destination in order to let any one lorry driver can transport the right kinds of goods and ensure the accurate goods number to transport to any one client home rapidly.

However, if this warehouse supervisor planed to buy several warehouse goods delivery robots to assist these warehouse workers to find the right kinds of goods from shelves and then deliver to the right destination location in the warehouse. So, these warehouse orkers can concentrate on counting the accurate goods number and ensuring the right kinds of goods in order to prepare to let lorry drivers to transport these goods to these goods of buyers themselvers homes rapidly. Consequently, in the first step, robots can concentrate on finding th right goods from shelves and delivers them to the right goods transportation of location destination. Then, in the second step, these warehouse workers can concentrate on counting the accurate goods number and ensuring the right kinds of goods in order to prepare to put them to the lorry. Consequently, when warehouse robots and warehouse workers can cooperate to work together, the most important, robots, can deal on finding the right kinds of goods and deal on delivering the accurate number of goods of job duty as well as these warehouse workers can only concentrte on counting the right kinds of goods number in order to avoid it has none any mistake of wrong kinds of goods and inaccurate goods of delivery number to be transported to the lorry and to deliver to any one buyer's home.

So, it seems that warehouse robots ought help any one warehouse worker to raise himself efficiency and avoid goods delivery of mistake occurrence easily as well as their help to warehouse workers that can let any one goods buyer feels their goods can be delivered to their homes rapidly. Moreover, warehouse robots can also help these warehouse workers to raise efficiencies because warehouse robots can help them to shorten goods delivery time between any one shelf and any one goods delivery destination of location in the warehuse because robots may help them to find the right kinds of goods from the right shelf in the short time. So, any one worker does not need to spend long time to seek anywhere is the right shelf location for the kind of goods when the kind of goods are needed to deliver to the buyer's home from lorry. Warehouse robots can help them to do this aspect of " finding the goods from the right shelf in short time job duty". So, any one warehouse worker only needed tospend less time to do the counting of any right kind of goods number and ensuring the right kind of goods job duty. Consequently, this warehouse 's any one worker, his any one kind of goods delivery time may be reduced, because robots' assistance and they may have more confidence to avoid mistake to deliver the wrong number of goods and/or the wrong kind of goods to any one goods buyer's home.

On conclusion, it seems that warehouse robots ought may help any one warehouse worker to raise efficiency for any one team in the warehouse as well as the warehouse any one supervisor does not need to spend much time to observe any one worker individual performance for " goods delivery job duty aspect" because their goods delivery job duty that had been replaced to do by these several warehouse robots. Robots can achieve the more accurate of right kinds of goods and the right number of goods delviery job performance to compare any one of human warehouse worker themselves right kinds of goods of delivery and right number of goods of delivery job performance. So, when robots can participate to cooperate with this warehouse's any one worker to do their goods of delivery job duty in this warehouse every day. Then, robots can raies any one of supervisor individual confidence in order to let they do not need to spend time to observe any one of worker individual whose goods of delivery job performane. They can concentrate on supervising any one worker whose goods transport to lorry in the final step in order to avoid to deliver wrong goods number and / or wrong kind of goods to any one goods buyer's home every day. Consequently, this warehouse's overall teams of their delivery of goods performance many be improved by robots' participation to goods of delivery task as well as this warehouse's overall teams themselves efficiencies may be influenced to raise by robots' goods of delivery task participation.

Why social behavior may influence organizational strategy needs to be changed ?

Why any organizations need to know whether nowadays social behaivor how has been changing in order to implement the kind of the most right strategy to achieve the profit aim pursue in possible. I shall indicate nowadays e-commerce or online, customer shopping behavior to explain above question concerns they ought have close relationship between social behavior and organizational strategic choice or organizational behavioral changing need.

On nowadays ecommerce business, or online shopping model, this kind of shopping model in global many young and old age consumers like to apply internet tool to choose any country sellers website stores in order to stay at home to buy any kinds of products from themselves webstores in global societies.

In fact, online shopping model had been popular for long time above to twenty years. Most of global sellers will make decision to design themselves webstores in order to attract global many online buyers to choose to buy their products from themselves webstores. So, it seems that social consumers purchase behaviors had been changed to online shopping from internet invention.

Hence, social consumers purchase behavioral changes may influence any organizations' strategies need to be changed from visiting shops purchase strategy model to online purchase strategy model, if the seller still concentrate on concentrate on considerate how to design itelf , but neglects to considerate how to design itself webstore, e.g. how to design attract product photos to put on itself webstore, how to arrange sale price information location to be putted on webstore and visa card payment location on itself webstore in order to let any one online buyer can feel very easier to buy itself any kinds of products from itself webstore. Then, its potential online buyers will be influenced to increase number when they can find this online seller itself any kinds of products photes and every kinds of product sale price information and visa card payment channel locations easily from itself webstore.

So, it implies that nowadays any one seller ought need to design one webstore to let any one online overseas and domestic consumers can have chance to click itself webstore to choose any one kind of product to buy conveniently when he/she does not hope to leave him/her home to go to shop, because nowadays social shopping behaviors had been influenced to change when internet invention, them it gives another online purchase method to replace visiting shops purchase method to global any one buyer in nowadays societies.

So, if nowadays any one seller still concentrate on how to design itself shop display in order to put any kinds of product on shelf in order to let any one visiting shop customer to find the kind of product to buy, but it neglects to change to choose to pursue another new technological shopping method, such as webstore purchase method in order to implement effective strategy to design the most right webstore as well as in order to attract global overseas and local consumers to find itself webstore easily from website and find its any one kind of product phots and sale price and visa card payment button in order to choose to buy itself any kinds of products in the short time. Consequently I believe that the seller will lose many customers from overseas and local when its other same or similar product sellers choose to design themselves webstores in order to let global any one product buyer can buy themselves any one kind of product when they can pay visa card to buy their products from them webstores conveniently when they stay at home habitly. Then, the seller will lose many global potential customers in long time.

On conclusion, in behavioral economic view, any consumer behavioral social changing, which will influence any in order to avoid customers number loses significantly . In future time, organizations need to make rapid decision in order to implement the most reasonable and the most useful strategy in order to avoid global potential customers number reduces or lose them in long time. So, social behavioral changing environment ought influence any global organizations need to decide how to change themselves strategies in order to avoid customers loses significantly in future time.

How and why human behavior may influence economic growth or recession?

May ourselves daily behaviors influence our global societial continue economic growth or recession? Do they have cause and effect close relationship between human behaviors and global economic growth or recession? I shall apply behavioral economic theory to analyze and explain whether ourselves daily behaviors and our global societial economic growth or recession which have close cause and effect relationship as below:

Every country itself economic development must depend on any business activities, otherwise, any kinds of business activities must need ourselves business activities or behaviors in order to achieve any business activities as well as achieve the country's overall economic development in macro view.

However, any country's overall business activities or behaviors which must depend on any kinds of individual businessmen, themselves employees daily working behavior or activity or performance in order to help them to attract or increase many clients number to achieve " earning profit" aim. So, it seems that any individual business, itself overall every department individual working behavior is one main factor to influence the company's overall business performance.

For agricultural fruit and meat food farming industry example, such as New Zealand is a farming main target industry country. It had had many New Zealanders were daily themselves own farming businesses for many years. Their farming businesses include growing fruit, sheep, cow, pig pork, meat etc. food sale business. If the New Zealand farmer owned a large size farming land, then he will choose either growing fruit or feeding sheeps, pigs, cows to be meat to to transport to New Zealand supermarkets to help them to sell to their farmers meet to New Zealanders in order to earn profit. Thus, if the New Zealand farmer owned large size of farming lands, then he needs to employ many farming employees (farming workers) to help him to carry on farming business daily tasks, e.g. picking up fruits, feeding pigs, cows, sheep to eat food daily. These daily farming jobs are very important to influence this New Zealand farmer's meats or fruits sale number whether they can be easy or difficult to sell in New Zealand supermarkets , if these farming workers can own enough farming knowledge or skill to know how to pick up fruits method and make judgment to know whether it is right time to pick up the kind of fruits from the trees , as well as know how feed this pigs, sheep, cows to eat food in order to let they are better health. Consequently, their farming behaviors which can let these animals can provide the best taste and enough meat from these animals to let New Zealander to buy to eat from New Zealand any one supermarket. Even these New Zealand farming workers can know whether the kinds of fruits, e.g. oranges, apples, gapes etc. fruits whether they ought be picked up from the trees at the right time. Consequently, they can make judgement to decide to pick up any kinds of the best taste fruits to let any one New Zealander to buy to eat from any one supermarket in New Zealand. Otherwise, if they do not make judegement to know whether the kind of fruit ought not be picked up because they still need longer time to continue grow up to increase fruit size and better taste from the trees in order to let any one fruit buyer can feel better taste when they eat this kind of fruit later. If they can buy this kind of fruit to eat later, then this New Zealand farmer's his fruit buyers can buy the best taste of this kind of fruit to eat from an yone supermarket in New Zealand. Consequently, many New Zealand supermarkets will choose to buy any kinds of fruits from this farmer fruit supplier when they feel this farmer's fruits can provide more better taste fruits to compare other farmers' fruits.

Thus, due to New Zealand is one farming main income source country. It's any kinds of fruits and meats need to be export to overseas to sell , instead of local sale. It's GDP percent is very high to whole country 's overall income source. So, any one New Zealand farmer individual and any one farming worker individual working behavior will influence its economy whether it is influenced to grow or recession possible. Moreover, it also seems that farming workers' farming knowledge and skill will influence themselves farming daily activities to achieve the aim of the number of increase or decrease to any kinds of fruits whether they are better taste or the number of increase of decrease to any kinds of meats whether they are better taste to supply to any one New Zealand fruit or meat buyers to eat from any one New Zealand supermarket. So, it implies that any one New Zealand farming worker individual farming behavior may influence any kinds of fruits or any kinds of meat taste because they are transported to any one supermarket to sell in New Zealand.

Consequently, if New Zealans had many farmers can teach god farming knowledge and skill to let their any one farming workers know how to decide judgement to decide when it is right time to pick up any kinds of fruits from trees , or how to grow them on soil in order to let they can grow rapidly. Then, many different kinds of fruits can be provided to let any one New Zealanders can eat the best taste of fruits when their fruits are supplied to any one New Zealand supermarkets. Even, if they knew how to feed foods to pigs, cows, sheeps to eat daily. Then they can be more health and they can provide the best taste of meats to let any one New Zealanders can buy their meats from any one New Zealand supermarkets. Moreover, their fruits and meats can be transported to overseas to let any one country fruits or meats buyers can choose any kinds of New Zealand meats and fruits to buy to eat from themselves countries supermarkets. Then, many overseas fruit and meat buyers will perfer to choose New Zealand any kinds of fruits or meats to buy to compare other countries fruits or meats to buy when they go to any one local supermarkets.

On conclusion, it seems that New Zealand farming workers themselves farming behavior may influence their farming employers any kinds of fruits or meats sale number and income because their farming task behaviors must influence whether their fruits or meats taste are the better taste or worse taste to compare their other local farmers (the farmer competitors) whose fruits or meats taste. If tthe farmer's any one farming worker can be trained to learn how to know to feed animals skill and when is the most right time to pick up any kinds of fruits from trees or how to grow them on the soil methods. Due to these farming worker individual farming behavior may influence his different finds of fruits and meats sale number to be increase or decrease, so these any one New Zealand farmer must need to depend on any one farming worker whose farming working methods, if their farming working behaviors can be the best to influence any kinds of fruits to grow rapid or any kinds of pigs, cows, sheeps animals grow up rapidly , then their sale number may be increase significantly and their taste can be improved to let any New Zealand or overseas meat or fruit buyer to buy to eat to feel from any one New Zealand or overseas supermarkets, then New Zealand's agriculture industry must be influenced to increase. In the world, any one fruit or meat buyer must choose to buy New Zealand's fruit and meat to eat in prefer to compare other countries' fruits and meats. So, New Zealand's GDP may be influenced to raise from any one New Zealand farming worker individual farming working behaviors.

Reasons why human behavior may influence economic recession or growth?

Can ourselves daily behaviors or activies influence ourselves countries' economic growth or recession? I shall attempt to explain the reasons why they have direct or indirect relationship between human behavior and economy growth or recession as below:

I shall indicate environment pollution case to attempt to explain above question. Our societies had been experiencing servious environment pollution challenge. However, environment pollution , such as air pollution is caused by air planes and vehicles emission by air planes and vehicles emission as well as water pollution is caused by plastic rubblish, or dirty water or oil or gas chemical material, these both kinds of pollution ought may bring economic recession and this both kinds of pollution are caused by human ourselves daily foolish activities.

I believe human behavior and economy and pollution which have cause and effect relationship. I shall analyze this environment pollution case to explain why they have case and effect relationship between human foolish behavior and environment pollution and economic recession as below:

When global societies had many people like to buy cars to drive to bring emission to fresh air on the roads as well as many manufacturing factories will bring emission to pollute fresh air in their manufacturing processes. Factories and cars will bring air pollution , due to factories need to pollute fresh air in order to manufacture many products and car owners need to drive their cars to go to offices or leisure places. Their cars will also bring emisson to pollute fresh air. On consequence, car owners themselves frequent driving behaviors and factory workers themselves frequent manufacturing behaviors may bring environment pollution. Technology or human behavior whether may influence economic growth or recession. Moreover, air planes also brings emission to pollute air when they are flying in sky. Also, when ships bring oil pollution or sea plastic rubblishs bring pollution to global oceans.

In fact, manufactucrs and cars owners, such as factories workers manufacturing behaviours ans car owners driving behaviors and pilots driving air planes flying behaviors and ships transport behaviors, which may cause plastic rubblish, oil or gas emission to sky or sea or on the road to cause ocean and air pollution is serious. However, human ourselves need to buy cars to drive to satisfy ourselves driving leisure or enjoyment, travelers need to catch air planes to travel to enjoy leisure needs, factories workers need help factories to manufacture many products to sell to customers to satisfy their using needs. oil exploration needs to find lands to explore new oil lands.

All of these business and leisure activites may bring serious air and water pollution. However, due to serious air and water pollution will bring earth warming challenge , such as some countries temperature will be influences to rise up to 40 degree or higher br earth warming. However, earth warming is caused by air and ocean pollution. Pollution must be caused by human ourselves, driving cars leisure and factories manufacturing business activities. Hence, if human decided to continue to do these foolish behaviors, we only pursue to manufacture different kinds of industrial products or drive cars to enjoy leisure aims, but we also neglect ourselves behaviors may bring environment pollution. Then, earth warming or earth temperature will be influenced to rise up absolutely in long term. Moreover, if our future earth will be influenced to bring serious high temperature effect by human ourselves these foolish behaviors.

On consequencey, warth warming will bring serious economic losses in possible because when ourselves earth temperature had been influenced to rise up to 40 degree or high. Ourselves health will be caused poor, due to we will feel difficult breath, we must need often tried and hard to work, due to our nervous and health will be influenced to poor by pollution and earth warming effect. Also, we need to pay more money to see doctors when we had long life. Then, our societies will lose may strong labors to help manufacturers to work, e.g. factories will reduce workers number to help manufacturers to produce more different kinds of products, due to workers health is general poor. Due to lacking enough workers to manufacture products, our societies will begin to reduce enough supply number of products to sell to global consumers to satisfy their use needs.

On conclusion, in behaviroal economic view, our societies will lose many labors due to their bodies are not health by air and water pollution. Global economic and business activities will be influenced to worse by global workers reducing number reason. So, economic recession will begin to occur in possible when pollution reaches the serious level.

How employee behavior influences organizational development?

Can any organizational department employee individual behavior may help the organization to bring long term development? When one employee individual behavior, manager won't feel whose task behavior may help organizational development, but when the department has many teams cooperate to work together , all of these team employees whose task behaviors may help their organization to bring long term development.

I shall explain how any why when the organization has many departments, as well as when every team member individual behavior may help whole organization to bring long term development in possible as below:

Every organization must need efficient department to cooperate to work together. They may include human resource, finance, logistic, facility management, sales, marketing , operateional , warehouse , factory manufacture , research and development, purchase, customer service etc. different kinds of departments to cooperate to work together. So, any one employee individual behavior, include manager, leader, supervisor, worker, salesperson, manufacture worker, administration staff, factory or logistic worker etc. themselves task behavior whether his/ her performance is worse or better , whose task behavior ought bring long term good or bad influence to cause the organization's whose efficiency, or performance , whether it can be influenced to improve significantly. For car factory manufacture workers department example, it employs 100 car manufacturing workers. They need to manufacture at least 50 cars in order to bring enough car manufacture number to supply to global car buyers to choose to buy (satisfaction to car buyers their driving leisure activity needs). However, if this car manufacture firm employs many low skilful car manufacture workers, their inefficient car skill may bring cars manufacture number reduces, they can not achieve to reach the at least 50 cars manufacture number, if these 100 car manufacture workers. They have half number of workers, they only manufacture 30 to 40 cars number at least daily. So, it seems that this car manufacture firm will have half car manufacture workers bring the low cars manufacture number to compare the another half cars manufacture workers, when this proficient car manufacture workers may manufacture at least 60 or more cars manufacture number daily. So, it explains that this inefficient car manufacture workers will not help this car manufacture company to manufacture enough cars number in order to supply to global car market to sell to satisfy global car buyers needs, when car buyers demand number is more than car manufacture supply number in supply and demand view. Hence, in long term, if this car manufacture company can not employ new proficient car manufacture workers to replace those inefficient or low skillful car workers. Consequently, its car manufacture number must be influenced to reduce and it can not satisfy global car buyers driving leisure needs.

However, if this car manufacture firm also has shop to sell itself any kinds of cars, instead of manufacturing cars product. So, it needs have both main departments to help it to earn profit. The first step, it needs have proficient car manufacture workers to help it to manufacture at least 50 cars from every car worker in order to have enough cars number to be provided to global car sellers to help it to sell to global car customers. Second step, if it decided to attempt to sell itself cars. Then, it needs to set up car shops in global to different countries in order to let global car buyers may visit its global any one car shop to enquire any one car etc. salesperson about any car quality, speed, gas useful, price, safety, etc. information questions and they can attempt to sit in any one car to feel whether which car can let them to feel more comfortable to make final car purchase decision in any one shop. So, if this car company can provide good sale speaking skillful training to any one car salesperson to let his/her to know whether how to explain every kind of car function and feature, manufacture method etc. questions, then I believe that they can influence any one car buyer to make car purchase choice decision more easily. So, it this car manufacturer hopes it may attempt to earn profit from different countries car sellers and car buyers both. It ought also provide training course to all general car salespeople to be proficient owning sale speaking skillful professional skill in order to prepare having more confidence to persuade any one car customer to make car purchase choice from any one car salesperson more easily to compare global other car sellers.

Hence, if this car manufacturer could build both car manufacturing team and car sale team more proficient. However, if this car manufacturer hopes to develop itself car manufacture business to expend to car sale business both in success. It must need to spend long term to provide training courses to general car manufacture workers and general car salespeople both to be proficient car skillful manufacture workers and proficient car skillful salespeople in order to help they can manufacture enough car numbers and help they can persuade may car customers can make car purchase decision in short time when they visit its any one car shop.

However, this car manufacture company explains why every car manufacture worker whose manufacturing behavior and every car salesperson sale persuading speaking ability may help this car manufacture company to expand from its car manufacture market to car sale market development in sussess in possible. So, this car manufacture firm must need these two kinds of essential human resource elements in order to achieve its cars sale number and cars manufacture number increasing aim. They may include proficient car manufacture workers and proficient car salespeople both human resource elements. These both human resource daily task behavior may influence its long term task efficient performance in order to expand itself car sale business in success from itself car manufacture business easily. If it hopes to expand its car manufacture business to car sale business in success. It must need to provide training to these two departments general staffs to be proficient staffs in order to supply enough cars number to its global car shops to let global car buyers can choose its any kinds of cars to buy in any time.

Moreover, if this car manufacture company can have good skillful of car research and development department , it aims to research and innovate any new technological cars invention in order to improve its any traditional old kinds of cars to be innovative new kinds of cars from every year. Consequently, its any new innovative cars ought attract global any one car buyer to make car purchase choice final decision more easily, because its any kinds of manufacture cars can be innovated rapidly to compare its any one car manufacturing competitors, when its nay kinds of cars can be shorten time to innovate within three months, but its any one car manufacturing competitors need to spend more than three months, even one year to innovate themselves traditional old cars products in long term.

Hence, its car staffs research and development department staffs must need own good car product design ability, proficient car engineering knowledge , even car invention knowledge in order to innovate its any one kind of car product in short time and introduce to let its global car proficient car buyers feel surprise to its any one kind of innovative car products to compare its any one car manufacturer.Hence, these four departments: car manufacture, car sale and car research and development and car training departments must need concentrate resource to provide enough training to any one staffs in order to achieve the best performance.

On conclusion, all these departments staffs their performance can influence car manufacture aim to chance to car manufacture and sale aim more significantly. it explains why some main department staffs whole behaviors may influence any organizational performance significantly.

Artificial intelligent Human clever and art creating ability methods

How robots create human clever and art creating ability? Nowadays robots invention may help businesses to reduce employees number, improve performance, raise productivities, reduce cost in service industry,manufacturing industry, office , warehouse, restaurant, hotel , factory, cinema etc. different kinds of business environments, even public transport tools. However, instead of robots may bring these above advantages to any kinds of business working and service environments, whether robots may also help human to create clever and image creating ability. I shall attempt to answer this question:

On the one hand, I believe that past technology ,e.g. machine , it should not have ability to help human to create clever and image creative ability,but nowadays, robots invention that I believe it had had enough ability to help future human to raise more clever and more creating image or painting picture, art design etr. image ability, after robots had been experienced above more than ten years improvement stage from early research stage to invention stage, till to nowadays improvement stage, e.g. non-manual driving auto vehicels, even future non-manual driving skill may be improved to apply to public transport tools, e.g. trams, trains,buses, airplanes, ships etc. public transport tools, when non-manual driving skills can be improved to own the most safe driving skillful ability to compare human driving skills.

On another hand, when robots could be invented to be applied to medical or hospital surgery aspect, e.g. roboting surgerys may help surgery doctors to do complex surgery in surgery rooms, or serving patients tasks in any hospital working environments. They can help nurses and doctors to spend more time to do more important tasks urgently, so medical or surgery serving robots may help nurses and surgery doctors to reduce task load pressure and create clever or improve their surgery skills to when they can cooperate to work in hospitals.

On the other hand, robots can be invented to help any public transport drivers to avoid more traffic accidents occurrence on any countries roads. So, it seems that non-manual driving public transport tools invention may also help human drivers to improve driving skills in possible, when they can learn how to avoid sudden traffic accidents occurrence in any countries roads in any time. so, any kindsof public transport tool drivers ought learn how to avoid traffic accidents skills from future non-manual driving robots invention. Instead of non-manual driving robots and hospital patients medical care or surgery service robots may help public transport tools drivers and hospital nurses and doctors to concentrate on spending time to treat any more important and urgent matters every days. Even, future restaurants may let cooking restaurants may let cooking robots to help human cookers to cook more different kinds of good taste food, to human cookers may learn cooking robots cooking skills in order to improve themselves traditional cooking skills often, in order to compare their cooking skills between human cookers and cooking robots.

On conclusion, it seems that cooking robots ought help human cookers to create any kinds of new cooking skills. Moremove, futuer robot cookers ought be future human cookers their cooking coaches. These robot cookers will help human cookers to create clever cooking skills in possible. Also, future non-manual driving robots ought help human drivers to create new driving skills in order to improve their driving skills to reduce sudden traffic accidents occurrence easily on any countries roads in any time, future hospital surgery or patient care service robots may help surgeons or nurses to do any surgerys in surgery rooms or looking care patients in hospitals. So, when robot surgeons help human surgeons to do complex surgerys in surgerical rooms, human surgeons can learn how to do more complex surgerical tasks for every surgeons when human surgeons can observate every surgerical robots how to do surgeons together. Hence, it seems that robot surgeons also may create future human surgeons themselves innovate surgerical skills from traditional surgerical skills improvement. So, future artificial intelligent technology ought help any kinds of human occupations to create clever, even improvement themselves traditional skills to new innovative skills absolutely.

Why does technology raise online products sale demand and reduces shops products sale demand?

Nowadays robot technology is popular to be applied to different aspects of our daily lives. They may include: non-manual driving vehicles, smart phones, space rockets, kitchen cookers, shopping centres service, cinema ticket sale, etc. different kinds of businesses demand. However, instead of internet invention may influence global communication, media channel is changed to computer internet, media channel is changed to computer internet, media communication from traditional newspaper, letter, TV, radio etc. communication channel. So, any internet users may click to yahoo.com news website to read global news from computer yahoo.com website easily.

In fact, internet technology is also used from businesses. They attempt to set up themselves web stores to sell their products from themselves webstores. So, any one product buyers may buy any kinds of products from any one webstores when they stay at homes. It is very convenient and common to future any one webstore shoppers. It brings this question: Can webstores help online product purchases needs raise and influence shop product purchases need reduce?

In demand and supply view, when one product price raises, its sale demand ought reduce, unless, it can attract to influence customers need consideration or its supply number decreases. But, when one product is increasing sale price to seel from the seller's webstore, whether its sale number will be influenced to reduce. Also, when the kind of product is selling and its sale price is raised, whether it can still keep demand number increase as well as whether it can influence its similar kinds of competitor their products sale demand number to reduce from shop sale channel.

In demand and supply view, when one product price raises, its sale demand ought reduce, unless, it can attract to influence customers need consideration or its supply number decreases. But when one product is increasing sale price to sell from the seller's webstore, whether its sale number will be influenced to reduce. Also, when the kind of product is selling and its sale price is raised, whether it can still keep demand number increases as well as whether it can influence its similar kinds of competitors their products sale demand number to reduce from shop sale channel.

I suppose that webstore sale may influence shop sale demand number decreases, because when internet is popular to use, when one country's buyer wants to buy one kind of product, but he/she can not find the kind of product can be bought from himself/herself home country. If he/she can findthe kind of product to buy from any one of overseas webstore from internet channel at home in any time. Then, he/she will be influenced to make purchase decision from the seller's websote immediately. So, it implies that when on consumer plans to buy one kind of product, he / she will attempt to find the kind of product from any one seller's webstore in preferat home, if he/she spend long time to find the kind of product from many of webstores, but he /she still does not find the kind of product from many of webstores, then he/she will choose to visit any one shop to attempt to buy the kind of product.Hence, online shopping purchase channel will be prefer choice to compare visiting shopd purchase channel in nowadays society.

So, it explains that why the kind of product online sale number may influence the kind of similar product visiting shop sale number either increases or decreases. It means that the kind of product visiting shops sale number may still increases , if the kind of similar products supply number is not enough , they are difficult to let any one online buyer to find to buy from any one webstore. Otherwise, if the kind of similar products sale supply number is enough to let any one online buyer to find from many webstores. Then, they can influence the similar kinds of shop products purchase demand to reduce and their shops purchase demand will be also influenced to reduce from webstores purchase channel.

On conclusion, it explains that the kind of shop products demand number ought be influenced to increase or decrease, when the similar kind of products can be bought easily from many webstores from internet (e-commerce) shopping channel. Internet (online) technology may help the seller to raise the kind of product competitive ability on purchase demand aspect, when there are not many other sellers can provide webstores to sell the similar kind of products and they only concentrate on selling the kind of similar products from shops to let any one online buyer to frind from may webstores. Then, they can influence the similar kinds of shop products purchase demand to reduce and their shops purchase demand will be also influenced to reduce from webstores purchase channel. Hence, webstore and shop both purchase channel explains that the similar kinds of shop products demand number will be influenced to increase or decrease , when the kinds of product can be bought easily from many webstores from internet shopping channel. Internet technology may help the seller to raise the kind of product competitive abilty to raise purchase demand when there are not many other sellers can provide webstores to sell the kind of similar products and they only concentrate on selling the kind of similar products from shops.

Does car technological development reach mature stage to help economic development?

Our societies had been developing too many years. In our past technological aspect, machine invention had began till to computer invention till to internet invention. It seems that our technological development stage may reach mature stage. Why do I feel our technological development had reached mature stage. I shall apply demand and supply economic theory to explain this question as below:

I shall indicate car development industry to explain whether when car development stage can reach mature stage, it may help global economic growth. In our car technological development stage, it is from gas energy car invention till to nowadays battery energy car invention till to even future non-manual driving car invention. Do you feel that when human (car buyers) felt environmental protecion need to avoid air pollution. So, battery energy cars demand number may increase , it will influence gas energy cars demand number reduces. Even, if future non0manula driving cars invention succeed, lazy driving car buyers will choose to buy non-manual driving (robot driving cars) in preference. So, it is possible that , it will influence future gas energy cars demand number reduces much. I mean that when car buyers can choose many different kinds of non-manual driving cars and battery energy cars to buy. Then, gas energy cars demand number must be influenced to reduce very much as well as gas energy cars supply number will be influenced to reduce to avoid sale prices reduce.

Hence, it explains why future car technological development will reach mature stage when both kinds of non-manual driving cars and battery energy cars are invented to the mature stage. When these two kinds of cars invention can satisfy future global car buyers driving needs. Then, car manufacture won't need to spend too much time to continue to attempt to invent any new kinds of cars in order to excite future car buyers' purchase decision. So, I believe that car technological development will reach mature stage within five years, if non-manual driving cars and battery energy cars are invented in success and they can be popular to accept to drive to global car buyers.

On conclusion, when car technological development reaches mature stage, it will help future economy continue grows because when car manufacturers had invented many new kinds of non-manual driving cars and new kinds of non-manual driving cars and new battery energy car sale market. Then, they will encourage or attract global many car buyers choose to buy these both kinds of cars products in preference to compare to traditional gas energy car products. So, they will influence many traditional gas- energy car buyers forgive to drive gas energy cars to avoid non pollution and lazy driving behavioral feeling. So, gas energy car reselling number will increase between gas energy car drivers and past non-owning any car buyers. Also, non-manual driving cars and battery energy car supplying number will be influenced to increase when battery energy car buyers and non-manual driving car buyers driving needs increase.

Consequently, these factors will influence global gas energy cars, non-manual driving cars and battery energy cars their cars purchase and sale transactions increase in future global car market. So, I believe that global car technological development could reach mature stage, then it will influence global car buyers number increases as well as this car technological mature development stage may also bring global rapid economic growth future non-manual driving car buyers and battery energy car buyers both number increases.

CHAPTER V

Introduction organizational behavioral economy

What does organizational behavioral economic mean? How organizational behavior may bring organizational itself economic benefit? I shall explain as below:

Understanding Behavioral Economics.This theory assumes that people, given their preferences and constraints, are capable of making rational decisions by effectively weighing the costs and benefits of each option available to them. The final decision made will be the best choice for the individual.

What are the principles of supply and demand?

Supply is generally considered to slope upward: as the price rises, suppliers are willing to produce more. Demand is generally considered to slope downward: at higher prices, consumers buy less.

What is the behavioral economic theory?

Behavioral economics combines elements of economics and psychology to understand how and why people behave the way they do in the real world. It differs from neoclassical economics, which assumes that most people have well-defined preferences and make well-informed, self-interested decisions based on those preferences.

What are the principles of behavior economics?

Behavioral economists embrace the core principles of economics—optimization and equilibrium—and seek to develop and extend those ideas to make them more empirically accurate. Behavioral models assume that economic actors try to pick the best feasible option and those actors sometimes make mistakes.

What is the advantage of behavioural economics?

Behavioural economics can be a powerful tool in achieving consumer policy goals, by nudging people to make healthy, sustainable and cost-conscious choices. It can also, however, be used against consumers' interests by misleading and deceiving them by exploiting their biases.

What is behavioural economic theory?

Behavioral economics is the field of understanding why people do things financially that may be irrational. Blended between cognitive bias, heuristics, bounded rationalities and herd mentality, people tend to do things that may not always be in their best interest.

How does behavioral economics affect consumer decision-making?

Behavioural economics recognizes the importance of emotions in decision-making. Studies using techniques such as facial expression analysis and self-reported emotions may be used to determine the impact of emotions on consumer decision-making.

What are the 5 basic economic principles of economics?

The 5 basic economic principles include scarcity, supply and demand, marginal costs, marginal benefits, and incentives. Scarcity states that resources are limited, and the allocation of resources is based on supply and demand. Consumers consider marginal costs, benefits, and incentives when purchasing decisions

What are the problems with behavioural economics?

Many experiments are rough and ready - they are sensitive to how they are constructed/delivered by psychologists. Discoveries about the past from behavioural experiments do not easily generalise to the future - the social context for one generation is often different from another.

What is the concept of economic organization?

The way in which the means of production and distribution of goods are organized, such as capitalism or socialism.

How does behavioral economics play a role in your decisions?

Behavioral economics is a field of study that combines economics and psychology to understand how people make decisions. It argues that people are not always rational actors, and that their decisions are often influenced by factors such as emotions, biases, and social pressure.

What is a real life application of behavioral economics?

Behavioral Econ has shown that people make predictable choices when faced with risk. People tend to be risk averse and loss averse. They take on less risk than traditional economics would expect and feel losses more than gains of equal proportion. This has applications in personal finances and daily decision making.

How is behavioral economics used today?

Behavioral economic theories are used to explain most everyday decisions, such as what people buy, how they manage their finances, and whether or not they make healthy lifestyle choices.

What are the three behavioral economics?

Behavioral economics is the study of the psychological, cognitive, emotional, cultural and social factors involved in the decisions of individuals or institutions, and how these decisions deviate from those implied by classical economic theory.

Is Behavioural economics part of economics?

Behavioral economics combines psychology and economic theory to examine why people sometimes make irrational decisions. Behavioral economists understand that humans are emotional, easily distracted by the modern world, and susceptible to outside influences.

What is economic theory or economic model?

Sometimes economists use the term model instead of theory. Strictly speaking, a theory is a more abstract representation, while a model is more applied or empirical representation. Models are used to test theories, but for this course we will use the terms interchangeably.

What is the organizational economics theory?

Organizational economics is used to study transactions within individual firms and determine management approaches to managing resources. It can involve a wide variety of ideas and theories including agency theory, transaction cost economics, and property rights theory.

How does economics affect organizational behavior?

Organizations are also heavily influenced by economic factors. A market crash or a recession will directly impact the sales of an organization. When people are no longer able to afford a product or choose to spend their money elsewhere, companies are directly impacted.

What are the limitations of Organisational Behaviour?

The document outlines several shortcomings and limitations of organizational behavior (OB). It states that OB will not solve problems like unemployment or conflicts, and has a narrow focus on people rather than social elements. OB also cannot prevent recurring behaviors and some may develop a behavioral bias.

What is organizational behavior in economics?

Organizational behavior is the study of how individuals and groups interact within an organization and how these interactions affect an organization's performance toward its goal or goals. The field examines the impact of various factors on behavior within an

organization. The study of organisational behaviour principles is applied to make businesses operate more effectively. Attracting and retaining the employees can be achieved by implementing the principles of the Study of organisational Behaviour. What is organization in economics with example? The way in which the means of production and distribution of goods are organized, such as capitalism or socialism.

What is the organizational behavior theory?

Organizational behavior theory is the study of human behavior within an organizational environment. This means that organizational behavior asks questions about why humans behave the way they do in working environments. However, behavioral economics studies irrational behavior and decisions, such as skipping work and going on a shopping spree. Its foundational principles are different from classical economic theory which assumes people make decisions based on self-interest.

What are the three organizational theories?

There are different theories of organization to predict and explain the process and also behavior patterns in an organizational setting. There are three different types of organizational theory: Classical Organization Theory, Neo-Classical Organizational Theory, and Modern Organizational Theory.

What is the most influential organizational theory?

Generally, Weber's bureaucratic model has been one of the most crucial and influential concepts in the modern history of organizational theory, especially given the current global political climate (Waters & Waters, 2015). The bureaucracy model is commonly accepted by many organizations across boards and institutions.

What are the 4 elements of organizational behavior?

But regardless of how much material there is, there are four key elements to keep in mind when applying organizational behavior theory to the workplace. They are people, structure, technology, and environment.

What is organizational behavior example?

Here are some of the key concepts and examples of organizational behavior in action: Leadership Styles: An effective leader can make a huge impact on an organization's success. Different leadership styles can be used to manage and motivate employees, such as autocratic, democratic, and laissez-faire.

What is economy in organization and management?

Organizational economics applies the theoretical and empirical methods of eco- nomics to study the nature, roles and performance of organizations, especially managed ones like business firms.

What do economic organizations include?

The Internal Revenue Service (the IRS—the government tax-collection agency), the U.S. Federal Reserve (the government producer of money), the National Bureau of Economic Research (a private research agency) are all examples of economic institutions.

What is economic pressure in organizational behavior?

Economic pressure refers to the various economic factors that affect a business's growth and profitability. In OB, it can present different challenges like affecting employee morale, destabilising the organisation, and forcing tough decisions regarding resource allocation.

How does economics contribute to organizational behaviour?

In OB, economics helps understand how incentives, rewards, and decision-making processes affect employee behaviour and performance. Economic principles are used in OB to design compensation systems, incentive plans, and cost-effective HR policies.

What is an example of an organization in economics?

The three major international economic organizations are聽the World Bank, the International Monetary Fund (IMF), and the World Trade Organization (WTO).

What are two forms of economic organization?

Although some form of capitalism is the basis for nearly all economies today, for much of the past century it was but one of two major approaches to economic organization. In the other, socialism, the state owns the means of production, and state-owned enterprises seek to maximize social good rather than profits

What are the functions of economic organization?

Economic institutions are responsible for organizing the production, exchange, distribution and consumption of goods and services. — Economic institution is also one of the basic institutions. For the sake of survival each society has an economic system ranging from simple to complex.

Why is organizational economics important?

Organizational economics is primarily concerned with the obstacles to coordination of activities inside and between organizations (firms, alliances, institutions, and market as a whole).

What are economic activities in business organization?

An economic activity takes place when resources such as capital goods, labour, manufacturing techniques or intermediary products are combined to produce specific goods or services. Thus, an economic activity is characterised by an input of resources, a production process and an output of products (goods or services).

What is economy in organization and management?

Organizational economics applies the theoretical and empirical methods of eco- nomics to study the nature, roles and performance of organizations, especially managed ones like business firms.

What are the economic factors affecting individual Behaviour?

Economic Factors – In an economic environment, the behavior of an individual is largely affected due to certain factors including: (a)Employment Level – The employment opportunities available to an individual directly influence the behavior of an individual.

What is the standard economic theory?

Standard economic theory is based on the assumption that consumers are rational and aim to maximize their utility. A rational person will know what is best for them (selfish motive) and will not be influenced by emotions or other external factors while making a decision.

What is the principle of behavioral management theory?

Specifically, behavioral management theory is concerned with how to manage productivity by understanding worker motivation, including expectations, needs and interests, and group dynamics.

How does globalization affect organizational behavior?

Globalization affects an organization's business approach in that the business will have to formulate strategies that address the globe as a market and not just a nation where it is located. This will require the business to produce high quality products at globally viable prices.

What are the three forms of economic organization?

Communism, socialism, and capitalism are the three forms of economic organization that have emerged in the world.

How business economics helps in decision-making to an organization?

Business economics equips managers with an arsenal of conceptual tools that expedite the identification, analysis, and resolution of problems. It empowers businesses to make enlightened decisions by applying concepts such as demand and supply analysis, cost structures, and the law of diminishing marginal utility.

How does economic growth affect an organisation?

The increase in the demand for goods/services within the economy means that firms are likely to experience an increase in sales revenue. This often causes an increase in the amount of profit that firms receive. Therefore, an increase in economic growth often benefits firms through increased revenues and profits.

What is the organizational structure in economics?

An organizational structure is a system that outlines how certain activities are directed in order to achieve the goals of an organization. These activities can include rules, roles, and responsibilities. The organizational structure also determines how information flows between levels within the company.

What are the three types of business organization in economics?

There are three main types of business organizations:sole proprietorship, partnership and corporation.

What type of economy is most commonly used today?

The U.S. has a mixed economy which exhibits characteristics of both capitalism and socialism. A mixed economy embraces the free market when it comes to capital use, but it also involves government intervention for the public good.

What are the two types of economic activities explain with example?

Economic activities have two parts :i Market activities. ii Non-market activities. Market activities :i These are the activities performed for payment or profit. ii They include production of goods and services.

What are the four different ways that economic societies can be Organised?

Economic systems can be categorized into four main types:traditional economies, command economies, mixed economies, and market economies.

What is functional economy?

The functionality economy replaces the sale of a product with the sale of a service fulfilling the same functions as the product. It is based on the value of using the product and not of owning of the product. In effect, the product remains the property of the producer and its use is invoiced to the customer.

How organizations apply behavioral economy theory to achieve their development or profit pursue aim?

Organizational learning is a topic to which March has devoted much of his attention in recent years, primarily in articles scattered throughout the literature, but also in a book (March 1999). This pursuit of organizational learning is in fact another extrapolation from his behavioral theory of the firm theorizing . However, March's ideas have developed gradually from that early beginning, with a particular acceleration occurring in the late 1980s and thereafter.

For Donald fast food restaurant , it had applied behavioral economic principle to implement how to design its health fast foods to persuade fast food consumer choice. While Ms Donald fast food restaurant its behavioral food decision research has found a number of stunning results that demonstrate effective ways to encourage healthier diets, many key questions remain unanswered. We have not yet been able to create a comprehensive intervention that effectively addressed both food scarcity and obesity–the key challenge facing the poor worldwide. The initial forays into this realm show promise and the potential for substantive policy intervention.

We observed higher consumption of soft drinks and fast food in children with increased exposure to TV advertising for CSDs and fast food. These findings suggest that children's exposure to advertising for calorie-dense nutrient-poor foods is associated with increased overall consumption of the unhealthy food categories commonly advertised to children. This may contribute to poor diet in children in the short-term, with potential long-term effects on BMI and health, especially among the heaviest .

Research on determinants of food choice has used models grounded in the social-psychological theories of decision making and behavior . Value expectancy theory provides a framework for systematically evaluating the issues a person may consider in deciding whether to take a specific course of action, and can help to specify how people define and evaluate the elements of decision making about performing a specific behavior.

Hence, it seems that Donald fast food chain restaurant had implemented health fast food manufacture industry to persuade global fast food eaters make preference choice to buy its any kinds of fast foods. Donald had advertised its different kinds of soft drink and fast foods to let global customers to know from different countries televisions, online advertisement promotion channels in order to achieve health fast food and soft drink food aim to influence global fast food buyers make eating choice in preference. So, Donald fast food chain restaurant is one good case to apply behavioral economic theory to implement fast food sale strategy to global market.

The economic benefits of applying organizational behavior to development center on the concept of "institutional quality" and "human agency." In authoritative texts on development economics, it is argued that the efficiency of an economy is constrained by the "transaction costs" associated with human interaction within firms.When organizational behavior principles—such as motivation theory, leadership efficacy, and group dynamics—are applied, they reduce these transaction costs, thereby increasing total factor productivity (TFP).In the context of economic development, TFP is often modeled as:

$$Y=A\cdot F(K,L)$$

Where Y represents output, K is capital, L is labor, and A represents the efficiency parameter (often interpreted as the state of technology and organizational effectiveness). By optimizing organizational behavior, firms can effectively increase A, leading to higher output without requiring additional capital or labor inputs.

Furthermore, scholars in the field of institutional economics suggest that organizational behavior fosters "social capital," which is essential for economic growth in developing regions.When employees are managed through frameworks that prioritize psychological safety, clear communication, and goal alignment, the resulting organizational stability attracts foreign direct investment (FDI) and encourages domestic entrepreneurship. This shift from hierarchical, rigid management to behaviorally informed, adaptive management allows economies to pivot more rapidly in response to global market fluctuations, a key requirement for sustainable development in the 21st century.

The synthesis of these behavioral insights suggests that the "micro-foundations" of macroeconomics are found in how individuals behave within the workplace. By fostering environments that encourage innovation and reduce organizational friction, nations can achieve higher levels of economic resilience and long-term prosperity.

The Nexus of Organizational Behavior and Economic Growth According to my view

In my analysis of the intersection between management science and macroeconomics, posits that organizational behavior (OB) is not merely an internal corporate concern but a fundamental driver of national and global economic trajectories. By examining the micro-foundations of firm performance, Lok argues that the collective decision-making processes of employees and the strategic adaptations of organizations serve as the bedrock for economic expansion or contraction. My framework suggests that when organizations optimize their internal behavioral dynamics—such as motivation, leadership efficacy, and team cohesion—they directly enhance productivity, which in turn fuels aggregate economic growth.

Behavioral Economics and Organizational Performance

My view integrates behavioral economics to explain why consumers and employees act in ways that either stimulate or stifle economic activity. My view emphasizes that understanding the psychological underpinnings of decision-making allows organizations to predict market shifts more accurately.In traditional economic models, agents are often assumed to be perfectly rational; however, my view aligns with the perspective found in foundational texts like Daniel Kahneman's Thinking, Fast and Slow, which highlights that cognitive biases significantly influence economic outcomes.

My view extends this by suggesting that organizations that account for these behavioral nuances in their workforce and customer base can better manage their output and pricing strategies, thereby contributing to a more stable economic environment.

The Role of Human Networks and E-commerce

A central tenet of my thesis is the role of "human network behavior" in the digital age. My view asserts that e-commerce acts as a modern network that facilitates the rapid exchange of goods and information, creating a multiplier effect on economic growth.This aligns with the theories presented in The Wealth of Networks by Yochai Benkler, which explores how decentralized human collaboration transforms economic production.

My view argues that the way employees interact within these digital networks—and how they utilize artificial intelligence to predict consumer demand—determines the competitive advantage of a firm. By leveraging AI to evaluate the "most reasonable sale price," organizations can optimize their sales volume, which serves as a micro-level engine for macro-level economic health.

Macro and Micro Economic Implications

My work bridges the gap between micro-level organizational behavior and macro-level economic performance. My view suggests that if an organization fails to align its internal culture with the demands of the modern, interconnected economy, it risks contributing to localized recessions.This perspective is supported by organizational theorists such as Peter Drucker, who famously noted that the purpose of an organization is to make human strengths productive, thereby creating economic value. My contribution is the explicit connection of these internal productivity gains to the broader economic cycle, suggesting that the "behavioral economy" is the invisible hand guiding modern market fluctuations.

Technological Integration and Future Outlook

Finally, my view emphasizes the necessity of artificial intelligence in modern organizational management. He posits that AI is not just a tool for efficiency but a behavioral assistant that helps leaders understand the "why" behind employee performance and consumer choice. As organizations become more adept at utilizing data to understand human behavior, they become more resilient to economic shocks. This aligns with the research found in The Second Machine Age by Brynjolfsson and McAfee, which discusses how digital technologies are fundamentally altering the structure of the economy.

My view concludes that by mastering the behavioral aspects of the workplace, organizations can navigate the complexities of the 21st-century economy more effectively, ensuring long-term growth rather than stagnation.

Would you like to explore how specific psychological theories, such as Prospect Theory, are applied by modern organizations to influence consumer behavior and drive economic growth?

CHAPTER VI

The Cost Of Progress

Technology is advancing at an unprecedented pace, the integration of robots and artificial intelligence into our daily lives has become a topic of intense debate. While many herald these innovations as harbingers of efficiency and progress. This story sets the stage for an exploration of the darker side of robotic advancement, examining how these technologies may inadvertently lead to societal challenges that could undermine human well-being.

As we stand on the brink of a new technological revolution, it is essential to scrutinize the implications of our reliance on machines. While robots can enhance productivity and streamline operations across various sectors, they also pose significant risks to employment, social structures, and ethical standards. The narrative unfolds with real-world examples illustrating how automation can displace workers, particularly those in low-skilled jobs, leading to increased unemployment rates and economic disparity.

This story can bring readers into the psychological impacts of living in a society increasingly dominated by machines. This story raises critical questions about human identity and purpose in a world where robots perform tasks once reserved for people. As we navigate this complex landscape, my readers are invited to reflect on what it means to be human in an age where our roles may be supplanted by artificial entities.

This story serves as a cautionary tale urging us to consider not only the benefits but also the potential pitfalls of embracing robotic technology without due diligence. Through rigorous analysis and compelling arguments, this story challenges us to rethink our trajectory towards an automated future and its implications for humanity.

Introduction to robots

Robots -driven automation industry will create wealth and expand economy growth to any countries, but it will be accompanied by changed in the skills that workers need to learn. One of main ways that technology increases productivity is by decreasing the number of labor hours needed to create a unit of output. It implies (AI) technology will influence low educated and low skillful labor number to be decreased (reduction employment number).

In contrast, technological change tended to work in a different direction throughout the nowadays. The advance of computer and the internet raised the relative productivity of higher skilled workers. So, routine-intensive occupations that focused on predictable tasks disappearance, such as switch board, operators, filming checkers, travel agents and assembling line workers etc. were particularly replaced by new technologies.

However, today, it may be challenging to predict exactly which jobs will be most immediately affected by (AI) driven-automation. The reason is because (AI) is not a single technology, but rather a collection of technologies that are felt unevenly through the economy to influence job changing both negatively and positively. In positively view point, (AI) driven-automation will make many workers more productive and increase demand for certain skills. Consequently, new jobs are likely to be directly create in areas , such as the development and supervision of (AI) as well as indirectly created in a range of areas throughout the economy as higher incomes lead to expanded demand. Otherwise, in negatively view point, many traditional human needed (demand) skillful jobs will be threatened by automation are highly concentrated among lower-paid, lower-skilled and less -educated workers. It means automation will cause pressure on demand for this group, pressure and employment, if (AI) can replace the low skilled and less educated workers' jobs. Thus, (AI) will have negative influence to impact on the labor market. (AI) capabilities will enable automation of some tasks that have long required human labor. Why can (AI) replace some simple human jobs? For example, advances in robotics are expanding machines' abilities to interact with and sharp the physical world. Combined , (AI) and robotics will give rise to smarter machines that can perform more sophisticated functions than ever before and brings more advantages that humans have exercised. This will permit automation of many tasks now performed by human workers and could change the shape of the labor market and human activity.

Today, it may be challenging to predict exactly which jobs will be most immediately affected by (AI)-driven automation. Because (AI) is not a single technology, but rather a collection of technologies that are applied to specific tasks.

Some specific predictions are possible based on the current (AI) technology. For example, driving jobs and house cleaning jobs, bank counter service jobs, telephone service operators. Restaurant cooking jobs, simple accounting record service jobs etc. that require relatively less education to perform. Advancements in computer vision and related technologies have made the feasibility of fully appear more likely, potentially displacing some workers in driving-dominant professions. Seemingly similar robot, for which the operational tasks is less specific of navigating to a specific destination when following a set of given rules and preserving safety.

In the future, the effects of (AI) on the labor market in the decade ahead will continue the trend toward skill-biased change that computerization and communication innovations have driven in recent decades. Thus, some human driving occupation will be disappeared or replaced by (AI) automation driven. For example, bus drivers, light truck or delivery services drivers, heavy and tractor-trailer truck drivers, school drivers, tax drivers, travel bus drivers.

However, (AI) technology could enable some workers to focus time on other job responsibilities, boosting their productivity, and actually raised wage growth among those still holding the reshaped jobs. For example, salespeople, who currently spend a considerable amount of time driving could find themselves able to do other work when a car drives them from place to place, or inspectors and appraisers could fill out paperwork, when their car drives itself. This (AI) -driven technology should make these workers more productive, with (AI) -driven technology serving as a complement, not a substitute. New jobs will also likely be created, both in existing occupations cheaper transportation costs with lower prices and increase demand for products and all the related occupations, such as service and fulfillment, and in new occupations not currently foreseeable.

What kind of jobs will be created by (AI) technology? Predicting future job growth is extremely difficult, due to it depends on technologies or substitute for existing today as well as they may complement or substitute for existing human skills and jobs. However, (AI) will also lead to substantial indirect job creation to the degree it raises productivity and wages, it may also lead to higher consumption that would support additional jobs from high-end draft production to restaurant and retail. The future(AI) " augmented intelligence", the technology's role is as assisting and expanding the productivity of individuals rather than replacing human work. Thus, based on the biased-technical change framework, demand for labor will likely increase the most in the areas where humans complement (AI) automation technologies. For example, (AI) technology , such as IBM's Watson may improve early detection of some cancers or other illnesses, but a human health care professional is needed to work with patients to understand and translate patients' symptoms, inform patients of treatment options, and guide patients through treatment plans. Shipping companies may also partner workers who pick up and deliver products over the last feet with (AI) enabled autonomous vehicles that move workers efficiently from site to site. In such cases, (AI) augments what a human is able to do and allows individuals to either be move effective in their specially task or to operate on a larger scale. Thus, it seems (AI) technology will also create new jobs, raise productivity and workers' efficiency..

The rise of automation

In the future, due to artificial intelligence influences to some kind of human jobs nature. So, the kind of human jobs of management methods will also need to change to adapt the artificial intelligence technology input to their organizations. It will cause challenges for every executive and manager if who won't have effort to manage their teams how to apply artificial intelligence technology to work efficiently and easily. For example, division of labor will change among humans and machines will increase. Thus, companies will have to adapt their training performance and talent strategies how to emphasize on work that how to make human judgment and skills and experimentation. Thus, (IA)'s greatest impact will be on administrative coordination and control tasks, such as scheduling , resource allocation.

In fact, mangers will encounter this challenges: How to apply human experience and expertise to judge critical business decisions and practices when the information available is insufficient to suggest a successful course of action? Due to this kind of work will require new skills and mindsets. I shall indicate these change management methods to adapt (AI) technology. Such as: administration and routine tasks, scheduling , allocation of resources and reporting will fall within the intelligence machines, responsibilities that have long been reserved for humans. For example, a typical store manager or a lead nurse at a nursing home most constantly arrange shift schedules, accounting for staff members' absences owing to illness, vacation time or sudden departures.

Thus, the managers need to learn how to arrange new division of labor within the organizations after (AI) technology had been implemented to the organization. Artificial intelligence is currently influencing into once considered exclusive to humans: assessing and acting on human emotions and personality traits. The influences to managers need to change their strategies to adapt (AI) technology implements include such as below:

Firstly, managers need to spend the bulk of their time on coordination and control tasks from intelligent system implements. Their time spending on these major three aspects from impact of intelligent system: coordinate and control, solve problems and collaborate and people and community , strategy and innovation three aspects. Thus (AI) will influence managers need to change their judgment method to teach whose teams how to adapt the (AI) system operations in any organizations.

Secondly, (AI) will influence top, middle and low level management needs to change to adapt the (AI) technology operations to any owned (AI) technology organizations in the future. Intelligent machines must be trained in context. Just like humans , on-the-job training is a requirement for such machines because they typically arrive with only very general capabilities. To get the most from (AI), managers at all levels must participate in the instructional experience and in the learning process and provides managers' familiarity with such systems on these aspects, e.g. How the system works and generate advice, how the system has a proven track record , how the system provides convincing explanations , how the system can make simple rule- based decisions.

Thirdly, managers need to learn how to make judgment more accurate (AI) systems assistance. Although (AI) will invariably take on more routine work and even augment human decision-making, it won't judgment work, the application of human experience and expertise to critical business decisions when the information available is insufficient to suggest a successful course of action or reliable enough to suggest an obvious course of action. For a sense of the nature of judgment work, consider big data marketing and sales analytic. Such analytic often provide insights that can inform promotional campaigns, including predicting which promotions will generate desired sales brand further into the future, marketing executives need use judgment, combining analytic with their own and others‘ insight and experience.

The application of experience and expertise to critical business decisions and practice represents the real value of human judgment. But, when artificial intelligent machines are implemented to any organizations to assist the low, middle and top level management to make any business judgment. These forms of judgment work that managers can gather data interpretation, idea development more absolute from (AI) machine assistance. Thus, why these level management executives need to learn how to apply (AI) machines to help them to make any business judgment more accurate.

Consequently creative and social intelligence will be in even greater demand as (AI) makes in management and the workforce. This development will represent a long term trend in labor markets , one characterized by intensifying demand and reward for social skills with a growing desire for creative capabilities, managers will seek

to fashion of ideas and hypotheses from inside and outside of the enterprise to shape solutions to their most pressing business problems. Thus, (AI) will influence overall organizational team members who have chance to participate any decision to make more accurate business judgment.
Many managers mistakenly view judgment work as only an individual discipline, failing to appreciate that it can also involve decide interpersonal and organizational practices. In more complex settings, judgment is typically a collective outcome of individuals' and teams' diverse perspectives, insights and experiences. And often , the resulting choices are better informed than decisions that an individual would have arrived at on his or her own.

Thus, when any organizations apply (AI) technology to assist managers to gather data and ideas to make any judgment. In these cases, organizations can create the conditions for effective collective judgment by establishing structures , such as " shadow advisory boards" that prompt managers and employees to source and synthesize multiple perspectives. Thus, a traditional organization (firm) might freshen its thinking is t put together a shadow advisory board, comprised of young, digital people who can apply (AI) machine assistance to make judgment work more accurate whether related to people development, problem-solving or strategy and innovating for considerable degrees of creative and social intelligence.
Thus, on the one hand, (AI) technology machine augmentation and automation can give these advantages to human (organization managers) , e.g. developing people and community, solving problems and collaborating, coordinating and controlling work, shaping strategy and leading innovation. Besides, on the other hand, the next generation managers need have these individual attitude to treat intelligent machines to be as colleagues.

When, judgment is a human skill, intelligent machines can accelerate human learning that supports it, assisting in data -driven simulations, scenarios and search and discovery activities. Focuses on judgment work, some decisions require insight beyond what data can tell them. This is the sweet sport for human judgment, the application of experience and expertise to critical business decisions and practices. Thus, managers will also need to find ways to learn how to use digital (AI) technologies to tap into the knowledge and judgment of partners, customer external stakeholders and role models in other industries after the (AI) machine had been implemented to the organization.

Job displacement crisis

Human future " micro to macro" industry trends will be affected business strategy and public policy by (AI) technology. In the future (AI) technology will influence those six themes: productivity and growth, natural resources, labor markets, the evolution of global financial markets, the economic impact of technology and innovation and urbanization. However, (AI) technology will bring economic benefits of tackling gender inequality, a new global competition, Chinese innovation and digital globalization.
Nowadays, advances in robotics artificial intelligence, and machine learning are in a new age of automation, as machines match or outperform human performance in a development to any countries. For example, automation of activities can enable businesses to improve performance by reducing errors and improving quality and speed, and in

some cases achieving outcomes that go beyond human capabilities. For example, some research indicated automation could raise productivity growth globally by 0.8 to 1.4 % annually; more than 2,000 work activities across 800 occupations. When less than 5% of all occupations can be automated using demonstrated technologies about 60% of all occupations have at least 30% of constituent activities that could be automated. Many occupations will change that will be automated away: Activities most susceptible to automation involve physical activities, in highly structured and predictable environments, as well as the collection and processing of data. They are most prevalent in manufacturing , accommodation and food service and retail trade and include some middle-skill jobs. For example, such as natural language processing is a key factor. Beyond technical feasibility, the cost of technology competition with labor including skills and supply and demand dynamics, performance benefits including and beyond labor cost savings, and social and regulatory acceptance will be affected by (AI) automation technology. Thus, (AI) automation will impact to influence global employment in those aspects as below:

Firstly, assuming that people are displaced by automation will find other employment. The anticipated shift in the activities in the labor force is of a similar order as the long-term shift away from agriculture and decreases in manufacturing share of employment. Both of manufacturing and agriculture industries which would be accompanied by the creation of new types of work not foreseen at the time.
Secondly, for business, the performance benefits of automation are relatively clear. Thus, the businessmen have opportunities for their micro economies to benefits from the productivity growth potential and macro economies to benefit to encourage continued progress and innovation , investment and market incentives. At the same time, employers must innovate policies to help workers and institutions adapt to the impact on employment.

This will likely include rethinking education and training, income support and safety nets , as well as support for those dislocated, when employees need to leave themselves homes to move to other cities to learn new (AI) automation works. Thus, individuals in the workplace will need to engage move comprehensively with machines as part of their everyday activities, and acquire new skills that will be in demand in the new automation age. Consequently , the scale of shifts in the labor force over many decades that automation technologies can be a similar order to the long -term technology -enables shifts in the developed countries' work forces away from agriculture in the 21 st century. Those shifts did not result in long-term mass unemployment because they were accompanied by the creation of new types of work not foreseen at the time. However, human will still be needed in the workforce when the total productivity gains are caused by (AI) technology.

In the future, scientists predict that these occupations will be influenced by (AI) technology mostly. They include : retail salespeople, food and beverage service workers, language or translation teachers, health practitioners. Since these work activities have a more relevant occupations are made up of a range of activities with different potential for (AI) automation . For example, a retail salesperson will spend more time interacting with customers, stocking shelves , or ringing up sales. Each of these activities is distinct and requires different

capabilities to perform successfully.
Thus, these job activities have similar simple control characteristics. Simple activities include greet customers, answer questions about products and services, clean and maintain work areas, demonstrate product feature process sales and transactions. All these activities can have similar simple activities in order to (AI) machines can be learn how to do these activities from (AI) technology . For example, the capability perception includes sensory perception, cognitive capabilities, such as retrieving automation, recognizing known patterns(supervised learning), logical reasoning problem solving.

Thus, (AI) machine is such human, which has feeling and emotion, such as social and emotional sensing, judgment reasoning methods, natural language understanding and physical capabilities, such as mobility , navigation, gross motor skill, fine motor skills. It seems that the future, (AI) human invents machines which will have these human characteristics to do human similar behavioral job duties more easily and efficiently. It implies these above human occupations will be replaced by (AI) human invention machines in the future. Due to (AI) creation, it is possible to cause unemployment number of these above workers will increase because (AI) machines can do their similar job behavioral activities.
Consequently, employers won't need to employ many of these skillful labor. Otherwise, they can buy less number (AI) machines to attempt to do whose job activities more easily and efficiently. So, it seems (AI) machines will have more high work performance to replace these occupation workers' work performance. Finally, these occupation worker unemployment number will only increase when the (AI) machines had been invented to achieve to do their work behavioral activities absolutely success in the future.

There is no single agreed definition of a robot how outcome of a task that is completed without human intervention. When some definitions require the task to be completed by a physical machine moves and respond to its environment, other definitions use the term robot in connection with tasks completed by software , without physical embodiment.

However, to answer the question : Whether (AI) technology machine labor will replace human worker more or assist human worker more. I shall indicate some examples to let readers to judge whether (AI) technology can create new jobs or reduce old jobs.

Firstly, I shall explain what (AI) function is. (AI) is a service robot that performs useful tasks for humans or equipment excluding industrial automation application . Thus, the classification of a robot into industrial robot or service robot is done according to its intended application. It is also a personal service robot or a service robot for personal used for a non commercial task, usually by lay persons . Examples are domestic servant robot, and pet exercising robot. It is also a professional service robot or a service robot for professional used for a commercial task, usually operated by a properly trained operator. Examples, are cleaning robot for public places, delivery robot in offices or hospitals, fire-fighting robot, rehabilitation robot and surgery robot in hospitals. Thus, these functions will be future (AI) application to our daily life necessaries or business necessaries.

However, some authors agree (AI) will bring negative outcomes of automation, due to raise competitiveness, reduce human job nature. Otherwise, other authors argue (AI) will bring positive outcomes of automation, due to raise productivity, job creation, assist humans work.

On the positive outcome hand, robots can increase productivity . This is particularly important for small-to medium sized businesses both are in developed and developing countries economies. It also enables large companies to increase their competitiveness through faster product development and delivery. Increased use of robot is also enabling companies in high cost countries to re shore, or bring back to their domestic base parts of the supply chain that will have previously outsourced to sources of cheaper labor. Currently , the greater threat to employment is not a automation, but an inability to remain competitive. Automation has led overall to an increase in labor demand and positive impact on wages. The reason is that the middle-income/middle-skilled jobs have reduced as a proportion of overall contribution to employment and earnings leading to fears of increasing income inequality, the skills range within the middle income bracket is large. Thus, robots are driving an increase in demand for workers at the higher -skilled and with a positive impact on wages. This issue is how to enable middle-income earners in the lower-income range to unskilled or retain. Finally, the (AI) positive impact supporter who argue the future will be robots and humans can work together.

However, on the negative outcome hand, robots can substitute labor activities, but don't replace jobs. They believe that less than 10% of jobs are fully auto. Increasingly , robots are used to complement and augment labor activities, the net impact on jobs and the quality of work is positive. Automation can provide the opportunity for humans to focus on higher-skilled, higher-quality and higher-paid tasks. Robots can improve productivity when they are applied to tasks that which perform more efficiently and to a higher and more consistent level of quality than humans. For example, increased productivity is enabling some firms, such as Whirlpool, Caterpillar and Ford Motors company in the US restructure their supply chains, bringing back parts of the manufacturing process to the country of origin. Thus, productivity gains due to robotics and automation are important not just at the company lcvcl, but also for build industry and nation compctitivcncss.

I suppose that productivity can be raised. What are the impacts of robots on employment? Firstly, the main focus of development has been on personal entertainment, which does not drive worker productivity (manufacturing production). When the internet (information and communication technology (ICT)) innovation. This is borne and by findings that manufacturing productivity, which has been driven by innovations in automation rather than consumer technologies, has government strongly than productivity in the services sectors of the economy in most nature economies. It seems (AI) automation will create many jobs in internet communication entertainment game industry. For example, many young people like to use internet to play any electronic games from computer or mobile at home or outside home conveniently. Thus, (AI) automation will increase demand to be invented to any new entertainment game from internet channel. It will need to employ many (AI) entertainment game inventors to create many automation entertainment games. Thus, (AI) automation in internet entertainment game industry will need human (AI) entertainment game inventors to invent the knowledge-based capital of (AI) automation entertainment games. The (AI) entertainment game inventors will need own research and development skills, form specific skills, organizational know-how skills, data based knowledge, design and various forms of intellectual property to do these (AI) automation entertainment game invention occupations in the future.

China will be as a major robotics manufacturer and user of robots, benefiting from jobs created by robot manufacturing and productivity gains from robot use. Chins had sold of robots to any one single market every year since 2017 year. The Chinese government has included a focus on robotics in its 10 year strategy. In order to achieve its target of a robot density of 150 units per 10, 000 workers by 2020 year. Thus, Chinese companies will have to install around 650,000 new industrial robots between 2016 to 2020 year, 2.5 times more than installed globally in 2015 year.
Hence, China (AI) manufacturing industry will need to employ many workers . It implies (AI) manufacturing industry will create many new occupations in China. Also, ministry of economy, trade and industry (2015) also showed that Japan currently has the largest stock of industrial robots in operations, primarily in the automation industry. Driven by a rapidly aging population and low productivity rates, the Japanese government has sights on a 20-fold increase in the use of robots in the non-manufacturing sector and a three-fold growth rate of labor productivity in the service sector both by 2020 year. Thus, it also implies Japan will need many robots to be provide to service industry. Due to robots will provide to serve any businessmen clients. Thus, it is possible that the service workers won't be dismissed as well as it is depended on the serving job nature to decide whether Japan's service workers can still serve to their employer when the service (AI) robots are applied to whose employers.

Consequently, it seems that (AI) can create employment, Ministry of economy, trade and industry (2015) showed that such as China will develop the major (AI) automation manufacturing industry. The (AI) employers will need to employ many workers to manufacture any these different kinds of (AI) robots to satisfy China or overseas individual or business buyers needs. But, (AI) can also cause unemployment to the low skillful service workers. Such as if Japan some service businesses choose to buy any (AI) service robots to replace their service staffs to serve their clients. It is possible that the service staffs will be dismissed, due to (AI) robots can do such as their same service job duties to achieve better service performance.

Thus, today, it is increasingly common for people to use robots in various situations at home and in retail stores, hotels and hospitals these service industries. Robots are classified into server types based on their functionality (service and utility robots or those designed to communicate with humans) and appearance (humanoid robots or mechanical robots). The type of robot, to which each country allocated particular importance in the advance of robotics, reflects the sense of values and preferences of its population. Thus, if the country has high population needs to use robots, then they will influence either more new jobs creation or more old job loss in the country's (AI) manufacturing or (AI) service industries both. For example, Japan respondents often associate the term " robot " with humanoid robots that can communicate with human and they have a high level of familiarity with robot. The US has the highest level of robot utilization at home and in retail stores with its people being the most enthusiastic about the future use of robots. Germany shows a strong tendency to consider robots for industrial purposes and its people feel strong effort to the presence of robots in their households.

In conclusion, to judge whether how (AI) will influence the country's employment to be better or worse. It will depend on the country home buyers (users) or business buyers (users) how to use (AI) for their daily needs. If the country , such as US retail stores need to use (AI) , it will have possible to reduce some or many retail service workers. Even, if the country , such as Japan has many home users need to use (AI) , it will not influence the employment market. Otherwise, it will raise (AI) salespeople numbers. Even, if the country, such as Germany and China will have many (AI) manufacturers, then it will create many (AI) manufacturing occupations for these (AI) manufacture workers.

Consequently, (AI) robots manufacturing and service needs will have positive or negative impact to any country's employment. It will depend on the (AI) service provision and service workers' job nature as well as the manufacturing workers of (AI) knowledge level to decide their employment chance in their country's employment market.

Today, it may be challenging to predict exactly which jobs will be most immediately affected by (AI)-driven automation. Because (AI) is not a single technology, but rather a collection of technologies that are applied to specific tasks.

Nowadays, (AI) related industrial applications will replace most human power in fields, including call centers, customer services and air cargo transportation. (AI) technologies also help weather forecasting based on repeated rainfall pattern (data) recognition, through robotics (i.e. floor cleaning, moving lawns etc.) transporting people and products with unmanned vehicles, sending space unmanned smart shuttles, developing robotic arms, predicting market values in stock exchanges by internet, making homes safer, helping elderly and disabled using robotic servants etc.

Among the (AI) related technologies , there are a few that significance for the impact on society and especially on digital economy . (AI) is particularly influential in machine learning. Such as robotics, transportation, finance, health and bioinformatics, e-commerce , e-games, big online data gathering and internet-of-things. For example, machine e-learning is based in bioinformatics and robots that can learn new skills for better caregiving in healthcare. What is machine e-learning? Machines can e-learn from e-data gathering, coming up generalizations and making decisions to act in certain ways from internet.

There are important applications , such as e-machine perception, electronic online natural language learning processing, online search engines, online bioinformatics, online brain –computer interface, online game playing, online robot locomotion, online advertising, online computations finances, online health monitoring, online DNA classification and decision making, online in chemistry –cheminformatics . So, online machine learning can positively impact productivity and it can enhance information and analytical system from (AI) online channel.

What is robotics? Robotics is one of the most strongly influenced fields in (AI). For example, heavy manufacturing industries, robots and used and man power is replaced for effectiveness, precision, and accuracy, especially in respective or dangerous tasks, including welding, assembling , picking and placing .

So, robots can acquire new skills or adapt the changing dynamic environment. Also, artificial intelligence can be applied in developing transportation. For example, automated vehicles, driver assistance systems , safety systems, collision avoidance systems and public transportation. Moreover, (AI) technology has proven to produce some of the best tools to predict stock market fluctuations from internet data gathering method. It's predictions are based on ever-evolving predictions algorithms and systems learn new models and make connections between historical data and new data to measure stock market trading more accurate from internet data gathering channel.

In health field, especially in health data processing , analysis, decision making support and medical diagnosis. So, online data can show which patients will need what treatment and what alternative drugs could be used more accurate from (AI) online data gathering method. Bioinformatics is an interdisciplinary field combining statistics, (AI) online technology can help in discovering data patterns and modeling through the application of machine learning, artificial neural networks and genetic algorithms. For example, further (AI) technology development of human genome project of online data sequences.

Online shopping can be facilitated by virtual assistants developed through (AI) technology and these assistants can offer the best advice. (AI) online purchase coming after every product image recommendations and personalization bring important revenue to shopping online sites, like Amazon . Smart computer graphics and games, artificial intelligence is useful in smarter computer, graphics, scene modeling , scene rendering processes in order to create, for example, effective human –robot interactions , online machine learning, online strategic games techniques etc. online computer related (AI) software.

So, online big data analysis and big data does have a critical need in the world of online intelligence machines and software in our future. In other words, (AI) offers online technology to enable online big data analysis to provide industrial organizations with valuable information for effective decision making in short time. For example, what IBM's Watson achieved: this machine used 200 million of structured and unstructured content with a special technology of hypothesis generation, massive evidence gathering, analysis and scoring from internet channel.

Finally, (AI) online technology another related internet invention (internet of things) (IOT) is the network of machines or objects connected through internet. These connected objects can sense their internal and external environment, communicate with each other, can send critical data and finally can make decisions to act or correct their environment from (AI) online technology. For example, factories can monitor and automatically change production processes, hospitals can monitor and regulate the health conditions of their patients , schools can collect data from facilities and cars can send data to car makers from (AI) online technology.

Some specific predictions are possible based on the current (AI) technology. For example, driving jobs and house cleaning jobs, bank counter service jobs, telephone service operators. Restaurant cooking jobs, simple accounting record service jobs etc. that require relatively less education to perform. Advancements in computer vision and related technologies have made the feasibility of fully appear more likely, potentially displacing some workers in driving-dominant professions. Seemingly similar robot, for which the operational tasks is less specific of navigating to a specific destination when following a set of given rules and preserving safety.

In the future, the effects of (AI) on the labor market in the decade ahead will continue the trend toward skill-biased change that computerization and communication innovations have driven in recent decades. Thus, some human driving occupation will be disappeared or replaced by (AI) automation driven. For example, bus drivers, light truck or delivery services drivers, heavy and tractor-trailer truck drivers, school drivers, tax drivers, travel bus drivers.

However, (AI) technology could enable some workers to focus time on other job responsibilities, boosting their productivity, and actually raised wage growth among those still holding the reshaped jobs. For example, salespeople, who currently spend a considerable amount of time driving could find themselves able to do other work when a car drives them from place to place, or inspectors and appraisers could fill out paperwork, when their car drives itself. This (AI) -driven technology should make these workers more productive, with (AI) -driven technology serving as a complement, not a substitute. New jobs will also likely be created, both in existing occupations cheaper transportation costs with lower prices and increase demand for products and all the related occupations, such as service and fulfillment, and in new occupations not currently foreseeable.

What kind of jobs will be created by (AI) technology? Predicting future job growth is extremely difficult, due to it depends on technologies or substitute for existing today as well as they may complement or substitute for existing human skills and jobs. However, (AI) will also lead to substantial indirect job creation to the degree it raises productivity and wages, it may also lead to higher consumption that would support additional jobs from high-end draft production to restaurant and retail. The future(AI) " augmented intelligence", the technology's role is as assisting and expanding the productivity of individuals rather than replacing human work. Thus, based on the biascd-tcchnical changc framcwork, dcmand for labor will likcly increase the most in the areas where humans complement (AI) automation technologies. For example, (AI) technology , such as IBM's Watson may improve early detection of some cancers or other illnesses, but a human health care professional is needed to work with patients to understand and translate patients' symptoms, inform patients of treatment options, and guide patients through treatment plans. Shipping companies may also partner workers who pick up and deliver products over the last feet with (AI) enabled autonomous vehicles that move workers efficiently from site to site. In such cases, (AI) augments what a human is able to do and allows individuals to either be move effective in their specially task or to operate on a larger scale. Thus, it seems (AI) technology will also create new jobs, raise productivity and workers' efficiency.

Consequently creative and social intelligence will be in even greater demand as (AI) makes in management and the workforce. This development will represent a long term trend in labor markets , one characterized by intensifying demand and reward for social skills with a growing desire for creative capabilities, managers will seek to fashion of ideas and hypotheses from inside and outside of the enterprise to shape solutions to their most pressing business problems. Thus, (AI) will influence overall organizational team members who have chance to participate any decision to make more accurate business judgment.

Many managers mistakenly view judgment work as only an individual discipline, failing to appreciate that it can also involve decide interpersonal and organizational practices. In more complex settings, judgment is typically a collective outcome of individuals‘ and teams’ diverse perspectives, insights and experiences. And often , the resulting choices are better informed than decisions that an individual would have arrived at on his or her own.

Thus, when any organizations apply (AI) technology to assist managers to gather data and ideas to make any judgment. In these cases, organizations can create the conditions for effective collective judgment by establishing structures , such as " shadow advisory boards" that prompt managers and employees to source and synthesize multiple perspectives. Thus, a traditional organization (firm) might freshen its thinking is t put together a shadow advisory board, comprised of young, digital people who can apply (AI) machine assistance to make judgment work more accurate whether related to people development, problem-solving or strategy and innovating for considerable degrees of creative and social intelligence.

Thus, on the one hand, (AI) technology machine augmentation and automation can give these advantages to human (organization managers) , e.g. developing people and community, solving problems and collaborating, coordinating and controlling work, shaping strategy and leading innovation. Besides, on the other hand, the next generation managers need have these individual attitude to treat intelligent machines to be as colleagues.

When, judgment is a human skill, intelligent machines can accelerate human learning that supports it, assisting in data -driven simulations, scenarios and search and discovery activities. Focuses on judgment work, some decisions require insight beyond what data can tell them. This is the sweet sport for human judgment, the application of experience and expertise to critical business decisions and practices. Thus, managers will also need to find ways to learn how to use digital (AI) technologies to tap into the knowledge and judgment of partners, customer external stakeholders and role models in other industries after the (AI) machine had been implemented to the organization.

In the future, scientists predict that these occupations will be influenced by (AI) technology mostly. They include : retail salespeople, food and beverage service workers, language or translation teachers, health practitioners. Since these work activities have a more relevant occupations are made up of a range of activities with different potential for (AI) automation . For example, a retail salesperson will spend more time interacting with customers, stocking shelves , or ringing up sales. Each of these activities is distinct and requires different capabilities to perform successfully.

Thus, these job activities have similar simple control characteristics. Simple activities include greet customers, answer questions about products and services, clean and maintain work areas, demonstrate product feature process sales and transactions. All these activities can have similar simple activities in order to (AI) machines can be learn how to do these activities from (AI) technology . For example, the capability perception includes sensory perception, cognitive capabilities, such as retrieving automation, recognizing known patterns(supervised learning), logical reasoning problem solving.

Thus, (AI) machine is such human, which has feeling and emotion, such as social and emotional sensing, judgment reasoning methods, natural language understanding and physical capabilities, such as mobility , navigation, gross motor skill, fine motor skills. It seems that the future, (AI) human invents machines which will have these human characteristics to do human similar behavioral job duties more easily and efficiently. It implies these above human occupations will be replaced by (AI) human invention machines in the future. Due to (AI) creation, it is possible to cause unemployment number of these above workers will increase because (AI) machines can do their similar job behavioral activities.

Modern information technologies and the labor economy growth of machines is powered by artificial intelligence have already strongly influenced the world of work in the 21 ST century. Computers, algorithms and software simplify every tasks and it is impossible to image how most of our life could be managed without them. How can be the information economy characterized by exponential growth replaces the most production industry based on economy of scales? What will the future world of work look like and how long will it take to get? Will the future world of work be a world where humans spend less time earning their livelihood? Alternatively, are mass unemployment, mass poverty and social distortions also possible scenario for the future, where robots, artificial intelligence systems play an increasingly central role? These questions concern how artificial intelligence further development . Can influence labor economy growth on workplace ? When the labor market has widespread impact on intelligence property, information technology, product liability, competition and labor and employment laws.

The future influence any organizations how labor economies use of (AI) can be analyzed, such as deep machine learning is based on a set of model high level data. Unlike human workers, the machines are connected the whole time in workplace. If one machine makes a mistake, all autonomous systems will keep this in mind and will avoid the same mistake the next time.

Over the long run intelligent machines will win against every human expert. Production robots have been replacing employees because of the (AI) technology. They work more precisely than humans and cost loss. Creative solutions like 3D printers and the self learning ability of these production robots will replace human workers, the automatic data recording and data processing, traditional back office activities are no longer in demand. Autonomous software will collect necessary information and will send it to the employee who needs it. Additionally, dematerialization leads to the phenomenon that traditional physical products are becoming software. For example, CD or DVDs are being replaced by streaming services. The replacement of traditional event ticket, e-travel ticket service products or hard cash will be the next step, due to the possibility of payment by smart phone.

So, (AI) technology will impact human's daily life consumption behaviors in the future. For another example, transportation tools, such as boats and ferries and private vehicles will use sensors and navigating without human input. Taxi and truck drivers will become obsolete, the stock store applies to stock managers and postal carriers of the delivery is distributed by (AI) machine delivery method.

Consequently, employers won't need to employ many of these skillful labor. Otherwise, they can buy less number (AI) machines to attempt to do whose job activities more easily and efficiently. So, it seems (AI) machines will have more high work performance to replace these occupation workers' work performance. Finally, these occupation worker unemployment number will only increase when the (AI) machines had been invented to achieve to do their work behavioral activities absolutely success in the future.

Can (AI) technology influence China economy? Could China workers be affected and jobs made up of routine work activities and predictable? Will programmable tasks be particularly impact to China employment market ? When impact on labor market is likely to be gradual at the aggregate level, it can be sudden and dramatic at the level of specific work activities, rending some job obsolete fairly. Overall (AI) technology will raise digital skills when reducing demand for medium incomer inequality for China workers. It seems (AI) technology's effect on productivity could be crucial to China's future economic growth as the population ages are increasing.

In China, some biggest technological companies driving significant investments in research and development. Moreover, China is one of the leading global (AI) technology development county. However, China will need to focus on building its innovation capacity. For example, United States and United Kingdom are currently producing more influential (AI) technological research. However, if China planed to achieve (AI) technology success, it's traditional industries will need to develop technical know-how –to and overcoming implementation costs prepare to develop (AI) . When (AI) technology is introduced into China society, China government needs to raise concerning ethical, legal, technological security etc. business questions. Also, surrounding issues include privacy, discrimination, legal liability and regulation. It aims to encourage overseas investors to choose to invest (AI) technological industry to raise GDP growth and manufacturing industries income growth for long term in China.

If China encouraged overseas (AI) technology investment in its country. It is possible to influence China employment market to be changed. Because (AI) technology will impact to influence China people daily life. Due to (AI) technology is introduced to China society, many rich people will prefer to spend to buy any high (AI) technological products for entertainment or learning or machine man driving etc. daily necessity activities. Then it will raise GDP growth and will raise (AI) manufacturers or related-(AI) technological manufacturers profit. It is beneficial to China because it can become one high knowledgeable and (AI) technological economical society.

But it will bring bad influences to raise unemployment chance for the low skillful labor. In labor economy aspect influence , how (AI) technology can influence China low skillful labor unemployment ratio raising. The raising low skill labor unemployment reason is because China low skillful human labors are argued or are replaced by (AI) technology creating new challenges to introduce to influence China society of simply human manufacturing job nature to be changed to be high (AI) technology manufacturing job nature in any China factories. Moreover, when

(AI) technology introduction to China, it will cause other related social challenges in China. The varied (AI) related challenges, including the difficulty of creating safe and reliable hardware for sensing and affecting (transportation and education), the challenges of gaining public trust, a low resource comities and public safety and security, the challenges of overcoming fears or marginalizing humans in China employment and workplace and the risk of diminishing interpersonal trust because the low skillful labors won't believe any China employers will give chance to employ them , due to (AI) technology will replace their skills and man manufacturing of productivity is much less to compare to (AI) technology manufacturing method.

Are future nature of jobs changed to computerization from (AI) technology? Where are the probability of computing occupations from (AI) technology influence? What is expected impacts of future computing on labor market from (AI) technology influence? In the future, (AI) technology will impact some nature of occupations to change computing. This chance will also influence some countries' economic change. For example, some factory human labors hand routine manufacturing tasks will be changed to computerization of routine manufacturing tasks by (AI) technological machine men hand manufacturing method. it will cause a structured shift in the labor market, with workers reallocating their labor supply from middle-income manufacturing to low-income service occupations.

Arguably, this is because the manual tasks of service occupations are less computerization, as who require a higher degree of flexibility and physical adaptability. So, (AI) technology will influence the human hand labor skillful occupation nature of task cheaper , such as vehicle manufacturing , ship manufacturing, computer manufacturing, steel manufacturing, television, radio etc. home electronic products of heavy machine industry change. Due to (AI) technology machine man will be proper to be used to manufacturing these electronic products when the (AI) technology innovation can develop to the mature stage. Then, any countries manufacturers will choose to use (AI) technology machine man, instead of human hand production.

Supposing the future prices of computing are fallen, seriously, problem solving skills are becoming relatively productive, explaining the substantial employment growth in manufacturing occupations, involving cognitive tasks where skilled labor has a comparative advantage, as well as the increase education needs for (AI) technology computing of machine man subject study.

Prediction of education needs for (AI) technology student numbers will increase, due to manufacturing industry needs many (AI) technology students in future employment market. Another (AI) technology influence if the future (AI) technological innovation, e.g. machine man manufacturing or machine man service industries will both increase demand, then with more sophistic software technologies will be disrupted labor markets by marketing workers redundant.

For publishing industry, what is striking about the case in paper book publishing industry will be unpopular? Due to the electronic book publishing industry will be popular, e.g. Amazon publish . (AI) technology can influence paper book manufacturing method which is replaced by machine man electronic book manufacturing method as well as it will cause the computerization is no longer confined to routine manufacturing tasks. Due to (AI) machine man manufacturing technology will be proper to be used to manufacture any products in short time efficiently and effectively , e.g. electronic book products. In the future, if it is fact to occur this case, such as (AI) technological machine man manufacturing method will be adopted (applied) to manufacture electronic books or any products in possible. (AI) technology will cause many manufacturing workers are unemployed. It is beneficial to employers, who can reduce to spend much wages expenditure to employ manufacturing workers, but it will cause many manufacturing workers loss jobs and reduce income to support whose families lives. It will cause social challenges, e.g. increasing stealing crimes if the manufacturing workers had not other skills to find other jobs to do easily. So, manufacturers need to concern over technological unemployment which will be hardly future phenomenon if who decided to dismiss all manufacturing workers, due to (AI) technology machine men replace to them.

If (AI) technology can be innovated to produce any kinds of machine man to serve any service or manufacturing industries successfully. Then, it will bring these questions: Can future that workers be influenced to be automation employment and productivity by (AI) technology influence? Does it impact to influence the (AI) technology countries‘ productivity and growth and natural resources development and labor markets and evolution of global financial markets and economic impact of technology and innovation and urbanization etc. issues? How will automation transform the workplace? What will be the implication for employment? What is likely to be its impact both on productivity in the global economy and on employment?

In fact, automatic of activities can enable businesses to improve performance by reducing errors chance and improving quality and speed, and same cases achieving outcomes that go beyond human capabilities. Some economists indicate (AI) technology would give a needed boost to economic growth and prosperity have of the working age population in many countries. Based on the scenario modeling, they estimate automation could raise productivity growth globally by 0.8 to 1.4 % annually. They also indicated that almost half the activities people are almost $1.6 trillion in wages to do in the global economy have the potential to be automated adapting current demonstrates technology, according to their analysis of more than 2,000 work activities across 800 occupations. When less than 5% of all occupations can be automated entirely using demonstrated technology, about 60% of all occupations have at least 30% of worker made activities, that would be automated. More occupation will change to be automated. They also indicated for business performance benefits of automation are relatively clear, but the issues are more complicated by policy making to attract foreign investors. Beyond technical feasibility, the cost of technology, competition labor will include skills and supply and demand dynamics, performance benefits and beyond labor cost savings and social and regulatory acceptance will affect the automation. Their predictions suggest that half of today work activities could be automated by 2055 year, but this could happen 10 to 20 years earlier or latter depending on the various factors in addition to their wider economic condition.

Some scientists suggest (AI) technology is finally starting to deliver real-life business benefits. Computer power is growing significantly , algorithms are becoming more sophisticated and perhaps most important of all, the world is generating vast quantities of the fuel that powers (AI) technology data billions of gigabytes of it every day. Also, online firms are digital natives, such as Google online search service company is investing on (AI) technology. For new though most of the news if coming from the suppliers of (AI) technologies. And many new users are only in the experimental phase. Few products are on the market or are likely to arrive these soon to drive immediate and widespread adoption. As a result, analysts believe (AI) technology's potential will give true economic benefit in the future. (AI) industry will introduce to suppliers and users to raise economic potential of (AI) technology.

In the future, (AI) technology systems can solve business problems. Some scientists categorized those into five technology systems that are key areas of (AI) technology development: robotics and autonomous vehicles, computer vision language virtual agents and machine learning , which is based on algorithms that learn from data without replying on rules-based programming in order to draw conclusions or direct an action.

Such as computer vision and language includes natural language processing, analytic, speech recognition technology, some are about learning from information, such as about machine learning and others are related to acting on information, such as robotics, autonomous vehicles and virtual agents, which are computer programs that can converse with humans. Machine learning and a sub field called deep learning are artificial intelligence applications.

What does AI prediction machine mean? Why AI machine can make more accurate economic prediction to compare human economists? How to apply AI machine to make more accurate economic prediciton to compare human economists? In tradition, economists can gather data to make statistics to analysis how to predict this year or next year either economic growth or recession occurrence in possible.

But, since AI machine tool, it can apply to manufacturing, service , logistic , office, hospital, shopping center etc. difference business working environment aspects, whether it can help economists to make more economic prediction in possible or economists will need AI machine to help them to make more accurate economic prediction for businessmen or societies needs. I shall attempt to give evidence to explain as below:

Economists view our world is differently than most people. Businessmen are influenced everything by forces such as supply and demand, production and consumption, prices and costs economic concept.

However, AI machine is needed to everywhere, such as packed into your smart phones apps, warehouse logistic workers, non manual vehicles. So, AI machine may innovate our lives. Human needs AI machine to assist our tasks from complex to simple. Businessmen may bring economic time and saving long time cost benefits. Such as online shopping method, AI can help consumers find any kinds of different products prices and photos to compare in order to make reasonable purchase decision more easily from webstores channel as well as businessmen can apply ecommerce sale channel to help them to sell products to different countries in short time.

Prediction is being used for traditional tasks in business environment, such as inventional management and demand and supply forecasting. For example, because the smart phone seller predicts smart phone buyers number will reduce when he feels every family, old and young age adult who have owned at least one smart phone to every family in the country. SO, the smart phone seller ought reduce to manufacture and sell the old smart phones in order to avoid the kind of old smart phone price to reduce, due to the kind of smart phone demand purchase number will reduce,but he ouhgt to continue to innovate new kind of smart phone in order to supply new innovative smart phones products to satisfy future smart phone users needs. It is general economists judgement.Such as this smart phone case, when smart phone prediction is cheap, there has two simple economic forces drive the new opportunities, such as new kind of innovative smart phones need that predction new kind of innovative smart phones will be needed to creat in order to keep this smart phone manufacturer competitive ability in the country.

However, at low levels, a prediction machine, such as AI machine can relieve humans of predictive tasks and save on costs, when AI machine help economists or businessmen to do gather this smart phone manufacturer to manufacturing and selling this kind of smart phones data in this country consumption market every day. AI machine can gather data in short time and then it can give this kind of smart phone manufacturing and sale number data to this smart phone company every day in order to make statistic conclusion. So, AI will affect the economic of a business so dramatically, that they will no longer be used to simply enchance productivity in executing against the strategy, they will help this smart phone manufacturewr to change the strategy itself, such as whether

it ought continue to improve or innovate another kind of new smart phone design and function in order to satisfy future smart phone users needs. So, smart phones daily manufacturing and selling data is the most influential point to help this smart phone manufacturer to make decision whether it is the right time to innovate its another new kind of smart phone design and function or not in order to keep its smart phone sale competitive ability in this country.

Amazon can apply AI machine to help it reduces warehouse seeking goods time from shelves. Because Amazon has many shevles, it putted many kinds of products in shelves. Every one of worker will need long time to seek the kind of goods in order to transport to customers when they had bought the kind of goods. Amazon found this long time seeking goods problem to avoid transport time waste. It applied AI transport machine to help human worker to seek any kinds of goods from shelves. On consequently, AI transport machine help every warehouse worker to reduce at least 5 to 10 minutes to seek ths right kind of product from shelves. So, if the warehouse has 600 different kinds of products to prepare to transport to global buyers homes in the day. Every product seeking time from shelves will reduce 600 x 5 minutes or 600 x 10 minutes seeking time. So, this 600 different kinds of products will reduce 3,000 minutes or 6,000 minutes transport time to deliver to global buyers homes. So, AI machine had helped Amazon to reduce goods transport time in this day. It can help Amazon bring economic transport time shorten benefits to let global buyers can get their products within the day or tomorrow rapidly. In this case, AI machine help Amazon 's business model from shopping -then -shipping to shipping -then -shopping , AI helps Amazon to avoid buyers whose purchase goods return occurrence chance when they can be transported to their homes in short time. and accelerates the timing of investment.

Hence, it seems that AI machine may help businesses to bring these economic benefits: mahcine learning is often referred to as advances in artificial intelligence because systems prediction on this technique learn and improve over time, these systems produce significantly more accurate predictions than human economists or businessmen, traditoinal statistics methods require the articulation of hypotheses or at least of human economists analysis. In fact, AI technology is called " machine learning) for a reason. The mahines leearn form data. The prediction machine has to learn how the data is associated with actual incidences of irregular heart problem, such as Amazon transport time reducing case, when Amazon discover it will have many buyers choose either goods return decision more than non -goods return decision. AI mahcine help Amazon to seek goods from shelves to avoid goods long time seeking from human workers when AI transport delivery machine help human workers to do " goods seeking from shelves tasks working first step, then human worker only need to spend time to put the goods to lorry to transport to lorries to drive to airport in order to fly the goods to overseas customers in second time. So, AI machine may help Amazon to gather warehouse different kinds of goods shelves location data any where in order to help human workers to reduce goods seeking timr from shelves. AI mahcine may Amazon warehouse workers to avoid to spend long time to seek goods from shelves, they can concentrate on spending time to put goods on lorries.Also, AI machine help Amazon to reduce warehouse workers number or reduce salaries expenditure, when AI warehouse machine can replace human workers to do goods seeking tasks from shelves.

Ai machine help organizaitons to achieve new division of labour aim. Such as, a law firm may apply AI mahcine help human lawyers to take legal documents and predicted which

information was condfidential. This product is valuable to law firms because when they are required to disclose documents, they have to black out comnfidential information. Historically,

redaction was done by hand, with humans reading documents and blacking out confidential information. SO, AI machine help lawyers to save time and effort. Such as Amazon case, AI machine

creates new division of labor strategy in any one of Amazon warehouse. AI machine will concentrate time on doing " goods seeking tasks from shelves in first step", then human workers will concentrate on time on doing " goods are putting on lorries tasks in second step ". Traditoinal , warehouse workers need to spend time to do seek goods from shelves task and putting goods to lorries tasks both. Nowadays,warehouse AI machine only need to spend time to do seek goods from shelves task , but human workers only need to spend time to do goods are putting to lorries tasks. So, AI machine will change traditional divisoin of labor to warehouse tasks in the future. Because AI machine will help workers to reduce goods transportation time and reducing goods return chance occurrence.

Whether human social job change it depends on social job demand more or job supply more? What does human network job mean ? Why may human network job be popular? Why human network job behavior may influence economy ?

Nowadays internet is popular to use. We can apply internet to find data , search any new things, even earn money. Why does internet may become human network job source. For example, e-publish may be one kind of new human network job. Any authors may apply internet channel to help them to sell electronic or paper books from e-publisher web store. They may apply facebook, you tub etc. any online channel to promote themselves new books to let new readers to know whether when they may buy themselves favorable new topic books to read from electronic publisher web store.

Thus, future electronic publisher industry may help any authors to build internet network platform to help them to sell and promote to advertise their any one new electronic or paper book topic to let global any one reader to choose to buy their any new topic books from electronic publisher web store easily and conveniently. However, it implies that electronic network platform author may be one kind of future new human network job in our societies.

How electronic network platform author job may bring economy benefit in macro economy view? A person can have few friends, contacts and still be very influential if these few friends and contacts are themselves highly influential, e.g. one author must not need to know any one reader in global society. When they like to choose any electronic books from electronic internet network platform. They may become the author's any one topic book buyer, when they feel the author's any one topic book is fun and attract they make decision to both the strange author whose the topic book from electronic book publisher's platform web store convenience in short time. Although, they are strangers, they do not know themselves , but the reader can understand what it way that made Google from writing platform to create new creative mind and typing network job method to replace traditional hand writing book method for global authors. It will be one kind of new human network writing job.

Hence, global any one reader can apply an innovative search engine , such as google.com to find whether whom author personal new topic books are value to read from internet. Then, the electronic publisher's web store may be new book store platform sale network to help the author to sell many electronic or paper books from electronic network platform in short time. So, internet may be future new network platform to help global any one author to create network writing job absolutely. Furthermore, internet may be popular social media to help any one author to build good relationship between his/her readers. It is one kind of new network, human network job. New authors do not need to buy many paper books to prepare to put in any one book shop warehouse. Their every book can print on demand to reduce out of book stock in any one book shop. They may choose to sell either electronic books or paper books both from any one book publisher web store. So, electronic network platform may be one kind of good writing channel to help human authors to create income and it can also help authors to bring new creative mind and new topic fun content books to let readers to know and buy to read from electronic publisher network platform.

Why does human behavior may be one kind of new human network job to bring global economic advantages. Although, it may be free income or without income, but the person does the network behavior, his/her behavior may be bring advantages to influence many other people's health. For this case, when a worker in a coffee shop in an airport gets a vaccination aganist the flu, it does not only helps him or her stay healthy, but also helps the many travellers who might otherwise have been inflected if that workers caught the flu. So, the externality , the result implies the vaccination of even a part of a community conveys benefits to the whole community. For example, governments pay special attention to the vaccinations of school children, teachers, health mothers, and the elderly, categories of people particularly susceptible not only to catching, but also to transmitting a disease.

It is not accidental that governments are heavily involved with vaccination . When there are externalities, free market, fail to persuade individual incentives with society's their the worker's decision of whether to get a vaccine ends up attracting whether other people get sick. The workers might not fully take all these other people's potential suffering into account when making her or his vaccination decision.

Whether robot labor needs are depended on employer labor demand more or robot labor number supply more? If one day robots can replace human to do simple, even complex jobs. They will bring what influences to our global societal economy.The popular economic refrain declares that the

global middle class is dying and robots will soon take our jobs, e.g. shopping center customer service jobs, library service jobs, cinema ticket sale jobs, restaurant kitchen cooker jobs,

even, bus drivers, taxi drivers etc. public transport driving jobs, accountant, doctors etc. professional jobs. Whether it is beautiful or petty matter if our future societies have many human jobs can be replaced to do from robots. Businessman must may reduce to employ employees and reduce to pay salary or wage, when robots can be replaced to do their employees tasks. But, societies must bring unemployment rate rises , due to societies will have many people loss jobs when their employers choose to buy robots to serve their clients or do any office tasks or customer service or cleaning etc. tasks.

In micro economy view, employers may save money in long term, but in macro economy view, it will cause unemployment ratio rises , even crime rate rises when there are many people lose

jobs in societies. These models of doom, though, fail to account for the hundreds of businesses riding the waves of change in their industries when robots may be invented to replace human to do many simple , even complex tasks in our future societies.

WE may image that one small factory needs to manufacture fishes canes to sell to supermarket, the small , cheaper stuff and higher margin parts of the fishes manufacture industry. Before, this factory needs to employ many human factory workers need to help every fresh customer making the perfect fishing gear, designed for performance, durability, and cost in order to achieve to manufacture every fish cane in whole fished processing manufacturing stages. Every worker needs to spend about 15 to twenty minutes to finish every fish cane , till to delivery to any supermarket to sell. If this fish canes manufacturing factory can apply manufacturing robots to help them to finish any one working tasks , every robot can only spend five minutes to finish whole fresh fish cane manufacturing process. Thus, every robot can

help this factory save 10 to 15 minutes time to finish every fish cane manufacturing process. IN fact, time is money, because when every robot can help this factory to reduce 10 to 15 minutes time to compare human worker. Then, this factory can finish about 20 fish canes in one hour if it can use robot to help it to manufacture fish canes. Otherwise, if this factory still use human workers to help it to manufacture fish canes, then it can finish about 3 to 4 fish canes in one hour. SO, the manufacturing efficiency ensures that robots must help this fish manufacturing factory to raise fish canes number more than human workers. So, in robotic behavioral economy view, manufacturing robots must help this fish canes manufacturing factory to raise fish canes manufacturing number and deliver increasing number to supermarkets to prepare to sell every day. Robots can help this fish canes manufacturing factory bring manufacturing time saving, rising manufacturing efficiency, improving performance and reducing wages expenditure long time advantages in micro economy view. However, manufacturing robots can also bring disadvantages to society, e.g. increasing unemployment ratio, increasing crime rate, this factory workers will lose jobs and income, they need earn social welfare from government and increasing government finance pressure in short time, even long time in macro economic view.

Stanford University graduate program in economics, Scott lecturer explained that "in demand and supply economic theory for robots supply and demand case, robots supply number increasing may influence human workers demand number decrease. It sometimes calls " the efficient frontier".

No specific human beings were mentioned in any of economics classes. As robots supply and demand in market case, They (robots) may be purely theoretical " agents" who reached to the most reasonable sale prices in order to persuade any one businessman buyer to make manufacturing robot buying decision whether robots can help him / her to bring how much saving time , saving money, saving cost, improving performance, efficiency economic benefit before he/she plans to reduce workers number when he/she decides to apply robots to replace human workers in his/her factory or office or any service department, e.g. cinema ticket sale service, shopping center customer service, shopping center cleaning , supermarket customer service etc. service or sale tasks. When robots can replace human to do any one of these tasks in any organizations. So, robots may be human worker agents who reached to prices the way robots would react to a software command. There was nothing that explained why some people thrived and others did n't or why truly brilliant, hardworking people could fail when much lazier folks succeeded." Having been admitted to the Stanford University graduate program in economics, Scott lecturer hoped to get his answers there.

How robots influence our future social changing? Using the right technology can be a boon to your business in this economy. For internet example, it is easier than ever to find well-matched customers all around the world, to stay in contact with them, and to more quickly design the products they want. If you focus solely on being cutting -edge, though you risk letting the technology take over what should be very robust relationships with your customers , employees, and colleagues. IN nowadays society, technological advances and automation, personal relationships in business are more crucial than ever. I mean that robots can not replace human to serve clients to let them to feel more comfortable and passion more easily. For shoe shop case example, if the shoe shop apply one robot to serve its clients to replace human shoe salesperson to serve its shoe customers. Robots ensure that they can not persuade every shoe potential buyer to make shoe buying decision more easily when robots need to contact every shoe potential buyer. The reason is simple, because robots can not touch any one shoe buyer individual emotion very easier.

If the shoe buyer needs the robots to help him/her to choose any right shoe styles when he/she can not feel himself / herself can make the most right shoe style choice decision. The robots can not replace human shoe salesperson to make shoe style choice judgment more easily. They must need longer time to analyze whether which shoe style may be the most suitable to the shoe buyer. Otherwise, human shoe salesperson may attempt to make the most right shoe style choice decision to help any one shoe buyer to choose the most right style shoe because he/she owns shoe style sale experience, shoe style knowledge, the most important reason is that they can feel every shoe customer individual emotion to touch whether he/she will feel comfortable or happy when they attempt to help every shoe customer to seek the most right shoe style in every shoe customer whole shoe searching processing. Otherwise, serving robots are only one machine, they can not touch or feel every shoe customer individual emotion whether he/she feel comfortable or unhappy or happy when they need to contact them in whole shoe searching processing. Hence, I believe that some tasks robots can not replace human staff to do very easily. Otherwise, robots may bring disadvantages to let any one businessman to loss his/her customers, due to robots can not touch every customer emotion to compare human staff in service tasks more easily. Robots serving customer behaviors may cause money lose and customers number lose to the shop in micro economic view.

On conclusion, in demand and supply economic theory for robots supply and demand case, robots supply number increasing may influence human workers demand number decrease. So, it seems that robots number supply will be depended on global robots supply number more than robots demand number because when human began to accept robots to replace human to do general simple jobs in global labor market. Then, it means that global robots labor number must need to be increased in order to satisfy global businessmen workers number need. If any kinds of robot workers manufacture number is not enough to be supplied to let global future businessmen to buy, then robot supply will be shortage and they can not provide to satisfy global businessmen robots labour purchase need. So, future robot number will be depended on supply more than demand.

Ethical scenarios of AI

Some scientists explain that artificial intelligence means which is an expert system, computer software that embodies a portion of the specialized knowledge of a human portion in a specific, narrow domain, owns decision making ability of human expert. The (AI)technology is based on the premise that what makes a person an expert is years of experience that enables who recognizes certain patterns in a problem as being similar to pattern. For example, in the future artificial intelligence system can be applied to control air traffic, design to computer configuration, medical diagnosis, instruction/training, speech/interpretation, monitoring to (nuclear plant), planning to mission, factory scheduling, prediction weather, repairing telephone, automatic driving etc. different industries.

Artificial intelligence characteristics include: creative, adaptive , common sense, fact processing, quick replication, broad focus permanent and consistent skill. Otherwise, traditional computer expert system disadvantage includes perishable, unpredictable, slow reproduction, expensive, slow reproduction, slow processing lacks inspiration, needs instruction, narrow focus only machine knowledge. So, artificial intelligence is a branch of computer science devoted to creating computer to influence software and hardware to attempt to create human intelligence or human intelligent behavior. It is learning from experience, responds flexibility in situation that are, new or not anticipated.

Thus, (AI) can be learn programmed knowledge to solve problems, using reasoning in solving problem, understanding and inferring facts and rules, recognizing the relative importance of different elements in a situation.

In summary, artificial intelligence is concerned with two basic ideas mainly: The first idea, it involves studying the thought processes of humans to understand what intelligence is; the second idea, it deals with representing thought processes using companies to create artificially intelligent entities for testing the theories of intelligence. It brings this question: Whether Ethical scenarios of AI robots which will bring negative impact to influence human future societies?

Human need concern this question: Will artificial intelligence (AI) reduce some human jobs in order to instead of replacing machines to do? Due to artificial intelligence is the ability of machines to do thing, that people would require intelligence. For example, artificial intelligence machine man driving(self-driver), it (AI) machine man driving research is an attempt to discover and describe aspects of human intelligence that can be simulated by driving machine functions. Alternatively, (AI) mathematical research may be another viewed as an attempt to develop a mathematical theory function to describe the abilities and actions of things (natural or man-made) exhibiting intelligent behavior and server as a design of intelligent calculation machine function.

Why do humans need artificial intelligence machines to instead of traditional human service job? For example, can artificial intelligence machine man (self-driving) driver drive to replace human driver? I shall compare the differences between humans and computers : The characteristics of humans are good at recognizing various things, either seen before or not, recognizing the relationship patterns between things. Human thinking is common sense reasoning, combining all types of sensory input, acting appropriately in novel situations, learning new things and changing behavior patterns, making decisions , even when given incomplete information, working with noisy, incomplete information gathering behaviors . However, characteristics of computers are good at: The tasks humans do naturally are extremely difficult for a computer program as intelligent, which must be able to do the same kind of tack as humans do naturally.

Hence, (AI) is an combination of many different success and technologies: Linguistics - computational and social, philosophy-logic, philosophy of mind and of language, electronic engineering -image and speech processing, pattern recognition, robotics, machine learning, neural networks, optimization scheduling, management information system and decision making. So, it is possible that (AI) can bring negative impact to influence human job nature to instead of human working behavior in the future. So, robots may influence global human losses many jobs in different countries occupations in possible. When employers make decision to choose robots do human jobs when robots are invented to own talent mind, human will lose jobs, due to employers hope to use robots to reduce salary expense in long term.

(AI) researchers are native in a variety of domains, e.g. formal tasks (mathematics, games), tasks (perception, robotics, natural language, common sense reasoning), expert tasks (financial analysis, medical diagnostics, engineering, scientific analysis and other areas).

From the second business perspective reason view point, (AI) is a set of many powerful tools, and methodologies for using those tools to solve business problems. From a programming perspective reason view point, (AI) includes the study of symbolic programming problem solving and search .

From the third human technological perspective reason view point, today's computer can do many well-defined tasks, for example, arithmetic operations, are much faster and more accurate than human beings. However, the computers' interaction with their environment is not very sophisticated yet. How can human test whether a computer has reached the general intelligence level of a human being? Can a computer convince a human interrogator that it is a human? But before thinking of such advanced kinds of machines, human will start developing our own extremely simple " intelligent" machines.

Not just intelligence, but also debating, if machines are capable of having a conscious minds. Artificial intelligence has those characteristics as below:

On functionalism aspect, artificial intelligence inputs mental states, sensory inputs, (beliefs, desires being in pain feeling) and behavioral outputs. Since mental states are identified by a functional role, which are thoughts to be manifested in various systems. Even, perhaps computers which are physical devices with electronic substrate that inform computations on inputs to give outputs similar to brains which are artificial intelligence composed of part any intrinsic relationship to each other. Thus, artificial intelligence activities is not the whole itself, but into parts or on external influence on the parts.

On dualism aspect, artificial intelligence is a set of views about the relationship between mind are matter. On materialism aspect, it builds the only thing that exists is matter, including consciousness.

On biological naturalism aspect, it is similar a human brain than feels pains makes mental situation. So, artificial intelligence is similar biologist which might to be excited to human labor work. Hence, it seems artificial intelligence can change (alter) or replace human labor work of nature in possible in the future.

So, it is possible that **human society job nature will to be changed to artificial intelligent society when (AI) technology is developed to the mature stage in the future.**

Future vision

One of major division in (AI) is between humans who think (AI) is the only serious way of finding out how we (human) work and human who want companies to do very smart things, independently of how we (human) work. This is the important distinction between cognitive scientists vs engineers. One of another major division in (AI) is between symbolic (AI), which represents information through symbols and their relationships. Specific Algorithms are used to process these symbols to solve problems or deduce new knowledge and connectionist. So (AI) , which represents information in network. Biological processes underlying learning, task performance and problem solving are imitated from human mind behaviors. Thus, it is possible that **artificial intelligence machines can do the better judgicious behavior to compare human.**

In the automation changing influence aspect, as companies increasingly use robots on production lines or algorithms to optimize their logistics manage inventory, any carry out other core business functions. Technological advances are creating a new automation age in which ever-smarter and more flexible machines will be deployed on an ever larger scale in the marketplace. However, researching artificial intelligence with how influences human working nature. We need to answer these questions: How will automation transform the workplace? What will the implications for employment? And what is likely to be its impact both on productivity in the global economy and on employment?

Advances in robotics, artificial intelligence, and machine learning are growing in a new age of automation as machines match or outperform human performance in a range of work activities, including ones requiring cognitive capabilities. What factors are determined the changing in workplace adoption by artificial intelligence innovation? What advantages are automation? Automation of activities can be enabled businesses to improve performance by reducing errors and improving quality and speed, and achieving outcomes that go beyond human capabilities.

Some scientists indicated based on their scenario modeling. They estimated automation could raise producing growth globally by 0.8 to 1.4 percent annually. Almost, the activities people are paid almost $16 trillion in wages to do in global economy have the potential to be automated by adopting currently demonstrated technology. According to their analysis of more than 2,000 work activities across 800 occupations. When less than 5% of all occupations have of least 30% of activities that could be automated. They also indicated that technical economic and social factors will determine automation. Continued technical progress, for example, in areas such as natural language processing is a key factor beyond technical feasibility , the cost of technology, competition with labor including skills, and supply and demand dynamics, performance benefits including and beyond labor cost savings and social and regulatory acceptance will affect (alter) the scope of automation.

Other some scientists also indicate U.S. country for example, the anticipate shift in the activities in labor force of a similar order of magnitude as the long term sight away from agriculture and decreases in manufacturing. Share of employment in the United States both which were achieved. So, those factors can influence why artificial intelligence technology needs. So, it is possible that future agriculture and manufacturing both industries will apply (AI) technology manufacturer-kind of job nature to raise productivity instead of farmers, fruit picking workers, farming transportation labors as well as factory manufacturing workers and supervisors etc. human-kind of job nature.

On technological innovation reason view point, the history development of artificial intelligence studying the intelligence is one of most ancient scientific discipline. The history development of artificial intelligence what aims to achieve human use to sense, learn remember and think, logic probability, decision making and calculation develop from mathematics, instead of replacement human labor functions.

Artificial intelligence history development aim is the scientific analysis of skills in connection and practice with the appearance of computers from 1950 year beginning. The artificial intelligence (AI) can deal with the ultimate challenges. How can (either biological or electronic) mind sense, understand and manipulate a world that is much simple and more complex than itself? And what if would human like to construct something with such capabilities?

The general-purpose software of the early period of (AI) were only able to solve simple tasks effectively and failed when which should be used in a wider range or an more difficult tasks. One of the sources of difficulty was that early software had very few or mix knowledge about the problems which handled, and activities successes by simply syntactic manipulation. Moreover, the other difficulty was that many problems that were tried to solve by the (AI) were untreatable.

The early (AI) software whether trying step sequences based on the basic facts about the problem that should be solved, experimented with different combinations till which found a solution. From the end the 1960 year, developing the so-called expert systems were emphasized. These systems had (sue-based) knowledge base about the field which handled. Till to the beginning of the 1970 year, (Prolog) the logical programming language was born, which was built in the computation realization of a version of the resolution calculus. (Prolog) is a remarkably prevalent tool in developing expert systems (on medical, judiciary and other scopes), but natural language parsers were implemented in this language. Then, in 1981 s, the Japanese announced the fifth generation computer system project, a 10 years plan to build an intelligent computer system that use the (Prolog) language as a machine code. Nowadays, (AI) can be applied any industries, such as car manufacturing industry can use (AI) technological machine-men manufacture car, instead of replacing human labors in factory. Even, in the future, using (AI) machine-men drivers can drive any private cars or public transportation tools, instead of replacing human drivers, e.g. bus, train, tram, ferry etc. Also in the future, machine-men can replace housewives to serve families to do housekeeping clean job , e.g. cleaning toilets, bathrooms, kitchens, even cooking functions at home. So (AI) machine-man can reduce housewives works at home. Moreover, (AI) machine man can take care old people , when who are living at homes or elder care centers.

So, it seems artificial intelligence (AI) will be possible developed to manufacture a new generation machine-man to assist (serve) families to do any simply cleaning or cooking jobs at homes. Moreover, the overall demand of (AI) general social needs will also rise, such as security, driving transportation tools, restaurant cleaning, elder centers care service etc. So, it seems that individual or families or social needs of (AI) will be increase in the future. Thus, it will influence macro economy growth (GDP) if there are large house family consumer group and hotel or bus or taxis or ferry etc. different business consumer group demand any artificial intelligence machine numbers increasing. Then, the artificial intelligence products and material manufacturers must need to buy many artificial intelligence materials to produce any kinds of artificial intelligence machines to prepare to satisfy consumer individual needs. Consequently, macro economy will grow to the owned artificial intelligence development countries, e.g. US, China, UK.

I assume that technology and human behavior which have close relationship (e.g. working behavior , living behavior), For robot case example, if robots can influence human behavioral change, and future human working environment will need to cooperate with robots or human living environment will depend on robots' helping. How human behavior will be influenced to change in order to adapt to accept robots invention when human needs to live or work with robots together in the same time.

In organizational working environment, staffs will need to accept digital, data and robot technology in our industries or implementing a business strategy , why organizations need to be made decision making by robots. However, staffs have possible to depend on robots to help them to make decision, e.g. staffs behavior on analysis or judgement which can be controlled or managed by robots in possible. CEO, or manager leaders , their managing ability will be supervised or managed by robots in any organizations . So, it seems that robots may be any organizational top leader, if they can manage CEO or manager or supervisor in any organizations.

Business organizational leader individual managing behavior must be controlled by robots. Robots (supervised learning) is the most popular type of machine learning and robots can learn any new kinds of knowledge to compare human easily and rapidly. So, any organizational business decision or strategy decision may be made or influenced by supervising robots in organizations in possible. CEO, manager, supervisor their managing ability or managing skill may be influenced to reduce by supervising learning supervising or leading robots cooperation.

However, we can follow these aspects to explain how robots may influence our behavior change. Robots may be applied to participate in sales and marketing , HR, finance, customer service, education, legal and government organizations. Robots will be super intelligence to impact human lives in due time, In future, robots has insight , such as perceives, learns, understands, comprehends. It is one deep learning machines. It can make right or wrong , true or wrong judgment or answer and make good or bad predictions.

Hence, if robots can be applied to work in our future societies in popular, they may be social leader to replace human leader, e.g. government leader, organizational leader, CEO, manager, supervisor. Robots can not only human's worker role, e.g. home servants, shopping center cleaner, kitchen cooker. If robots can be organizational leaders, they may supervise worker individual working attitude or working performance whether his/her performance is satisfactory or perfect or to be needed to improve.

In organization, robots won't be only workers role. They may be supervisor role to supervise, manage or dominate or control all organizational top, middle , low level staffs their behavior and make judgment whether whom staffs can either stay to work or leave the organization.

However, some behavioral economists feel robots are Unfair to make judgment on staff individual working behavior. But on behavioral economic view, robots may help business owners to make judgment whether whom staffs ought stay the firm to work or leave the firm. They can help the organization to bring long term economic benefit. Hence, robots may be right to be future any organizational leader, such as CEO, manager, supervisor role more than worker role. If robots can be supervisor role in any organizations, I believe that they can help the organizations to bring much long term economic benefits to compare human CEO, manager, or supervisor for future global business economic development environment because robots may help any organizations to improve efficiency , or raise productivity to compare human staff decision making abilities.

Ought robots be leader role? In any organizations robots can bring this economic benefits to customer service aspect. For example, in order to reduce mind-numbing repetition for human workers, some economists recommend that future organizations seriously consider use of robots to field calls and process requests at a basic level. Such robots could be used to authenticate users for basic access to the organization in order for staffs to obtain the least risky information that they need. As customer need rise is complexity and business risk failure to satisfy that customer's need and to cause the customer chooses to buy another product or use another service. The work of ticket creation and case routing can be enhanced by robots, but a human should oversee it according to business risk assessment.

Hence, robot analytic can help to any organizations to predict those cases most likely headed for escalation in real time, all the date of the chat bot need to be presented to the human , so that the poor, annoyed customer does not have to start all over again with self-identification and description of the problem.

So, future robots can be perfect customer service leader, they can help satisfy your customers and retain them. Robots can know whether what the customer's real need , how to let the customer feels satisfactory more compare human customer service staffs. They can be customer service leader, service recommendation professionals. They can help organizations to retain old customers , even increase new customers easily to compare human customer service staffs. Hence, robots ought participate to marketing, customer service teams to help staffs how to do right customer service decision with human customer service staffs together. Hence, customer service staffs need to follow up customer service robots' ideas how to help them to solve any customer complain or enquiry in order to improve customer service performance. Consequently, the organization will increase new customer number and retain old customers easily if robots can be applied to participate on marketing, customer service departments.

How be robots in business? They may include three main areas: More intelligence products, services and business process. The first perspective is external. AI enhanced product and service means what you need to deliver to your customers. Both product and service -based business, which means they're all about making customers' lives easier, understanding and anticipating their needs, and solving their problems.

The second perspective is internal, making business processes more intelligent means looking at your business from the inside, assessing every aspect of your operations. To see how to make the business more efficient and enhance from manufacturing to the supply chain.

The third perspective is creating more intelligent products. How robots influence human living behavior? The internet of things means a whole host of everyday products are getting smart. Smart devices like smart phones, smart TV, smart watches on the market, smart office buildings, smart houses, they can influence staffs work or households live whom feel more comfortable.

On AI products aspect,. Intelligent smart running shoes products are like a fitness tracker, but provide more specialist information for runners. A smart AI chip that and how monitors movement (including gait and how feet strike the ground), the shoes provide feed- that helps runners improve their form and reduce the risk of injury. SO, AI smart shoes can influence runners feel comfortable and safe when runners run long time on gardens and they will predict or know whether the running places are dangerous or safe as well as smart running shoes can help runners to collect data on their running style , and the accompanying app provides real -time analysis of the runners' performance and running technique.

Smart running shoes can be runner coach on how to run better and avoid running injuries. It's not only running shoes that are being fitted with sensors to gather data and provide feedback.

The " wearable" technology sector is booming due to AI technology development to influence human needs to pursue more comfortable lives. Hence, AI smart products may help human to build health lives daily. Human begins to attempt to learn how to live more health by robots (AI) products.

When robots can be applied to human ourselves living environment , e.g. working, home, social , transport (non manual driving public transport tools service) , leisure environment. How behavioral economists feel they can bring positive or negative economic influence to our future societies?

Robots will bring human to experience economic anxiety. Why? After centuries of development, basic science, applied science and technology had been rapidly developing. Material science, additive manufacturing , nanotechnology, bio-tech , new batteries, smart phones, non human driving public transport or non public transport tools invention. All of these new technological products include robots may help human to create new technological economic social development and technology also impacts human behavioral change.

Future, (AI) online teaching method will be popular to be applied to teach to any university in possible, even secondary and primary schools. Because internet service is free charge to any students in any countries. Many different age students who can know how to apply internet as well as internet studying is very convenient to any students who can to internet to learn or study in home or public library or school library conveniently. Teachers do not need spend much time to teach students in classroom. They can use internet to teach teachers by face to face seeing and talking to their individual student from every student's computer. So, students do not also often spend much time to go to school to learn. So, developing any fast speed and time saving and talking and listening online teaching methods will be popular needs to any UK primary and secondary and university students in the future. It will be one new technological teaching method to change the traditional classroom educational method in UK and schools. For example, when one UK student who had left UK and is living in another country long time. If any UK school did not provide online teaching service to any UK students. It means that the UK citizen can not choose study himself/herself any UK school if who still hope to study any UK course when who is living in another country. Even one foreign student who does not go to UK to study, if he/she can find any UK primary or secondary or university to study from online. Then, the UK school won't lose one foreign student, due to it does not provide online teaching method to any foreign students. So, online Technology educational learning method will be one popular learning method which is enhanced, supported, mediated or assessed by the use of electronic media. Technology also enhanced learning may involve the use of new or established technology and/or the creation of new learning material. It may be deployed both locally and at a distance (i.e. a combination of traditional and e-learning approaches), to learning that is delivered entirely online. Online learning technology characteristics (features) include identification of a project lead for each area of any learning strategy, identification of two " quick win" for example lecture capture, electronic submission and feedback.

How can online technology enhance learning at UK any schools? It will include these several aspects to analyze. On identifying, prioritizing and innovation hand, online technology is a process for resourcing, prioritizing, acquiring and evaluating school software and hardware for UK any school needs. On staff development learning plan and a student skills development plan hand, UK schools need to establish a base-line policy on the standard (minimum) technology enhanced learning expectation for education each program and module and a mechanism for updating the schools' policies. On evaluation and research hand, a mechanism for engaging the owners of the technology enhanced learning strategy with best practice in the sector including contributing to and benefiting from pedagogical research and the evaluation of the student experience to UK any school.

Thus, UK schools can apply (AI) teachers to teach their students from online technological teaching channel to develop on educational aspect, such as (AI) teachers' digital literacies and appropriate technical skills that equip UK students for life-long learning, graduate level employment and professional practice, be empowered to learn how to learn with online teaching technology, using online technology to engage in interactive, creative and co-constructed learning with the potential for online learning in an interdisciplinary and international context, using online teaching technology to engage in learning with and from people from anywhere in the world, be supported on placement and in workplace learning through mobile applications and other supportive technologies that facilitate their online learning when away from the classroom, having access to innovative methods of online learning teaching and assessment that are the foundation of a research-lead academic environment, engaging with UK schools in developing , implementing and reviewing the technology enhanced learning strategy. Thus, in the future, it is important to build a capacity to apply (AI) teaching robots to teach their students from the online education technology to adopt future learning innovation and student individual online learning need (demand) to UK any school (AI) robotic online teaching trend.

There are many examples where UK academics working in isolation or in small UK teaching organizations or classroom learning groups have developed (AI) robotic teaching innovation that have a positive impact on UK students' academic experience , but these have remained isolated to particular modules or occasionally program. The aim of education researching online learning process is to identify the good (AI) robotic teachers' online teaching innovation that is being developed and to prioritize those that have the potential to make a significant contribution to improving the academic student experience at UK any schools. This online teaching process will need any UK schools which can plan how to apply limited resources necessary to achieve online teaching. In addition, the online teaching research process would evaluate and prioritize large scale educational software and hardware requests for primary, secondary and university students' requests. An important part to this process will be to ensure the integration of (AI) robotic teaching tools and their educational method to be applied to online educational products and packages that school staff and students regular use to make routine working and access as seamless as possible.

Decisions about school administrative online technologies should not be taken in isolation before assessing the impact on UK teaching staff. In addition, a range of techniques such as, (AI) robotic online expert facilitation, (AI) robotic coaching and peer support will be used to support individuals, groups or longer academic units, who are learning on major technology enhanced (AI) robotic teching online learning projects. Staff engagement may also facilitated through incorporating technology that is used in teaching staff research and/or professional activity that can be cooperated into their teaching.

Consequently, (AI) robotic online learning technology can develop UK students skills, UK schools need to understand how UK students understand technology and learn with it, therefore the digital literacy strategy needs to be considered as part of the overall strategy as well as the relevant skills development in UK employability strategy. So, in the future, (AI) teaching robotic online learning and teaching technology will make it clear that students will develop technical skills the appropriate level for graduate employability and professional practice. Also, in the future, the (AI) robotic teaching online technology can enhance learning working group to discuss external development, that are of educational strategic importance, understanding and evaluating current best practice and research and understanding and evaluating the online educational strategic contribution that pedagogical research and student feedback can have on online educational strategy, policy and practice. The (AI) robotic teaching e-learning unit is responsible for informing and educating. This could be done by, for example, providing a short digest of relevant information for each meeting and by setting aside a proportion of each school meeting to discuss a topic of particular (AI) robotic teachers to be applied to online educational strategic interest to every school. Academics that have not got a specialist interest in (AI) robotic teaching online educational technology enhanced learning will need relevant information at an appropriate time. This could be provided at a school department or faculty level and this will have clear links to the staff and (AI) robotic teaching online teaching development plan. Hence, future (AI) robotic teaching online educational development strategy will influence any UK or US educational school technological improvement in the future (AI) robotic online teaching method.

2 (AI) robotic environmental protection technology

Can future (AI) robotic environment technology be valid to human to develop? Nowadays, global air and water pollution is serious. For example, UK has many farming is polluted by the water and air pollution. It will influence UK farmers' income if whose farm land (natural resource) is polluted by water or air (natural resource). Even it will influence UK citizen will encounter food shortage if UK farmers can not grow any fresh and health food to provide the enough food numbers to eat every day. Moreover, air and water pollution will influence UK citizen drink the polluted water and breathe the dirty air to live every day. This natural resource (air and water challenge) will influence UK citizen health to cause illness , even death every easily. So, UK government can not neglect the natural environment pollution challenge. The environmental protection technology will help the UK and development countries to solve the challenge of climate change to avoid or reduce farming, foods, or vegetable or fruits or rice, pork, livestock numbers loss threats, i.e. the development and deployment of low carbon energy technology, including technology for the efficient use of energy. The commercialization of low carbon energy and energy efficiency technologies in the UK, with a specific focus on the demonstration and deployment phases of bringing low carbon technologies to UK market.

The UK Government needs to deliver a low carbon economy and to meet UK ambitions emission reduction target. So, low carbon and environmental protection technology researching and development will reduce the carbon intensity of energy production as well as reduce energy demand, towards meeting the contributing UK's ambitions production as well as reduce energy demand, and renewable energy goals. The use of energy (including transportation fuel) and the UK's targets on climate change, for example, by helping the UK make a step change in increasing deployment of renewable energy, improving UK energy efficiency and helping low carbon technologies reach the market. The development of low carbon technologies, and to realize the benefits of doing so in terms ensuring security of energy supply for the UK future economy development.

In UK, private sector investment in technology innovation in the low carbon energy sector will other sectors of the economy. So, in UK energy technologies are likely needed to be developed to avoid dangerous climate change, or an acceptable cost. So, in the future, UK government will need to consider to research environment protection and low carbon energy technology. The activities will reduce carbon emissions, or have the potential to reduce carbon emissions on the longer term, through the use of energy technology will accelerate development and deployment of low-carbon energy and energy efficiency technologies will capacity in the demonstration and deployment of low carbon technologies. Innovation in the energy sector is the only way to identify, develop and reduce the costs of new and improved technologies for the extractions, generation, distribution and use of energy. It has long been an important means of achieving the UK's energy policy aims of a secure and affordable energy supply, as well as to develop the environmentally friendly technologies that are required in UK response to climate change, i.e. nuclear, wind or water, sun energy technology, which is future new energy technology is suitable to research to create to apply instead of current electricity energy.

How global warming influences UK agriculture growth. Scientists have also been fighting the use of chlorine in municipal water systems to kill various strands of bacteria. Chlorine reduces by about 80% the number of alimentary tract diseases relative to polluted, unchlorinated water. A relatively new genetically modified agricultural products. They were partly successful in Europe, such as UK (some countries banned genetically modified products) in spite of the fact that neither history nor research supports their case. People began to modify plants as early as the beginning of the agricultural revolution (8000 to 10,000 years ago), when they started seed selection and who have continued ever since. The green revolution of the 1960 year brought about strains of grans and rice more resistant to a variety of local conditions. The effects have been that countries like India, which had suffered from recurrent famines over the millennia, became self-sufficient in food due to the resultant sharp increase in agricultural productivity. It was a real science and technology over the poverty dominating most of human history. But it is precisely the products of science and technology that ecologists are so deathly afraid of. In an interesting study in a quarter (28%) of clinically analyzed cases of obsessive compulsive disorder were cases resulting from the fear of global warming.

To destroy the modern, whether industrial or postindustrial, civilization, human have to destroy an important engine of economic growth, that is its energy sources. And this is what eco-warriors try to achieve under the banner of against global warming. Thus, UK government will have responsibility to attempt to research new technology to fight global warming challenge for itself farmer benefits and even global benefits both on the future.

Hence, future (AI) robotic development can be applied to environment protection aspect. Future (AI) robotic tools can help human to predict when and how any why environment pollution will occur in which countries and (AI) robotic tools can be one environment protection machine to gather environment pollution information to give opinions to human how we ought need to do in anywhere in order to avoid the places' environment pollution will become serious in influence our health. So, future (AI) robotic machince will be one predictive environmental pollution and bad climate change machine and it can give opinions to avoid serious environment pollution and give solutions to solve environment pollution any country.

(AI) will give global warming technological protection economic influence opinion to human

Some future economists indicated reasons to explain why UK government and businessmen needed to consider how to develop natural environment protection technology to avoid global warming challenge to influence UK economy development. They indicated the anthropogenic (human-made) global warming resulting from the increase in "greenhouse gas". They offered their perspectives on the scientific valid of anthropogenic global warming phenomenon, its probability of occur and expected consequences and is dominated by technologists, economists and political scientists, who considered the need to make the horribly costly adjustments in energy generation and usage suggested by climate alarmists.

Many stress that global warming is primarily caused by other phenomena than human use of fossil fuels or human activities in general. They are looking at the activities of the sun and impact of the larger universe as the main source of global warming and stress that global warmings (plural) happen intermittently with global cooling. I shall explain why global climate warming will influence to the political and economics of the issue to UK country. For it is the latter, rather than the global warming itself, that will pose a challenge to the Western world, such as UK and the world at large in the future. Scientists concerned who should move forward with policy measures to avert the alleged disaster. They also apply manufacturing theories to support enough to frighten politicians into action and scare societies into acceptance of measures that would sharply reduce UK citizen their living standards. Otherwise, UK politicians had support that bureaucracies were established, money allocated and lobbies created dependent on the new kind of subsidies. In consequences, climate alarmism and resultant interventions in national economies and human activities have become the increasingly wide spread and increasingly cost reality. With the growing availability of money distributed, and even more promised, a range of benefit of the global warming machinery has been on the increase. So, if UK government did not concern how to innovate new weather protection technology to avoid climate change adverse (poor) influence. It is possible that billions of dollars of UK public money are needed to spend on research global warming challenge because global warming will influence UK agricultural industry. UK agricultural industry is one important export income source to raise UK GDP income every year. If global warming become very serious to influence UK weather to be bad to cause UK farmers who can not grow good taste food and vegetable to supply to domestic and overseas food consumers to eat. Then, UK will loss much GDP income from local agricultural export sale. It seems global warming and agricultural production which has direct relationship to influence UK economy development in the future.

The main problem with climatology is that it must be based as already stressed on very many variables affecting climate and too few hard data necessity. Differences apply not only with respect to the scale of changes obtained, but even to their direction (rising or declining temperature). Some weather scientists indicated to concern global warming challenge. In consequence, it would be impossible to discover if and where errors were made not only in estimating relationships between variables but also in the quality of data used. (Hauser, J. Tellis, G. J; Griffin, A. 2006) They were comparing average temperatures measured some 30, 40 or 50 years ago by, say, 90 % weather stations in the countryside and 10 % stations in the cities with contemporary average temperatures measured by weather stations located today on 50:50 basis in the countryside and cities. Then, one could obtain the increasing temperatures without any real world climate or even weather changes. Comparability would be ensured if the same number of countryside-located and city-located weather stations had been compared for different periods. The alarmists intentionally mix up " temperature growth" with the trend of temperature growth. To give an example, if in the first decade the temperature grew by 0.5 % degree, in second decade it grew by 0.3 % and in third decade it grew by 0.1%, what was registered was a growth in the temperature, but certainly not a trend of growing temperature. A fourth decade should, on the basis of the trend, bring about no change in the temperature.

To conclude, scientists believed that global warming was caused by human's bad behavior more than natural environment influence. So, it is human's responsibility needs to solve this challenge, due to who feel earning profit aim is more important to protect natural environment, e.g. air and water pollution , due to manufacturing process is the main factor. So, UK has responsibility to attempt to research how to solve global warming challenge , such as it has many famous scientists who can devote their scientific skills to cooperate to solve global warming challenge with other countries' scientists. Some weather scientists also hypothesized that human may be at the end of the present warming period. If they are right, it would be bad for humanity, as warmer periods have always been associated with better conditions for economic activity. To sum up, scientists believed that global warming will influence human economic activity to be bad.

Future (AI) robotic environmental protection machine can give opinions to UK farmers:
Climate alarmists were able to convince a large part of the Western public and a majority of Western politicians of the cause of fighting against the global warming. It supposes itself in an instinctive preference for collectivist

solutions in economic and social spheres, with negative to disastrous consequences when scientists are applied in practice, so UK government needs to concern global warming challenge, due to it is possible that it will influence UK natural environment weather to be poor to influence many UK farmers' agricultural and vegetable and fruit and rice wheat etc. food growth successfully. What is the global warming influence to cause disease? For example, ecological alarmists and activists (eco-warriors) never admit they are wrong, they long pursued their fear mongering campaign against chlorine. Their success in branding DDT a dangerous substance had a negative impact on the malaria eradication campaign in poorer parts of the world. Alternatives to be have been far less effective and the result has been the resurgence of malaria cases and the manifold increase in malaria -caused deaths to the largest extent in Africa.

3 (AI) robotic automation technology in manufacturing industry

Future, (AI) robotic automation technology can be applied to manufacturing industry. For example, nowadays, UK computer and space explore technology had reached the mature stage. It means that UK government ought not need to continue spend much resource to research these two kind technologies. Otherwise, the (AI)robotic automatic manufacturing technology, e.g. human intelligence new product. It has need to develop because human intelligence machines will bring beneficial to satisfy human everyday life need, e.g. hospital patients' activities need, if the patent who can not walk easily, but the human intelligence machine can assist the patient walk to anywhere conveniently. So, he/she does not need to sit on wheel chair and apply the human intelligence machine man to help him/her to drive on the intelligence automatic driving vehicle to go to anywhere conveniently.

Otherwise, increased automation in low wage countries, e.g. China, Korea, Africa, Hong Kong etc. which have traditionally manufacturing firms, could use automatic technological manufacturing to bring lose cost advantage and potentially lose their ability of achieving rapid economy growth by shifting workers to factory jobs. So, UK government and businessmen needs to consider automation technology development, i.e. 3D printing manufacturing industry will encourage UK companies to move manufacturing process, closer to gain the biggest advantage from this 3D automation technology development.

A growing concern of premature de-industrialization in energy and developing countries could require new models and a need un-skillful the UK workforce. In the future, the best way toward for UK cities will reduce their exposure to automation is to boost their technological dynamic and attract more UK skilled workers. Automation technology progress can give UK manufacturers' employee benefits, such as long term healthy productivity improvement, raising productivity efficiency and product quality, macroeconomic and microeconomic effects of automation technological change, it's change will be beneficial to UK society, i.e. automation active labor market policies, which could help UK job seekers find jobs from training to incentive to support self-employment to create high technological job employment chance in UK society. So, raising science, technology, engineering and math subjects update skills level are needed to UK any universities, which can be increasingly important in UK society, these factors could complicate the ability of UK high automation technology education to adopt to the UK automation

manufacturing technological change. A talent mismatch already exists in UK, with many well UK educated workers can find employment in lower-skilled jobs. To combat this, greater coordination will be needed between the education, training and employment sectors in UK society.
Why are high automatic technology product development models needed to research to UK any manufacturers? UK government and manufacturers need to consider how to achieve high technology product development models. According to Hauser et al. (2006) indicated the high technology (high tech.) development process, is influenced by the innovative process, bringing products on exception value which stimulate product market demand. Innovation provides products the specific basis for which world economies compete with each other on the global market. Able to find new solutions, innovations generate significant changes in existing markets, destroy them, or create new marketing (Hauser et al. 2006). So, UK manufacturers need to concern on any manufacturing high technology product development process because which can influence any new products development to manufacture to sell to any overseas or domestic both markets successfully.

What is high tech. product meaning? Mohr et al. (2010) argues that there are two reasons why it is important to clarify and specific high technology : (1) due to the impact of technologies on the economy, attempts are made to classify economic production and incomes ; (2) due to the impact of high tech. on the environment. Standard marketing strategies are being modified and adopted , therefore, it is necessary to know the products to focus on. Why UK manufacturers need to consider high technological product process. Nowadays, high tech. products are complex, advanced, requiring specific technical knowledge, which is technologically not discontinued and being produced at the companies which have twice as many technical personnel and invest twice as many in scientific research and development than other companies. Moreover, these products are time-sensitive as scientists are continuously searching for new approaches for invention of more advanced technologies which make all preceding ones lower-ranking. The most important, nowadays global consumers will adopt the particular technology. It means that global customers may delay adopting new high-tech. products and in order to mitigate the prolonged uncertainty require a high degree of education and information about the product and need post-purchase reassurance.
Anyway, nowadays customer individual needs in high tech. environments are characterized by sudden changes related to unpredictable fashion. Even, consumers concern about how to preserve new product' competitive technological standard is completely incompatible with technological uncertainty. The most important factor is the prevalence rate of any new products development process, which is influenced by slower than of traditional products. In many cases high-tech. automatic product market are being materialized slower than which are expected. The technological uncertainty challenges will exist in development process, such as uncertainty related to the timetable for development of the question whether the new product will be function as promised. In automatic high-tech. industries, the time requires for product development is difficult to predict as , commonly, it takes longer than expected , uncertainty related to unanticipated consequences and uncertainty about the product life cycle

related to competition products. In conclusion, these factors will influence new automatic technology product development process unsuccessful, so UK manufacturers will need to concern on any high technological automatic product's manufacturing process.

Future economists predict automatic technology how to influence future UK economy

Before, all over the world presented picture of demonstrate in London on the occasion of the meeting of the G20. Some economists indicated disastrous economy consequences will occur to any one of Western country , such as UK, so if any one of Western country did not consider automatic technology development to itself country. They indicated one example, such as material incentives to produce disappeared throughout Russia and, when Society leadership called off the experiment, the country faced industrial output reduced to 10% of what had been registered in 1914 and agricultural output reduced to such low levels as to cause widespread famine.

Why would UK encounter disastrous economy consequences if UK government did not encourage manufacturers spend money to invest to innovate automatic technology industry? According to a variety of anthropological studies, a collectivity is unable to operate efficiently with everybody giving talent workers have chance to devote whose best effort to manufacture any high technological products, e.g. human intelligence vehicle or airplane. Hence, economic incentives are needed to UK manufacturers to invest high technological automatic industry development. Because the economists predict UK will have many talent worker numbers, their number will be more than a certain number of normal effort workers, due to UK technological education level is very excellent to provide to train many young technological manufacturing students to find this kind of high technological manufacturing job. So, the high technological manufacturing job seekers will increase and it won't decrease to UK job market in the future.

Assuming that UK high technological automatic manufacturing workers who would desire only to introduce changes in the workings of the international economic order and policies of countries participating in the present economic order rather than change the order itself, what will be UK manufacturers their specific economic preferences in the future? It implies tnat either concentrate on spending more investment to automatic high technological development, e.g. human intelligence automatic high technological products or still concentrate on spending more investment to common traditional technological products.

However, UK was a developed Western country which had had strong automatic high technological development effort very long time. Otherwise, it compared to some developing countries, such as Asian China, Hong Kong, Korea etc. Asian countries their future economic growth rate will show un- surprising , different patterns, so the Asian countries has weak effort to invest high automatic technological product development, such as human intelligence technological development. The catching-up process suggests low economic growth rate in the high automatic technological product development to the Asian developing countries in the future.

Hence, the future economists predict that it views as probable successors of the Western world economic leadership if any Western country , such as UK manufacturers who prefer to invest to any high automatic technological products development , e.g. developing on human intelligence automatic technological products more than traditional common technological products development. On the one side, but it seems important to stress that two very poor countries among the challengers-China and India-are examples of countries that changed their institutions and economic policies from no or little economic freedom to more economic freedom. Because there two countries whose governments prefer to lend loans to encourage their country manufacturers prefer to invest high automatic technological products manufacturing. On the other side, attitudes toward foreign direct investment (FDI) have undergone change since the 1960 s and a large majority of less developed countries, e.g. China and India are now competing strongly among themselves and with developed market economies for direct investment from multinational companies. So, UK will face China and India high automatic technological product competitors in the future. And in fact, all countries that joined Western developed economies did that without much (if any) external inflow of public resources. It is right time that UK government needs to lend loans to encourage domestic manufacturers to invest high automatic technological products to raise whose international high technological products sale effort to win its future competitors. So, machine resources will be increased demand to o UK manufacturers if who chose to spend machine resources to innovate to manufacture any new and high technological automatic products to raise human daily life needs in the future. It means that it is right time UK manufacturers need buy much machines to prepare to manufacture many future high technological automatic products when these machine prices are low. Because the future global machine prices will possible be raised if many China and India manufacturers will also buy many machines in the future. For example, USA government had provided much financial support to assist sugar cane producers to develop their businesses. And they are dependent to a much larger extent than sugar cane producers and sugar processors in the USA on government. Without very high subsidies to renewable energy generation, they would not have survived at all. So, USA government had been the first country which could lent much financial assistance to encourage domestic renewable energy generation manufacturers to develop high technological energy manufacturing business. So, UK government needs follow USA to lend financial assistance to encourage domestic high technological automatic industry development.

Future economists also predict China and India will be competitors for future leadership in the global economy, special high technological products. China has been the media and analyst's favorite for quite some time. Quantitative projections have seemingly supported such expectation. Such as China and India had manufactured many high technological new space rockets products, ocean war large ships etc. Moreover, China has become one of the major world trade players in the early twenty-first century.

Many long-term forecasts, assuming similarly high economic growth rates in the decades ahead, predict that China will surpass the USA in terms of aggregate GDP somewhere between 2020 and 2030 or later, say between 2030 and

2050 year. The future economists conclude on the basis of these predictions that China will not only pass the USA in aggregate product (GDP), but its economy and economic policies will influence the rest of the world to a similar extent that the USA does at present.

I stressed a very important point, namely that the UK future high technological automatic product competitor China and India, namely that economies not only grow, but in the process change their structure. China and India have been industry very rapidly (the first transition) and building the physical infrastructure that accompanies industrialization changes to technology in the future. However, at a certain per capita GNP level the two countries, such as China and India will face another structural shift when which technological development will reach the mature stage in the future. China and India had been primarily historical pattern of economic development because the shift in the role of engine of growth from industry to services is to a much greater extent a qualitative shift. Both higher and different skills are required. And, even more importantly, interactions generating ideas driving the highly human-capital-intensive service economy require a much freer environment, not only in the economic area. Chinese exports have been heavily labor-intensive. This being the case, they contributed to the expansion of industrial employment, offering for the first time in the history of China a taste of (very modest) prosperity to more than 100 million new industrial workers and their families. This is the major component of the success accomplished by Chinese economic growth. Richer trade partners create room for more trade, so the Chinese should hope that intra-South trade, that is, trade between the emerging economies of Asia, the Middle East, Africa and Latin America, will open up new and growing opportunities. I presume that if Western economy , such as UK did not developed high technological automatic industry to stable their social welfare, so thoroughly slowed down their economic growth.

Will it allow China to accomplish the transition to a mature, innovation, service-sector-based market economy? It has allowed the economy to industrialize much more successfully, even if the labor shift from agriculture to industry has not yet been completed. But it is a long way off the next major test: the second high technological industry transition of the economic structure to China. Bear in mind that Russia attempted it twice and failed at both attempts.

But even, assuming that China at some point in the future does succeed in accomplishing the second transition, will it be able to supersede the USA, for example, as the main global high automatic technological innovation center if it wants to become the No.1 global high technological industry economy? Given the nature of the centralized state and its stability to collect financial resources , China's ability to increase research and development expenditure to high automatic technological products and to hire a mass of researchers, engineers, technicians and other specialists should not be doubted. This process in already taking place.

But , again, Soviet Russia already exceed the USA in the R&D/GDP ratio in the 1970s, long before the communist collapse, with no effects on its innovativeness. Inputs matter less than outputs, quantity in the innovation process mean much less than quality. The latter characteristics depends importantly on economic, civic and even political

institutions. Otherwise, independent India had three options open to it in 1946s. It could pursue spontaneous economic development, with some state intervention to be sure, along the lines of basically free market capitalism; it could turn the clock back and try to recreate the rural-agricultural and handicraft based. The dominant way of thinking was Society -style priority to industrialization and , within industralization , priority to heavy industry. In other words, not textiles and clothing, which has been developing well in India since the mid- nine teen century, but production of sewing machines and , even better, production of machines the produce sewing machines.
The results were only to be expected. The heavy stress on the expansion of capital-intensive heavy industries in a very poor country quickly strained the ability of the Indian economy to generate adequate savings. Moreover, some of these industries were above the level of industrial competence of an underdeveloped economy. Thus, the amount of required resources (capital, skilled labor) was usually larger per unit of output than in the same industries in more mature, richer industries economies. In another view point, India will develop light industries, just as any other poor country with a great deal of unskilled labor, had a comparative advantage and no less importantly, an economy in which, due to their low capital/labor ratio, light industries could employ many more people, spreading prosperity more widely in a poor country. So, it explain that why China will have more effort to develop heavy high technological industry in the future. Thus, India got less economic efficiency, less employment than in a spontaneously developing economy, less ability to compete internationally in light industries suitable for an underdeveloped economy and finally got heavy industry unable to compete even on the domestic market and, therefore requiring no less heavy a dose of protection. Overall India got an underperforming economy, in particular in its relations with the rest of the world.

To conclude by comparing the performance of the traditional sectors of the Indian economy and the performance of its modern, human -capital-intensive subsector of manufacturing and skill intensive service sector. The latter both employ workers with high-and medium -high skillful level (in branches ranging from computer software and biotechnology and pharmaceutical high technological light industry). India is ahead of China in terms of the output and export of such products and services. Thus, it implies that UK ought concentrate on developing high automatic heavy high technological industry, e.g. human intelligence technological products because these industry is not better development to other many countries' strong effort , such China and India large population countries.

Consequently, future (AI) robotic technology can be applied to medical service industry, e.g. in hospital and clinic environment to let patients to live in these places to feel more comfortable. It can also be applied to manufacturing industry to assist productivity performance rasing and computer software and biotechnology and pharmaceutical high technological light industry to improve computer technological software development and invention of much new biotechnology and pharmaceutical medicines for human health.

Increase development in genetics, human intelligence, robotics, nanotechnology, 3D printing and biotechnology technological industry

In US future, (AI) robotic tools will assist nanotechnology, 3D printing and biotechnology technological industry development, these kinds of jobs will be needed to increase development in genetics, human intelligence, robotics, nanotechnology, 3D printing and biotechnology. For example, smart systems homes, factories, farms grids or cities will help tackle problems ranging from supply chain management to climate change. The rise of US economy growth will allow US people to monetize everything from their empty house to their car in US. These new technological products development will change US patterns of consumption, production and employment adaption are also be changed by US corporations, US government and individuals.

Why will the technological revolution be broader socio-economic, geopolitical and demographic drivers of change to influence future US social economic and consumption pattern change? Future US most occupations will also be changed. When some traditional old jobs are threatened by redundancy and other new technological jobs will grow rapidly, existing jobs are also changed in the skill sets required to do them. The debate is between some economists foresee limitless new job opportunities and foresee massive dislocation of US jobs. In fact, the reality is highly specific to future US high technological production industry, region and high technological occupation in question as well as how US production workers can be raised themselves ability to actions the upgrade level of high technological production ability from various stakeholders to manage high technological production method change.

Overall, this is a modestly positive outlook of US high technological production employment across future most high technological production industries with jobs growth expected in several sectors. However, it is also clear that this need for more talent in certain job categories is accompanied by high skills instability across all job categories. Combined together, future US net job growth and skills instability result in most US businesses with face major recruitment challenges and talent shortages, a pattern already evident in the result and set to get worse over next five years in possible.

The question is how US businesses, government and individuals will react to these new technological job changes, due to talent shortage, mass unemployment and growing inequality challenges will encounter in future US society.

The current technological revolution does not need become a race between humans and machines , but rather an opportunity for work to truly become a channel through which US people recognize their potential. So, if US traditional low manufacturing skillful workers lack talent to learn new skills to prepare to do future new technological manufacturing jobs, such as 3 D printing, robotics, nanotechnology, biotechnological high technological products manufacturing jobs. Then, it will cause increasing of unemployment rate to some not talent US low manufacturing skillful workers. So, US government or high technological product industry employers need to consider this future unemployment challenge will be caused by high technological products manufacturing changing influences. It seems high technological development will cause these low manufacturing skillful workers

unemployed rising numbers as well as high manufacturing skillful workers human capital shortage global challenges will exist.
In the future, the driver of changes to influence US demographic and socio-economic growth. They may include: changing work environments and flexible working arrangements. It means new technologies are enabling workplace innovations , such as remote working, co-working spaces and teleconferencing. Rising of the middle class in Asia markets. It means the world's economic center is shifting towards the Asia developing countries.

Some economists predict that Asia will be projected to account for 66% of the global middle class and for 59% of middle class consumption by 2030 year. In addition, climate change, natural resource will be constraints to a greener economy. It means that climate change is a major driver of innovation as organizations search for measures to help adjust to its effects. As global economic growth consumers are needed to lead to demand for natural resources and raw materials, over explanation implies higher extraction most and degradation ecosystem and these challenges will also impact US employment changes needs. All US government also needs to concern future global economic change influence. Hence , future (AI) robotic tools will assist these industries‘ technological development and creates more new jobs.

Although (AI) can influnence technological development to bring positive impact to bring beneficial welfare to provide human life. But, I also feel (AI) can bring new military to attack weak effort countries enemy from strong owning (AI) military defense wepon countries. If one day, some owning strong (AI) technological development countries' leaders who applied (AI) technology to manufacture social military defense weapon robots. Then, it will cause the third World war in possible. So, different countries‘ leaders need to consider (AI) invention ethic issue to keep world peace.Nowadays, artificial intelligence (AI) is widely knowledge to be one kind of the dramatic technology. However, it is expected to continue, to have a disruptive impact on human's private and public life, so defense and security will be no exception. But how exactly will these be affected ? How will (AI) defense and security is incremental in nature?

To research why artificial intelligence (AI) has possible to be used to cause autonomous weapons by human. We need to understand these three aspects of relationship. They include cybersecurity and artificial intelligence and machine learning and autonomous weapon systems relationship between of them.Firstly, we need to know what is the mean of artificial intelligence and cyber defense/offense? It means defense of critical networks: real time, pattern finding, anomaly seeking, it must utilize machine (AI) learning algorithms to efficiently, and instantaneously respond to potential network threats as well as it means human on or out of the loop. On the loop : it means anomaly detection: human notified, IT analysis, response. Out of the loop: it means anomaly detection: (AI) decides best method of response: quarantine, honey pot monitoring, hack-back. Thus, it is possible that (AI) can be used , such as autonomous cyber weapon.

What is artificial intelligence and autonomous weapons? Autonomous weapons mean one kind of weapon that can be selected and engaged a target, without intervention by a human operator. Are these machines artificially intelligent? I believe the answer is not, because present weapons systems are not capable of human level reasoning. But, (AI) algorithms are presently employed to process sensor data, monitor system health, take and respond to vocal commands manage data, navigate. This, future autonomous weapons systems will require stronger (AI) to be secure and operationally and cost effective. Moreover, self-aware autonomous cyber systems are crucial.

What is cybersecurity mean? It means the ability to control access to networked systems and the information they contain. It is acted to prevent , detect, recover, react. It is application objects concern people, process, technology and it's application goals are confidentiality, integrity and popular availability. Thus, what is cyber weapon mean? Walware means viruses, Trojans, zero-days, worms ransomware, spyware etc. Does it require a particular objective? E.g. military paramilitary or intelligence. Does it require physical harm? E.g. functional harm or interruption? Mental harm? Is (AI) a technological weapon that it is an object or tool? What about when it is an weapon agent?

In simplicity, (AI) can be one of scientific weapons platform. When one day, it is invented to be applied to control war planes to fly to any countries to attack enemies or it is invented to be seemed to human to replace soldiers to bring guns or any weapons go to other countries to attack. So, it is possible that future any war defense planes, (AI) technological automatic control weapon can be replaced of human soldiers or war plane pilots to control any war defense planes to go to different enemy countries to attack them easily. It is very horror matter to threaten global human's ourselves life in the future , if (AI) automatic control war defense planes or (AI) automatic control machine soldiers were invented successfully.Hence , when (AI) can be applied to weapons platforms, it structures that launch weapons, i.e. jets, ships, vehicles. (AI) platform and weapon and software architecture components are be done one (AI) technological weapons systems. Thus, human will encounter any (AI) benefits or risks (threats) causes in the same time as soon as possible. If we can predict when (AI) weapon system will be manufactured or invented successfully. Then, we can reduce (AI) weapon systems risks , if we can threaten any (AI) scientists continue to invent any undiscovered (AI) weapons in any time to avoid the future first time (AI) weapon war occurrence in possible.

The (AI) weapon system risk means autonomy: the ability to problem solve technological war , when (AI) weapon system is manufactured successfully, the power to act, how to damage the (AI) weapon system. The power to chance to stop (AI) weapon system manufacturing processes, ability to create a new goals, how to change the (AI) weapon system inventors' or scientists' minds to avoid to apply (AI) tools to achieve attack goals to change to another positive goal. Due to human can't know a prior what an autonomous (AI) weapon system will do.Although, human is known what (AI) is , but human is also known when (AI) scientists whose emergent behaviors will do to change to do any negative behaviors from positive behaviors. Whatever (AI) weapon system design we use, there will be cybersecurity, problems arising from computation design/complexity. Due to any one (AI) scientist can manipulate the system to act against itself, or who can utilize traditional " cyber weapons" against the (AI) weapon system, or who can manipulate the system to lie to humans, but also due to complexity, there is no way to know if it is lying or not or bounded rationality : satisficing.Finally, the most serious (AI) technological invention risks are human is unknown these aspects of (AI) absolutely: They are not simple automatic systems, learning reasoning, communication of " self-aware" systems. Thus, human will face (AI) technological invention risks or threats. We need to find any methods to avoid (AI) weapon system is manufactured successfully to avoid (AI) technological war can occur in future anyone day.

Why (AI) system can be invented to damage our society ? IS it possible to achieve this (AI) damage system successfully? ON (AI) attribution hand, it can be applied to cars, aircraft, which are subject to regulation designed to protect the public from harm and ensure fairness in economic competition. Thus, (AI) safety issue is important to scientists to consider. IN general, the approach to regulation of (AI)-enabled products protect public safety issue should be informed by assessment of the aspects of risk that the addition of (AI) way reduce any respects of risk that it may increase. Also, where regulatory responses to the addition of (AI) threaten to increase the cost of compliance, or slow the development or adoption of beneficial innovations, policymakers should consider how those responses could be adjusted to lower costs and barriers to innovation without adversely impacting safety or market fairness.

For example, regulatory challenges that (AI) enabled present are found in the cases of automated vehicles. (AI)s, such as self-driving cars and (AI)-equipped unmanned aircraft systems. IN the long run, self-driving cars will likely save many lives by reducing driver error and increasing personal mobility, it will offer many economic benefits. Thus, public safety must be protected as these technologies are tested and begin to mature. Creating safe spaces and test beds for experimentation , and working with industry and civil society to evolve performance based regulations that will enable more uses as evidence of safe operation accumulates. Thus, it implies that any scientists can also invent (AI) system to control weapon defense planes or (AI) automatic machine human to do any soldier's behaviors to attack to any countries easily, instead of none driver automatic control vehicle invention. Thus, (AI) system can be applied to harm to human or achieve to damage our society aim by ourselves in possible.

The rapid growth of (AI) has dramatically increased the need for people with relevant skills to support and advance the field. AN (AI) –enables would demand a data literate citizenry that is able to read, use, interpret and communicate about data and participate in policy debates about matters affected by (AI). Thus, if (AI) technology is applied to assist human's social development and raising life enjoyment or benefits. It will bring positive impact to influence human's future life. Otherwise, if (AI) technology is unsafe to be applied to threaten human's society. It will bring negative impact to influence human's future life. Thus, (AI) scientists need to consider how to apply (AI) technology.As (AI) technologies move toward deployment, technical expects, policy analysts and ethicists have raised concerns about unintended, consequences of adoption. Use one (AI) to make consequential decisions about people, often replacing decisions made by human –driven bureaucratic processes, leads to concerns about how to ensure justice, fairness, and accountability, the same concerns of human's safety issue. Thus,)AI) expects have cautioned that there are challenges in trying to understand and predict the behaviors of advanced (AI) systems. Use of (AI) to control physical-world equipment leads to concerns about safety, especially as systems are exposed to the full complexity of human environment. A major challenge in (AI) safety is building systems that can safety transition from the closed world of the laboratory into the outside open world, when unpredictable things can happen. Adapting to unforeseen situations are difficult necessary for safe operation. Experience in building other types of safety artificial systems and, such as aircraft, power plants, bridges and vehicles has much to teach (AI) practitioners about verification and validation, how to build a safety case for a technology, how to manage risks, and how to communicate with stakeholders about risk. The risk means the harm of human's safety of (AI) damage system control machine invention. Thus, any (AI) scientists need consider moral responsibility when who decide to invent what kind of (AI) system machine to aim to bring human's benefits or attribute to human's welfare intention.Thus, (AI) products safe invention matter will need any scientists' considerations. Because , if (AI) any products are unsafe or harm human's invention in the manufacturing process, it will bring any human's life danger when the (AI) system damage tools are invented successfully and are provided weapons to humans to use to attack other countries easily. It will cause future global human (AI) technological war occurrence.

I shall recommend the solution is necessary of ethical training for (AI) practitioners and students. Ideally, every student learning (AI) , computer science, or data science would be exposed to curriculum and discussion on related ethics and security topics. However, ethics alone is not sufficient. Ethics can help practitioners understand their responsibilities to all stakeholders, but ethical training should be methods for deciding good intentions into practice by doing the technical work needed to prevent unacceptable or immoral (AI) invention outcomes.Hence, global human needs to concern (AI) weapon system invention security issue. Nowadays, (AI) has important application is increasing role for both defensive and offensive cyber measures. Currently, designing and operating secure systems requires significant time and attention from experts.

Challenges issues are raised by the potential use of (AI) in weapon systems. The United States has incorporated autonomy in certain weapon systems for decades, allowing for greater precision in the use of weapons and safer, more humane military operations. Nonetheless, direct human control of weapon systems involves some risks and can raise legal and ethical questions concern (AI) manufacturing process intention.

The key to incorporating autonomous and semi-autonomous weapon system into American defense planning is to ensure that U.S. Government entities are always acting in accordance with international humanitarian law, taking appropriate steps to control , to develop standards related to the development and use of such weapon systems. The United States has activity participated in ongoing international discussion on Lethal autonomous weapon systems and anticipates continued robust international discussion of those potential weapons systems. Thus, (AI) scientists have responsibilities to manage the potential to be a major driver of economic growth and social progress only, their (AI) intentions are not the global dominance aims absolutely, if (AI) product industry , civil society, government and the public work together to support (AI) positive development of the technology with thoughtful attention to its potential and to managing its invention threat risks to avoid (AI) products to manufacture to be used weapon tools.

Finally, I recommend that as the technology of (AI) continues to develop, practitioners must ensure that (AI) enables systems are governable, that what their inventions need to be openness to let public to know clearly and understandable; that they can work effectively with people and that their operation will remain consistent with human values and aspirations. Researchers and practitioners have increased their attention to these challenges , and should continue to focus on their future any (AI) inventions.

Hence, (AI) safe system ought to be applied to solve the biggest challenges that society faces, such as mobility for the elderly and those with disabilities, smart buildings may save energy and reduce carbon emissions, precision medicine may extend life and increase quality of life, smarter government may solve citizens more quickly and precisely., better protect those at any immoral invention risk and save money.Moreover, (AI) enhanced education may help teachers give every child on education that opens doors to a secure and fulfilling life. Thus, these are the future human's potential benefits if the (AI) technology is developed to its benefits and scientists ought avoid to manufacture (AI) tools to cause weapon risks and challenges.

Consequently, the main point is that how experts invent (AI) systems. (AI) systems ought not be advanced weapon systems, it doesn't seem to be thought similar human soldiers mind and behaviors. (AI) system ought be systems that think like humans. (e.g. cognitive architectures and neural networks), systems that act like humans (e.g. pass the test via natural language process, knowledge representation, automated reasoning, and learning), systems that think rationally , e.g. logic solvers, inference and optimization and systems that act rationally e.g. intelligence software agents and embodies robots that achieve goals via perception, planning reasoning, learning , communicating, decision-making and acting function.In conclusion, it is horror (AI) scientists will invent (AI) systems to be owned human's (soldier's) mind and attack strategic behavior to attack other countries easily, who must need to consider (AI) system ought be invented to own scientists' creating mind and non manual assistance functions for positive attribution to human's society. I expect that (AI) system can only be invented to create human's welfare in our future.

In the future, how human can avoid (AI) technological ethical, social and economic negative impact. Scientists need to concern these questions: how to develop of a good (AI) society, how the role and responsibility of the government, the private sector, and the reserch community(including education), in pursuing such a development, whether how the recommendation to support , such a (AI) system development may be in need of improvement. However, none appers to deliver a comprehensive explicit vision of the role that (AI) system should play in mature information societies. Thus, (AI) 's potential contribution to social good shoud include an in-depth plan for linking in a comprehensive socio-political design questions of responsibility of the different stakeholders, of cooperation between them and of sharable values to understand of a good (AI) positive impact society, not a bad (AI) negative impact society.Thus, the notion of mature information societies is introduced to stree the importance of addressing the current ethical challenges that (AI) poses in a comprehensive fashion.

It seems (AI) wil invention will be human's moral societal consideration issue. It concerns our (AI) scientists' moral issue, how who invent (AI) system to apply to which kind aspects. IF (AI) system was one direction on war weapon tools to similar to soldier's personal mind or attacking behavior. Then, it will bring poor social safety and poor economy growth our world, due to (AI) scientists' moral is low level.
Thus, the developed country US (AI) technological leader needs to focuse on the impacts of (AI)-driven customatin on the US job market and economy. It represents three specific policy responses to the perceived impact of (AI) on the US economy. They include these three aspects such as: How to invest in and develop (AI) for its many benefits, how to educate and train Americans for the jobs of the future and how to aid workers in the transition and empower workers to ensure broadly shared growth.The future of (AI) influenced cyber conflicts need more than just the application of current and past solutions in order to ensure security and stability of societies, and avoid risks of escalation. To achieve this end, efforts to regulate cyber conflicts require an in-depth understanding of this new phenomenon, identify the changes brought about by cyber conflicts and the information revoluation, and defines a set of shared values that will guide the stakeholders operating to avoid the international (AI) war occurrence. This becomes clear when considering for example, cyber deterrence. Deploying conventional (cold war) strategies to deter (AI)-influenced cyber conflicts proves highly problematic and the urgent need to foster and coordinate new solutions able to account for the any kinds of conflicts of the cyber demain and of mature information societies to avoid (AI) technological war occurrence in the future.We hope that in the on-going international conversations and reviews, the US government with further specify how " (AI) system invention law" fit into their vision of the future of society in this case the future of (AI) technological war and conflicts. Hence, (AI) scientists need to concern ethical issues related to (AI), like fairness, accountability and social justice can be addressed through increasing needs. Such as: how the creation of a new body focused on robotics and related (AI) system development to avoid to intent to apply weapon tools to provide advice on the policy, legl and consumer protection issues arising in these fields should be considered.

How to achieve ethical training of (AI) staff and ethical education of the public is certainly important responsibility for (AI) tools ethical behavior and design to the private sector and the citizens : of unique challenges that (AI) brings to society in terms in fairness, social equity and accountability are addresses. Thus, the development of the (AI) technology and defining good (AI) remains problematic. In particular, the US government's innovation driven approach to defining the potential, positive impact of (AI) shows that more could be done to ensure that the opportunities and advantages brought about by (AI) are shared by all society.

An initial on Robotics, based upon the ethical framework and guiding principles is proposed. It should be complementary to legislaton and comprise ethical codes of conduct for Robotics researchers and designers, codes for research ethics committees as well as licenses (rights and duties) for designers and users. Thus, (AI) robotics invention of safety issues is very important considertion to any (AI) inventions or researchers. Every country's government ought have legal guiding to control their robotics' manufacturing intention. If their robotics (AI) is applied to seem to be soldiers to attack other countries to threaten their people's safety. Then, those (AI) inventors or researchers need to be punished by law.

In conclusion, I believe (AI) technology will be applied to weapon, when it's technological development is nearly mature to able to learn human's mind to do any behavior. During (AI) technology reachs thie mature stage, I predict the (AI) weapon tool , e.g. (AI) soldiers will have chance to be caused. This (AI) invention mature stage has these characteristics such as:When (AI) invetion reachs this mature stage, computers and robots will develop conscious, intelligent, personified minds. Further, information technology devices and (AI) systems will be implanted into humans, enhancing, psychological and behavioral abilities and allowing for direct communication with artificial intelligent minds. There will be both artificial intelligence (AI) and intelligence amplification (AI) in the relatively near future stage.

During the (AI) invention reachs this mature stage, these will be an ongoing mulit-faceted integration of information technologies and human life. Humans and information technology will cooperate. Humans will increasingly immerse their lives and minds in (AI) systems of technological intelligence and virtual reality. The distinction between humanity and technology will increasingly close dependence.
During the (AI) invention mature stage reachs that the environment will be infused with information technology, becoming animated, communicative and more intelligent. The destinction between the artificial and the natural will increasing close dependence.
During the (AI) invention mature stage will expand through virtual reality, simulated and virtual reality will increasingly into normal reality, e.g. the (AI) weapons is virtual reality to seem to be soldier weapon.Finally, during the (AI) invention mature stage is as the global expression of the evolving human-technology integration a " world brain" and " world mind" will emerge on the earth. This psychophysical (AI) weapon system will enhance and enrich the capacities of both individual and collective cogniton. This (AI) weapon system is a potential starting point toward the evolution of a cosmic brain and cosmic mind.Thus, it is possible that the workship raw data was a

unique way in which (AI) could be weaponized to cause war, during the (AI) invention stage reachs the invention mature stage. However, (AI) weapon manufacturing factory will be built possibly. In the future, how will we defins and locate (AI) weapon factories. Especially, as these factories are no longer solely buildings , but a mil of virtual and substantially different facilities, particularly as it shifts from a physical assemly and development model to a distributed and flexible network. Needing minimal raw materials to develop (AI) weapons, the phsysical location of their (AI) factories could be anywhere and their identification from the outside, nearly impossible. Given the expanding uses for intelligent and super-intelligent (AI). How will we tell the different form a location that is manufacturing (AI) for the creation of weapons versus creating (AI) for an innovative new gaming platform?

In conclusion, human needs to consider every (AI) scientist's personal ethical or moral mind and research intention and (AI) system invention of (AI) weapon factories cause. During (AI) invention reachs the mature stage if human expects to avoid (AI) technological war occurrence in future one day. The technological development on autonomous military robots, ideally among relevant social groups and actors including human-rights, activists, researchers developers, engineers, philosophers, policy-makers, military authorities, lawyers, journalists and the publis need to consider when human has effort to invent autonomous military robots successfully in the future one day. Finally, some ambitious countries or dominant global countries must like to apply (AI) autonomous military robots to be machine soldiers more than human soldiers if (AI) technology had reached the mature stage. So, future (AI) autonomous military robots will be the next choice of weapon to follow nuclear weapon. If civilians were used as a human (AI) soldiers, the weapon simply ignored them and targeted anyway. This scenario highlighted the dangers of proliferation and quick replication of autonomous weapons. Unlike nuclear weapon, a piece of code for (AI) artificial intelligent soldier could be obtained on the black market and replicated at little cost and the hardware for this type of weapon doesn't require costly or hard to obtain components and materials. Thus, (AI) artificial intelligent soldiers can be manufactured many at cheaper cost. Otherwise, manufacturing one nuclear bomb weapon will spend too much cost. Hence , it is possible that (AI) artificial intelligent soldier will be future new technological weapon to follow nuclear bomb weapon. Hence, any country government needs to legislate to control any (AI) scientists' inventions whether they are attributed benefits or welfares to human or damage human's safety.

Why China's computer manufacturing and product development industry will be global leader to compete US computer dominant market. The reason is because that China will have possible to dominate global computer industry development if it can invent new (AI) learning tool to assist global computer systems to raise more efficient performance effort. Nowadays, China's computer industry is the largetest hardware producer production and experts is dominated by Taiwanese firms. It is also the second largest personal computer (pc) market and domestic pc companies are top three sellers in global computer manufacturing and product development market. Forx example, Lenovo buys BM pc business in 2004 year. It implies US, IBM pc manufacturing leader can not dominate global computer market in possible in the future. Reed Electronic Research, Yearbook Of World Electronic Data (2003) indicated that the leading computer producing countries of hardware production in US

$millions and share share of total gogal production: The world region US was the global rank number one. In 1995 year, US had US $76,284 value, market value 26.5%. Then in 2000 year, US had increased up to US $ 90, 430 value, market share 24%. Till to 2003 year, US had fallen down to US $ 69,102 value, market share 21.7%. However, US hardware production was still the global rank number one , although its hardware production value had been falling down.

But, the following second rank country, Japan and the third rank country, Singapore and the fourth rank country, Taiwan and the fifth rank county China which hardware production value could not exceed US till to 2003 year. However, although China had the lowest hardware production value US $5,600 to compare to among of these countries in 1995 year, but China had increased the value to US $65,000 and market share to 20.5%. Otherwise, Japan, Singapore and Taiwan value and market share had surprisingly fallen down below than China value in 2003 year. Thus, it seemed that China will be a potential country to compete US hardware production industry after 2003 year.Reed Electronic Research, Year book Of World Electronic Data (2003) also showed that these computer companies of China had these % of market share : Beijing Founder had 9.9%, Tsinghua Tongtang had 7.8%, dell had 7.2 % , IBM had 5.1% , HP had 4.8% of market share. Thus, it also seemed that China some computer companies will have impotant large market share percentage in global pc sale market. In the future, global hardware production and pc sale industry. China and Taiwan both countries will be one pc manufacturing and design and sale partner. The reason is that China and Taiwan had been the number one rank of markers of notebook pcs, motherboards, scanners, keyboards, add-on card optical drives, monitors and some network equipment etc. pc (personal computer) relative computer function products. It seems that these both countries had co-operated to research any computer relative products to sell to global computer market.

They are also the original design manufacturers (DDMS) develop and manufacture over half the world's notebook pcs as well as their customers include all major branded pc vendors (OEMS). Taiwan Minstry Of Economic Affairs (2003) indicated Taiwan's top notebook ODMS include: In 2003 year volume (thousands) Quanta had $8,500 sale volume thousands , for example, Quanta major OEM partners include Gateway, Dell, HP, IBM, Apple , Sharp, Sony, Fujitsu-Siemens (F/S). Compal had $6,000 sale volume (thousands) , Compal major OEM partners include Dell, HP, F/S, Toshiba, Acer. Thus, it also implied Taiwan had many small size and non famous brand of computer companies which choose to co-operate to be partners with some global large size and famous brand of computer companies to raise competitive effort in global computer markct, such as Dell, IBM, HP, Gatway, Apple etc. Thus, the future trend of computer new product manufacturing development will shift from US to Taiwan and SE Asia, then to China. However, what kind of knowledge work factors will be needed to China and Taiwan . In general, notebook manufacturing stages will include: The first process is design stage, it includes concept design, such as analyze need, create concept and set brand image as well as product planning, such as business case, specifications, industrial design and sourcing strategy. The second process is development stage, it includes design review steps, such as design review, such as mock-ups, electrical test as well as prototype build, such as commercial samples, integrated system test as well as pilot production, such as production process design, pilot. Final process is production stage, it includes mass production, such as ramp-up, volume production, production testing and global distribution as well as sustaining support, such as speed bump, component replacement, technical support and warranty support.

Thus, I believe that China and Taiwan must own thee knowledge work skillful of computer design and development professionals who can assist these two countries how to innovate their future computer development to change global traditional computer model to be renew and innovate computer model in the future. Due to computer industry's stages of development and manufacturing are closely linked , need manufacturability , testing of sample products, concept design and product planning stay together in lead markets and branded vendors, design and development can be separated organizationally and geographically. Thus, China and Taiwan choose to co-operate to exchange their different skill, such as either China has own more concept design and product planning skill or more development skill or more production skill. Then, China will choose either one of the most beneficial comparative advantage among of them. To bring this one of the most beneficial co-operative advantage to attract Taiwan to choose either one of the beneficial comparative advantage of skill, such as either design or development or producton to already co-operate to compete the Western developed country US together. Thus, US won't be the global computer industry development leader if both US country famous and large employee number computer companies, such as IBM and Apple which choose to outsource their pc design and development and production skill to China and Taiwan both countries to help them to develop global computer design and development and production skill to be upgraded. Thus, I feel these both countries will plan how to co-operate to compete US to win the global computer industry leader position in the future. When China invented its (AI) learning system success. Why does it influence global computer industry market change? For example, in the future, instead of global computer manufacters need to consider the design, development and production processes, who also need to consider what factors can influence consumers' laptop purchases. Because any consumers have much different computer model and brand to choose to make final decision to buy any computers. If the computer manufacturer can predict what factors will be whose weakness(es) to influence global computer consumers to change whose mind or attitude to choose to buy other brands of computers, then it won't lose its many old computer customer numbers and reduces it market share in global computer market share.

Nowadays, in general computer has three kinds to provide to global consumers to choose to buy , such as laptop, notebook computers, desktops. it seems that laptop and notebook computers and desktops will have different factors to influence any consumers to choose to buy any brand of computer products. Thus, computer indsutry can divide three consumer groups, such as (stayers, satisfied switchers and dissatisfied switchers) of a computer company with respect to the factors influencing consumers' laptops or notebook computers or desktops purchases. However, I feel the factors can include such as core technicl features, post purchase services, prices and payment conditions, peripheral specification, physical appearance, value added features and connectivity and mobility seven main factors that are influencing consumers' laptop or notebook computer or desktop purchases in global computer industry market.

Ganesh et al., (2000) indicates the customer base of a company consists of three groups of consumers: stayers, satisfied switchers and dissatisfied switchers. Therefore, the consumers in this study replied to the question about whether the current brand that who were using was their first laptop brand or whether who had switched from a previous laptop brand. As a following question, consumers who had switched were asked to state the reason of why who switched from a previous laptop brand brand to their current brand. The options include overall dissatisfaction from the previous laptop brand and reasons other than dissatisfaction. Thus, computer companies need to know what factors influence either whose prior computer customers why who don't choose repeat to buy its any computer products or whose new potential computer customers why who don't choose to buy its any computer products in the first time choice.

Thus, future computer manufacturers need to consider intangible salespeople service attitude or performance, such as salespeople current purchase and post purchase service, e.g. technical repair, model function explanation how to use the computer, instead of tangible product performance, e.g. computer appearance design , function , mobility and internet and document download speed connectivity function. Because salespeople and technicians‘ service performance can be represented to the computer image. If they can provide excellent service to let computer buyers to feel satisfactory, then they can help their computer company employer to build good image. So, staff service performance will be one important factor to influence computer consumers to make the final decision to choose to buy the brand of computer products more easily. Even, one famous brand computer company, such as IBM, Apple, Gateway, these any one of famous brand computer company must not attract any new (the first time) or repeat computer buyers to choose to buy their any kind of computer products , such as laptop, desktop or notebook more easily due to their famous brand. Althoug, these famous computer companies had built good image to let consumers have more confidence to buy any kind of their computer products.

But, if these famous computer companies' salepeople or repair technicians can not provide excellent customer service or performance to satisfy their computer buyers‘ service need, e.g. explaining how to use the new computer, repair post purchase service etc. I believe these famous brands of computer consumers will not have more desire to prefer to chose to buy any one of these famous computer brand's products. Otherwise, if the other less famous computer companies' any kind of laptop, desktop or notebook sale price is higher than the famous brand of computer companies‘ products sale price, but their salepeople or technicians can provide more excellent service attitude or performance to satisfy their consumers' needs. It is possible that the new or first time computer buyers or repeat computer buyers will still choose to buy their computers. So, the famous or less famous computer brand is not one important factor to influence the computer buyer to decide either to buy the computer or not buy the computer. Otherwise, computer company's salepeople and repair technician whose service performance or attitude will be one important intangible factors to influence any first time (new) or repeat computer consumers to choose to buy any famous or less famous brand of computer company's product, instead of the tangible computer design appearance and reliable function and convenient mobility and long term durability etc. factors influences. Thus, China has possible to influence global office and home computer comsumers to choose to buy its any brands of computers to use if it can invent (AI) learning systems to assist global computers to raise their performance efficiency. So, it will influence global computer consumers to choose its country's any brands of computers to buy to use, due to themselves new (AI) learning computers can help office and home computer users to raise efficiency and provide the excellent productive performance to them more than the traditional computers. When China's (AI) computer learning system has developed in success. Then, it will possible to influence global consumers' traditional computer applying culture to change to new innovation (AI) learning computer applying culture. It means that China will dominate global computer consumer choice to be trended to choose to buy China's any computer brands' produducts , due to it 's (AI) technology can be invented to apply to traditional computers in order to raise their efficiency and reduce office staffs' workload and provide excellent performance to serve office or home (AI) learning computer users.

Durmza and Zengin, (2011:53) indicted marketers closely interested in this issue to know the family which changed and renewed in course in time. It provides an advantage for a marketer to know the family structure and its consumption characteristics. Nowadays, consumer behavior is influenced not only by consumer personalities and motivation, but also by the relationships within families. Family is a social group and it can be considered a crucial place in th perception of marketing (Durmaz, Yakup, CELLK, Mucahit and ORUC, Reyhan, (2011).

The consumer buying behaviors examined through an empirical study. Then, it brings this question: Whether cultural factors will influnece the computer consumer choice. Choice and include computer brand choice, computer price choice, computer model choice, computer design choice, laptop or desktop or notebook product choice, new or second-hand old computer choice, the computer of manufacturing country choice, computer package choice etc. So, any consumer will consider to choose any one of these to decide to buy which kind of computer. Every country computer consumers had different culture to influence their computer shopping choice. I feel culture can be explained how to influence to computer shopping such as: How do the country computer consumers buy and use their computer products habitually ? How do the country computer consumers react to th computer price changes, attractive advertising methods to satisfy whose needs and computer company store interiors? What underlying mechanisms operate to produce any one of the country computer consumers' responses? If computer marketers have answers to such these questions, who can make better managerial decisions how to adopt which computer target country (countries) consumers' culture.

Consumer behavior deals with many other issues, for instance (Priest, Carter and Statt, 2013: 19). How do we get information about products? How do we assess alternative products? How do different people choose or use different products? How do we decide on value for money ? How much risk do we take with what products? Who influences our buying decisions and our use of the product? How are brand loyalties formed and changed? For computer industry, it means that how computer consumers get information about computer products, how computer consumers assess alternative notebook, desktop, laptop computer products, how different age, country, culture, sex, student or working people or retired people computer consumers choose or use different kind of computer products, such as notebook, desktop, laptop computer products, how much risk computer consumers take with notebook, desktop, laptop computer products, the computer consumers' buying decisons and their use of the desktop or notebook or laptop computer products will be influenced by whom, e.g. family, friends, teacher, employer, computer salepeople, advertisement marketer etc. , computer company brands how are formed and changed by whom, e.g. computer consumers, computer company competitors, marketers, different countries' culture etc.

Durmaz and Jablonski, (2012:56) also explained culture is the essential character of a society that distinguishes it from other cultural groups. The underlying elements of every culture are the values, language, myths, customs, laws and the artifacts or products that are transmitted from one generation to the next (Lamb, Hair and Deniel, 2011: 371). Culture is the most fundamental determinant of a person's wants and behavior. Whereas, lower creatives are governed by instinct, human behavior is largely learned. The child growing up in a society leans a basic set of values, perceptions, preferences and behaviors through a process of socialization involving the family and other social roles. So, I feel different country have different culture to influence as well as different country computer consumers who have different computer purchase and consume habitually. So, computer manufacturers ought focus on manufacturing the unique need and characteristics to satisfy any country's consumers' needs.

What is my idea about future global computer competition and factors influence computer consumer behavior ? In conclusion, future computer industry development will trend that computer manufacturers need to consider every country's computer comsumer culture. Because every country computer consumers who will have different computer consumption habitually if who can predict what the country most computer consumers culture, then they can have more confidence to sell their computers to different country markets. Moreover, US computer manufacturers need to consider China and Taiwan computer manufacturing technology because it is possible that these both countries will be its main competitor among different computer manufacuring countries. Because thess both countries will cooperate to research new model of different computers to attract global computer consumers to choose to buy their new model of computer products in the future. Finally, computer manufacturers need to consider salepspeople and repair technicians service performance because computer consumers will consider intangible service performance , instead of tangible computer quality and price and style etc. factors . The main reason is that any computer have chance to be needed to repair and salespeople' skill will influence the computer consumer to make final decision to choose to buy the brand of computer. Thus, these factors will influence global computer development and trend in the future.

Robots eliminate dangerous jobs for humans because they are capable of working in hazardous environments. They can handle lifting heavy loads, toxic substances and repetitive tasks. This has helped companies to prevent many accidents, also saving time and money.

They increase productivity: Robots are wired to perform repetitive tasks ad infinitum; the human brain is not. Industries use robots to accomplish the tedious, redundant work, freeing employees to tackle more challenging tasks and even learn new skills. Everyday robots have already found a place in homes. Also referred to as domestic robots, they are generally used to help with chores. They deliver easy cleaning solutions for the average household. Examples of robots in daily life include social family robots, cleaning robots, and cooking aids

The goal of most robotics is to design machines that can help and assist humans. Many robots are built to do jobs that are hazardous to people, such as finding survivors in unstable ruins, and exploring space, mines and shipwrecks.So, it seems that robots help human to reduce time to work, reduce cost. Finally, robots have the potential to improve our standard of living. They may be able to improve healthcare, make transportation more efficient, and give us more freedom to pursue creative endeavors in addition to shouldering the burden of physically demanding or repetitive tasks.

Robots have the potential to revolutionize our lives in the near future by performing tasks that are dangerous, repetitive, or time-consuming. They can enhance efficiency, productivity, and accuracy in various industries, such as manufacturing, healthcare, and agriculture. HRI boosts productivity, quality of life, teamwork, and self-awareness. Safety, ethics, employment displacement, and social and cultural acceptance are issues. As robots grow more advanced and affordable, they will be used in more applications, enabling new human-robot collaboration opportunities. For example, AI-enabled robots greet customers in stores and provide them with personalized information and directions. They harvest ripe vegetables in farm fields and serve made-to-order lattes in coffee shops. In industrial settings, AI-enabled robots keep workers safe by operating in shared spaces.

Fosters Logical Thinking and Problem Solving. Educational robotics involves young learners in creating, programming, setting up, and controlling robots. This activity requires the use of logical thinking and problem-solving skills, in other words, the development of computational thinking.

Assistive robots for people with disabilities

Exoskeletons to aid walking and rehabilitation processes. Also known as robot suits or motorised armours, they adapt to the body's movements through intelligent algorithms. ...

Bionic limbs or prosthetics. ...

Devices for visual and hearing impairment. ...

Autonomous vehicles.

As programmed, robots are able to complete tasks quicker and in a more precise manner than humans. As industrial robots are less likely to get exhausted over periods of time, this can speed up manufacturing on the production line by being able to work for longer and create shorter cycle times, as a result.

I assume that technology and human behavior which have close relationship (e.g. working behavior , living behavior), For robot case example, if robots can influence human behavioral change, and future human working environment will need to cooperate with robots or human living environment will depend on robots' helping. How human behavior will be influenced to change in order to adapt to accept robots invention when human needs to live or work with robots together in the same time.

In organizational working environment, staffs will need to accept digital, data and robot technology in our industries or implementing a business strategy , why organizations need to be made decision making by robots. However, staffs have possible to depend on robots to help them to make decision, e.g. staffs behavior on analysis or judgement which can be controlled or managed by robots in possible. CEO, or manager leaders , their managing ability will be supervised or managed by robots in any organizations . So, it seems that robots may be any organizational top leader, if they can manage CEO or manager or supervisor in any organizations.

Business organizational leader individual managing behavior must be controlled by robots. Robots (supervised learning) is the most popular type of machine learning and robots can learn any new kinds of knowledge to compare human easily and rapidly. So, any organizational business decision or strategy decision may be made or influenced by supervising robots in organizations in possible. CEO, manager, supervisor their managing ability or managing skill may be influenced to reduce by supervising learning supervising or leading robots cooperation.

However, we can follow these aspects to explain how robots may influence our behavior change. Robots may be applied to participate in sales and marketing , HR, finance, customer service, education, legal and government organizations. Robots will be superintelligence to impact human lives in due time, In future, robots has insight , such as perceives, learns, understands, comprehends. It is one deep learning machines. It can make right or wrong , true or wrong judgement or answer and make good or bad predictions.

Hence, if robots can be applied to work in our future societies in popular, they may be social leader to replace human leader, e.g. government leader, organizational leader, CEO, manager, supervisor. Robots can not only human's worker role, e.g. home servants, shopping center cleaner, kitchen cooker. If robots can be organizational leaders, they may supervise worker individual working attitude or working performance whether his/her performance is satisfactory or perfect or to be needed to improve.

In organization, robots won't be only workers role. They may be supervisor role to supervise, manage or dominate or control all organizational top, middle , low level staffs their behavior and make judgement whether whom staffs can either stay to work or leave the organization.

However, some behavioral economists feel robots are Unfair to make judgement on staff individual working behavior. But on behavioral economic view, robots may help business owners to make judgement whether whom staffs ought stay the firm to work or leave the firm. They can help the organization to bring long term economic benefit. Hence, robots may be right to be future any organizational leader, such as CEO, manager, supervisor role more than worker role. If robots can be supervisor role in any organizations, I believe that they can help the organizations to bring much long term economic benefits to compare human CEO, manager, or supervisor for future global business economic development environment because robots may help any organizations to improve efficiency , or raise productivity to compare human staff decision making abilities.

Ought robots be leader role? In any organizations robots can bring this economic benefits to customer service aspect. For example, in order to reduce mind-numbing repetition for human workers, some economists recommend that future organizations seriously consider use of robots to field calls and process requests at a basic level. Such robots could be used to authenticate users for basic access to the organization in order for staffs to obtain the least risky information that they need. As customer need rise is complexity and business risk failure to satisfy that customer's need and to cause the customer chooses to buy another product or use another service. The work of ticket creation and case routing can be enhanced by robots, but a human should oversee it according to business risk assessment.

Hence, robot analytics can help to any organizations to predict those cases most likely headed for escalation in real time, all the date of the chatbot need to be presented to the human , so that the poor, annoyed customer does not have to start all over again with self-identification and description of the problem.

So, future robots can be perfect customer service leader, they can help satisfy your customers and retain them. Robots can know whether what the customer's real need , how to let the customer feels satisfactory more compare human customer service staffs. They can be customer service leader, service recommendation professionals. They can help organizations to retain old customers , even increase new customers easily to compare human customer service staffs. Hence, robots ought participate to marketing, customer service teams to help staffs how to do right customer service decision with human customer service staffs together. Hence, customer service staffs need to follow up customer service robots' ideas how to help them to solve any customer complain or enquiry in order to improve customer service performance. Consequently, the organization will increase new customer number and retain old customers easily if robots can be applied to participate on marketing, customer service departments.

How be robots in business? They may include three main areas: More intelligence products, services and business process. The first perspective is external. AI enhanced product and service means what you need to deliver to your customers. Both product and service -based business, which means they're all about making customers' lives easier, understanding and anticipating their needs, and solving their problems.

The second perspective is internal, making business processes more intelligent means looking at your business from the inside, assessing every aspect of your operations. To see how to make the business more efficient and enhance from manufacturing to the supply chain.

The third perspective is creating more intelligent products. How robots influence human living behavior? The internet of things means a whole host of everyday products are getting smart. Smart devices like smart phones, smart TV, smart watches on the market, smart office buildings, smart houses, they can influence staffs work or households live whom feel more comfortable.

On AI products aspect,. Intelligent smart running shoes products are like a fitness tracker, but provide more specialist information for runners. A smart AI chip that and how monitors movement (including gait and how feet strike the ground), the shoes provide feed- that helps runners improve their form and reduce the risk of injury. SO, AI smart shoes can influence runners feel comfortable and safe when runners run long time on gardens and they will predict or know whether the running places are dangerous or safe as well as smart running shoes can help runners to collect data on their running style , and the accompanying app provides real -time analysis of the runners' performance and running technique.

Smart running shoes can be runner coach on how to run better and avoid running injuries. It's not only running shoes that are being fitted with sensors to gather data and provide feedback.

The " wearable" technology sector is booming due to AI technology development to influence human needs to pursue more comfortable lives. Hence, AI smart products may help human to build health lives daily. Human begins to attempt to learn how to live more health by robots (AI) products.

When robots can be applied to human ourselves living environment , e.g. working, home, social , transport (non manual driving public transport tools service) , leisure environment. How behavioral economists feel they can bring positive or negative economic influence to our future societies?

Robots will bring human to experience economic anxiety. Wy? After centuries of development, basic science, applied science and technology had been rapidly developing. Material science, additive manufacturing , nanotechnology, bio-tech , new batteries, smart phones, non human driving public transport or non public transport tools invention. All of these new technological products include robots may help human to create new technological economic social development and technology also impacts human behavioral change.

Consequently, this leads us to the Fourth industrial revolution" or Klaus Schwab for the world economic forum in his 2015 article and 2016 book, he indicated

The first industrial revolution used water and stream power to mechanize production . The second used electric power to create production. The third used electronic and information technology to automate production. How a Fourth industrial revolution is building on the third, the digital revolution that has been occurring since the middle of the last century. It is characterized by a fusion of technology that is developed by scientists between the physical, digital and biological science.

Ref: Excerpts from the fourth industrial revolution.

Consequently, human have expanded capabilities to communicate, to connect, to work without actual physical environment. Human behavior may be influenced alone or live lonely because robots can help organizations to reduce many workers to work together and working hours. When robots can replace human workers to do their tasks. Moreover, human will have driverless vehicles and drones, which help in more than moving people and goods. They assist us in farming, in pollution control, human have machine-aided surgery, and human have smart cities, smart contract, smart product to use. So, any kinds of new invention of technological tools will be needed to use in any organizations in order to improve performance. Even our homes also need (AI) tools to help us to live more comfortable.

Technological invention have changed our lives to be Better, continuing a trend in previous experiencing of

Industrial revolutions, smartphones, connected with Computing power, change the many we decide on Travelling, entertaining purchasing or connecting with Friends. Our day-to-day behavior and decisions are seriously affected by and dependent on the digital network technology.

In fact, machines are more than substitute for people In routine jobs, they can even take over some jobs, that require cognitive functions. Consequently, it may bring unemployment ratio rises or jobs need reduce in our societies. Machine-search changes the life of lawyers, accountants, engineers, even doctors when (AI) tools help them to deal every tasks. So, many professionals will have chance to lose jobs if robots can do their most tasks.

On conclusion, the fast process in machine-human – capital substitution means that experts need to seek new competitive advantages, this time against intelligence machines . So, technology may change human behavior to bring positive and negative both impact in our societies, such as the usefulness in -skill sets as capital labor substitution has become capital -human capital substitution. All of these will raise economic anxiety, because companies will have a reduced staffs number and increase robots number sense of security. Also, workers need to spend time to learn new skills in order to adapt to work with robots together in any organizations. So, technology can not influence workers become lazy. Otherwise, they influence workers become hard because they need to spend time to learn how to work with machine together in organizations. But, technology can also influence human pursue more comfortable to live.

Can technology influence consumers reduce spending on visiting shopping

Why may knowledge influence economic growth? Have they close relationship between knowledge and economic growth or recession in behavioral

economy view? I shall attempt to indicate evidences to explain these two questions as below:

IN fact, human development had been experiencing from agricultural stage to industrial manufacturing stage, till to nowadays, service section stage,e.g. hotel tourism leisure development, and technological development stage, e.g. computer and robot development. All of these stages, which are created by ourselves knowledge, it means that how we decide choice, what social development direction will be caused. It it is true, it seems that global human knowledge may influence how our social future continue development. Our social economic growth or recession will be brought to influence from knowledge

indirectly.

It is focus on " behavioral economic concept" Economists define scarcity as the condition of wanting more than we can get with available resources. Scarcity is a fact of

life. So, human can arrange ourselves resources in a lot of different ways, such as watching TV, buying a book, a car or traveling, but at any given time, ourselves have a fixed range of possibilities. SO, scarcity also describes the world on a collective level. As a society, we can produce only so many things, and we have to decide how those things are divided among many people. But, when social development, knowledge is very important to cause human (scientists) choose how to decide to invent any new things in order to satisfy human not limited need and using desire. So, the total quantity of available knowledge does not diminish as more and more people acquire it. So, ourselves every behavioral decision in life involves weighing the trade off between costs and benefits . We look at our options and decide whether it is worth giving up in order to get the other.

Economists explain this time cost of choice the " opportunity cost", opportunity cost is the value you could gained by choosing your next best alternative, the opportunity you have to pass up in order to take your first choice. Why may ourselves behavior have relationship between opportunity cost and economic growth? For computer invention example, when scientists feel compute products will be future human needs daily, for student learning using need, office tasks needs, watching movie, listening music leisure need,even playing game need. So, scientists had chose to spend time and resource and labor to invent computer products , they forgave to spend time and resource

and labor to invent other products. They computer invention is their opportunity cost, includes time, money, resource, labour, knowledge, mind on computer scientists , they had forgiven to spend these resources to research how to invent other kinds of new products.

However, when computer new products had been invented in success, e.g. desktop, laptop, can be popular to be accept to provide to global computer users to use. This kind of computer

invention , its users number had been increasing, manufacturing computer number will be influenced to grow, due to computer invention will help developing and developed countries GDP

growth rapidly since 1980 year , the early first stage of computer invention had been experiencing during our global technological development history.

So, it implies that computer scientists had been confirmed to do right choice decision to forgive to spend resources, time, money and labour and knowledge to research how to invent any kinds of new products. They make right decision to research how to invent new computer products,even improve desktop to laptop and smart phone , hand carrying smart phone and computer both functions new products to satisfy computer users daily using needs. It is true opportunity cost to computer scientists case. Also, when past, our scientists do right choice to invent this kind of computer product, this kind of computer products can bring global economic benefits, such as government can increase profit tax form computer sellers, offices can use computers to reduce employees number, when computers can help offices to save much document, clerical employees number may be influenced to reduce, tasks can be simple from complex tasks, spending tasks time may be influenced to reduce by computerization of office, factories can apply computers or robots to replace workers to manufacture any kinds of products, such as cars, washing machine, rice cookers, radios, fans ,television etc. different kinds of electrical products.

So workers number may be influenced to reduce and wage expenditure must be reduce.

Hence, new knowledge may help global societies to bring economic growth, such as past scientists had decided to forgive to spend time, resource, money, labor, skill, knowledge to research how to invent any kinds of new products, it is possible that they have some different kinds of new products concept choices, computer concept is only one kinds of choice among these new different kinds of new products invention concepts. However, they need to choose only one kind of new product invention among of these different kinds of new product concept choices, because they have not enough resource to provide to them to invent in the past. Finally, they evaluate the weigh and cost between computer invention concept and other new products invention concepts. In fact, computer is one kind of "the bringing much economic benefits" new concept invention product choice.

I believe that if computer will be continue improved in order to bring more economic growth in possible. SO, scientists need to spend more time, resource, money, labor, skill, knowledge to research how to continue to improve traditional computers to bring more using functions, in order to help global different industries to reduce resource, time, labour , money aim to bring reducing cost spending expenditure benefits to global industries , due to societies had been experiencing " knowledge social stage". If societies need to apply computer technology to assist our societies can continue develop, when our societies' different industries, such as service, manufacturing, even agricultrial sectors, e.g. robots may help farmers to predict when it is right time to grow vegetable, or replace farmers to grow vegetable, fruit in farms to provide human have enough food to eat, or robots can help hotel to clean rooms, serve clients, robots can help cinemas to sell tickets, robots can help manufacturers to product new products in factories. So, technological products may help any kinds of industries to reduce employees number, improve efficiencies and productivities and reduce wages expenditure economic cost benefits.

Production possibilites economic concept knowledge indicates about who produces which goods and why. The fact that millions of people and firms around the global coordinate their activities to provide consumers with the right combination of goods and services seem like magic.

In fact, coordination doe snot happen by chance, nor does super-planner tells every one where to go and what to do. Instead, the global production time is a natural outcome of people every acting in their own self interest to improve their own lives. Economists call this coordination mechanism the " invisible hand", an idea that was first suggested by economic thinker Adam Smith.

To get some insight into the who and why of production, such as shirt production case, most shirts are made in China, and other countries when factory wages are low. Have American workers become worse at making shirts over the last two countries? Definitely not, In fact, as are better than American workers at making shirts. Instead , each good tends to be produced by that country, company, or person with the lowest opportunity cost of producing that shirt kind of product, such as scientists make cooperation decision to invent computer products together, they can earn high invention royalty income, computer sale and manufacturing number increases, governments can earn more profit tax, different kinds of service, manufacturing industries can reduce workers number, wage expenditure, improving performance economic benefits . So, countries and firms and persons need a specialize in making goods for which they have the lowest opportunity cost. They than trade with one another to get the coordination of goods. They want to consume, such as computer manufacturing , if IBM and Microsoft both companies can cooperate to research how to improve themselves traditional model of laptops and desktops to create new improved and more using functions laptops and desktops, e.g. small size, more new using functions, clear colour and easier visible screen, or small book cover design, new computer model. I believe that the resulting, gains from themselves computer trade can be shared much that every computer buyers ends up better offer, global computer users will choose to buy and use these both IBM and Microsoft future new computer invention products to compare other kinds of computer manufacturers.

In production possibilities frontier economic concept, it explains why IBM and Microsoft ought cooperate to manufacturer computers, their cooperation can bring more economic benefits to themselves and global computer users, e.g. more computer functions, reducing sale price, reduce computer workers manufacturing wages, and computer manufacturing workers number, increasing computer manufacturing and demand number, increasing profit to themselves and government profit tax income, increasing buyers number, offices can improve efficiencies and employees performance, reducing manufacturing cost expenditure, improving student learning ability, etc. different kinds of global economic benefits. Hence, in production possibilities frontier economic concept, IBM and Microsoft ought make cooperation decision in order to bring global economic benefits.

In fact, computer manufacturing industry is one competitive market, it is one in which truly informed, prices taking buyers and seller easily trade a standardized good or service. IBM and Microsoft need to cooperate in order to win their computer manufacturing competitors , if they hope to earn in global computer manufacturing top leader position. Otherwise, if IBM and Microsoft do not choose to cooperate to invent new kind of computer products, their traditional computer products will be not popular to be accept to use to compare their computer manufacturing competitors. Because, future computer trends to cheap, more using functions, small size, light weight , clear visible and touch feeling screen. in order to attract computer buyers choices more easily.

On conclusion, it is possible that scientists invention knowledge may bring economic growth indirectly. Their invention choice or invention decision may assist our future economy development rapidly or slowly. Hence, knowledge is one invisible hand to influence global economy either it can bring growth or recession in possible.

Knowledge how influences global online shopping times increase

Why may knowledge influence economic growth? Have they close relationship between knowledge and economic growth or recession in behavioral economy view? I shall attempt to indicate evidences to explain these two questions as below:

IN fact, human development had been experiencing from agricultural stage to industrial manufacturing stage, till to nowadays, service section stage,e.g. hotel tourism leisure development, and technological development stage, e.g. computer and robot development. All of these stages, which are created by ourselves knowledge, it means that how we decide choice, what social development direction will be caused. It it is true, it seems that global human knowledge may influence how our social future continue development. Our social economic growth or recession will be brought to influence from knowledge

indirectly.

It is focus on " behavioral economic concept" Economists define scarcity as the condition of wanting more than we can get with available resources. Scarcity is a fact of life. So, human can arrange ourselves resources in a lot of different ways, such as watching TV, buying a book, a car or traveling, but at any given time, ourselves have a fixed range of possibilities. SO, scarcity also describes the world on a collective level. As a society, we can produce only so many things, and we have to decide how those things are divided among many people. But, when social development, knowledge is very important to cause human (scientists) choose how to decide to invent any new things in order to satisfy human not limited need and using desire. So, the total quantity of available knowledge does not diminish as more and more people acquire it. So, ourselves every behavioral decision in life involves weighing the trade off between costs and benefits . We look at our options and decide whether it is worth giving up in order to get the other.

Economists explain this time cost of choice the " opportunity cost", opportunity cost is the value you could gained by choosing your next best alternative, the opportunity you have to pass up in order to take your first choice. Why may ourselves behavior have relationship between opportunity cost and economic growth? For computer invention example, when scientists feel compute products will be future human needs daily, for student learning using need, office tasks needs, watching movie, listening music leisure need,even playing game need. So, scientists had chose to spend time and resource and labor to invent computer products , they forgave to spend time and resource and labor to invent other products. They computer invention is their opportunity cost, includes time, money, resource, labour, knowledge, mind on computer scientists , they had forgiven to spend these resources to research how to invent other kinds of new products.

However, when computer new products had been invented in success, e.g. desktop, laptop, can be popular to be accept to provide to global computer users to use. This kind of computer invention , its users number had been increasing, manufacturing computer number will be influenced to grow, due to computer invention will help developing and developed countries GDP growth rapidly since 1980 year , the earily first stage of computer invention had been experiencing during our global technological development history.

So, it implies that computer scientists had been confirmed to do right choice decision to forgive to spend resources, time, money and labour and knowledge to research how to invent any kinds of new products. They make right decision to research how to invent new computer products,even improve desktop to laptop and smart phone , hand carrying smart phone and computer both functions new products to satisfy computer users daily using needs. It is true opportunity cost to computer scientists case. Also, when past, our scientists do right choice to invent this kind of computer product, this kind of computer products can bring global economic benefits, such as government can increase profit tax form computer sellers, offices can use computers to reduce employees number, when computers can help offices to save much document, clerical employees number may be influenced to reduce, tasks can be simple from complex tasks, spending tasks time may be influenced to reduce by computerization of office, factories can apply computers or robots to replace workers to manufacture any kinds of products, such as cars, washing machine, rice cookers, radios, fans ,television etc. different kinds of electrical products. So workers number may be influenced to reduce and wage expenditure must be reduce.

Hence, new knowledge may help global societies to bring economic growth, such as past scientists had decided to forgive to spend time, resource, money, labor, skill, knowledge to research how to invent any kinds of new products, it is possible that they have some different kinds of new products concept choices, computer concept is only one kinds of choice among these new different kinds of new products invention concepts. However, they need to choose only one kind of new product invention among of these different kinds of new product concept choices, because they have not enough resource to provide to them to invent in the past. Finally, they evaluate the weigh and cost between computer invention concept and other new products invention concepts. In fact, computer is one kind of "the bringing much economic benefits" new concept invention product choice.

I believe that if computer will be continue improved in order to bring more economic growth in possible. SO, scientists need to spend more time, resource, money, labor, skill, knowledge to research how to continue to improve traditional computers to bring more using functions, in order to help global different industries to reduce resource, time, labour , money aim to bring reducing cost spending expenditure benefits to global industries , due to societies had been experiencing " knowledge social stage". If societies need to apply computer technology to assist our societies can continue develop, when our societies‘ different industries, such as service, manufacturing, even agricultrial sectors, e.g. robots may help farmers to predict when it is right time to grow vegetable, or replace farmers to grow vegetable, fruit in farms to provide human have enough food to eat, or robots can help hotel to clean rooms, serve clients, robots can help cinemas to sell tickets, robots can help manufacturers to product new products in factories. So, technological products may help any kinds of industries to reduce employees number, improve efficiencies and productivities and reduce wages expenditure economic cost benefits.

Production possibilities economic concept knowledge indicates about who produces which goods and why. The fact that millions of people and firms around the global coordinate their activities to provide consumers with the right combination of goods and services seem like magic.

In fact, coordination doe snot happen by chance, nor does super-planner tells every one where to go and what to do. Instead, the global production time is a natural outcome of people every acting in their own self interest to improve their own lives. Economists call this coordination mechanism the " invisible hand", an idea that was first suggested by economic thinker Adam Smith.

In production possibilities frontier economic concept, it explains why IBM and Microsoft ought cooperate to manufacturer computers, their cooperation can bring more economic benefits to themselves and global computer users, e.g. more computer functions, reducing sale price, reduce computer workers manufacturing wages, and computer manufacturing workers number, increasing computer manufacturing and demand number, increasing profit to themselves and government profit tax income, increasing buyers number, offices can improve efficiencies and employees performance, reducing manufacturing cost expenditure, improving student learning ability, etc. different kinds of global economic benefits. Hence, in production possibilities frontier economic concept, IBM and Microsoft ought make cooperation decision in order to bring global economic benefits.

In fact, computer manufaturing industry is one competitive market, it is one in which truly informed, prices taking buyers and seller easily trade a standardized good or service. IBM and Microsoft need to cooperate in order to win their computer manufacturing competitors , if they hope to earn in global computer manufacturing top leader position. Otherwise, if IBM and Microsoft do not choose to cooperate to invent new kind of computer products, their traditional computer products will be not popular to be accept to use to compare their computer manufacturing competitors. Because, future computer trends to cheap, more using functions, small size, light weight , clear visible and touch feeling screen. in order to attract computer buyers choices more easily.

On conclusion, it is possible that scientists invention knowledge may bring eocnomic growth indirectly. Their invention choice or invention decision may assist our future economy development rapidly or slowly. Hence, knowledge is one invisible hand to influence global economy either it can bring growth or recession in possible.

Technology how influences consumer behavioral change

Can human behavior may help economic growth? Why human behavior and economic growth have close relationship? I believe that productivity growth in different industries, how the shares of

wages and profits, how taxation affects growth, how inventions which can bring global economic growth, create working chance, sale income chance, consumption chance, productivity chance,

wealth chance. These factors may bring global short term or long term economic growth. All of these factors hace close relationship between human invention and economic growth. I shall

explain as below:

For any kinds of things inventions example, are best regarded as a form of investments, and their volume depends in like manner, on their expected profitability. Investments opportunities

are recreated by inventions investment. However, inventions may not be economig growth factor, but there is a high profitability that prior circumstances will bring them about,

so learning from human past prior experience is important not just in scientific or engineering matters, but in other fields, such as business and social organization. So, research and development,

such as human invention behavior which has chance to bring long term or short term economic growth.

I mean that human invention may be one kind of investment opportunity to bring global economic growth in possibility, because human new knowledge learning behavior may attribute to global new business invention chance to bring unlimited economic growth chance in nowadays society.

Hence, human can not neglect to create ourselves " invention mind or invention behavior" in order to help global economic growth more easily. SO, human invention may be one kind helping

global economic growth new investment opportunity, which is created from " human learning behavior". IN fact, an improvement in investment opportunity method may be created by human " any

kinds of new inventions behavior". SO, nowadays society, any kinds of new inventions of product, which ought help global societies to bring economic growth chance.

The theory of economic growth may be based on income, labor and land which every one knows and which are adequate. However, nowadays society had changed, such as scientific invention example,

it can bring profit chance to business, creating job opportunities in global labor markets, such as smart phones, laptops, desktops, non-manual driving vehicles, electric energy cars invention

etc. any kinds of new scientific invention products, they can bring new science products business chance, they must need to employ may manufacture labour, salespeople,

transport workers,logistic store workers, admin staffs, transport workers, product invention staffs , marketing promotion staffs etc. different job positions to let global human can have chance to find these jobs to do in order to earn income. Moreover, any kinds of scientific product inventions , which can bring many new jobs positions chance to let global unemployed people have chance to work and earn income.Also, any kinds of new scientific products invention may create many new jobs chance to global and solve unequal wealth and income allocation problem to global human, even businesses have chance to sell these new scientific invention products to sell to global buyers to earn more profit.

I mean that " new products invention" may help global societies to reduce unemployment challenge and it can bring long term economic growth in global labour market view. Moreover, when any

kinds of new product inventions, such as battery energy vehicle, non-manual driving auto vehicle or public transport tools, home washing machines, televisions, radios, fans, smart phomnes,

laptops, electronic book reading tools, internet invention etc, different kinds of new scientific product inventions, they can bring " consumption opportunity" to let global consumers

have chance to buy any kinds of new scientific inventionw which can also encourage global consumption rate raises in order to increase global wealth improvement rate speed rises up rapidly.

So, global wealth rising rate whether which is rapid or slow, it depends on whether how many different kinds of new scientific products invention may be confirmed to sccess to sell in

global business market.

Hence, investment on invention, which may be tangible evidence to create economic growth in the distribution of income , wages and profits between global labor, scientific inventions of products sellers,and global scientific inventions of products consumers. They have close relationship to be influenced to increase economic growth speed whether they are rapid or slow from " global scientific new products inventions". If human product invention scientists can attempt to research how to invent any kinds of undiscovered new kinds of products inventions, for example, if global any kinds of scientific product invention scientists can attempt to invest time to invent 100 kinds of new scientific products inventions in order to provide global human have chance to buy to use. Then, these 100 different kinds of scientific invention products may help global new invention of scientific products sellers to provide many different kinds of new jobs vacancies to let global unemployed or job seekers have chance to work and earn income.

So, global unemployed rate will have chance to reduce in global societies. Moreover, they can also help these new scientific products sellers to bring " earning profit chance", even these global

" new product invention scientists who have earn product invention royalty income chance after they can invent any kinds of products in success.

Finally, global consumption market growth rate will be influenced to rise up, when in the year, there are 100 new kinds of new scientific products invention have been already sold to let global consumers have chance to choose the kind of target of scientific product to buy to use. So, global new economic growth rate speed , it can rise up rapid up or slow down, it depends on whether the year, global has how many kinds of new invention of scientific products" have been invented to prepare to sell in global scientific products sale market

in macro economic view.

Hence, economic growth and human invention behavior, which have cloase relationship . The list of anti-growth factors could be extended perhaps however. Hartwell (1983) has pointed out that

economies have always contained a mixture of three main systems for making production, consumption, and distribution decisions namely, administered and market free enterprise. It was the gradual freeing

of man's entrepreneurial talents from the bonds of custom and command that finally resulted in the remarkable economic growth of the industrial revolution. However, in the twrms of human history, sustained economic growth is rare, and this suggests that several conditions (Needham's Packet), rather than memely one or two , have had to be met before it earns occur.

It is also the case, however, that its occurrence has at least in some respects made its survival more probable. HUman scientific investment has improved communications, such as smart phone, internet email and increased education (learning) chance, such as distancel learning, AI learning writing method, listening language learning method, reading e-books from smart phone, laptop channel method, which can chance traditional classroom leanring method to new scientific channel learning method or which can change traditional telephone or post lewtter communication method to nowadays sending email, smart phone calling, whataps new scientific tool communication methos.

ON conclusion, the free societies are influenced by any kinds of new scientific products inventions, Human had began to accept how attempted to buy any kinds of new scientific products inventions to use. New scientific inventions of products, which has bring more fashable of undiscovered new scientifical inventions of products choice to satisfy human ourselves daily new products invention using needs in our daily lives. SO, human scientists whose any kinds of new products inventions which will bring more chance to help global societies to create new social economic growth in global societies.

Finding balance conclusion

Nowadays, new technology development is popular. However, artificial intelligence is one kind of new technology choice among different technologies innovation. So it brings this question: Is artificial intelligence technology value to invest? To answer this question. I shall indicate some other new technology developments to compare (AI) technology development to judge which has urgent needs to achieve human expectation nowadays.

For example, why is green peace interested in new technologies? New technologies features prominently in our ongoing campaigns against genetic modified crops and number power. However, which are also an integral part of our solutions to environmental challenges, including renewable energy technologies, such as solar, wind and wave (water) power energy as well as waste treatment technologies, such as mechanical, biological treatment.

It seems humans need concern how to apply (AI) technology to solve environment pollution challenges in our future. So, environment protective, agriculture, natural energy technology will be popular demand to attempt to apply (AI) technology to solve their challenges or apply (AI) to assist to develop their industry.

First, On machine-man satisfactory demand aspect view point, it makes computers that think, it is the automation of activities. We associate with human thinking: like decision making, learning. It is the act of creating machine that perform function that require intelligence when performed by people. It is the study of mental faculties through the use of computational models. It is the study of computations that make it possible to perceive, reason and act. It is a branch of computer science that is concerned with the automation of intelligent behavior. It is anything in computing service that human don't yet know how to do property.

Second, on thought aspect artificial intelligence means systems thank think like humans, systems that think rationally.

Third, on behavioral aspect, artificial intelligence systems that act like human and that systems act rationally. However, the basic objective of (AI) is to represent human's thought processes in computation . These machines are supposed to exhibit behavior that. It is performed by a human being, would be considered intelligent. However, some authors feel (AI) has disadvantages, such as it is not creative, it is excited in the use of sensory devices, it can't make use of a very wide context of experiences and it does not use common sense.

For speech recognition and understanding function needs example, (AI) can be applied in speech recognition and understanding function, which (AI) speech or voice recognition is a data input method. For example, the computer recognizes and understands one (or a few) word commands. Speech understanding on the other hand is the computer's ability to understanding a spoken language. That is , the computer understands the meaning of sentences, an paragraphs through (AI).

So, (AI) can be attempted to learn human language how to speak. It is similar to translate human language skill, instead of actual human speaking skill. Also, (AI) can assist handicap learning or language student how to listen different languages by machine-man sounds from computers more accurately. So, it seems that it (AI) can replace human language teachers speaking function and can change teaching language nature of job in language speaking and listening education industry.

Advances in artificial intelligence (AI) technology and related fields have opened up new markets and new opportunities progress in critical areas, such as health, education, energy, economic development, social welfare and the environment pollution.

(AI) automation will continue to create wealth and expand the global economy development in the future. However, when many will benefits that growth won't be cost less and will be accompanied by changes in the skills, that workers need to increase productivity in the economy and structural changes in the economy. So, in the skills that workers need to succeed in the economy and structural changes.

I shall indicate why aggressive policy action will be needed to help Americans who are disadvantaged by these changes , due to (AI) technology is caused. For automation industry change example, artificial intelligence (AI) capabilities will enable automation of some tasks that have long required human labor. These artificial intelligence technology introduction can increase new opportunities for individuals. The economy and society, but (AI) has also the potential to disrupt be current livelihoods of many Americans. However, (AI) leads to unemployment and increase in inequality over the long run depends not only on the (AI) technology itself, but also on the institutions and policies that are changed.

Thus, it is possible that (AI) technology will raise some countries unemployment number if the employer apply (AI) technology workers to work instead of human labor in their factories, but it can also raise productivity for these employers.

Technological progress is main driver of growth of GDP per capita, allowing output to increase faster than labor and capital . However, technology can increase productivity, but also decrease the number of labor hours needed to create a unit of output. So (AI) causes unequal to labor wage decreases, even reduces the number of labor to manufacture, e.g. artificial intelligence technology of automation car manufacturing industry; clothing manufacturing industry; plane manufacturing etc. high technology of artificial intelligence manufacturing method. But (AI) should be potential environment benefit, although it raises unemployment ratio. Moreover, it can rise production , due to many skilled craft were replaced by the combination of machines and lower-skilled labor. The result of (AI) technology introduction , it causes output per hour risen when inequality declined, driving up average living standards, but the labor of some high-skill workers was no longer as valuable in the market. Otherwise, if (AI) technology is continue developed to be success. Some routine intensive occupations will be loss, which focused on predictable, e.g. easily programmable tasks, such as switchboard operators, filing clerks, travel agents, and assembly line workers would be particularly replaced by new (AI) technology. However, at the same time, (AI) technology development will bring these benefits: improvement in education (training (AI) technology scientists) , due to (AI) manufacturing technology needs are raising to businesses and institutional changes, such as the reduction in unionization and raising in the minimum wage to the (AI) manufacturing technology skilled labor in factories.

Because (AI) technology is not a single technology, but rather a collection of technologies that are applied to specific tasks, the effects of (AI) will be felt unevenly though the economy. It will bring some tasks will be most easily automated than others , and some jobs will be affected more than others, both negatively and positively. Finally, new jobs are likely to be directly created in areas , such as the development and supervision of (AI) as well as indirectly created in a range areas though out the economy as higher incomes lead to expanded demand.

However, if (AI) technology could dominate global labor markets. If labor productivity increases, do not influence into wage increases, then the large economic gains brought about by (AI) technology could be increased wealth inequality, due to employers can reduce production cost, but workers (labors) wages will not be increased, even will be decreased. Hence, it seems the (AI) technology will bring disadvantages to labor market to cause unemployment or reduce wages in possible, although it can reduce employer individual salary (wage) expenditure and it can raise productivity.

Artificial intelligence (AI) technology is a branch of computer science that aims to create intelligent machines that work and react like humans. So, (AI) is a technology that appears to impact (influence) human preference by learning, understanding complex contents, enhancing humans in executing both routine and non-routine tasks. In the future, (AI) technology that can be virtual personal assistant, as well as it may exist, such as robots with human-like processing capabilities.

How can (AI) technology impact global economy growth over the next 10 years? During this time period, (AI) technology is predicted to have wide-ranging applications including: Machine learning that automates analytic model building by using algorithms that allow machines to operate without human assistance.

In global education aspect, potential applications include predicting cause-and-effect relationships from biological data, identifying new drugs, self-driving cars, and protecting against fraud, improved natural language processing that allows computers to continue to better analysis, understand and generate language to interface with humans using natural human languages. For example, transcribing notes dictated by physicians, automatically drafting articles and translating text and speech. So (AI) technology can be applied to education aspect to improve humans' knowledge level.

In visual art aspect, (AI) machine vision that allows computers to identify objects, scenes and activities in images. Current applications of (AI) machine vision include providing objective descriptions for the blind seeing(visual) needs.

We except the economic effects of (AI) technology to include both direct GDP growth from sectors that develop or manufacture. (AI) technology and indirect GDP growth through increased productivity in existing sectors that employ some form of (AI). If (AI) technology is an increasingly critical component of more products, it will become an integral part of many people's lives. Thus, (AI)'s ability to influence economic activity, rather than the economic or development status of the region. (AI) has the potential to impact income classes and to bring significant gains to both developed and developing countries. For example, (AI) has the potential to optimize good production around the world by analyzing agricultural regions and identifying what is necessary to improve crop yields.

In estimating the future economic effects by (AI) technology innovation, it is important to note that it is challenging to accurately predict which applications of (AI) will ultimately be commercially successful. In micro level economic influence, we need to apply methodologies to estimate the economic effects of investment in firms developing (AI) technology since investment levels in a technology are a telling sign of the future potential of that

(AI) technology.

How (AI)'s development may affect the global economy over the next ten years. In fact, (AI) technology has the potential to affect business across the global in a wide range of industries in ways only a number of technologies have done in the parts. For example, (AI) technology's expected to be a useful tool for enhancing human capabilities and in some instances replacing functions, such as driving a car, adoption of broadband internet, mobile telephone, industrial robotic automation have served to enhance human capabilities.

However, significant public debate has focused on projections of (AI) technology's effect on the labor force. However, large companies prefer to invest in (AI) technological industry. For example, face book's (AI) research lab., google machine intelligence lab. and micro soft machine learning and artificial intelligence research division are all making advances in (AI) technology and investing in the industry's top talent. Additionally, between 2010 year and 2015 year, nearly $5 billion in venture capital funding invested in firms across the global developing and employing (AI) technology (Facebook (AI) Research).

Can encourage consumption develop economy? Can new technology products develop economy? Can creating new jobs develop economy? Can human behaviour influence economic development? Can encouraging new energy education knowledge development economy? I shall attempt to answer these questions as below:

How consumption can develop economy? Economists explain that if a resource used in production, such as labour or equipment, becomes more expensive,, firms have an incentive to find new methods of production that economize on that resource. When economists study the behaviour of people or firms , they look at the incentive being faced. So, I feel that when new technology resource is needed to apply to manufacture any kinds of products, it can help the kind of product to bring consumer purchase desire increases to choose to make purchase decision more easily and quickly. Hence, new technology is one factor to bring new incentive to manufacture the kind of product, when the kind of product can be manufactured by the kind of new resource. Consequently, it can attract many consumers to choose to buy the kind of new product, e.g. smart mobile. This kind of smart mobile product is invented and is applied to manufacture by new resource, e.g. manufacturing phone equipment, labour smart phone inventors, and phone designers. They can bring new incentive to find new methods of production that encourage on that resource to help new smart mobile products to develop to global phone market.

SO, any kinds smart mobile products can be increased to phone product sale market and they can replace traditional mobile product products. Due to different kinds of smart mobiles need increases. They bring new incentive to global mobile products users accept to use smart mobile popularly as well as their smart phone use needs increase their smart mobile using desire.

IN behavioural economic view, new method of production technology need can bring new technique products market development, then when new technological products can be popular to be accepted by global general users. They can feel more satisfactory to use this kind of new technological product to replace old technological product, such as innovative smart mobile phone products can be accepted to use to replace traditional mobile phone or home telephone products.

ON consequence, global smart mobile demand needs will be influenced to increase by cost of production reducing factor. It explains that when new production of technological resource needs increase, it can influence the new kind of technological products demand and supply number also be influenced to increase. Consequently, these both of factors can encourage consumption desire increases to consumers as well as the country's economic growth GDP is also influenced to climb up rapidly in possible. So, I believe that " new production technological resource is main factor to cause consumption desire increases and economic growth effect in nowadays society.

Can creating new jobs develop economy? Some economist believe that cost of production determines supply, supply determines final degree of utility, final degree of utility determines value. They bring this question: If all of these factors have concern to any kinds of products need increases or decreases , when the cost of production increases, then the kind of product supply will be influenced to decrease.

Due to the kind of product supply decreases , but consumers demand to the kind of product increases. SO, the kind of product utility increases, when the kind of product utility increases, it can increase the kind of product sale value. When the kind of product sale value increases, it will bring creating new jobs need increases. Can this kind of new creating jobs of increasing need develop economic growth? For laptop new style of computer product example, if any kinds of laptop cost of production decreases, then laptop manufacturers can decrease expenditure to any kinds of laptop cost of production. Consequently, laptop supply of manufacture number may be influenced to increase, they must need many laptop labours help to manufacture many laptops to satisfy global laptop computer users need. So, laptop is popular to be accepted to use to global computer users, due to their utilities values are also influenced to increase. Laptop sale value must be influenced to increase by raising laptop utility factor. SO, global laptop computer manufacturers must need to increase labour number in order to manufacture many different kinds of laptop products to satisfy global laptop users needs. Consequently, in behaviour economic view, due to laptop cost of production decreasing factor, which can bring laptop manufacturing number needs increase and creating new jobs need for laptop market development. On conclusion, laptop market development can create new jobs chance to help the country economic growth in possible. So, creating new jobs chance can help the country to bring economic growth in possible.

Can human behaviour influence economic development?

Can ourselves daily behaviour help economic growth? Some economists believe that unemployment causes become real wage were too high. In other words,, workers were looking for too much money, relative to the rate of inflation and output in the economy. To reduce the number and of work, therefore it was just a case of " lowering salary demand".

In behaviour economic view, if one country has many workers can accept lowering salary demand, whether they can influence the country will develop economy rapidly or slowly, or whether they have cause and effect relationship in behaviour economic view.

I assume that when the country can have many labours accept low salary demand, their daily working behaviour and working attitude may influence the country develop economy speed slowly. For China example, nowadays,

China has many labours or workers, their salaries level are very low to compare developed countries, e.g. US , UK due to in general China labours their salaries. SO, low salaries demand factor may influence China laze labours number increases. When China has many labours number are laze more than hard labours number. Their working behaviours and performance may influence any kinds of products manufacture number reduces to compare US, UK labours. Consequently, the same kind of products manufacture number will be influenced to reduce by low inefficiency factor in China as well as China will have many businesses will earn less sale income from global consumers. When these China's products their sale number decreases, it will influence China economic growth speed slowly in possible in macro economic environment. SO, it seems that labour behaviour and their working performance may bring indirect negative influence to the country's economic growth speed to be sloe. I mean that human behaviour may influence the country's economic growth speed rapidly or slowly.

It explains that how human behaviour influences an economy grows to the country. It depends on " each country has how many workers , natural resource (may be coal or metals) or non natural resource e.g. machine, equipment and capital and land which all bound together by technology. Using those in the right combination will make the country's economy grows rapidly or slowly. For another case example, it explains how human behaviour may influence economy grows. I shall indicate the circular flow income theory to explain. It indicates that when one person (working people) who earns wages, he/she makes decision either saves to bank or investment aspect or spends on cash purchase goods aspect. In the year, for US country example, if the year US faces economic recession, US has high unemployment rates, it will have many workers loss jobs or US has many workers reduce wages.

ON consequence, reducing wages or lose jobs both factors which will influence many US people reduce much living expenditure spending , e.g. shopping or leisure expenditure. They will prefer to make decision to save money to bank or invest, e.g. buying shares. To finance aspect. SO, in the year, US will have many businesses reduce products sale number. In behavior economic view, due to US has many people make decision to save money to bank or invest to shares market more than spending to buy any kinds of products or leisure activities aspect. So, in the year, US's economic growth speed will be influenced to be slow by reducing spending behaviour on human behavior factor aspect.SO, it explains why human behaviors may bring positive or negative influence to the country's economic growth speed, whether it's economic growth speed is either rapid or slow.

How robotic helps to solve recession

Is the use of robots to job market increasing during the Great Recession?

Some researchers constructed a measure of the use of robots—commonly referred to as "robot intensity"—to estimate trends in robot exposure across more than 250 metropolitan areas and over time, finding that: During the Great Recession, robot intensity plummeted. But since 2009, robot intensity has sharply increased nationwide. They felt that robots may influence recession in possible. How are robots going to affect our jobs? Most analysis tends to be prospective in nature, and estimates of future impacts on employment vary widely, with some studies predicting that as many as 50 percent of all workers are at risk of losing their jobs to automation. Even less is understood about the actual impacts of robots on jobs, wages, and workers today. If there are many low skillful jobs e.g. cleaner, warehouse deliver, cooker, restaurant waitor etc., even high skillful jobs, e.g. accountant, lawyer, doctors etc. occupations are replaced by robotics. Then, our societies will increase unemployed people number. Consequently, great recession will be caused by robotic workers because when our societies have many people lose jobs, then many people loss income, then our consumption desires may be influenced to reduce. Consequently, many businesses may lose many customers. Low consumption desires may bring serious recession to any countries, due to robotic workers number increases to replace human workers in global societies.

The reason is that new technologies of the period have enabled people to be very productive while working part-time. Businesses do not need large numbers of employees, so individuals can devote most of their waking hours to hobbies, volunteering, and community service. In conjunction with periodic work stints, they have time to pursue new skills and personal identities that are independent of their jobs. Developed countries may be on the verge of a similar transition. Robotics and machine learning have improved productivity and enhanced the economies of many nations. Artificial intelligence (AI) has advanced into finance, transportation, defense, and energy management. The internet of things (IoT) is facilitated by high-speed networks and remote sensors to connect people and businesses. In all of this, there is a possibility of a new robotic society that could improve the lives of many people, but it also encourage future businesses apply robotics to replace human workers to do many jobs in finance, transportation, defense and energy management, medical health, hotel, tourism, cinema, theater etc. entertainment service fields. So, robotics may bring reducing cost benefits to businessmen, but they can also increase workers losing jobs number in our societies if future many businesses make decision to apply robotics to replace human workers to do any simple or complex jobs in global job market.

However, robotic architects or engineers may bring advantages and disadvantages both aspects:

On advantages aspect:

Artificial intelligence allows us to do all of the following:

•The completion of mundane tasks that would otherwise take a lot of labour hours. Automating such tasks frees up skilled workers to work on more important tasks.

•A.I. is not as prone to making errors as a person. As long as the A.I.'s programming is good enough, you should find that calculating errors and similar issues become problems of the past.

•Speed is a key feature of artificial intelligence. Huge datasets no longer provide any problems to businesses, as automation allows for much faster processing. This means that a business can spend money elsewhere.

•The most complex A.I.s reduce the amount of risk attached to the decision-making process. The "Curiosity" Mars rover is a good example. It's programmed to choose the best course of action depending on its position.

On disadvantages aspect:

It's not all good, unfortunately. The following are some of the bad points of artificial intelligence:

•The previously mentioned job losses can cause all sorts of problems for staff morale.

•Some believe that artificial intelligence gets rid of the human element. The nightmare scenarios in films like “The Terminator” may seem far-flung, but that doesn’t mean there isn’t a risk in letting machines make all the decisions.

•A.I. relies on pre-existing knowledge, which means it lacks creativity. Attempting to use it for creative endeavours may result in failure.

•Algorithms may not be able to make judgment calls in disaster situations. Again, the A.I. may not take the human element into account, no matter what’s actually happening on the ground.

On people management aspect, what do you think would be the reaction to a robot attempting to manage people? It’s likely that a lot of people won’t take to kindly to artificial intelligence telling them what to do. Many underestimate the importance of people skills in the architecture and engineering profession. Architects and engineers must be able to organize workloads and manage individuals. It is sure, A.I. device could handle the former. Scheduling is a task that many already automate. However, A.I. will fall down when it comes to the human relationships that are so vital in a team environment. An A.I. won’t understand when somebody is demotivated, or why. It won’t make allowances for the human issues that affect every problem. This makes skilled team members even more valuable. As A.I. takes an increasing role in the workplace, the need for people management will become more important. Architects and engineers with those skills may even find they make more money to employ them. Although, it is possible that AI can replace human architects or engineers to do their tasks to be better , it can help any one architectural or engineering firms to improve design performance in order to satisfy customers design demand, but our societies will increase unemployment ratio to engineers and architects number, even universities will reduce architect and engineering students number. Our traditional professional knowledge will be felt to be rubbish when these professional subjects won’t be useful to help us to find jobs easily. So, AI invention will influence many students won’t choose to study these two subjects. Our societies will be influence to experience knowledge recession when knowledge will become rubbish because robotics invention , it can do many human professional jobs to do. " knowledge recession" will be important factor to bring economic recession, because human can not be encouraged to learn any new knowledge to prepare to enter job market due to robotic invention can replace us to do more complex tasks in our future societies.

Can robotic leadership be good solution method when recession had come to the country?

On leadership management aspect, can robots become clever leadership to any organizations? As artificial intelligence becomes further embedded into our everyday working lives, we are already seeing the footprint of machine learning, automation, algorithms and robots in many of our professions and sectors. However, when we look at the upper levels of business management and leadership, these technological shifts are less evident, with C level Executives continuing to lead and strategize as they have done before. In Ireland, there are more than 500 CEOs. The question is, when will we start to see machines and robots play a more central role in the CEO sphere, and is a ‘Robot CEO’ realistic in the short to medium term?

New research shows that 24% of people aged 25-29 would replace their boss with a robot, demonstrating an interesting trend among Generation Z. However, these data sets are perhaps less founded in AI and robotics and more in current employee engagement. It's telling that the 20-30% of people who would willingly replace their human boss with a robot is about the same percentage of people who are consistently classified as "actively disengaged" at work. In addition, research from analytic giant Gallup demonstrates that 70% of how we feel about work, namely our emotional commitment, is driven by who our manager is, again underlining the centrality of human behavioural traits when making decisions on leadership.

CHAPTER VII

How Technology or human behavior may influence economic development

I am an author with a background in behavioral economics, explores the intricate relationship between technology and the economy through the lens of human behavior. My work, often integrating insights from psychology with traditional economic theories, aims to provide a comprehensive understanding of how these factors interact to influence economic development, organizational performance, and societal changes

My opinion on the technology and economy relationship can be broken down into several key areas:

1. Technology as a Driver and Influencer of Economic Development

My view consistently investigates whether technology influences economic development, often posing it as a central question in his books . My view examines how technological advancements, including the rise of robots and artificial intelligence (AI), can impact economic growth and recession at both macro and microeconomic levels . My view considers technology as a potential production resource that can help organizations reduce costs, thereby contributing to economic benefits .

2. The Role of Human Behavior in Economic Outcomes

A core tenet of my work is the exploration of how human behavior influences economic development . My view emphasizes that psychological factors, such as cognitive biases (e.g., overconfidence, loss aversion) and emotional influences, significantly shape economic decision-making . By understanding these behavioral elements, My view argues that we can gain a more complete picture of consumer behavior, market dynamics, and the overall economic landscape .

3. Interplay Between Technology, Human Behavior, and Organizational Change

My view delves into how technology can influence human and organizational behavioral change to achieve economic benefits . My questions whether robots can drive such changes and explores the impact of technology on organizational behavior for economic gains . My view research also considers how technology influences human social activities, leading to shifts in consumer behavior and ultimately affecting economic performance . For instance,

My view examines how e-services bring organizational innovation and how auto food sale machines help organizations reduce staff numbers .

4. Positive and Negative Impacts of Technology

My view acknowledges that technology can bring both positive and negative influences to organizational development and society . While he explores how technology can reduce costs and improve efficiency, my view also raises concerns about potential negative impacts, such as the displacement of human jobs by AI, particularly for low-skilled workers, which could lead to increased unemployment rates . This balanced perspective highlights the complex nature of technological integration into the economy.

5. Bridging Theory and Practical Application

Through his academic pursuits and writing, my view aims to bridge the gap between theoretical economics and practical applications influenced by human behavior . My view suggests ways policymakers can utilize behavioral insights to design more effective interventions for improving economic outcomes .

In essence, my opinion is that the relationship between technology and the economy is deeply intertwined with human behavior. Technology acts as a powerful force that can drive economic development, reduce costs, and reshape organizational structures. However, its ultimate impact is mediated and often determined by how humans interact with it, their psychological biases, and the resulting behavioral changes. Therefore, a holistic understanding of economic development requires considering the dynamic interplay of technology, human psychology, and organizational responses .

Nowadays, our global economy seems to continue grow, but it also has possible to bring recession by any factors. This question concerns whether either human behavior can influence future global social economic growth or recession or technology can influence future global social economic growth or recession more? I shall attempt to indicate evidences to explain as below:

Firstly, on the one hand, when one country can manufacture new technological products, e.g. laptops, war weapons (non-manual driving flying war air planes, space rocket, smart phone etc. different
kinds of high technological products. For America example, US is one export high technogical products country. When its these different kinds of high development products manufacturers can sell to local and overseas customers. Then, they may earn high profit from both. Alsn US government can charge high profit tax from these high technologicalproducts manufacturers, when they can attract global many customers to buy their any kinds of high technological products. So, it seems that high technological products manufacturers may help US government and US high technological products manufacturers to earn more US technological products sale income. Moreover,

technology can help US country to grow up its economic development in long term, due to US manufacturers can concentrate on effort to invent any kinds of new technological products in order to persuade global buyers to chooce to
buy their products in preference.

However, but on the other hand, I feel human behavior, such as talent high technological products inventors , they are the beginning main factor to help US to grow economy. The reason is because US which any kinds of high technological products must need talent human product scientists) themselves idea to invention. If themselves idea can influence global high technological products buyers feel needs to buy to use. Then, they must choose to buy US country's any kinds of these products in preference. So, talent high technological product scientists will be US future economic growth source. If one high technological product scientists did wrong idea to the high technological
product manufacturers to manufacture the kind technological products. They can not influence global buyers feel needs to buy the kind of high technological product to use. Then, whose
idea of innovationm may not help US to develop itself eocnomy.

Hence, such as technological product case example, talent product scientists their idea innovation factor can bring more influential to US future economic growth easily. So, I conclude this criticism to explain why human behavior is more important factor to compare technology to influence the country's economy, because if the high technological product inventor whose dreams and iea to invent the kind of high technological product, if it can influence users feel useful feeling, e.g. smart phone product, it can attract phone users buy to use because it can use internet to gather global data, or read online news, read electonic books, listen music, watch movie, take photos, know the day weather, send and receive email, download document etx. different kinds of fuctions. SO, can let phone users feel smart phones can replace past traditional innovation of mobile phones and smart phones can influence global mobile users feel human ourselves can make phone calls in convenient in anywhere. Hence, smart phone product manufacturers can help themselves countries to earn high GDP income and increase high profit tax to give themselves governments. Otherwise, the traditional mobile phone products can not persuade phone buyers to choose to buy forever, because they lack more functions to compare smart phones.

So, it explains why smart phone users personal using phone behavior is more important to influence the country's economy because when global every family begin to feel to use smart phones is themselve daily habit, they need smart phone to help them to do any matters, instead of general phone call at streets. So, their using smart phone behavior will influence they feel often need to change new mobdel of smart phone invention of product to replace old model of smart phone. Consequently, smart phone manufacturers need to continue to invent new and more functions of new model of smart phone products to satisfy future global smart phone users' need. Henvce, smart phone users' habitual using new model smart phone using behavior may bring global smart phone manufactuers long term manufacturing benefits in order to increase sale number chance. So, smart phone is one kind of high technological product may help any smart phone manufacturing countries to grow up economic growth easily. Also, smart phone inventor individual idea and smart phone improvement skillful technology and smart phone user individual frequent chaning new model using behavior which may be main factors to influence the country's smart phone sellers sale number. Such as, UK, US, Germany , CHina. Korea , they are global main smart phone manufacturers.

Economists call it " production -side growth" , which means that most companies, most of the time, made their (such as those countries smart phone manufacturers profit by cutting the cost of production). If these countries' smart phone manufacturers can cooperate to research how to improve more new functions of new model of smart phones to sellin global smart phone market. Consequently, it is possible that their production of smart phone cost may be influenced to reduce. Then, themselves future invention of new model of smart phone product sale price may also be influenced to reduce, due to reducing production cost. Then, the global smart phone buyers number may be influenced to increase by reducing smart phone production cost. When these manufacturing smart phone countries, every year , their smart phone sale number Ccan increase to double time , even more.

I believe that smart phone technological product may help these countries to earn more profit tax, if these countries smart phone manufacturers need to research how to improve future smat phone functions to satisfy global future smart phone user individuia; " frequent changing new model of smart phone habitual satisfactory need". So, future smart phone technological product may be one kind of high technological product to help the smart phone manufacturing countries themselves economic growth.

Ecommerce may also help the country to grow economy. In the past, before twentieth century , this efficiency extends to the ways our economic goods spread around the country and the world. As the begining of the twentieth century , most markets , more local, most people bought things made nearby. But with the expansion system and then commercial air travel and the super-efficiency of containerized shipping, markets became national and eventually, global. Till to first century, since internet technological invention, it brings economic chance to let any countries local merchants may apply web-store internet platform to help them to sell products to overseas buyers. They only need click to the overseas seller whose web store and then they canpay visa to buy the kind of product frm the online seller's web-store. So, many merchants , they own webstores to let overseas buyers can pay visa to buy the kind of product from themselves web-stores at their home countries conveniently. Then, the owning " more number of web-store sellers " countries government will have possible to earn high profit tax from these local webstore sellers. So, ecommercal sale internet technological platforms and global online buyers purchase behaviors , these two factors mau also influence the country's economy. If the country had many people like to buy any kinds of products from webstore, then they may influence the " owning more number of online sellers countries" their online seller profit increases, whether it is more or less sale number. Hence, whether e-commerce technology may help the country's government to grow GDP in technological product sale view. It depends on whether the country owns how many number of online sellers as well as how many online buyers number both for their products choice purchase chance. For example, when the country own high number people like to spend more time to stay at home to use internet. They do not like to walk on streets, they like to listen music and read books at homes more than going outside to do sports. Then, the country's people individual living habit will influence they choose to apply webstores to buy any things, if the country had many people like to stay at homes more than leaving homes. SO, individual living behavior may also influence the country economy on online purchase view.

Finally, nowadays, some economists indicate that human ourselves behavior may be as full participants in Earth's cyclical processes of life and economy. They think that human behavior, such as we are rational economic man, social adaptable humans, our daily behaviuors may bring direct or indirect influences

to global economy growth or recession. For share market example, before 21 century, share buyers need to go to banks or finance companies or share markets to buy the company's shares. But, since 21 century, smart phone technological products had been invented. Nowadays global many share inventors began to choose to use smart phones to buy and sell any companies shares in any time and any where conveniently. So, smart phone invention had brought indirect influence to global share buyers'carrying on

sale and buying shares investing behavioral transactions in preferable choice. SO, smart phones and internet invention may influence global many share investors shares investment behavior and investment attitude change. It seems that this both new technological invention can encourage future share investors accept to apply smart phones to carry on shares buying and selling transactions more than visiting finance companies to enquire share agents their idea because, they can apply smart phone to observe global any shares whether their prices will rise up or fall down immedicately. SO, smart phone and internet will changfe future share investors investment behavior.

Two economic sociologists, DOnald Mackenzie and Yuval Miko, decided to reseach how share traders behaviors, however, by interviewing some of

the share traders themselves. What did they discover? That the theory's increasing accuracy ovdr time was because the share traders had started to behave as if the theory ware true and so were using the model's predicted prices as a benchark for selling, their owning bids. FInancial economics, they

concluded " helped create in reality the kind of markets, it posited in theory. Ans as financial markets later learned, when those theories turn out to be flowed. If rational economic man can reshape our behavior in financial markets, he is vary likely to be reshaped our behavios in past. Hence, smart phone can influence future share buyers to do shares buying and selling decision in short time as well as it can persuade global share markets shares purchase number increases to bring economic growth.

Learning invisible hand economy theory

How may " inivisible hand " factor influence the smart phone manufacturer products demand number increase? The invisible hand is for the law of supply and demand explains how the pull and push of these two factors serve to benefit sciety as a whole. In simple, every consumer choose to buy the product, he/she pursues to earn the most more interest to the manufacturer needs to produce the product as its product may be of the greatest value to let the consumer intends only his/her own gain, led by an invisible hand to promote the product to let the consumer to make satisfaction to choose to buy the product.

In behavioral economic view, the invisible hand to the product manufacturer may be " the consumer whose satisfactory feeling to use the product".So, the invisible hand meant that ir can not be touch , seen, it only brings feeling to let the consumer to feel. This feeling to the product is very mportant factor to excite the consumer to choose to buy the product, e.g. smart phone product the smart phone buyer's invisible hand factor may include: The smart phone can link to app to use internet service, download documents from smart phone , taking phonoes, watching movie, listening music, clock time etc. function, seeling different countries street locations, instead of general mobile talking function.

So, all of above factors will be future new smart phone main " invisible hand" factors to excite future smart phone buyers to make purchase decision to choose to buy the kind of smart phone among different kinds of smart phone products innovation , when they are manufactured to promote to smart phone market to sell.
So, in smart phone market supply and demand view, the smart phone manufacturer needs to innovate new smart phone products in order to let smart phone buyers fee its news phone buyers feel itsnew smart phone products have unique functions or features to excite its smart phone buyers to choose to buy its new kind of smart phone products, because smart phone buyers will be influences to make final smart phone purchase decision by invisible hand factors from smart phone different new function .
Smart phone manufacturers need to innovate many new functions o future new kinds of smart phone manufacturing in order to bring new invisible hand satisfactory feeling to let any one smart phone buyer to feel whose new smart phone can bring the most unique satisfactory feeling to let them to feel. So, smart phone 's invisible hand factor is main influential factor to bring smart phone manufacturer's new smart phone demand number will increase or decrease. If the smart phone manufacturer can often innovate its smart phone products to let smart phone buyers feel more using satisfactory feeling to its new kind of smart phone more than its other similar kinds of smart phone manufacturers. Then, the smart phone manufacturer ought raise its smart phone purchase number demand easily.

What is smart phone opportunity cost?
Hence, the concept of opportunity cost factor means smart phone manufacturers need to forgone opportunities of time cost , design new kinds of smart phone products, e.g. smart phone pictures, colour and shape , future smart phone manufacturers need to concentrate more time to research how to innovate new featurers and function to let every potential smart phone buyers to bring more functions using satisfactory feeling in order to attract they choose to buy its smart phone product.
On conclusion, opportunity cost to smart phone manufacturers may be forgone spend more time on smart phone design, colour choice, shape choice aspects. Smart phone manufacturers need to spend more time on innovate new feature and function aspects in order to satisfy future smart phone using needs in global competitive smart phone smart.

Why ought any kinds of businesses need to invest in technology to offices when businessmen began to do businesses? The reason is simple, such as any offices need email to communicate to let different departments staffs can contact to do any tasks in short time. So, email can replace telephone calling communication channel between departments in offices. Moreover, for paper files, electronic files may replace to keep to save any office confident documents or general memos, letters, reports etc. documents. So, paper printing number may reduce. Even some businesses began to sell their products from online webstores to let customers to pat visa to buy their products from their webstores conveniently. Hence, computer technology is essential to nowadays any kinds of businesses offices.

The best are developed with the entire project-focused organization in mind. For example, a question on resourcing could involve looking a cariety of systems and files with no way to automatically generate the rught combination of data. Hence, any business offices ought need a single, centralised database which keeps accounting, project and even HR information and can integrate data when required.

ON the office investing in technology web-based system with mobile access benefit, due to investing globalization and pressure on fee rates means staff are in the office less
frequently than ever. A web-based system means data can be accessed from PCs and networked laptops with no other software needed. So, instead of offices can apply laptops and intra-internet communication technological tool, which can also offer the option of a mobile applications suite which means personnel working on -site can enter timesheet and expense reports from laptops, even when not connected to the central data base. This helps minimise time delays, streamlining the billing process and improving cash flow. So, office mobile onlinesite technology may help thme to bring real- time , easy access benefits. For exmaple, if a staff is still making decisions based on information that is seven or eight weeks old, the staff will be surprised by the power of having real-time information at the
staff's fingertips. At any time this will give the staff an accurate "snapshot" of the health of the staff's project, enabling the staff to take preventive action if the problems arise before it is too late.

This visualisation ensures that all key stakeholders can identify project problems immediately they happen . It's also an ideal way for directors or other managers to grab headline information before a short notice meeting, for example, all of office laptop, mobile intra-internet, onsite technology may help to ensure more targeted decisions and better project control. Hence, office technology may help any business offices to save more time deal urgent tasks daiuly. It means that office technology may help any offices to save much time in long term.

For some businesses office technology may help their businesses to manage on projects to achieve rapid finishing in short time, such as all projects of harbour construction business aspect, some projects may face complex to prolong time to finish. SO, defining a discipline as " complex project management assumes that one can find projects cause of complexity". Also, any the harbour business projects do not really exist. The term project is a contract used to describe a particular human activity. Hence, if the harbour construction company managers can let its all harbour construction managers to apply mobile onsite technology, intra-internet communication channel to do daily communication tasks in short time between their different construction teams. Then, these new harbour onsite mobile intra-internet communication technology ought help all onsite harbour construction managers can supervise all harbour onsite workers to construct all harbour construction projects in short time efficiently and effectively.

Sp, on-site mobile intra-internet communication technology may be future construction industry which a kind of essential onsite mobile intra-internet communication technoogy.Moreover, on-site mobile intra-internet communication technology can bring future construction industry on time to save cost and construction quality improvement benefits. Due to increasingly construction industry and clients demand more for less and this is in a traditionalty high risk industry. The problem of
construction and its relatively slow pace of change seem to stem from its competive building living demand role in providing building buyer value. With its attendant professions, it is often too remote from the customers' experience of their buildings.

When if the construction company really knew how to add value for building clients? What if the construction firm could improve productivity among those using the building?
How much is that worth? What if the school could improve performance of students in shcools and the recovery of patients in hospitals? Such improvements represent much cost
benefits that could mean that the building pays for itself. However, nowadays building technology can bring these key benefical features to any construction companies, such as value success are committed leadership providing the vision, suitable values and effective shared processes.

How office technology brings intelligent thinking to office staffs? Finally, I beleive that if the company can invest technology in office. It will bring intelligent thinking to office staffs in order to improve efficient and performance, because investing in office technology , which is a way to reduce risk without
going over the top through effective use of the company networks. Why can office technology working environment can help staffs to bring intelligent thinking in order to
improve performance and raise efficiency?

The reason of office technology working environment can excite staffs their intelligent thining to be raise. What's lacking is a way of mitigating against these risks and doing so cost- effectively. Because more recently, a new stage has been reached where office staffs rely not only on their technical and business knowledge, but now have methodologies and tools so sophisticated that they can forward predict and control any office projects to finish before due date more easily.Hence, with good technical knowledge, sound business underatanding, a good way of methodologies, and training in the very latest software technology to hand, these are the not investing in office technology staffs, those who still find it impossible to deliver projects successfully more easily before any their office projects finishing due date. What needs to be addressed to change this situation?
The main factors critical to improve office staffs performance and improve efficiency, the non-investing in office technology working environment ought to changed to invest technology to office working environment in order to excite staff individual working emotion to bring raising efficiency, even improve performance effectiveness.

ON conclusion, any offices need to invest technology to offices in order to bring " improving technical skill to staffs their working environment", because they need to know that skill does not equate to competence , and there fore, a competence and therefore a competency based assessment is essential so that a prospective office employee knowledge and understanding, attitude and skills can be evaluated. So, technological office can help managers to evaluate office employee individual job skill more easily in order to make decision whether skill is high or low to let high skillful staffs can continue to be trained to work in offices as well as fire the low skillful staffs. So, when the office can attempt to spend more money to invest to its office working environment, it means that the organization should be investing in training for permanent staffs in the scarce skills working markets. A small investment in office technology can reap significant benefits further down the live, such as planning for skills scarcity on investing nowadays office technological working environment.

Human Behavioral network job brings social economic benefits

What does human network job mean ? Why may human network job be popular? Why human network job behavior may influence economy ? Nowadays internet is popular to use. We can apply internet to find data , search any new things, even earn money. Why does internet may become huma network job source. For example, e-publish may be one kind of new human network job. Any authors may apply internet channel to help them to sell electronic or paper books from e-publisher web store. They may apply facebook, you tub etc. any online channel to promote themselves new books to let new readers to know whether when they may buy themselves favourable new topic books to read from electronic publisher web store.

Thus, future electronic publisher industry may help any authors to build internet network platform to help them to sell and promote to advertise their any one new electronic or paper book topic to let global any one reader to choose to buy their any new topic books from electronic publisher web store easily and conveniently. However, it implies that electronic network platform author may be one kind of future new human network job in our societies.

How electronic network platform author job may bring economy benefit in macro economy view? A person can have few friends, contacts and still be very influential if these few friends and contacts are themselves highly influential, e.g. one author must not need to know any one reader in global society. When they like to choose any electronic books from electronic internet network platform. They may become the author's any one topic book buyer, when they feel the author's any one topic book is fun and attract they make decision to buth the strange author whose the topic book from electronic book publisher's platform web store conventiently in short time. Although, they are strangers, they do not know themselves , but the reader can understand what it way that made Google from writing platofrm to create new creative mind and typing network job method to replace traditional hand writing book method for global authors. It will be one kind of new human network writing job.

Hence, global any one reader can apply an innovative search engine , such as google.com to find whether whom author personal new topic books are value to read from internet.
Then, the electroniuc publisher's web store may be new book store platform sale network to help the author to sell many electronic or paper books from electronic network platform
in short time. So, internet may be future new network plaform to help global any one author to create network writing job absolutely. Furthermore, internet may be popular social media
to help any one author to build goold relationship between his/her readers. It is one kind of new network, human network job. New authors do not need to buy many paper books to prepare to put in any one book shop warehouse. Their every book can print on demand to reduce out of book stock in any one book shop. They may choose to sell either electronic books or paper books both from any one book publisher web store. So, electronic network platform may be one kind of good writing channel to help human authors to create income and it can also help authors to bring new creative mind and new topic fun content books to let readers to know and buy to read from electronic publisher network platform.

Why does human behavior may be one kind of new human network job to bring global economic advantages. ALthough, it may be free income or without inocme, but the person does the network behavior, his/her behavior may be bring advantages to influence many other people's health. For this case, when a worker in a coffee shop in an airport gets a vaccination aganinst the flu, it does not only helps him or her stay healthy, but also helps the many travellers who might otherwise have been inflected if that workers caught the flu. So, the externality , the result implies the vaccination of even a part of a community conveys benefits to the whole community. For example, governments pay special attention to the vaccinations of school children, teachers, health mothers, and the elderly, categories of people particularly susceptible not only to catching, but also to transmitting a disease.

It is not accidential that governments are heavily involved with vaccination . When there are externalities, free market, fail to persuade individual incentives with society's
their the worker's decision of whether to get a vaccine ends up attracting whether other people get sick. The workers might not fully take all these other people's potential suffering into account when making her or his vaccination decision.

As Stanford University does many suggestions, understand this and tries to help them make the right decisions and so providers free flu vaccines for its staff and students.
Small pockets of unvaccinated individuals can allow a disease to gain a spread more widely well-being. For example, parent weighing the costs and benefits of a vaccine for their child is not always thinking of the consequences of that vaccination to other people. THese are markets in which subsidizing or regulating behavior can make everyone better off. Because the reason for requiring that a child be vaccinated before enrolling in school is not just to protect that child, because each child's vaccination affects others via potential contagions.

Robots take our jobs behavioral and economy influences

Robot job behavior brings economy influences

If one day robots can replace human to do simple, even complex jobs. They will bring what influences to our global societial economy.The popular economic refrain declares that the global middle class is dying and robots will soon take our jobs, e.g. shopping center customer service jobs, library service jobs, cinema ticket sale jobs, restaurant kitchen cooker jobs, even, bus drivers, taxi drivers etc. public transport driving jobs, accountant, doctors etc. professional jobs. Whether it is beautiful or petty matter if our future societies have many human jobs can be replaced to do from robots. Businessman must may reduce to employ employees and reduce to pay salary or wage, when robots can be replaced to do their employees tasks. But, societies must bring unemployement rate rises , due to societies will have many people loss jobs when their employers choose to buy robots to serve their clients or do any office tasks or customer service or cleaning etc. tasks.

In micro economy view, employers may save money in long term, but in macro economy view, it will cause unemployment ratio rises , even crime rate rises when there are many people lose jobs in societies. These models of doom, though, fail to account for the hundreds of businesses riding the waves of change in their industries when robots may be invented to replace human to do many simple , even complex tasks in our future societies.

WE may image that one small factory needs to manufacture fishes canes to sell to supermarket, the small , cheaper stuff and higher margin parts of the fishes manufacture industry. Before, this factory needs to employe many human factory workers need to help every fresh customer makeing the perfect fishing gear, designed for performance, durability, and cost in order to achieve to manufacture every fish cane in whole fished processing manufacturing stages. Every worker needs to spend about 15 to twenty minutes to finish every fish cane , till to delivery to any supermarket to sell. If this fish canes manufacturing factory can apply manufacturing robots to help them to finish any one working tasks , every robot can only spend five minutes to finish whole fresh fish cane manufacturing process. Thus, every robot can help this factory save 10 to 15 minutes time to finsh every fish cane manufacturing process. IN fact, time is money, because when every robot can help this factory to reduce 10 to 15 minutes time to compare human worker. Then, this factory can finish about 20 fish canes in one hour if it can use robot to help it to manufacture fish canes. Otherwise, if this factory still use human workers to help it to manufacture fish canes, then it can finsh about 3 to 4 fish canes in one hour. SO, the manufacturing efficiency ensures that robots must help this fish manufacturing factory to raise fish canes number more than human workers. So, in robotic behavioral economy view, manufacturing robots must help this fish canes manufacturing factory to raise fish canes manufacturing number and deliver increasing number to supermarkets to prepare to sell every day. Robots can help this fish canes manufacturing factory bring manufacturing time saving, rising manufacturing efficiency, improving performance and reducing wages expenditure long time advantages in micro economy view. However, manufacturing robots can also bring disadvanages to society, e.g. increasing unemployment ratio, increasing crime rate, this factory workers will lose jobs and income, they need earn social welfare from government and increasing government finance pressure in short time, even long time in macro economic view.

Stanford University graduate program in economics, Scott lecturer explained that "in demand and supply economic theory for robots supply and demand case, robots supply number increasing may influence human workers demand number decrease. It sometimes calls " the efficient frontier".

No specific human beings were mentioned in any of economics classes. As robots supply and demand in market case, They (robots) may be purely theoretical " agents" who reached to the most reasonable sale prices in order to persuade any one businessman buyer to make manufacturing robot buying decision whether robots can help him / her to bring how much saving time , saving money, saving cost, improving performance, efficiency economic benefit before he/she plans to reduce workers number when he/she decides to apply robots to replace human workers in his/her factory or office or any service department, e.g. cinema ticket sale service, shopping center customer service, shopping center cleaning , supermarket customer service etc. service or sale tasks. When robots can replace human to do any one of these tasks in any organizations. So, robots may be human worker agents who reached to prices the way robots would react to a software command. There was nothing that explained why some people thrived and others did n't or why truly brilliant, hardworking people could fail when much lazier folks succeeded." Having been admitted to the Stanford University graduate program in economics, Scott lecturer hoped to get his answers there.

How robots influence our future social changing? Using the right technology can be a boon to your business in this economy. For internet example, it is easier than ever to find well-matched customers all around the world, to stay in contact with them, and to more quickly design the products they want. If you focus solely on being cutting -edge, though you risk letting the technology take over what should be very robust relationships with your customers , employees, and colleagues. IN nowaddays society, technoligical advances and cutomation, personal relationships in business are more crucial than ever. I mean that robots can not replace human to serve clients to let them to feel more comfortable and passion more easily. For shoe shop case example, if the shoe shop apply one robot to serve its clients to replace human shoe salesperson to serve its shoe customers. Robots ensure that they can not persuade every shoe potential buyer to make shoe buying decision more easily when robots need to contact every shoe potential buyer. The reason is simple, because robots can not touch any one shoe buyer individual emotion very easier.

If the shoe buyer needs the robots to help him/her to choose any right shoe styles when he/she can not feel himself / herself can make the most right shoe style choice decision. The robots can not replace human shoe salesperson to make shoe style choice judgement more easily. They must need longer time to analyze whether which shoe style may be the most suitable to the shoe buyer. Otherwise, human shoe salesperson may attempt to make the most right shoe style choice decision to help any one shoe buyer to chooce the most right style shoe because he/she owns shoe style sale experience, shoe style knowledge, the most important reason is that they can feel every shoe customer individual emotion to touch whether he/she will feel comfortable or happy when they attempt to help every shoe customer to seek the most right shoe style in every shoe customer whole shoe searching processing. Othwerwise, serving robots are only one machine, they can not touch or feel every shoe customer individual emotion whether he/she feel comfortable or unhappy or happy when they need to contact them in whole shoe searching processing. Hence, I believe that some tasks robots can not repalce human staff to do very easily. Otherwise, robots may bring disadvanatges to let any one businessman to loss his/her customers, due to robots can not touch every customer emotion to compare human staff in service tasks more easily. Robots serving customer behaviors may cause money lose and customers number lose to the shop in micro economic view.

Intellectual human economic behaviors

What does intellectual human economic behaviors mean ? I believe that when we choose or decide to do intellectual behaviors, then our societies will be influenced to bring economic growth in consequence.I shall attempt to indicate pollution case to explain how and why eithet our intellectual or foolish behaviors may bring economic growth or recession in consequence as below:

On one hand, for air pollution social case aspect example, if we only consider to buy cars to drive for working aimr or holiday leisure aim. Then, our societies air will be polluted. Our health will be influenced to bad. Our car driving behaviors may cause global environment air pollution serously. In long tiem, global air pollution will bring our bodies health to be bad. Although, ourselves car driving behaviors may bring our driving travelling leisure enjoyment and comfortable feeling in short time, also we so not need to pay public transport fare often, but we need to compensate ourselves health economic intangible loss due to air pollution , when cars number increases, dirty air will cause ouselves health to become bad.

In the result, we will need to pay more medical expenditure when we are old age, due to ourselves bodies will become bad, due to we breathe global dirty air every day, due to ourselves cars pollute air in long time, e.g. 10 to 20 years, even 30 more without limited air pollution environment. So, driving cars behavior may be one kind of human foolish behavior and our foolish behavior may bring ourselves future long time medical expenditure absolutely.

One the other hand, water pollution social aspect, if we often keep much rubblish to pollute sea, oil exploration porcessing pollute ocean , ships gas pollute ocaen, then fishes will eat polluted food and drive dirty water, due to global ocean is polluted.

In fact, because human only to conside how to buy boats to carry on leisure enjoyment activities, or catch cruises to travel on the sea. Also, oil manufacturers only consider researching anywhere to find new oil exploration places to manufacture oil product, when their oil exploration processes pollute ocarn . Consequently, global fishes drink polluted warer or eat polluted food. They will have poison. SO, human will have high chance to eat poison polluted fishes, due to fishes are poison or are polluted.

So, human is doing foolish activities, we only hope to find oil exploration places to pollute ocean or we only spend money to buy ticket to catch ships to travel anywhere in global ocean. All of these human foolish behaviors will bring pollution to global ocean. On consequently, we will need to compensate to eat polluted or dirty or poision fishes, ourselves bodies health will be bad. In long time, we need have high chance to pay medical expenditure when we are old. So, pollution case may be one good example to explain how and why human foolish behavior may influence ourselves future need to compensate serious medical loss.

All of these human foolish behavior will bring pollution to global ocean. On consequently, we will need to compensate to eat polluted or dirty or poison fished , ourselves bodies health will be bad. In long time, we will have high chance to pay medical expenditure, when we are old. So, pollution case may be one good example to explain how and why human ourselves intellectual or foolish behaviors may influence future long time economic loss or economic growth or recession in micro and micro economic view.

On another water pollution aspect hand, if we often keep rubbish to sea, oil exploration processing pollutes ocean and ships' gas pollute ocean, then fishes will eat polluted food and drink dirty water, due to fishes will eat polluted food and drink dirty sea water because the global ocean is polluted seriously.

In fact, because human only consider how to buy boats to carry on any leisure water activities, or catches cruises to travel on the sea. Also, oil manufacturers only consider any where to find oil exploratin places to manufacture oil products from ocean, when their pol exploration processes can plooute ocean. Consequently, global fishes drink polluted water or eat direty food. They will have poison. So, human will have high chance to eat poison fishes.

Otherwise, such as pollutin case, it can infuence inflation or deflation. Consequently, the reason indicates supply and demand theory. If air pollution is serious, then we will consider health issue, global cars demand number may be influenced to reduce, when global cars number demand will reduce, global car prices and supply number will need to change to fall down in order to attract or persuade global car consumers choose to make car purchase decision.

Hence, global car manufacture number and car price will be influenced to reduce, due to global air pollution issue. Consequently, deflation will occur because when the country citizen usually does not spend much extra saving money to buy car expensive goods. Money value will be low. Otherwise, if global cair pollution is not serious, human considers to buy cars to enjoy driving leisure lives. So, global car demand is influenced to increase , also global car price will also influenced to increase.

Consequently, gobal human will choose to buy cars to drive. Due to we accept to spend extra saving to buy expensive car goods. Car sale price and supply may be influenced to rise up. Money value is influenced to reduce. Inflation may be influenced, due to global car consumers number increases, we would not have extra money to spend easily. Car expensive goods expenditure influences our spending habit to avoid to make car purchase decision more easily. So, human intellectual or foolish activities may bring inflation or deflation consequency in possible indirectly in macro economic view.

On conclusion, above pollution case explain that how and why human intellectual or foolish economic behaviors may bring inflation or deflation consequency as wll as economic growth or recession consequency as well as any goods demand and supply increasing or decreasing consequency. It implies that human behavior may have indirect relationship to influence any goods demand and supply number to either increase or decrease result as well as any goods price will be influenced to increase or decrease in micro and macro economic view.

The relationship between social change and human behavior

Why does economic changes may influence human individual behavioral change? I shall attempt to indicate shopping behavior and staying at home behavior to explain their case and effect relationsip as below:

Human behavior can be influenced by economic change or economic change can be influenced by human behavior? Why does recession may influence consumers reduce shopping desire? In social recession suitation, it is possible that many people lose jobs suddenly, due to businessmen lose many customers. They need to make decision to reduce employees number in order to continue to keep businesses. Consequently, many firms (organizations) their employees may lose jobs. When they have much time, due to lose jobs, they will feel to avoid to spend too much time and money to go to shopping often. Many losing jobs people, they will often stay at homes.

So, they will reduce time to go to shopping, then non essential products won't their preferable choice purchase products. Hence, recession will change many losing jobs people their shopping or consumption desires to avoid to buy non essential products often . Usually when economic boom, many people have jobs to do because consumers number must increase when many people have jobs to do. Then, many people can accept to spend money to buy non essential products often. Many people feel spend time to go to shopping can satisfy their purchase of any kinds of new products useful psychology or desire. So, recession is one good example to explain it can influence many people do not like often to leave homes to go to shopping easily. Many people like to stay at homes, becaue they feel worry about spending too much shopping time when they leave homes. Their staying home time is one good negative shopping behavior example. So, economic change may influence human individual behavior changes , they have direct cause and efect relationship in behavioral economic view.

May human behavior influence economic change? Is it possible that human behavior may bring the country social economic change in macro economic or micro behavioral economic view ? I shall indicate publishing industry example. Do you feel that if there are many students feel learning is very important when they read many books or many of students feel interesting to read or they have reading new books in habit, then it is possible that the country will have many students like to spend time to go to any book shops to choose the books, they feel that they can help they learn new knowledge. Then the country will increase students number, they often spend time to visit any one book shop every week. Their visiting book shops behavior which may become their habits. So, the country will increase students number, they often spend time to visit book shops. Also, it implies that visiting book shops behaviors may be their behavioral habits.

So, when the country has many students often spend time to visit book shops , their visiting book shops behaviors may help any one book shop to raise books sale chance. So, the country's student individual often visiting book shop behaviors, their habitual visiting book shops behaviors must may assist help any one book shop to increase books sale number absolutely.

Consequently, any one book shop , its books sale bumber must be influenced to increase to increase because the country will have many students like or feel need visit book shops habit in order to choose any suitable books to buy to read at home in order to raise themselves learning effort. When the country has many bok shops often have many students visit their book shops, then their books sale number may be influenced to increase. It explain why student individual visiting book shop behavior may help any one book shop sale number increases also.

How human productive behavior may influence economic development

May any country which citizen behavior assist themselves country development? It is one cause and effect economic question. I mean that if the country itself citicen can not concentrate mind or energy to choose to do one kind of industry in order to let themselves country can bring the most benefit, then whether the counry itself economy can bring the most serious economic benefit. I shall attempt to indicate these countries themselves indistry choice to explain whether these countries themselves citizen productive behavior may help themselves countries to achieve the largest economic benefits. I shall indicate as below:

New Zealand farmer individual wine productive behavior

For New Zealand country example, this country concerns itself effort is foucs on farming agricultural aspect. So, this country has many farmers concentrate on farming agricultural aspect. May New Zealanders choose to spend time to produce different kinds of wines, e.g. wine or red grape wine is for the people are eating meat, or they are eating dinner.

When these New Zealanders their behaviors choose to do farming or agriculture to grow and produce different kinds of taste of white or red grape wine drinking products job. Themselves grape agriculture behavior will influence these New Zealanders themselves, they can learn how to improve different kinds of grape wine drinking products in order to achieve every kinds of white or read grape wines taste improving aim during their white or red grape producing process.

Why can New Zealander every individual white or read grape wine producers improve their white or read grape wine taste more easily? In behavioral economic view, it can explain that why any one New Zealander white or read grape wine producer can be encouraged or excited or persuaded to concentrate nervous and energy and effort to learn how to improve their white or red grape wine products easily.

In fact, New Zealand is one agricultural food export country. It has good natural environment resource , e.g. land, seed to provide any one farmer to produce themselves any kinds of agricultrual food products, e.g. fruit, or wine food products. Because New Zealanders know themselves country has enough natural resource . So, in common,

many New Zealanders choose to attempt to do farming agricultural jobs in order to export themselves any kinds of fruit or meat or wine products to overseas or sell to domestic in order to earn profit.
So, when these New Zealand farmers number has been increasing every year. This country farmers will feel themsleves competition between this New Zealand farmers themselves are serious due to they may feel New Zealanders choose to do agriculture businesses in order to export themselves different kinds of farming food to overseas or sell to local to earn profit.
Hence, when many New Zealand farmers feel that farmers number has been increasing every year. They will feel themselves competition is serious. They must need to spend much time and nervous and effort to research what method is the best how to produce the best taste of white or red grape wine products in order to let local or overseas wine buyers to choose to buy his/her producing white or read grpae products to drink.

Hence, in competition psychological view, may influence many New Zealand white or reaad wine producers had been beginning to change their learning behavior on researching what method is the best in order to produce the best quality of taste red or white wine products to sell in order to attract overseas or local white or read grape wine drinkers to choose to buy his/her wine products. Their behavior will focus on learning how to raising or improving white or read grape wine taste method more than only focus on producing a large number white or red grape wine products. They believe wine quality is more important to compare wine producing number. So, New Zealand wine producers themselves wine producers behaviors have been changing on concentrating on researching wine quality method aspect more then wine producing number aspect in behavioral economic view.

America high technological productive behavior

For America example, US is one high technological country, it owns many high technological knowledge talent inventors, e.g. computer science inventors. Hence, US must attract many diferent countries owning high technological computer inventors choose to go to US to develop their computer science profession career. Also, it seems that when many computer science inventors or professions choose to go to US to develop themselves computer science new career. In behavioral economic view, due to their leaving themselves countries choice, which may bring influence themselve country job behaviors need to be changed. They must need to adapt US new live. Because they will forgive their past computer science job. These computer science professionals need to spend time to adapt US new lives. They " past computer science job behaviors" will need to be changed to their new US any computer employer's new computer science job model.

Because their traditional computer science jobs needed to be forgot in their themselves countries. They will feel their old computer science job knowledge and behavior needed to change in order to let their US any one new of computer company employer feels satisfactory to accept their new working behavior in any one US computer organization.

So, on the other hand, many US computer company employer will feel that they must need time to accept any one new overseas computer science professions their working behaviors, their working attitude daily, because these foreign comouter science professional, their past computer working behaviors and working attitude must be different to US domestic computer science professions.
In behavioral economic view, these overseas computer science professions, their working behaviors and attitude must be needed to change in order to adapt any one US new computer company itself domestic or local computer science professional stafs themselves daily working behaviors and attitude because these overseas and local computer science professionals must need to team work together.
In behavioral economic view, it is only one way that foreign computer science professionals must need to change themselves past country traditiona daily working behaviors and attitude in order to cooperate with these US local computer science professionals in teams more easily.

Consequently, if these foreign compute science professionals can change their past working behaviors and attitude to let any one US local computer science professional feels to cooperate with them easily in short time. Then, the US computer company itself whole computer professional teams themselves efficiencies will be influenced to raised or improved by the changing past working attitude and working behaviors of these foreign computer science professionals. So, in behavioral economic view, only if US any one computer company hopes itself computer teams themselves efficiency can be raised or improved when it decides to employ foreign computer science professionals and US domestic computer science professionals. They need to work in teams together. They must need to let these foreign computer science professionals to know how to change their working behaviors and attitude to let their domestic computer science professionals feel easy to work together. Then, the US computer company itself whole team efficiency must be rasied or improved easily in short time.

- China share market investing behavior

For China share market example, economic development depends on financial market. Because if many Chinese have interest to invest to carry on shares buying and selling activities in orde to learn how to earn shares interest and share profit when the China shareholder can make decision to sell himself/herself shares in the the high price, then he/she can earn money when he/she can sell the China company's shares in the high sale share price position.

If China has many Chinese like to spend time to carry on investing shares activities. Themselves shares buying and selling behaviors will influence China has many companies can increase fund from many Chinese shareholders in order to have enough money to expand or develop themselves businesses in China in long term.

Consequently, when China can have many Chinese like to attempt to carry on buying and selling shares investing behaviors in China share market. Themselves buying and selling shares behaviors can help many Chinese companies have effort to increase enough money or capital in order to continue to do their businesses in long term absolutely. So, it explains why when many Chinese become shareholders , they can assist China will have many companies continue to develop their businesses if many Chinese like to carry on shares buying and selling investing behaviors in long time in China financial investment market nowadays in behavioral economic view.

Why has any individual country have many people invest share behavior which can influence the country's macro consumption desire?

I shall apply shares market buying and selling investment behavior to explaiin why shares investment behavior which may impact the country's overal consumption desire as below:

In behavioral economic view, I assume that when the coutry has many people have interest to attempt to carry on shares buying and selling investment behavior, then their frequent shares buying and selling behaviors which may bring negactive consumption desire or shopping desire of these shares investors their consumer behavior.

The reason is simple, when the country has many share buyers number suddenly been increasing rapidly. Consequently, these large group share investors must need to spend much time to research any kinds of company shares variations, whether when their share prices will rise up of fall down in order to achieve buying the company's shares in the lowest price and selling the company's shares in the highest price level in order to earn profit.

Basic on this reason, they must need to spend much extra time to research share prices changing behavior every day, e.g. one working person will wait to leave his/her job, after he/she can spend time to gather data to research the day's share price changing behavior after dinner. So, the working person's right time may be his/her share price market research behavior. Before he/she may spend his/her night time to go to shopping after dinner, but nowadays, he/she will fogive to do his/her shopping behavior before dinner or after dinner at hight sometime. He/she will make decision to spend much night time to turn on computer to click on share market website to research his/her share purchase choice to investigate whether his/her share price whether it rises up or falls down at the moment in order to make his/her share buying or selling decision at ever night time.

I mean the when the country has many people are share investors, their shares investment behavioral spenging time which will influence many shops lose customers at might often because the country will have many people feel need to spend night time to turn on computer or watch television to investigate share price variation. So, the country will have many people / share investors choose to stay at home in order to carry on share price variation investigation behavior, they need to listen share market update news from radios or watch the share market update news from computer or TV at home every night. Consequenly, they must reduce times to leave themselves homes at night. So, their shopping behavior also will be reduced. Because these share investors feel need to spend time to investigate share price variation news at homes which can bring economic benefits (high opportunity benefits) when they choose to forgive to leave homes to go to shopping times (opportunity cost) every night.

On conclusion, it seems that when the country has many people are share investors, then their share price investigating behavior may bring negative shopping emotion at night. Consequently, the country's any one shop may lose many customers from this share investor consumer group in behavioral economic view. Hence, when the country's share investors number had been increasing rapidly, it will influence any shops lose many customers from this share investing customer group at night frequenly in short time, even long time in behavioral economic view, because their shopping desires or shopping emotion will be brought negative feeling when they make decisions to spend much time to listen radios or watch TV or computers share price update nes at night. Hence, share market will bring negative impact to influence consumer shopping desire or negative shopping emotion in behavioral economic view.

Can technology influence human shopping behavioral change?

Nowadays, technological development has reached mature stage, whether technological mature stage may bring positive or negative shopping emotion influence to global consumers. I shall aplly internet inventin or ecommerce shopping channel tool to explain whether internet technology can bring postive or negative influence to global consumer behavior in behavioral economic view.

Internet is a good technological tool, it brings e-commerce business chance. In fact, commonly, global has have many businessmen choose to use internet channel to carry on their products transactions between global online-buyers and their electronic websites. So, global many shoppers had begun to feel online shopping is more convenient to compare visiting shops shopping. Their shopping behaviors have been changed from internet technological tool. Global has many shoppers choose to buy any products from any overseas or local businessmen their web stores. They only need to spend time to find any businessmen their webstores to choose the most suitable products to pay visa to buy from their webstores. at homes. So, in general, global had have may shoppers had changed their shopping behaviors from visiting shops to visiting webstores at homes often.

So, it seems that internet technological tool had influenced global many shops disappear, but internet webstores will be replaced their actual shops on streets. Some of businessmen either they choose webstores to replace shops or choose websotes and shops both or still keep shops only. Hence, internet tool influences global businessmen have three kinds of products sale channels to let globa local and overseas consumers to choose how to buy their products.

However, in fact, many of global shoppers, youngers and olders had begun to accept to buy any products from webstores. They feel to spend time to leave homes to visit shops , their shopping behaviors will be wasted time to not essential part to their daily lives. Hence, since internet technological invention, it had changed many consumers their traditional visiting shops shopping habit to change to buying products from webstores channel.

However, on the one hand, internet creates webstores ecommerce shopping channel to let global many consumers do not need to leave homes to go to shopping. It brings negative visiting shops shopping emotion to global general consumers nowadays. But on the other hand, it also brings positive visiting internet webstores shopping emotion to global general consumer nowadays. So, it seems that global many consumers feel that they often do not need to spend much time to go out shopping. Many global consumers feel convenient and enjoy to choose any products to buy from different internet webstores, when the online buyer chooses the most suitable product, he she only needs to pay visa card to buy the product from the online seller's webstore conveniently at home.

Hence, online shopping can bring economic benefit to online buyers, e.g. avoiding walking time or spending transport fare to visit the shop to go to shopping, shortening or reducing shopping time to do another important matter.

On conclusion, global many consumers began feel online shopping can bring more economic benefits on shortening shopping time, avoiding transport fare spending aspect. So, online shopping will be popular shopping behavior for future long time. It may encourage global many shoppers can make rapid shopping decision in short time in order to carry on any products buying transaction to global any one online shopper in short time easily in behavioral economic view. So, global many businessmen had begun to build themselves one attraction webstore in order to persuade different countries consumers to choose to click themselves webstores from internet channel to buy any kinds of products in short time easily.
So, internet technology had changed consumers traditional shopping behaviors to build positive online shopping emotion as well as raise online sellers‘ any products sale chance easily in behavioral economic view.
 Why and how human behavior may influence the country's economic growth or recession?
When one country has many people choose to do the same matter for one period, whether their behavior may influence the country's pvera; economic growth or recession . I shall attempt to indicate cases toexplain their relationship as below:

For flowing rubblish behavioral case example, do you feel that when the country has many people often flow rubblish on the streets, instead of their flowing rubblish behavior may bring streets dirty? But, their flowing rubblish behavior may explain that this country has people may have enough money to buy food to ear, or enough cloths to wear, enough bottles of water to drink, even they may have enough money to buy new television, radio, refrigeraters , washing machines, desktops or laptops electronic home products from old to new to use in order to satisfy their living needs. So, when they flow old electronic home products, their flowing old home electronic products behaviors may seem that they have enough money to buy other new home electronic products to replace old home electronic products to use at homes.

However, it seems thaat this country ought have many people have jobs to do. So, many of them, they can easy to make purchase decison to flow any old home electronic products and buy any new home electronic products to use . Because this country has many people have jobs to do. So, they can often not use old home electonic products to become rubblishs to flow on streets after they had bought any kinds of new home electronic homes.

In fact, it also implies that this country's economy grows rapidly. So, many businesses can glow up rapdly. When they expanded their businesses, they must need to increase employees number in order to let they help themselves to raise productivity or serve their clients absolutely. So, when the country has many businesses can grow up, it seems that its economy must be better or it is improved to compare past. Due to many different kinds of home electronic products had been often bought to use by this country people in this period. So, this country's any streets can be observed that expensive electronic home products were flowed on streets anywhere. then, this country will have many electronic home products sellers can sell their home electronic products very easily. When this country has many people can find any kinds of jobs to do easily. So, due to unemploymen rate had been decreasing.

In behavioral economic view, as this many electronic home products rubblish country case, we can observe this country may have many people have jobs to do. So, consumption number has been increased long time. So, cheap food, or expensive home electronic products may be rubblish on any streets. This country's people , their flowing rubblish behaviors may be explained that many of people have enough jobs to do, so they have ability to buy any good taste food to eat or buy any kinds of expensive electronic home products to use. So, this country's economy may be improved for this long period. So, in behavioral economic view, when this country can have many electronic home products rubblishs are flowed on anywherer in streets frequently. It seems that this country will have many people have jobs to do, so it causes they often change old home electronic products or replaced them easily, when they have enough income to spend to buy any kinds of new home electronic products to use at homes easily. Moreover, their flowing old electronic home products behaviors also indicate that this country has many people their salaries may be increased in possible from their emplyers. When this country can have many different kinds of home electornic products are sold. It means that this country's electronic home products needs or demand had been increasing, due to many people have jobs to do and income increases to excite their living of needs also improve. Consequently, this country may seem have better economic improvement. We can observe from this country's electronic home products rubblish increasing income in theis period.
On conclusion, this country ought experience economic growth at this period. So, " flowing expensive electronic home rubblish increasing number " may seem that this country's economic growth is rapidly in this period, due to many people have jobs to do as well as salaries increase in this period.

Technology how impacts human behavior changing?
Technology how influences human behavior to bring changing? For example, online share purchase and sale

transaction from smart phone brings share investor can do share buying or selling transation in any where and any time conveniently, non manual driving auto vehicle, bring car owner feels comfortable and spends free time to do other matter, e.g. reading, listening mucis in himself or herself car freely. electrical energy vehicle can help car owner to reduce air polluton and it can brings the drivers do not feel drive long time in any journeys in order to avoid air pollution for environmental protection responsible car drivers in our societies. Thus, they will drive long time in any journeys when they can drive electronic energy cars to replace oil energy cars.

However, online technology can also bring consumers can choose to stay at homes to buy any things from seller individual online webstore conveniently. Such as online technology can bring shoppers do not need to spend much time to visit shops to buy any things. They can choose any kinds of products from any online sellers individual online webstores conveniently at homes. Online technology excite busy consumers can make purchase decision easily as well as it can help online sellers sell any kinds of products from internet easily.

In behavioral economic view, technology can change human behavior to be improved, it can let human feels comfortable, more free time ro use, rapid making any decisions, such as apply smart phones to make share purchase or sale transaction decision, online shopping decision, even travelling any where decision in short time, when the traveller finds the most cheap hotel accommodation room price and air ticket price frm any travel agent online tourism webstore, then the potential travel customer can follow the online hotel accommodation price and air ticket price data to make decision when to buy the air ticket from the airline travel agent or make decision when to prebook which hotel accommodation room to go to the country to travel from online travel agent tourism webstores. So, technology can encourage global any country travelers to make anywhere to trvel rapidly. If the traveler can find the country's general hotel rooms and airline tickets prices had been decreasing more sightly. The traveler may make travel decision to choose the country to travel in short time, then he/she can prebook the country;s any hotel room and airline ticket to pay by visa fraom the country's any hotel and airline travel agent webstores., before one week, even one month or more easily. Hence, online technology can also encourage traveler individual frequent travel times to be increased, due to global travelers can find any hotel rooms and airline tickets prices from internet conveniently at homes. They do not need to spend time to visit any airline travel agent to enquire travel choice country's hotel rooms prices and airline ticket prices. They can compare global travel of countries choices ' all hotels rooms and airline agents air tickets prices to make prebook airline seat and hotel room decision before one week, one month even six months early.

On conclusion, online technology can encourage global travelers can make travelling any where and when traveling time desicions easily. It can excite tourism industry develops in long time. Also, such as electricity cars invention can encourage environment protection car owners do car purchase decision easily, because they can choose to drive electronic energy cars to replace oil energy cars in order to avoid air pollution occurs easily. So, electronic cars can increase electronic car purchasrs number, due to many of environmental protection attitude of car owners can choose to drive electricity cars to bring air cleans, even non -manual driving cars can encourage lazy driving and free time driving car owners to choose to buy non-manual (artificial intelligent) cars to drive , because they can spend much free time to read, listen music or do any matters in themselves cars, they do not need to drive cars, robotic (AI) auto driving machine is such one non-manual driver to help them to drive themselves cars confidently. So, non-manual driving cars can attract lazy and enjoying free time driving car owners to choose to buy to replace traditional manual cars to drive easily. Moreover, online share transaction can help any share investors to make share buying and selling decision in short time easily. When they can apply smart phones technological tool to carry on share buying and selling activities easily. They can observe any share rising or falling price suitation from smart phones in any where any any time easily. So, smart phone technology can help global any shareholders to make share purchase and sale transaction easily. So, technology can encourage human makes decision in short time rapidly.

How and why employees behaviors may influence economy development?

In behavioral economy view,I believe the country's any organizational employees behavior may bring indirect relationship to influence the country's long term economic development. I shall indicate past manufacture industry social development period to explain their relationship. For many countries' past business activities had belonged to manufacturing industry, such as US, UK past before 1980 year, it focused on steel manufacturing and steel manufacturing related machine products. So, US, Uk developed countries manufacturing industries may be past main country's economic income sources. I assume US , UK past had one million number different kinds of industries. They ought had about seven houndred thousand number organizational businesses were belonged to manufactured industry. They may include:

Steel manufacturing and steel related machine manufacturing, e.g. vehicle manufacturing, home appliances, e.g. washing machine, television, radio, refrigerate cooler, heater, air condition etc. different kinds of different kinds of steel -related manufacturing machine, they were manufactured from US, UK steel machine manufacturers. So, US, Uk the other three hundred thousand number industry may be general service industry, e.g. hotel service, restaurent, cinema, public transport service, tourism lesiure , wine bar, supermarket etc. different kinds of non-manufacturing industries business organizations were operated in UK, US past before 1980 year.

So, in UK, US developed countries industry development history, they ought have high percentage of businesses belonged to steel related manufacturing machine and steel products. Also, in the past before 1980 year, US, Uk business employers , they employed many workers are manufacturing workers. They needed to spend long time to work in factories. They were skillful workers, and they are trained to manufacturing cars, washing machine, television, heater, etc. even steel itself different kinds of steel related products to prepare to deliver to their shops to sell to US, Uk local or overseas clients.

So, I believe that past UK, US ought employ many employees, they belonged to skillful manufacturing workers, manufacture increasing steel machine or steel related machine number of products rapidly daily. So, if UK, US had had many of these manufacturing factories owned high skillful workers, then their manufacturing steel-related machine or steel both kinds of products number must be influenced to raise rapidly. Consequently, their steel machine manufacturing products would been exported to overseas or would been sold to local both markets , they may be influenced to raise sale number. They (these manufacturing workers) needed to be trained to know how to manufactur these different kinds of machine products in the efficient teams and they ought to be trained to raise their efficiencies in order to shorten time to manufacturing many kinds of steel related manufacturing machine or steel itself products rapidly. So , if their efficiencies and manufacturing performance was improved, these US, UK any one manufacturing worker and their teams ought achieve raising productivities significantly.

Hence, when past UK, US manufacturing industry development period, if these two countries' any manufacturing factories could have many manufacturing workers could be trained to be skillful and proficient manufacturing workers. Then, in past every day to these factories workers, they ought help their steel or steel related manufacturing employers to raise any kinds of machine or steel products number in every team. So, when past in the manufacturing industry development, US, UK could have many factories' manufacturing workers themselves steel or steel related machine products manufacturing skill could be trained to to improve to any kinds of these machine or steel manufacuring products quality as well as their products number could be influenced to raise by themselves skillful improvement significantly every day.
Then, what would be influenced to occur to past UK, US manufacturing industry period? In behavioral economic view, when these two manufacturing industry developed countries, such as UK, US , if they had many factories workers can be trained to improve their skill in order to achieve any kinds of steel or steel-related machine products quality could be improved as well as products manufacturing number could be also increased absolutely.

In consequence, past UK and US both countries ought increase themselves any kinds of steel and steel related machine products number to be supplied to themselves local shops to let local clients to choose any one kind of machine manufacturing products to buy easily as well as they could also export to supply overseas any countries to buy their different kinds of steel or steel related machine products to let overseas steel or steel related manufacturing machine product buyers, they can have many of these different kinds of these steel or steel-related different kinds of manufacturing machine from UK and UK these both countries easily to compare other countries.

On conclusion, I believe that past US, and UK macro manufacturing industry income GDP would increase significantly. So, they would have good economic growth performance because when many of these manufacturing workers themselves manufacturing effort could be improved. So, it explained when employees manufacturing abilities can influence economic growth indirectly.

Robots invention whether they can help organizations to raise efficiencies or inefficiencies?
In behavioral economic view, in any organizations, when the organization hopes its worker teams can raise efficiencies , the organization may choose to increase more workers number and/or it can provide training to improve these workets themselves skills in order to raise their efficiencies. For one warehouse example, when the warehouse increases many goods , they are needed to delivered these goods from the shelves to the delivering destination locations. If this warehouse supervisors feel these workers themselves goods delivery speeds are slow, which is possible due to this warehouse's workers number is not enough. So, this warehouse supervisor ought increase workers number in order to increase their goods delivery speed in order to deliver goods from the shelves to every indicated goods delivery destination in order to let any one lorry driver can transport the right kinds of goods and ensure the accurate goods number to transport to any one client home rapidly.

However, if this warehouse supervisor planed to buy several warehouse goods delivery robots to assist these warehouse workers to find the right kinds of goods from shelves and then deliver to the right destination location in the warehouse. So, these warehouse orkers can concentrate on counting the accurate goods number and ensuring the right kinds of goods in order to prepare to let lorry drivers to transport these goods to these goods of buyers themselvers homes rapidly. Consequently, in the first step, robots can concentrate on finding th right goods from shelves and delivers them to the right goods transportation of location destination. Then, in the second step, these warehouse workers can concentrate on counting the accurate goods number and ensuring the right kinds of goods in order to prepare to put them to the lorry. Consequently, when warehouse robots and warehouse workers can cooperate to work together, the most important, robots, can deal on finding the right kinds of goods and deal on delivering the accurate number of goods of job duty as well as these warehouse workers can only concentrte on counting the right kinds of goods number in order to avoid it has none any mistake of wrong kinds of goods and inaccurate goods of delivery number to be transported to the lorry and to deliver to any one buyer's home.
So, it seems that warehouse robots ought help any one warehouse worker to raise himself efficiency and avoid goods delivery of mistake occurrence easily as well as their help to warehouse workers that can let any one goods buyer feels their goods can be delivered to their homes rapidly. Moreover, warehouse robots can also help these warehouse workers to raise efficiencies because warehouse robots can help them to shorten goods delivery time between any one shelf and any one goods delivery destination of location in the warehuse because robots may help them to find the right kinds of goods from the right shelf in the short time. So, any one worker does not need to spend long time to seek anywhere is the right shelf location for the kind of goods when the kind of goods are needed to deliver to the buyer's home from lorry. Warehouse robots can help them to do this aspect of " finding the goods from the right shelf in short time job duty". So, any one warehouse worker only needed tospend less time to do the counting of any right kind of goods number and ensuring the right kind of goods job duty. Consequently, this warehouse 's any one worker, his any one kind of goods delivery time may be reduced, because robots' assistance

and they may have more confidence to avoid mistake to deliver the wrong number of goods and/or the wrong kind of goods to any one goods buyer's home.

On conclusion, it seems that warehouse robots ought may help any one warehouse worker to raise efficiency for any one team in the warehouse as well as the warehouse any one supervisor does not need to spend much time to observe any one worker individual performance for " goods delivery job duty aspect" because their goods delivery job duty that had been replaced to do by these several warehouse robots. Robots can achieve the more accurate of right kinds of goods and the right number of goods delviery job performance to compare any one of human warehouse worker themselves right kinds of goods of delivery and right number of goods of delivery job performance. So, when robots can participate to cooperate with this warehouse's any one worker to do their goods of delivery job duty in this warehouse every day. Then, robots can raies any one of supervisor individual confidence in order to let they do not need to spend time to observe any one of worker individual whose goods of delivery job performane. They can concentrate on supervising any one worker whose goods transport to lorry in the final step in order to avoid to deliver wrong goods number and / or wrong kind of goods to any one goods buyer's home every day. Consequently, this warehouse's overall teams of their delviery of goods performance many be improved by robotss' participatin to goods of delivery task as well as this warehouse's oveall teams themselves efficiencies may be influenced to raise by robots' goods of delivery task participation.

Why social behavior may influence organizational strategy needs to be changed ?
Why any organizations need to know whether nowadays social behaivor how has been changing in order to implement the kind of the most right strategy to achieve the profit aim pursue in possible. I shall indicate nowadays ecommerce or online, customer shopping behavior to explain above question concerns they ought have close relationship between social behavior and organizational strategic choice or organizational behavioral changing need.

On nowadays ecommerce business, or online shopping model, this kind of shopping model in global many young and old age consumers like to apply internet tool to choose any country sellers website stores in order to stay at home to buy any kinds of products from themselves webstores in global societies.
In fact, online shopping model had been popular for long time above to twenty years. Most of global sellers will make decision to design themselves webstores in order to attract global many online buyers to choose to buy their products from themselves webstores. So, it seems that social consumers purchase behaviors had been changed to online shopping from internet invention.

Hence, social consumers purchase behavioral changes may influence any organizations' strategies need to be changed from visiting shops purchase strategy model to online purchase strategy model, if the seller still concentrate on concentrate on considerate how to design itelf , but neglects to considerate how to design itself webstore, e.g. how to design attract product photos to put on itself webstore, how to arrange sale price information location to be putted on webstore and visa card payment location on itself webstore in order to let any one online buyer can feel very easier to buy itself any kinds of products from itself webstore. Then, its potential online buyers will be influenced to increase number when they can find this online seller itself any kinds of products photes and every kinds of product sale price information and visa card payment channel locations easily from itself webstore.

So, it implies that nowadays any one seller ought need to design one webstore to let any one online overseas and domestic consumers can have chance to click itself webstore to choose any one kind of product to buy conveniently when he/she does not hope to leave him/her home to go to shop, because nowadays social shopping behaviors had been influenced to change when internet invention, them it gives another online purchase method to replace visiting shops purchase method to global any one buyer in nowadays societies.

So, if nowadays any one seller still concentrate on how to design itself shop display in order to put any kinds of product on shelf in order to let any one visiting shop customer to find the kind of product to buy, but it neglects to change to choose to pursue another new technological shopping method, such as webstore purchase method in order to implement effective strategy to design the most right webstore as well as in order to attract global overseas and local consumers to find itself webstore easily from website and find its any one kind of product phots and sale price and visa card payment button in order to choose to buy itself any kinds of products in the short time. Consequently I believe that the seller will lose many customers from overseas and local when its other same or similar product sellers choose to design themselves webstores in order to let global any one product buyer can buy themselves any one kind of product when they can pay visa card to buy their products from them webstores conveniently when they stay at home habitly. Then, the seller will lose many global potential customers in long time.

On conclusion, in behavioral economic view, any consumer behavioral social changing, which will influence any in order to avoid customers number loses significantly . In future time, organizations need to make rapid decision in order to implement the most reasonable and the most useful strategy in order to avoid global potential customers number reduces or lose them in long time. So, social behavioral changing environment ought influence any global organizations need to decide how to change themselves strategies in order to avoid customers loses significantly in future time.

How and why human behavior may influence economic growth or recession?

May ourselves daily behaviors influence our global societial continue economic growth or recession? Do they have cause and effect close relationship between human behaviors and global economic growth or recession? I shall apply behavioral economic theory to analyze and explain whether ourselves daily behaviors and our global societial economic growth or recession which have close cause and effect relationship as below:

Every country itself economic development must depend on any business activities, otherwise, any kinds of business activities must need ourselves business activities or behaviors in order to achieve any business activities as well as achieve the country's overall economic development in macro view.
However, any country's overall business activites or behaviors which must depend on any kinds of individual businessmen, themselves employees daily working behavior or activity or performance in order to help them to attract or increase many clients number to acieve " earning profit" aim. So, it seems that any individual business, itself overall every department individual working behavior is one main factor to influence the company's overall business performance.

For agricultural fruit and meat food farming industry example, such as New Zealand is a farming main target industry country. It had had many New Zealanders were daily themselves own farming businesses for many years. Their farming businesses include growing fruit, sheep, cow, pig pork, meat etc. food sale business. If the New Zealand farmer owned a large size farming land, then he will choose either growing fruit or feeding sheeps, pigs, cows to be meat to to transport to New Zealand supermarkets to help them to sell to their farmers meet to New Zealanders in order to earn profit. Thus, if the New Zealand farmer owned large size of farming lands, then he needs to employ many farming employees (farming workers) to help him to carry on farming business daily tasks, e.g. picking up friuts, feeding pigs, cows, sheeps to eat food daily. These daily farming jobs are very important to influence this New Zealand farmer's meats or fruits sale number whether they can be easy or diffcult to sell in New Zealand supermarkets , if these farming workers can own encough farming knowledge or skill to know how to pick up fruits method and make judgement to know whether it is right time to pick up the kind of fruits from the trees , as well as know how feed this pigs, sheeps, cows to eat food in order to let they are better health. Consequently, their farming behaviors which can let these animals can provide the best taste and enough meat from these animals to let New Zealander to buy to eat from New Zealand any one supermarket. Even these New Zealand farming workers can know whether the kinds of fruits, e.g. oranges, apples, gapes etc. fruits whether they ought be picked up from the trees at the right time. Consequently, they can make judgement to decide to pick up any kinds of the best taste fruits to let any one New Zealander to buy to eat from any one supermarket in New Zealand. Otherwise, if they do not make judegement to know whether the kind of fruit ought not be picked up because they still need longer time to continue grow up to increase fruit size and better taste from the trees in order to let any one fruit buyer can feel better taste when they eat this kind of fruit later. If they can buy this kind of fruit to eat later, then this New Zealand farmer's his fruit buyers can buy the best taste of this kind of fruit to eat from an yone supermarket in New Zealand. Consequently, many New Zealand supermarkets will choose to buy any kinds of fruits from this farmer fruit supplier when they feel this farmer's fruits can provide more better taste fruits to compare other farmers' fruits.

Thus, due to New Zealand is one farming main income source country. It's any kinds of fruits and meats need to be export to overseas to sell , instead of local sale. It's GDP percent is very high to whole country 's overall income source. So, any one New Zealand farmer individual and any one farming worker individual working behavior will influence its economy whether it is influenced to grow or recession possible. Moreover, it also seems that farming workers' farming knowledge and skill will influence themselves farming daily activities to achieve the aim of the number of increase or decrease to any kinds of fruits whether they are better taste or the number of increase of decrease to any kinds of meats whether they are better taste to supply to any one New Zealand fruit or meat buyers to eat from any one New Zealand supermarket. So, it implies that any one New Zealand farming worker individual farming behavior may influence any kinds of fruits or any kinds of meat taste because they are transported to any one supermarket to sell in New Zealand.

Consequently, if New Zealans had many farmers can teach god farming knowledge and skill to let their any one farming workers know how to decide judgement to decide when it is right time to pick up any kinds of fruits from trees , or how to grow them on soil in order to let they can grow rapidly. Then, many different kinds of fruits can be provided to let any one New Zealanders can eat the best taste of fruits when their fruits are supplied to any one New Zealand supermarkets. Even, if they knew how to feed foods to pigs, cows, sheeps to eat daily. Then they can be more health and they can provide the best taste of meats to let any one New Zealanders can buy their meats from any one New Zealand supermarkets. Moreover, their fruits and meats can be transported to overseas to let any one country fruits or meats buyers can choose any kinds of New Zealand meats and fruits to buy to eat from themselves countries supermarkets. Then, many overseas fruit and meat buyers will perfer to choose New Zealand any kinds of fruits or meats to buy to compare other countries fruits or meats to buy when they go to any one local supermarkets.

On conclusion, it seems that New Zealand farming workers themselves farming behavior may influence their farming employers any kinds of fruits or meats sale number and income because their farming task behaviors must influence whether their fruits or meats taste are the better taste or worse taste to compare their other local farmers (the farmer competitors) whose fruits or meats taste. If tthe farmer's any one farming worker can be trained to learn how to know to feed animals skill and when is the most right time to pick up any kinds of fruits from trees or how to grow them on the soil methods. Due to these farming worker individual farming behavior may influence his different finds of fruits and meats sale number to be increase or decrease, so these any one New Zealand farmer must need to depend on any one farming worker whose farming working methods, if their farming working behaviors can be the best to influence any kinds of fruits to grow rapid or any kinds of pigs, cows, sheeps animals grow up rapidly , then their sale number may be increase significantly and their taste can be improved to let any New Zealand or overseas meat or fruit buyer to buy to eat to feel from any one New Zealand or overseas supermarkets, then New Zealand's agriculture industry must be influenced to increase. In the world, any one fruit or meat buyer must choose to buy New Zealand's fruit and meat to eat in prefer to compare other countries' fruits and meats. So, New Zealand's GDP may be influenced to raise from any one New Zealand farming worker individual farming working behaviors.

Reasons why human behavior may influence economic recession or growth?
Can ourselves daily behaviors or activies influence ourselves countries' economic growth or recession? I shall attempt to explain the reasons why they have direct or indirect relationship between human behavior and economy growth or recession as below:
I shall indicate environment pollution case to attempt to explain above question. Our societies had been experiencing servious environment pollution challenge. However, environment pollution , such as air pollution is caused by air planes and vehicles emission by air planes and vehicles emission as well as water pollution is caused by plastic rubblish, or dirty water or oil or gas chemical material, these both kinds of pollution ought may bring economic recession and this both kinds of pollution are caused by human ourselves daily foolish activities.

I believe human behavior and economy and pollution which have cause and effect relationship. I shall analyze this environment pollution case to explain why they have case and effect relationship between human foolish behavior and environment pollution and economic recession as below:
When global societies had many people like to buy cars to drive to bring emission to fresh air on the roads as well as many manufacturing factories will bring emission to pollute fresh air in their manufacturing processes. Factories and cars will bring air pollution , due to factories need to pollute fresh air in order to manufacture many products and car owners need to drive their cars to go to offices or leisure places. Their cars will also bring emisson to pollute fresh air. On consequence, car owners themselves frequent driving behaviors and factory workers themselves frequent manufacturing behaviors may bring environment pollution. Technology or human behavior whether may influence economic growth or recession. Moreover, air planes also brings emission to pollute air when they are flying in sky. Also, when ships bring oil pollution or sea plastic rubblishs bring pollution to global oceans.
In fact, manufactuers and cars owners, such as factories workers manufacturing behaviours ans car owners driving behaviors and pilots driving air planes flying behaviors and ships transport behaviors, which may cause plastic rubblish, oil or gas emission to sky or sea or on the road to cause ocean and air pollution is serious. However, human ourselves need to buy cars to drive to satisfy ourselves driving leisure or enjoyment, travelers need to catch air planes to travel to enjoy leisure needs, factories workers need help factories to manufacture many products to sell to customers to satisfy thei

r using needs. oil exploration needs to find lands to explore new oil lands.
All of these business and leisure activites may bring serious air and water pollution. However, due to serious air and water pollution will bring earth warming challenge , such as some countries temperature will be influences to rise up to 40 degree or higher br earth warming. However, earth warming is caused by air and ocean pollution. Pollution must be caused by human ourselves, driving cars leisure and factories manufacturing business activities. Hence, if human decided to continue to do these foolish behaviors, we only pursue to manufacture different kinds of

industrial products or drive cars to enjoy leisure aims, but we also neglect ourselves behaviors may bring environment pollution. Then, earth warming or earth temperature will be influenced to rise up absolutely in long term. Moreover, if our future earth will be influenced to bring serious high temperature effect by human ourselves these foolish behaviors.
On consequencey, warth warming will bring serious economic losses in possible because when ourselves earth temperature had been influenced to rise up to 40 degree or high. Ourselves health will be caused poor, due to we will feel difficult breath, we must need often tried and hard to work, due to our nervous and health will be influenced to poor by pollution and earth warming effect. Also, we need to pay more money to see doctors when we had long life. Then, our societies will lose may strong labors to help manufacturers to work, e.g. factories will reduce workers number to help manufacturers to produce more different kinds of products, due to workers health is general poor. Due to lacking enough workers to manufacture products, our societies will begin to reduce enough supply number of products to sell to global consumers to satisfy their use needs.

On conclusion, in behaviroal economic view, our societies will lose many labors due to their bodies are not health by air and water pollution. Global economic and business activities will be influenced to worse by global workers reducing number reason. So, economic recession will begin to occur in possible when pollution reaches the serious level.

How employee behavior influences organizational development?

Can any organizational department employee individual behavior may help the organization to bring long term development? When one employee individual behavior, manager won't feel whose task behavior may help organizational development, but when the department has many teams cooperate to work together , all of these team employees whose task behaviors may help their organization to bring long term development.

I shall explain how any why when the organization has many departments, as well as when every team memmber individual behavior may help whole organization to bring long term development in possible as below:

Every organization must need efficient department to cooperate to work together. They may include human resource, finance, logistic, facility management, sales, marketing , operateional , warehouse , factory manufacture , research and development, purchase, customer service etc. different kinds of departments to cooperate to work together. So, any one employee individual behavior, include manager, leader, supervisor, worker, salesperson, manufacture worker, adminisration staff, factory or logistic worker etc. themselves task behavior whether his/her performance is worse or better , whose task behavior ought bring long term good or bad influence to cause the organization's whose efficiency, or performance , whether it can be influenced to improve significantly. For car factory manufacture workers department example, it exmploys 100 car manufacturing workers. They need to manufacture at least 50 cars in order to bring enough car manufacture number to supply to global car buyers to choose to buy (satisfaction to car buyers their driving leisure activity needs). However, if this car manufacture firm employs many low skilful car manufacture workers, their inefficient car skill may bring cars manufacture number reduces, they can not achieve to reach the at least 50 cars manufacture number, if these 100 car manufacture workers. They have half number of workers, they only manufacture 30 to 40 cars number at least daily. So, it seems that this car manufacture firm will have half car manufacture workers bring the low cars manufacture number to compare the another half cars manufacture workers, when this proficient car manufacture workers may manufacture at least 60 or more cars manufacture number daily. So, it explains that this inefficient car manufacture workers will not help this car manufacture company to manufacture enough cars number in order to supply to global car market to sell to satisfy global car buyers needs, when car buyers demand number is more thn car manufacture supply number in supply and demand view. Hence, in long term, if this car manufacture company can not employ new proficient car manufacture workers to replace those inefficient or low skillful car workers. Consequently, its car manufacture number must be influenced to reduce and it can not satisfy global car buyers driving leisure needs.

However, if this car manufacture firm also has shop to sell itself any kinds of cars, instead of manufacturing cars product. So, it needs have both main departments to help it to earn profit. The first step, it needs have proficient car manufacture workers to help it to manufacture at least 50 cars from every car worker in order to have enough cars number to be provided to global car sellers to help it to sell to global car customers. Second step, if it decided to attempt to sell itself cars. Then, it needs to set up car shops in global to different countries in order to let global car buyers may visit its global any one car shop to enquire any one car etc. salesperson about any car quality, speed, gas useful, price, safety, etc. information questions and they can attempt to sit in any one car to feel whether which car can let them to feel more comfortable to make final car purchase decision in any one shop. So, if this car company can provide good sale speaking skillful training to any one car salesperson to let his/her to know whether how to explain every kind of car function and feature, manufacture method etc. questions, then I believe that they can influence any one car buyer to makecar purchase choice decision more easily. So, it this car manufacturer hopes it may attempt to earn profit from different countries car sellers and car buyers both. It ought also provide training course to all general car salespeople to be proficient owning sale speaking skillful professional skill in order to prepare having more confidence to persuade any one car customer to make car purchase choice from any one car salesperson more easily to compare global other car sellers.
Hence, if this car manufacturer could build both car manufacturing team and car sale team more proficient. However, if this car manufacturer hopes to develop itself car manufacture busness to expend to car sale business both in success. It must need to spend long term to provide training courses to general car manufacture workers and general car salespeople both to be proficient car skillful manufacture workers and proficient car skillful salespeople in order to help they can manufacture enough car numbers and help they can persuade may car customers can make car purchase decision in short time when they visit its any one car shop.

However, this car manufacture company explains why every car manufacture worker whose manufacturing behavior and every car salesperson sale persuading speaking ability may help this car manufacture company to expand from its car manufacture market to car sale market development in sussess in possible. So, this car manufacture firm must need these two kinds of essential human resource elements in order to achieve its cars sale number and cars manufacture number increasing aim. They may include proficient car manufacture workers and proficient car salespeople both human resource elements. These both human resource daily task behavior may influence its long term task efficient performance in order to expand itself car sale business in success from itself car manufacture business easily. If it hopes to expand its car manufacture business to car sale business in success. It must need to provide training to these two departments general staffs to be proficient staffs in order to supply enough cars number to its global car shops to let global car buyers can choose its any kinds of cars to buy in any time.

Morevoer, if this car manufacture company can have good skillful of car research and development department , it aims to research and innovate any new technological cars invention in order to improve its any traditional old kinds of cars to be innovative new kinds of cars from every year. Consequently, its any new innovative cars ought attract global any one car buyer to make car purchase choice final decision more easily, because its any kinds of manufacturng cars can be innovated rapidly to compare its any one car manufacturing competitors, when its nay kinds of cars can be shorten time to innovate within three months, but its any one car manufacturing competitors need to spend more than three months, even one year to innovate themselves traditional old cars products in long term.

Hence, its car staffs research and development department staffs must need own good car product design ability, proficient car engineering knowledge , even car invention knowledge in order to innovate its any one kind of car product in short time and introduce to let its global car proficient car buyers feel surprise to its any one kind of innovative car products to compare its any one car manufacturer.Hence, these four departments: car manufacture, car sale and car research and development anr car training departments must need concentrate resource to provide enough training to any one staffs in order to achieve the best performance.

On conclusion, all these departments staffs their performance can influence car manufacture aim to chance to car manufacture and sale aim more significantly. it explains why some main department staffs whole behaviors may influence any organizational performance significantly.

Artificial intelligent Human clever and art creating ability methods

How robots create human clever and art creating ability? Nowadays robots invention may help businesses to reduce employees number, improve performance, raise productivities, reduce cost in service industry,manufacturing

industry, office , warehouse, restaurant, hotel , factory, cinema etc. different kinds of business environments, even public transport tools. However, instead of robots may bring these above advantages to any kinds of business working and service environments, whether robots may also help human to create clever and image creating ability. I shall attempt to answer this question:
On the one hand, I believe that past technology ,e.g. machine , it should not have ability to help human to create clever and image creative ability,but nowadays, robots invention that I believe it had had enough ability to help future human to raise more clever and more creating image or painting picture, art design etr. image ability, after robots had been experienced above more than ten years improvement stage from early research stage to invention stage, till to nowadays improvement stage, e.g. non-manual driving auto vehicels, even future non-manual driving skill may be improved to apply to public transport tools, e.g. trams, trains,buses, airplanes, ships etc. public transport tools, when non-manual driving skills can be improved to own the most safe driving skillful ability to compare human driving skills.
On another hand, when robots could be invented to be applied to medical or hospital surgery aspect, e.g. roboting surgerys may help surgery doctors to do complex surgery in surgery rooms, or serving patients tasks in any hospital working environments. They can help nurses and doctors to spend more time to do more important tasks urgently, so medical or surgery serving robots may help nurses and surgery doctors to reduce task load pressure and create clever or improve their surgery skills to when they can cooperate to work in hospitals.

On the other hand, robots can be invented to help any public transport drivers to avoid more traffic accidents occurrence on any countries roads. So, it seems that non-manual driving public transport tools invention may also help human drivers to improve driving skills in possible, when they can learn how to avoid sudden traffic accidents occurrence in any countries roads in any time. so, any kindsof public transport tool drivers ought learn how to avoid traffic accidents skills from future non-manual driving robots invention. Instead of non-manual driving robots and hospital patients medical care or surgery service robots may help public transport tools drivers and hospital nurses and doctors to concentrate on spending time to treat any more important and urgent matters every days. Even, future restaurants may let cooking restaurants may let cooking robots to help human cookers to cook more different kinds of good taste food, to human cookers may learn cooking robots cooking skills in order to improve themselves traditional cooking skills often, in order to compare their cooking skills between human cookers and cooking robots.

On conclusion, it seems that cooking robots ought help human cookers to create any kinds of new cooking skills. Moremove, futuer robot cookers ought be future human cookers their cooking coaches. These robot cookers will help human cookers to create clever cooking skills in possible. Also, future non-manual driving robots ought help human drivers to create new driving skills in order to improve their driving skills to reduce sudden traffic accidents occurrence easily on any countries roads in any time, future hospital surgery or patient care service robots may help surgeons or nurses to do any surgerys in surgery rooms or looking care patients in hospitals. So, when robot surgeons help human surgeons to do complex surgerys in surgerical rooms, human surgeons can learn how to do more complex surgerical tasks for every surgeons when human surgeons can observate every surgerical robots how to do surgeons together. Hence, it seems that robot surgeons also may create future human surgeons themselves innovate surgerical skills from traditional surgerical skills improvement. So, future artificial intelligent technology ought help any kinds of human occupations to create clever, even improvement themselves traditional skills to new innovative skills absolutely.

Why does technology raise online products sale demand and reduces shops products sale demand? Nowadays robot technology is popular to be applied to different aspects of our daily lives. They may include: non-manual driving vehicles, smart phones, space rockets, kitchen cookers, shopping centres service, cinema ticket sale, etc. different kinds of businesses demand. However, instead of internet invention may influence global communication, media channel is changed to computer internet, media channel is changed to computer internet, media communication from traditional newspaper, letter, TV, radio etc. communication channel. So, any internet users may click to yahoo.com news website to read global news from computer yahoo.com website easily.

In fact, internet technology is also used from businesses. They attempt to set up themselves web stores to sell their products from themselves webstores. So, any one product buyers may buy any kinds of products from any one webstores when they stay at homes. It is very convenient and common to future any one webstore shoppers. It brings this question: Can webstores help online product purchases needs raise and influence shop product purchases need reduce?

In demand and supply view, when one product price raises, its sale demand ought reduce, unless, it can attract to influence customers need consideration or its supply number decreases. But, when one product is increasing sale price to seel from the seller's webstore, whether its sale number will be influenced to reduce. Also, when the kind of product is selling and its sale price is raised, whether it can still keep demand number increase as well as whether it can influence its similar kinds of competitor their products sale demand number to reduce from shop sale channel.

In demand and supply view, when one product price raises, its sale demand ought reduce, unless, it can attract to influence customers need consideration or its supply number decreases. But when one product is increasing sale price to sell from the seller's webstore, whether its sale number will be influenced to reduce. Also, when the kind of product is selling and its sale price is raised, whether it can still keep demand number increases as well as whether it can influence its similar kinds of competitors their products sale demand number to reduce from shop sale channel.

I suppose that webstore sale may influence shop sale demand number decreases, because when internet is popular to use, when one country's buyer wants to buy one kind of product, but he/she can not find the kind of product can be bought from himself/herself home country. If he/she can findthe kind of product to buy from any one of overseas webstore from internet channel at home in any time. Then, he/she will be influenced to make purchase decision from the seller's websote immediately. So, it implies that when on consumer plans to buy one kind of product, he / she will attempt to find the kind of product from any one seller's webstore in preferat home, if he/she spend long time to find the kind of product from many of webstores, but he /she still does not find the kind of product from many of webstores, then he/she will choose to visit any one shop to attempt to buy the kind of product.Hence, online shopping purchase channel will be prefer choice to compare visiting shopd purchase channel in nowadays society.
So, it explains that why the kind of product online sale number may influence the kind of similar product visiting shop sale number either increases or decreases. It means that the kind of product visiting shops sale number may still increases , if the kind of similar products supply number is not enough , they are difficult to let any one online buyer to find to buy from any one webstore. Otherwise, if the kind of similar products sale supply number is enough to let any one online buyer to find from many webstores. Then, they can influence the similar kinds of shop products purchase demand to reduce and their shops purchase demand will be also influenced to reduce from webstores purchase channel.

On conclusion, it explains that the kind of shop products demand number ought be influenced to increase or decrease, when the similar kind of products can be bought easily from many webstores from internet (e-commerce) shopping channel. Internet (online) technology may help the seller to raise the kind of product competitive ability on purchase demand aspect, when there are not many other sellers can provide webstores to sell the similar kind of products and they only concentrate on selling the kind of similar products from shops to let any one online buyer to frind from may webstores. Then, they can influence the similar kinds of shop products purchase demand to reduce and their shops purchase demand will be also influenced to reduce from webstores purchase channel. Hence, webstore and shop both purchase channel explains that the similar kinds of shop products demand number will be influenced to increase or decrease , when the kinds of product can be bought easily from many webstores from internet shopping channel. Internet technology may help the seller to raise the kind of product competitive abilty to raise purchase demand when there are not many other sellers can provide webstores to sell the kind of similar products and they only concentrate on selling the kind of similar products from shops.

Does car technological development reach mature stage to help economic development?
Our societies had been developing too many years. In our past technological aspect, machine invention had began

till to computer invention till to internet invention. It seems that our technological development stage may reach mature stage. Why do I feel our technological development had reached mature stage. I shall apply demand and supply economic theory to explain this question as below:

I shall indicate car development industry to explain whether when car development stage can reach mature stage, it may help global economic growth. In our car technological development stage, it is from gas energy car invention till to nowadays battery energy car invention till to even future non-manual driving car invention. Do you feel that when human (car buyers) felt environmental protecion need to avoid air pollution. So, battery energy cars demand number may increase , it will influence gas energy cars demand number reduces. Even, if future non0manula driving cars invention succeed, lazy driving car buyers will choose to buy non-manual driving (robot driving cars) in preference. So, it is possible that , it will influence future gas energy cars demand number reduces much. I mean that when car buyers can choose many different kinds of non-manual driving cars and battery energy cars to buy. Then, gas energy cars demand number must be influenced to reduce very much as well as gas energy cars supply number will be influenced to reduce to avoid sale prices reduce.

Hence, it explains why future car technological development will reach mature stage when both kinds of non-manual driving cars and battery energy cars are invented to the mature stage. When these two kinds of cars invention can satisfy future global car buyers driving needs. Then, car maufacturers won't need to spend too much time to continue to attempt to invent any new kinds of cars in order to excite future car buyers' purchase decision. So, I believe that car technological development will reach mature stage within five years, if non-manual driving cars and battery energy cars are invented in success and they can be popular to accept to drive to global car buyers.

Can non-manual driving cars dominate traditional car market

Nowadays, non-manual driving car invention may influence traditional car market development. In car development history, human had been habitly driving gas energy cars, but since battery energy cars invention, it can influence environmental protection car buyers feel gas energy cars may pollute global air. So, many different countries car buyers begin to choose to buy battery energy cars to replace traditional gas energy cars to drive. For example, US, Uk, China , they haver many big cities, their different cities living car buyers had begun to choose to buy battery energy cars to replace their old gas energy cars to drive to different destinations from their living cities every day. So, it seems that nettergy energy cars had been beginning to replace some old gas energy cars in some countries cities, e.g. China Shanghai large cities, US, New York, Washington large cities, UK London large city. However, it brings these questions: Can non-manual driving cars may dominate future traditonal gas energy cars market? Because, cattergy energy cars bring environmental protection advantages to reduce air pollution. So, battery energy cars may influence nowadays many gas energy car buyers to choose to buy battery energy cars to replace gas energy cars to replace gas energy cars to drive to avoid air pollution problem serious occurrence in our future societies.

In car market demand and supply view, I assume that if future many gas energy car owners accept to battery energy cars can reduce air polution continue influences our health when we often breathe dirty air due to gas energy cars' emission.

Hence, I estimate the demand number of battery energy cars pollution will be influenced to increase by air pollution. If future global air pollution will continue seriously influence global human health, it will influence global many car owners make choice either not buy any cars to drive, they will choose to catch public transport tools, e.g. bus, tram ,ferry, taxi, underground train etc. to go to anywhere or they will choose to buy battery energy cars to avoid gas continue pollute air to influence our health. So, it seems that battery energy cars will replace traditional gas energy cars to cause gas energy cars demand number decreases and battery energy cars demand number increases.

The other questions concern: Can battery energy cars influence future non-manual driving cars demand number reduces? Can non-manual driving cars replace battery energy cars and gas energy cars to dominate global car market?

In fact, non-manual driving cars may let many lazy car drivers or car buyers do not need to drive their cars, robots may help them to drive cars when they are sitting in themselves cars. So , they may read books, lsten music or sleep when their non-manual driving cars are still running on the roads. Although, non-manual driving cars can let many lazy car drivers feel comfortable and free when they are sitting in themselves cars. But non-manul driving cars can let they feel not safe, when robots help they to drive cars.

It means that their lifes are dominated by robots. However, traffic accidents may occur in any time, if robots help them to drive their cars in whole road journey time. So, they will feel more dangerous to compare they drive themselves cars on road busy time. Moreover, non-manual driving cars also need gas energy. So, non-manual driving cars still cause air pollution when many non-manual driving cars are being driving on the roads.

Hence, non-manual driving cars can also let environmental protection drivers feel that they can cause air pollution when they are driven on the roads by robots. Otherwise, battery energy cars must not pollute air , because they are using battery charge energy to replace gas or oil energy. Moreover battery energy cars won't let many car drivers feel safe to drive themselves cars on the road, due to they can still drive themselves cars and they won't need robots to help them to drive cars on the roads.

On conclusion, it seems that battery energy cars can attract many car buyers to choose to buy more than the kinds of both non-manual driving cars and gas energy cars. In supply and demand view, if future non-manual driving car manufacturers hope to raise sale price and demand purchase number. Unless, they can reduce their future any kinds of non-manual driving manufacture number to less than battery energy cars sale number to let future non-manual driving buyers feel that they can not buy any kinds of non-manual driving cars easily if they make purchase decision to buy them leter. Then, any kinds of non-manual driving cars prices may be influenced to raise to sell more easier when car buyers feel their supply number will begin to reduce to sell in global non-manual driving car market. However, future battery energy cars will be non-manual driving cars main competitive choice target to global car buyers. So, non-manual driving cars will be difficult to dominate the primary car choice tool to car buyers in future global car market.

On conclusion, when car technological development reaches matural stage, it will help future economy continue grows because when car manufacturers had invented many new kinds of non-manual driving cars and new kinds of non-manual driving cars and new battery energy car sale market. Then, they will encourage or attract global many car buyers choose to buy these both kinds of cars products in preference to compare to traditional gas energy car products. So, they will influence many traditional gas- energy car buyers forgive to drive gas energy cars to avoid non pollution and lazy driving behavioral feeling. So, gas energy car reselling number will increase between gas energy car drivers and past non-owning any car buyers. Also, non-manual driving cars and battery energy car supplying number will be influenced to increase when battery energy car buyers and non-manual driving car buyers driving needs increase.

Consequently, these factors will influence global gas energy cars, non-manual driving cars and battery energy cars their cars purchase and sale transactions increase in future global car market. So, I believe that global car technological development could reach matural stage, then it will infuence global car buyers number increases as well as this car technological mature development stage may also bring global rapid economic growth future non-manual driving car buyers and battery energy car buyers both number increases.

The relationship between technological advancement and global economic development is a foundational pillar of modern economic theory, characterized by a complex feedback loop between innovation, human behavior, and institutional frameworks. Historically, technological progress has acted as the primary engine for long-term economic growth, a concept famously formalized in the Solow-Swan growth model, which posits that technological change is the exogenous driver of output per worker.As economies transition from agrarian to industrial and now to digital-information paradigms, the nature of productivity has shifted from physical capital accumulation to the mastery of knowledge and technological integration.

The Mechanics of Technological Impact on Global Economies

Technological change influences the economy primarily through the creation of new products, the optimization of existing processes, and the reduction of transaction costs. In the context of advanced manufacturing, technologies such as robotics, additive manufacturing, and the Industrial Internet of Things (IIoT) have fundamentally altered the patterns of global labor.

These advancements allow for a higher degree of customization and efficiency, which can be represented by the production function $Y=A\cdot f(K,L)$, where Y is output, K is capital, L is labor, and A represents the level of technology. As A increases, the marginal productivity of both capital and labor shifts, often necessitating a workforce transition toward higher-skill requirements.

Human Behavior and Economic Development

While technology provides the tools for growth, human behavior—governed by psychological factors, institutional trust, and cultural norms—determines the efficacy of these tools. In my analysis of the interplay between technology and human behavior, suggests that while technology influences the economy, human behavior often dictates the direction and speed of adoption.

Trust, for instance, is a critical variable; economies with high levels of social capital and trust are better positioned to adopt disruptive technologies because the risks associated with innovation are mitigated by stable institutional frameworks.The behavioral economics perspective suggests that individuals do not always act with perfect rationality, and their response to technological displacement—such as fear of automation—can lead to policy shifts that either accelerate or stifle economic evolution.

Future Trajectories: AI and Sustainable Development

The future of global economic development is increasingly tied to artificial intelligence (AI) and sustainable technologies. These innovations are not merely additive; they are transformative. AI has the potential to reshape economies by automating cognitive tasks, thereby increasing the elasticity of labor supply in high-value sectors.

Furthermore, the transition toward a sustainable economy is being driven by "green" technologies that decouple economic growth from carbon emissions. This shift is essential for long-term resilience, as climate-related economic shocks pose a significant threat to global trade and supply chain stability.The interdependence of nations, accelerated by advancements in transportation and communication, means that the adoption of these technologies will likely be uneven, potentially widening the gap between technologically advanced nations and those lagging in digital infrastructure.

Key Factors Influencing Human Behavior in Economic Development

The study of human behavior within the context of economic development is a multifaceted discipline that bridges psychology, sociology, and classical economic theory. When examining the work of my view, specifically my analysis of how human behavior influences economic systems, one must distinguish his contemporary observations from the classical political philosophy of the 17th-century thinker John Locke.

My modern perspective emphasizes that economic development is not merely a product of capital accumulation or technological advancement, but is fundamentally driven by the psychological dispositions, cultural values, and social interactions of individuals within a market.According to my view, human behavior acts as the primary engine of economic change, where individual decision-making processes—influenced by risk perception, social trust, and long-term planning—determine the efficiency and sustainability of economic growth.

In the framework provided by my view, several key factors emerge as critical determinants of economic behavior. First, the role of "institutional trust" is paramount; individuals are more likely to engage in productive economic activity when they perceive that the legal and social systems are stable and fair.This mirrors broader economic literature which suggests that human behavior is highly responsive to the "rules of the game," a concept famously explored by Douglass North in his analysis of institutional economics.

Second, my highlights the importance of "cognitive biases" in economic decision-making. My view argues that human behavior is often bounded by irrationality, which can lead to market volatility or the misallocation of resources during periods of rapid development.This aligns with the behavioral economics movement, which posits that humans do not always act as the "rational agents" described in classical models, but are instead subject to heuristics and social pressures.

Furthermore, my view emphasizes the impact of education and cultural capital on economic development. My view posits that the behavioral traits fostered by educational systems—such as critical thinking, delayed gratification, and collaborative problem-solving—are essential for transitioning from agrarian or resource-based economies to innovation-driven ones.

This perspective is supported by extensive research in development economics, which demonstrates that human capital is the most significant predictor of long-term economic prosperity. Additionally, the influence of social networks and community cohesion cannot be overstated; my suggests that economic development is accelerated in environments where social capital is high, as this reduces transaction costs and encourages the sharing of knowledge and resources.

Finally, my view addresses the role of individual agency in the face of global economic shifts. He argues that while structural factors (such as geography or natural resources) provide the context for development, it is the behavioral response of the population—their willingness to adapt, innovate, and participate in global trade—that ultimately dictates the trajectory of an economy. This synthesis of behavioral psychology and economic theory provides a comprehensive view of how human choices, when aggregated, create the complex phenomena we observe as economic development.

Future space tourism development

Psychology and economic environment changing both factors influence whole space tourism market leisure desire

How can psychology method predict space tourism leisure desire? I believe that it has relationship between the space tourism planner and the economic environment as well as his/her psychology as below:
Firstly, on the economic environment influence hand, it includs these both economic situations, either in the good economic environment, many people can earn high income and employers can supply many job number to provide to many people to work, then it will influence the space travelling planner has more space travelling desire. Otherwise, or in the bad economic, less people can earn high income and employers can not supply many job number to provide to many people to work, it will influence the space travelling planner has less space travelling desire.

Secondly, on these both the space travelling planner individual psychology influence hand, the space travelling planner will have these both aspects of individual psychological influence, it includes these both either positive or negative psychological influence aspectsas below:

On the positive psychological influence aspect, if the space travelling planner has confidence to the space travelling leisure company can provide safe, comfortable, good quality of one space travelling trip arrangement, good taste food arrangement, reasonable space ticket price and every reasonable space trip for space hotel living arrangement and space garden and space farming land visiting journey arrangement, even, space swimming pool and space sport centre and space cinema leisure arrangement to let whom to stay on the planet at least one day trip, it means not one short time space trip, e.g. the spacecraft only flies about half hour or one half. It can not fly to the planet to arrive its space station destination to stay to let the space travelling planner to live at the space hotel at least one night. Then the space travelling planner will have more desire to choose to catch the space tourism leisure company's spacecraft to travel to space.
Otherwise, on the negative psychological influence aspect, if the space travelling planner lacks confidence to the space travelling leisure company can provide safe, comfortable, good quality of one space travelling trip arrangement, good taste food arrangement, reasonable space ticket price and every reasonable space trip for space hotel living arrangement and space garden and space farming land visiting journey arrangement, even, space swimming pool and space sport centre and space cinema leisure arrangement to let whom to stay on the planet at least one day trip, it means not one short time space trip, e.g. the spacecraft only flies about half hour or one half. It can not fly to the planet to arrive its space station destination to stay to let the space travelling planner to live at the space hotel at least one night. Then the space travelling planner will have less desire to choose to catch the space tourism leisure company's spacecraft to travel to space.

Hence, it seems economic environment changing factor and the space travelling planner's confidence factor to the space tourism leisure providers will influence the whole space travelling market whose space travelling consumer's space travelling leisure consumption desire to be more or less. So, any one space tourism provider can not neglect these both factors how to influence whose customer consumption desire.

● space tourism strategy
Future any space tourism leisure business needs have good business plan to outline the space tourism leisure business in these aspects , such as: different space tourism destinations of every space tourism journey, technical , financial and regulatory factors for growing space tourism leisure consumption into any one kind of unique artificial intelligent space tourism journey for identified passenger target group.
All how to design one space tourism business development plan to attempt to predict whether what trends will influence how every different kinds of identified space tourism journey in order to achieve passenger number growing aim as well as how to achieve one attractive space tourism leisure to satisfy future space tourism passenger individual space travel needs more easily.

I shall indicate what aspects to future every space tourism traveler who will consider in order to reduce the space tourism traveler personal worry to catch any pace boats to leave our Earth to fly to other planets to travel.
I recommend that any space tourism leisure organizations need to concern these aspects in their space tourism leisure business plan as below:

(1) safe space tourism journey

On first aspect concerns safe space tourism journey plan to let all space tourism travelers will considerate safe issue. They must ensure space boats that is safe to catch them to fly to planets in their space journeys. So, any space tourism leisure business will utilize previous flight rated and proven technologies to form the basis for manufacturing spacecraft vehicles, and will incorporate the latest modern avionics and flight systems for ensuring safety, reliability and economical operation in order to reduce any space tourism traveler personal worry to catch any spacecraft.

So, the space tourism safe journey plan is one very important factor to influence space tourism consumer number for them if any one of space tourism leisure business hoped they can grow the space tourism consumer number for long term. For example, the space boat flight hardware must often be maintained at the space station. It is needed to be considered by space boat experts as risky, extremely expensive and potentially sensitive. To aims to ensure spacecraft will offer an economical and safe alternative for any satellite manufacturers and other space tourism entertainment organizations have a desire or requirement for space tourism flight.

(2) reduction cost expense plan

On second aspect concerns reduction cost expense plan, any space tourism entertainment organizations need have the experience and capacity for safely launching a fully loaded , including space tourism passengers and passenger individual cargo for every spacecraft tourism journey. As a result of outsourcing the launch role to a major contractor, the space tourism pilot can concentrate on space boat crews flight training, planning space tourism passenger cargo capacity and preparing space flight manifests , and will as a result, avoid the expense of maintaining a launch operation on a daily basis.

In addition, by outsourcing the spacecraft manufacturing, it can avoid spending millions of dollar on facilities and equipment infrastructure and engineering manufacturing expertise.

(3) achieve any space tourism mission plan

On third aspect concerns how to achieve any space tourism mission. Every space tourism mission must be ensure that reliable service is provided to satisfy every space tourism passenger personal space traveler needs and let them to enjoy in their whole space tourism journey, let them to catch a big aircraft in comfortable environment of technologically sophisticated space boat, reasonable and competitive every time space tourism flight ticket price plan is developed and properly revised every time space tourism ticket price when performing their assigned every different space tourism journey mission.

Hence, the space tourism leisure company will provide one careful selected space tourism destination , e.g. Mar planet space tourism journey, Moon planet space tourism journey or no any space destination journey, it means that the space craft only needs to fly one circle around between Earth and Moon space journey etc. that are capable of meeting the requirements of travelling into Earth orbit. So, any space tourism journey must emphasize affordability, reliability, safety, customer service and responsiveness in responding to every client's space tourism journey requirements. Hence, any one of space tourism journey must have clear space journey mission and objective to satisfy any space traveler client target needs.

● Methods to raise space
traveler number

Future space tourism will be one kind of new travel leisure market for any new space travel leisure companies to enter this undiscovered market in the beginning. However, how to predict future 10 to 20 years , even more space traveler number that is one important issue to any new space tourism leisure companies.

I think that space tourism leisure companies need to define what kinds of space travel leisure service to be provided to space travelling passengers, however, what age group of space passengers who will be their space travelling target client. For example, their space travel leisure must provide any flight operation that takes one or more passengers beyond the altitude of 100 km and thus into space to let space travelling passengers who have fun, exciting space travelling feeling.

Anyway, for any kind of space tourism (leisure space travel) journey, space tourism leisure company needs anyone to be bring customer satisfaction, it is a plan or predictive methods to measure how to let every space travelling passenger to feel comfortable when they are catching the spacecraft (space flying product) and they can have enjoyable and fun or exciting feeling when they have need providing any space tourism journey, services meet or surpass customer expectations.

Thus, any space tourism leisure company needs to evaluate the degree of every time space tourism journey's customer satisfaction and customer satisfaction is also always evaluated in relationship to the every time ticket price of the space tourism journey. So, the space tourism leisure company will predict the next time of what the space tourism journey of passenger number is more accurate, after it has evaluated what degree of every time space tourism journey's customer satisfaction is. It aims to gather their opinions to find which aspects that they need to revise, e.g. choosing where will be the next time space tourism journey destination, how to improve spacecraft staff's service attitude and performance to serve to their space tourism passengers when they are catching the spacecraft, to evaluate whether the spacecraft can provide comfortable and safe environment to let them to catch in order to let the next time space travelling passengers can feel satisfactory and enjoyable when they are catching the space tourism leisure's spacecraft to fly to anywhere in space.

In general, the expectation of factors space passengers include the following customer value elements, such as below:

- viewing space and the Earth.
- experiencing weightlessness and being able to float freely in zero gravity.
- experiencing pre-flight astronaut training and related sensations.
- communicating from space to significant others.
- being able to discuss the adventure in an informed way.
- having astronaut like documentation and memorabilia.

These objectives need to be combined with, sometimes conflicting constraints, such as guaranteed safe return, limited training time, reasonable comfort, and minimum medical restrictions. All these above issues which will be every space travelling passenger considerate matters before they choose the space tourism leisure company to catch its spacecraft to fly to space. So, all these factors will influence the next time space passenger number. Any space tourism leisure company can not neglect how to solve these all matters before they decide when their next time space tourism journey to be achieved.

Consequently, if the space craft tourism leisure company could revise what aspects of its last space tourism journey to find what are its wrong or weakness or unattractive challenges to cause any one space travelling passenger who feels unsatisfactory. Then, it can have more effort to concentrate on improving its next space tourism journey to raise its space tourism service performance level , e.g. people, food, leisure etc. service aspects and its space tourism product quality level, e.g. proving comfortable spacecraft facilities to let space travelling passengers to catch in whole spacecraft tourism journey. Then, it will have more confidence to achieve the raising space travelling passenger number.

- What is the prediction space travelling passenger desire method ?

The prediction space travelling passenger individual desire method can be one survey investigation method. When every time spacecraft finishes space tourism journey mission, after all space tourism passengers catch the spacecraft to arrive earth from space. When they arrive earth space station destination, then the space tourism leisure company can arrange survey investigation staffs to enquire their feeling for this time space tourism journey immediately.

The survey content can include as below:

Do you feel satisfactory or unsatisfactory to which aspects of this time space tourism journey?

(1) On service aspect questions include as below:

(a) Do you feel space food taste is good?

(b) Do you enjoy this time space tourism journey arrangement?

(c) Do you feel satisfactory to space staff

service performance?
(d) If you have unsatisfactory feeling for any one of above questions, which aspect issue cause you feel unsatisfactory to explain to let us to know in order to us to revise our service performance.

(2) On product aspect questions include as below:
(a) Do you feel comfortable when you are catching our spacecraft in whole space tourism journey?
(b) If you feel comfortable , may you explain the reasons what aspects of our spacecraft has weakness to cause you feel uncomfortable?
(c) Do you feel safe when you are catching our spacecraft in whole space tourism journey?
(d) If you feel unsafe, may you explain the reasons what aspects of our spacecraft has weakness to cause you feel unsafe?

Finally, we thank your ideas to be given to let us know how to improve our every time future space tourism journey in order to find what challenge cause our service performance and product quality which can not satisfy your needs. So, we shall improve to avoid future challenges continue occur.
Our mission is achievement of 100% satisfactory level to our every space travelling passenger individual feeling. Also, we hope that you can choose our space tourism leisure service again, when you have another time space tourism leisure desire need. However, we shall revise to improve our service performance and product quality to be better, after collecting your ideas from this time survey investigation. I think you spend time to give your ideas from this survey investigation faithfully.
So, survey investigation method will be one important idea gathering tool to help any space tourism leisure company to revise the weaknesses to raise or improve future every time space tourism journey service performance and product quality to achieve raising competitive effort in this new space tourism leisure market.

Hence, survey investigation method will be the best idea gathering method to predict how space travelling passenger emotion or desire need will change in order to achieve the objective of raising every time space tourism journey future space travelling passenger number more easily for every space tourism leisure company.

- The prediction of price factor influences space traveler number

The space tourism leisure organizations indicate the total cost of a trip into space is rapidly coming down from the initial price level of about US$600,000, it is obvious that the space travelling customer base is going to be rather small. Typical customers tend to belong to the top 1% income bracket. They also indicate that the price comes down , it is expected that new space travelling customer groups will enter the space tourism leisure market.

Typical new customers include people in other brackets with one-of-a kind incomes, such as inheritance or business sold. There are indications that those types of customers are becoming interested in spending on an once-in-a lifetime space experience. Therefore, the growth of the space tourism market is highly sensitive to

customer satisfaction and how it is communicated through various media.
This will establish the status factors of space tourism and corresponding brand reputation service providers. They also suggest that any operator monitors space travelling customer satisfaction closely, as it will help developing increasingly accurate estimates of how the space tourism leisure market will develop.
Hence, it seems that every time space tourism journey price variable factor will influence the time space tourism of customer individual leisure desire and the space tourism passenger number. For example, the minimum price goal foe a variable space tourism business is currently estimate to be below US$3000-4000/kg for a round -trip depending on variable configuration and operation size. At this price, they estimate that somewhat over 1 % of the high income earners are potential customers.
However, for significant volume growth the longer term goal should be below US$2000/kg for a typical passenger, baggage and supplies. The lower price will probably open space tourism to a broader population, expanding the customer base and altering expectations. beyond this point space tourism will become into a travelling competitive leisure commodity, price competition will ensure and service providers need to rethink their space tourism marketing and branding and price strategies.

I shall also recommend how to attract the potential customers successfully. First, space operators need to pay special attention to the right level of customer services. Second, various preparatory customer operations cost, such as a travel to the launch site, space tourism destination accommodation, pre-flight training, medical check-ups and equipment my add up to between 10 to 15 % of the actual space travel cost. Thurs, solving the right balance between services offered and cost of client operation in order to earn the largest intangible benefits, such as loyalty, confidence, leisure enjoyment, comfortable space travelling journey as well as tangible benefits, such as profit, spacecraft manufacturing facilities, space stations, space hotels , space swimming pools, space gardens, space cinema etc. which are built to similar to earth building facilities to satisfy space travelers' needs.

The influential factors persuade travelers choose space tourism

Nowadays, our earth is no longer an adventurous enough place for some experienced tourists. Space tourism will be a new sector of adventure tourism, which is in the near future will be fast becoming a new tourism leisure opportunity for experiencing the unknown. Of one day, space tourism is able to reach the mass tourism phase, due to improved safety and decreased operation costs, a future space tourist will possibly only need minimal training to cope with the zero cost.
Space tourism is quite well established with visits to space attraction and launch sites, and it is a wealthy trips to the international space station for any space tourism travelers. However, if any space tourism leisure companies can attempt to find what the most influential factors are to persuade travelers feel attraction more than travelling in our earth.

It aims to let travelers to choose space travelling more than earth travelling when they feel travelling leisure need. I shall indicate what will be the most important influential factors to persuade travelers to choose space tourism more than earth tourism as below:
Firstly, I shall argue that the majority of different new space tourism journey destinations will be needed to find to satisfy different aged space travelers and different income space tourism consumers‘ needs. For example, the rich people have effort to consume longer time and reach any space tourism destinations where are far away from our earth of their every space tourism journey.
Otherwise, the middle income people will choose shorter space tourism journey distance from our earth and short time space tourism journey. Also, younger space tourism clients can accept more longer journey time, exciting fast speed spacecraft flying journey. Otherwise, old space tourism clients can only accept comfortable and shorter time safe space journey. So, it seems that safety, comfortable feeling, shorter time space tourism journey won't be one important influential factor to excite any young people who choose to consume space tourism leisure. Otherwise, safety, comfortable feeling, shorter time space tourism journey will be one important influential factor to excite any old people who choose to consume space tourism leisure.

Secondly, the another most important influential factor to excite space travelers to choose space tourism , it concerns whether the space travelers will feel what tourists benefits can be earned from a substantial variety of destinations choice. In general, space tourism with those of aviation, space travelers will hope space tourism will be travelling distances by air in a very short time, safely and comfortably, to bring them to arrive any space planet destinations when spacecraft reaches any space stations to stay in any space destinations.

Hence, space destination factor will bring important influential choice to any space destination journeys. As a result of the space technological tourism boom, the number of potential different space destination, choice attractions have grown with far fewer places on earth to which human do have access yet. However, the ultimate different space destinations to which many of us dream is not on earth, but as least 100 km above us, anywhere in space any planets.

If the space tourism leisure company can provide different space tourism destination choices to young or old age both space traveler target consumer groups. They will feel a real holiday when they will be able to enjoy a great image of the earth from planets. It might mean that every space tourism journey can provide different space tourism destination to let space travelers have another new travelling destinations where are far from our earth anywhere.

Hence, the different space tourism destinations will give them an unforgettable adventure. Think of how it would be to be able to check in at a " billion strategy" luxury hotel in space one planet, it means that the space planet destination can provide one luxury hotel to let space travelers to live one night or more in the space planet destination, how it would be to schedule the space traveler' vacation at one of the space tourism leisure company luxury resorts on the Moon or Mars.

This images seem from science fiction movies, but one should not forget that 100 years ago, the Wright brothers, aviation pioneers inventors and builders of the air plane, would not have imagined how, every day it is possible that future spacecraft can fly to any planets to let human have chance to stay in the space hotel one night or more.

Consequently, space destination choice and space tourism journey service performance, aviation safety, ticket price and leisure satisfactory feeling which will be important influential factors to attract future space travelers to choose space tourism leisure to replace earth tourism leisure in future one day.

● Raising space tourism leisure
consumption strategies

Although, space tourism industry is a real enjoyment and exciting travelling leisure to human. It is possible that human will choose to consume space tourism leisure to replace earth tourism leisure, if human felt that earth tourism leisure is not attractive to them to consume to go to anywhere to travel in their leisure time.
But, I believe that space tourism industry has still many factors to influence human to choose to consume space tourism leisure, even they will consider space tourism leisure consumption I is only one time space tourism in their life time. Hence, space tourism companies ought achieve this aim to persuade or attract everyone prefer to spend space tourism leisure at least one time in their life, then it can represent success. However, I think to achieve this aim, it has these challenges to influence their success, even they believe space tourism leisure business is one potential attractive travel entertainment business. These challenges include such as: expensive space tourism ticket price issue, catching spacecraft safe issue, space traveler personal body health issue, age issue, family and friend relationship influence issue, working time and holiday time arrangement issue, the space trip arrangement issue, weather issue etc. different challenges, which will have possible to influence every space tourism planner either who decide change to cancel the time space tourism plan, or forgive to choose space tourism leisure in their life forever.
Hence, how to raise space tourism leisure consumption desire will be one considerable matter for any space tourism leisure businessmen. I shall indicate my personal three aspect of strategical opinions to let them to know how to raise every space tourism planner individual space tourism leisure consumption desire to avoid every time space tourism passenger number will have decrease failure chance as below:

● (1) Strategic opinion

On the first aspect of strategic opinion, I feel that the space education tutor can teach new space knowledge to let every space traveler to learn any new space and earth knowledge during he/she is catching on the spacecraft in personal contact learning experience environment which can raise space tourism consumption desire. The reason is because the space tourism leisure traveler can raise extra space and earth learning knowledge when they can catch the spacecraft to fly and contact the space environment to learn and feel what the differences are between space and earth by himself or herself. Hence, it is very attractive to the space traveler student target group and I believe that their parents will encourage their sons or daughters to participate the time of space trip and they are more preferable to help them to buy the time space trip ticket, due to their sons and daughters can learn any space knowledge when they are studying. Moreover, every space traveler will feel surprise to learn any new space and earth knowledge from the space tutor's teaching, due to he/she is unknown that this space travel trip includes learning space and earth knowledge.

I suggest that the space tourism leisure businessmen can give learning opportunity to every travel trip space travelers to feel that this space actual environment can bring what disadvantages or advantages to influence our earth when they are catching aircraft to fly to space to travel in every space trip. The space and earth learning knowledge can include these two aspects of space learning knowledge and experience below:

On the teaching of space environment learning knowledge hand, the topics can include as below:
Firstly the space learning topic can concern how space environment influences water and hydrated minerals change , they can learn what our drinking water function how is applied to space environment. For example, in the space environment, they can learn and attempt to feel that how water can be used in protecting astronauts against harmful radiation from the sun and cosmic rays by cloaking spacecraft with a thin layer of water in the actual space environment as well as the space travelers can also feel water is same as fuel when they are catching the spacecraft, they can feel the water is heavy to transport into space when they are catching the spacecraft to fly to space during their whole space tourism journey.
Moreover, when their spacecraft reaches anyone of planets and it stays on the planet's space station, e.g. Moon space station. They can learn how to attempt to contact the hydrated minerals to learn and feel what they contained in some asteroids may be possible sources of water and fuel in the actual space environment. When they are walking in actual space environment, such as Moon planet, they can contact or touch this hydrated minerals to learn how water molecules can be extracted and separated chemically to produce hydrogen fuel knowledge in the actual space environment. This is one exciting space learning experience to the space travelling student passengers.

Secondly the space learning topic can concern how human fights space threats , even when their whole space leisure journey, the space science teacher can let the space trip student passengers to feel that they are learning new space knowledge between the space science teacher and whose space trip student passengers. Such as how to protect our earth knowledge: Teaching them to know when will be threats to our earth from space. The space science teacher can explain how this space threating environment influences our life safety and let them to feel that a mass extinction can be triggered if an asteroid 10 kilometers across hit the earth. Even being the apex species in the food chain did not space carnivorous dinosaurs from such disaster, who knows if this terrifying scene won't happen before our eyes? So, the space travelers can image and feel how the space threating environment can influence their life safety in the actual space environment as well as the space science teacher can let whose space travelers to feel and image the actual earth disaster will possible happen suddenly to let they feel afraid in the actual space environment. Also the space science teacher can teach how our earth can fright the space stones attack to let the space traveler to know, when an impactor targets an asteroid for a controlled well-times wallop. The collision will change the asteroid's momentum, deflecting it from its original orbital path which intersects with that of the earth. So, at the moment, the space travelers can image they are a larger spacecraft near an asteroid which can also change the path. Given enough time, the gravitational pull from the spacecraft will be able to steer the asteroid away from the earth. So, every space traveler will feel that they are catching the spacecraft in the safe space environment to avoid the Earth disaster from space sudden unpredictable attack.

It is more fun real space tourism knowledge learning feel to let every space traveler has chance to learn any new space science knowledge when he/she is catching the spacecraft to fly to space to travel. Hence, one successful space trip ought include trip and learning experience both contents in order to raise every the space tourism planner individual space trip consumption desire.

● (2) Strategic opinion

On the second aspect of strategic opinion, space tourism leisure companies need to let planning travelers feel that anyone of space tourism leisure is very different to general tourism leisure. In general, tourism leisure is visiting at least one night for leisure and holiday, business or other tourism purposes in Earth only. Otherwise, space tourism leisure is other kind of an unique trip leisure or entertainment method, e.g. the space traveler can catch the spacecraft to visit any planets to stay to live at the planet's space hotel at least one night, e.g. Future potential populated Moon or Mars space hotel space trip. Moreover, the space travel companies ought give chance to let them to feel what weightless feeling is in weightlessness environment when they are walking on Moon or other planets in possible. Even, they can attempt to build these entertainment facilities, instead of space hotels, such as space swimming pools, space gardens, space cinema etc. building facilities. It aims to let them to feel what the differences between Earth and space life when they are walking on the Moon, when they are swimming on the space pools, when they are living in space hotels, when they are watching movies in space cinemas, when they are seeing flowers and different species of planets and fruits. e.g. oranges, apples, bananas, and vegetable and potatoes and tomatoes in space gardens. It is very exciting and fun space trip life experience between one days to seven days. So, they believe that they must not feel these space life experience if they do not choose to participate this time space trip planning journey by the space trip company preparation.

Also, due to that the space tourism passengers need to the pre-flight checks and training before they ensure to qualify to permit to participate the space trip. So space travel companies need to concern how to take care their health check and training matter considerately. It aims to let every space traveler will feel a market segment with fitness and extreme experiences as well as he/she will become popular with a market segment passenger to the space tourism leisure company, although he/she must not guarantee to pass the space training and/or pre-flight health checks to permit to participate the space trip. However, he/she can believe that he/she is one worth space travelling passenger to the space tourism leisure company, even this time pre-flight health check or/and the short time space trip training requirements are failure. However, the space tourism leisure company must need to let all pre-flight health check and space trip training passengers to feel that it is only one space tourism which can give them and let customers view the space travel is as the ultimate showcase for health, even though a majority of the population can pass the pre-flight medical and other tests in order to raise their confidence and safety to catch the spacecraft to fly to space to travel when they are confirmed to pass these tests to permit to catch the spacecraft later.

In general, the expectations of future space passengers include the following customer value elements, such as below:

- Viewing space and the Earth.
- Experiencing weightlessness and experiencing pre-flight astronaut training and related sensations.
- Communicating from space to significant others.
- Being able to discuss the adventure in an informed way.
- Having astronaut-like documentation and memorabilia.
- Enjoying one exciting and fun space trip.

However, instead of considering these objectives need to be combined with, sometimes conflicting , constraints such as guaranteed safe, return , limited training time, reasonable comfort, and minimum medical restrictions. So, space tourism companies need to reduce every space traveler individual worries before they decide to make the time of space tourism journey. Then, it can increase their confidence to raise their space tourism consumption desire more successfully.

Consequently, instead of these consideration, a space travel operator must pay attention to the total customer experience over the entire customer process, starting from how the service is presented, proposed and sold. The service package must include training, instructions, travel to the launch site and various post. Travel activities to generate maximum customer satisfaction and brand building opportunity.

(3) Strategic opinion

On the final aspect of strategic opinion, I think any space tourism companies space tourism companies need to consider every time space tourism ticket price and space tourism trip issues. It is important factor to influence

every space traveler individual consumption desire. Due to space trip ticket price must be more expensive to compare common Earth trip travelling ticket price, so this kind of tourism leisure market target customer will be the rich and high income customer group.
On the space trip ticket challenge issue, despite that fact the total cost of a trip into space is rapidly coming down from the initial price level of about US$60,000, it is obvious that the customer base is going to be rather small and the client target customer is only high income or rich consumer group. Typical customers tend to belong to the top of the top 1% income bracket. So, ensures that space traveler number must be less than common Earth traveler number.

Also, such as the space trip ticket price, it is expected that new middle rich level or middle high level income customer target group will enter the space trip leisure market, when every space trip ticket price falls down about 1% Typical new customers include people in other income brackets with one-of-a-kind incomes, such as inheritance or business sold space traveler target group. These people will be space travel new client group, when its every space trip ticket price can be reduced to close 1 to 2 % nearly. If any space tourism leisure companies expect to attract new rich and/or high income target customer group to choose any one kind of space trip journey planning to consume.

These are indications that these types of customers are becoming interested in spending on an once-in-a-lifetime space experience. Therefore, the growth of the space tourism market is highly sensitive to customer satisfaction and how it is communicated through the various media. This will establish the status –factor of space tourism, and corresponding brand reputation of service providers. The minimum price goal for a variable space tourism business is currently estimate to be below US$3-4000/kg for a round-trip depending on vehicle configuration. So, space travel leisure companies need to concern every round space trip cost, it can depend on the space vehicle number and weight issue to influence every space trip ticket price variable to achieve how much it can earn.

On space journey design factor aspect, it includes these different facilities aspects how to design, because future space travelling consumers will concern whether the space travel company can provide special entertainment to satisfy their needs. The facilities include as below:

How to design space hotels to let them to live in comfortable space environment and eat the best taste and fresh food quality when the cookers need to cook in the space hotel in the space environment? How to design space swimming pools to let them to swim in safe space environment? How to design space sport centers to let them to run more easily in one space sport warm and safe environment? How to design one space garden to let them to see different species of Earth flowers, or plants? How to design one space farming land to let them to see different species of Earth fruits, vegetables, tomatoes, potatoes etc. fresh foods growth in warm and safe space farming land environment? How to design one space cinema to let them to watch movies in one safe and warm space cinema environment? All these facilities will be any one of future space trip's' important and attractive space trip leisure facilities to influence every space traveler to choose to buy the space tourism leisure company's space trip leisure service.

Instead of these space building entertainment facilities, they also need to concern how the space vehicle entertainment tools are provided the entertainment service to satisfy their needs. When the space travelers can sit on the space vehicles to move on any planets' lands, such as Moon. A number of space vehicle options exist in the market, mainly differing based on the seat capacity as well as the in-flight experience level offered. The typical space vehicle solution is a small, relatively light weight spacecraft taking between 2 to 10 passengers. The number of passengers depends on the service level, amenities and extra offered. The trip typically lasts about 10 hours and of which about 4 hours are spent in space. The main attraction is the weightless time after in space. The main attraction is the weightless time after re-entry has started. It is a rather low-G technology and therefore the medical requirements for participants are nor very high.

Consequently, the space vehicles, space leisure building facilities, the space trip reasonable price ticket level, every safe space trip journey arrangement, clean and fresh and good taste space food arrangement, space traveler individual real learning experience etc. these factors will be the main influential factors to raise the space tourism leisure company's competitive effort and the space traveler consumer individual consumption desire to the space tourism leisure company in the future.

Research how to raise space traveler individual leisure desire

The first factor may raise space traveler leisure desire is that space rocket needs have safe and clean inside environment. Future, space tourism may be another kind of possible popular tourism leisure activity, because since COVID 19 disease occurs, it may influence many travellers feel afraid to catch air planes in the high risk closed window airt plane inside environment, when many different countries people must need to body contact or air contact. Hence, it is possible that our tourism leisure will not be popular in our earth, if COVID 19 disease , even other unknown air disease may occur to cause global travellers feel fear to catch air planes to avoid life danger in the one hour, even more than 12 hours sitting air plane flying time. Otherwise, because any space tourism rockets are small and it only allows one to four space travellers and space rocket pilot to sit in the space rockets as well as any space journey is only spent 15 minutes to 30 minutes for view moon space journey or more than one day visiting moon space journey or up to one week visiting space station journey in the space rockets. So, owning COVID 19 disease travellers can permit to sit in the space rocket, the chance is low to get COVID 19 disease when the space rocket has less passengers are sitting in the space rocket. It means that when many space travellers feel any space rocket is safe and clean in the inside none window space rocket environment, this safe and clean space rocket inside environment feeling, it cam emcourage many future space passengers begin to choose to catch any one space rocket to leave earth to fly to space to travel in possible. Hence, when space rocket can be invented to bring equipment safe and comfortable feeling and guarantees none of any one owning COVID 19 disease patient can sit in the space rocket as well as all of they can catch this space rocket to earth and come back to earh safely . It means that any one space tourism leisure service provider can guarantee without any sudden accidents occurrence in space. The another most important factor may be every space tourism can charge reasonable ticket price to any one space trip to let any one space tourism leisure consumer to feel. All of these factors may influence the space tourism leisure consumers number increases to the space tourism leisure service provider.

Instead of above space trip ticket price and space rocket's safe and clean inside environment both aspects. I shall indicate how to raise space traveller individual leisure desire methods as below:
Firstly. attractive space trip is another important factor to influence any one space tourism leisure consumers to choose the space tourism leisure service provider's any one space tourism leisure activities. Because of the space trip's time is short, e.g. 15 minutes to 30 minutes leaving earth to stay on space for viewing our earth leisure , within this 15 to 30 minutes short space trip time, the space tourism leisure service provider needs to seek the different kinds of attractive space destinations to let every space tourism leisure passengers to feel enjoyable in space different locations when they see our earth from their rocket's staying different locations in space. Because different space locations, they can influence different viewing feeling of our earth from the rocket. So, choosing the suitable different space locations to stay in order to view earth , this short time space staying locations trip is very important to influence every passenger whose viewing earth feeling. Otherwise, if the space trip's time is longer, e.g. more than 5 hours sitting to visit moon space trip. The space trip must need to be arrangement have more attractive feeling to let they do not feel boring when they need to sit more than 5 hours in the space rocket to arrive the moon. So, their sitting space rocket times are needed to be feel leisure times for every passenger. They can not feel bore or non space trip arrangement leisure feeliing in the whole space trip. So, when the space trip is longer time, its space leisure activities arrangement ought need have enough different leisure activities to provide in order to avoid any one space passenger feels bore, e.g. spending one week to arrive space station space trip, the rocket must need have sport equipment or cinema provide to let they do not feel bore when they need to sit about one week time to go to the space station as well as spend another one week time to come back earth from the space station. Otherwise, short time space trip , e.g. only 15 minutes viewing earth space trip , it doe not any space trip leisure activities, because this space viewing earth trip aims to let passengers can feel comfortable and enjoyable to view our earth when they are sitting in the rocket in this 15 minutes. However, this rocket needs to fly to about 4 to 5 different space locations to let passengers to feel different viewing earth visable feeling. If the rocket is only staying in one same space location to let them to view our earth. They must feel bore to view the same visable feeling of our earth in this 15 minutes space viewing earh trip. So, space locations choice factor is very important for short time viewing earth space trip. Consequently, they may feel their this short time viewing earth space trip ticket price is unreasonable.

Hence, any one space trip lesiure activities and space staying locations choice arrangement, as well as its space trip time as well as its evaluated ticket price, they must have close relationship to influence any one space trip traveller individual leisure satisfactory feeling in this space tourism leisure development industry. Hence, if any one space tourism leisure service provider hopes that they can have many space travellers to choose their any one long or short time space trip lesisure activities. They must need to consider how to design space trip in order to attract their leisure choices , how to evaluate every space trip's time and space trip ticket price in order to achieve how to attract many future space traveller individual preference space trip choice among potentient different space trip lesiure providers. Because when future space tourism leisure is popular to accept. In this space tourism market, it will have many potential space tourism leisure service providers attempt to anticipate and implement any kinds of space trip leisure activities arrangement, it seems future space trip may influence our traditional tourism industry from earth travel changes to space travel lesisure direction development.

In earth tourism industry, every travel leisure service provider needs to design different kinds of travelling destinations in order to attract different countries travellers choose to play themselves designing trips packages, if their trips arrangements are attrractive, it will influence thr traveller chooses this travel agent's trip to visit the another country service. Hence, earth trip's travelling packages are very important to influence every traveller individual travel agent choice. It seems that space tourism trip arrangement may be another main factor to influence space passengers number increases or decreases to any one space leisure service provider. The question concerns how to design attract space trip to any one space traveller choice preference. I shall explain as below:

IN fact, space tourism's general price is expensive, so the wealthiest people ought be any ones space tourism leisure provider's main customer target. But advances in rocket and capsule design also also expected to lower the price to the point that people of more modest fortunes are able to afford a ticket. What space tourists can expect? What exactly is on store for space tourists? The excitment of a rocket ride and a chance to experience weightlessness for starters. And bragging rights are hard to beat. But some the biggest benefit of point into space is getting a dramatic new outlook on life when any one space traveller can try to catch rocket to leave our earth home.

For Virgin Galactic plans to offer suborbital space trips, with customers being treated to feel of weightlessness feeling. He says more than 600 customers have signed contracts to already to pay a ticket price US$250,000 for one time space trip. Another space tourism leisure provider, e.g. Blue Origin, Amazon CEO Jeff Bezos , thees space tourism leisure providers had begun to plan future space adventures leisures to satisfy future any one space traveller individual space trip leisure need. In general, average a ticket price is between US$75,000 to US$300,000. SO, wealth people must be space travel consumer targert customer.
Future space trip may include: Flying to space stations, it may be a big vacation will be able to buy a rocket ride into orbit, future NASA is not transfoming into a space travel agency, private companies will have to pay it about

US$35,000 a night per passenger to sleep in the space station's beds and use its amenities, including air, water , the internet and toilet. Hence, flying to space station may be one attract one to two weeks attractive space trip.

Another kind of space trips, such as a variety of options for private of spaceflight have started to emergy. Virgin Galactic, founded by the entrepreneur Richard Branson, and Blue Origin from Jeffrey P. Benos of Amazon, both plan to carry passengers on short suborbital flights, space X also announced that Yusaka Maezawa, a Japanese, clothing company founder, would pay for a trip around the moon on a spacecraft it is building. Hence, short time space trip, e.g. flying to moon or leaving earth short suborbital flights, staying on space to viewing our earth , even long time space trip, e.g. flying to space station,spends more than one to two weeks. They may be future any one wealth space traveller's space trip leisure choice.

Some companies already conduct modest experiments on the space station, such as Merall Research laboratories, which has grown crystals of antibodies, and mode in space, which is testing the manufacture of higher quality optical communications fiber in the weightlessness of orbit. Hence, flying to moon and staying on space to viewing our earth space trips both ticket prices miust be more cheaper to compare long time spce trip, e.g. visiting space stations space trip. Axion space, a houston based company that arranges training and all aspects of the flights, is charging as much as US$55 million for a week long trip to the international space station. Blus Origin , Virgin Galactic had been planning attractive space trip. It focuses on views of earth space leisure activities when its space travelling customers can sit in its space rocket. Virgin Galactic was charging as much as US$250, 000 per seat on its spaceship. HOwever, these both space planes have a waiting list of about 600 passengers.

ON conclusion, in the future, the different kinds of space trips may include: short journey viewing earth, 15 to 30 minutes, visiting to moon, about one days , even it is possible that visiting space station, one to two weeks. Even it is possible that any one space traveller can attempt to live one night in space hotel, if human can build hotels on moon, when human can confirm moon can build hotels , then flying to moon to live one night space trip experience may be implement in possible. I believe that any one space leisure provider can attract many space passengers to choose their viewing earth short time staying space trip, visiting moon, living space hotels, visiting space stations to live one night space leisure trip, So, any one space trip leisure provider can attempt to evaluaate whether implementing "living moon hotel" or " visiting space station" or viewing our earth any one space trip is possible in order to raise future any one potential space traveller individual leisure desire. However, the main considerable points, they need to evaluate whether they ought charge how much space trip ticket or seat price for every passenger. Also, they need build confidence to let every passenger feels their space rocket is safe to sit to leave our earth and come back our earth again absolutely. Hence, all of these are important factors to influence future any one space tourism leisure provider their success, if they expect to develop their space trips businesses in long time.

Space travel marketing strategy

Any space travel organization needs have good marketing strategy to prepare how to operate its space travelling leisure business in order to attract many space travelling clients to choose its space travelling service. I shall indicate these different strategies aspects whey they are needed to be concerned as below:

(1) On concept of spacecraft design aspect

Firstly, on concept aspect, any one space travelling leisure company needs have at least one spacecraft to catch clients to fly to space to travel. So how to design the spacecraft and its quality and safety and comfortable environment spacecraft machine concept aspect issue which is one challenge to be concerned. Because many space travelling passengers ususally concern whether the spacecraft is safe, comfortable , good quality, as well as the space travelling leisure providers also need to concern whether the spacecraft is less time and energy saving efficient use, less manufactory operating cost and durable.

In general, space travelling leisure provider expects the spacecraft or spacecraft vehicle can be uesed long time. The spacecraft will be expected to utilize previous flight rated and proven technologies to from the basis for manufacturing spacecraft vehicles , and will incorporate the latest modern avionics and flight system for answering safety, reliability and economical operation.

In general, the spacecraft will be designed to carry two crew and approximately, 10,000 pounds of cargo, depending on the ultimate weight of the spacecraft. Relying on flight hardware to maintain the space station, such as Moon or Mar space station is fpr any space travelling spacecrafts to reach these space travelling destinations to stay, it is also need to consider by many space travelling experts as risky, extremely, expensive cost sensitive for any space station travelling destination design arrangement in order to future every spacecraft can fly to any planets to stay on its space station safely.

● Outsourcing spacecraft concept design strategy

As a result, outsourcing strategy is one good method to help them to reduce cost in order to achieve to let every space travel passenger has safe space journey experience and capacity for safely launching a fully loaded (including crew and cargo). Outsourcing strategy is the launch role to a major contracor, they can concentrate on crew flight training, planning all passnegers and cargo capacoty, and preparing flight manifests, and will as a result, avoid the expense of maintaining a launch operation on a daily basis. In addition, by outsoucing the spacecraft manufacturing, the space travelling provider can avoid spending millions of dollars on facilities and equipment infrastructure and engineering manufacturing expertise.

(2) On deciding misson aspect

Secondly, on mission aspect, any space travelling journey needs have a clear mission to be planned how to achieve in order to ensure every space travelling passenger feel satisfactory in the space travelling journey. So, every whole space travelling journey arrangement, e.g. where will be the space travelling destination, how to check every space travelling planned passengers' bodies whether who are health to catch spacecraft to fly to space to travel or how to train every space travelling planned passenger to ensure whom can permit to catch spacecraft to fly to space to travel, how to arrange every space travelling journey entertainment and facilities to let either young or old age target passenger to enjoy the space trip to feel satisfactory, how to arrange different days of every space trip.

In the last few years, Virgin Galactic has been making new's headlines with its promises to provide space travel services, and announcement that it will soom offer, at quite a hefty price, trips to sub-orbit. It is generally agreed that sub-orbit exists 100 kilometres above the earth's sea-level (Von Der Dunk, 2012). Hence, Virgin Galactic will provide travel to where customers may experience weightlessness, as well as the sight of earth's curvature. Even more interesting is that Virgin Galactic is not the only company with such a mission,there are a few more that wish to offer the same type of service. For example, some companies even aim to provide an orbital type of flight.

Orbit flight suggests that humans would venture into outer space, where they might either orbit the earth or board the international space station (hereinafter: ISS). In addition, some envision space hotels, moon visitations and mining asteroids. Although at first such statement might seem for one must point out that a "space hotel" is already in earth's orbit and that diligent progress through flight tests is almost made the commercial aspect of regular space travel a reality; it is only the question of time and readiness for the companies to make their long-awaited and open a new industry of present day economics (Klemm & Markkanen, 2011; Berry , 2012).

So, every space travelling mission is to ensure that reliable, technologically-sophisicated competitively-priced flight certified spacecraft are designed and properly maintained when performing their every assigned space travelling journey mission. The space traveller leisure provider will need to provide a carefully selected array of techologies that are capable of meeting the requirements of travelling into earth orbit. It will emphasize affordability, reliability, safety, customer service and responsiveness in responding to customer's space travelling requirements.

For this space tourism leisure mission example, it many include these objectives , such as below:
One trip into space, sending a space vehicle of a certain make and with a specify capacity on a space mission, provides the various grades of a core service, such as a space mission including issues such as waiting and delivery times, personal attention and advice, amenities and facilities, ensure quality assurance, it is the planned and system activities implemented in a quality system. So that quality requirements for a product or service will be fulfilled. It aims at preventing high-risk adverse events, or reducing thei impact, provides excellent customer satisfaction, it is a measure of how products and services meet the space travelling customer expectations, customer satisfaction is also

always evaluated in relationship of every space travelling ticket price of the space travelling entertainment service and spacecraft product comfortable environment feeling and good leisure arrangement for every space travelling leisure journey.

(3) On space tourism leisure organization managment aspect

Thirdly, on space tourism leisure organization management aspect, it is also important to influence efficient and excellent space service performance to be provided to satisfy every space travel organization management team needs to be consists of experienced professionals who have successfully management and operated companies specializing in the aerospace industry for a number of years.

Their knowledge and contacts within the space industry will prove invaluable in assisting the space tourism leisure provider in the achievement of its goals and objectives. In individuals on the team components that up a spacecraft tourism development organization, and have unique experience in the design, construction, operations and maintenance of the major functions will developing spacecraft for launching into orbit. Every spacecraft will be built and maintained utilizing the same high standards of quality, within budget and well within time constraints.

Hence, every space tourism provider needs have one excellent management leaders to manage every space tourism service staffs to serve passengers in order to achieve excellent service performance to let them every one to feel satisfactory, during their every space tourism journey (trip).

(4) On target audience prediction aspect

On target audience prediction aspect, every space trip needs have identifies target travelling passenger in order to concentrate to choose the most popular and satisfactory space travelling journey for their identified needs.

For primary audiences example, it can include space enthusiasts and educational families both. Space enthusiasts target are usually young people and they are only 20% over 65 age old people target space ethusiasts who will be the future potential space tourism target consumers as well as the educational families target who will aspect owning educational experience for children , who is the explicit reason to visit space, either he/she has interest in history of space exploration or he/she has interest in future of space exploration or he/she feels that spce trip looked like fun. KSCVC Visots (2013) indicated that future top markets, ranked by high visitation against space enthusiasts and educational families space tourism passengers, the US cities will include: Orlando, NYC, Miami, Tampa Bay, Chicago, West plam, Philadelphia, Atlanta, Boston, Washington, DC and San Francisco cities. So, future US space travelling market will be the top one in the world.

(5) On space objective aspect

On space objective aspect, instead of any one space tourism leisure organization concerns how to achieve its mission to satisfy all space tourism passengers leisure needs. Although, it is the major missin for space tourism leisure industry. But they can not neglect what the objectives are in order to develop or achieve long term space tourism leisure missions more easily.

The objectives main open space key issues can include such as: Providing an adequate supply of land to meet the future needs of strategic opn space links, natural areas and recreational facilities on any future space tourism destinations, increasing pressure for public access to open space areas with conservation values, competing interests between adjoining land use and development on public open space and its user groups, use of public open space and recreational resources for drainage purposes, raising higher space traveller hotel residential development placing increased pressure on the demand for public open space planet land use aim and developing public open space mor intensive leisure and sport activities on any future new space tourism planet destinations.

When the space tourism leisure providers have long term objectives to attempt to solve above these any one of key issues. It will ahve a more clear objective to achieve its long term space tourism leisure business market. It's long term objectives can include such as below:

To identify existing and future active and passive recreation needs and social trends of future space tourism visitors; to provide a wide range of high quality and accessible public open space public land areas to encourage physical activity and social interaction to meet the existing and future needs of space travelling visitors; to identify existing gaps in the public open space network and develop any different kinds of space trip arrangement to satisfy the different identified target space traveller individual needs; to protect enhance and increase landcrapt values of public open space land use; to recognize the hierarchy of public open space assets; equitably distributing open space resources; access to facilities and a diverse range of opportunities to incorporate the drainage function in public open space travelling destination areas without detriment to safely, environmental, visual and recreational values.

So, these development of any space planets howo to use their lands objectives will bring long term space travelling destination beneficial advantages to raise to build the space hotels, space swimming pools, space gardens, space cinemas, space sport places to let future space travelers can stay in Mars or Moon planet destinations to enjoy these leisure facilities and they can feel which are similar to our earth leisure facilities attractively.

These space buildings are important to attract future space travellers to catch spacecraft to fly to Mars or Moon planet to travel in possible because it is fun and exciting space trip when these leisure facilities can be built on Moon or Mars to let space travellers to stay short days in either these two planets to live their space hotels. So how to build any one of these space leisure building which is another important objective for any future space tourism leisure business, instead of how to arrange any space destination trip objective. So, any space tourism leisure provider ought not neglect how to achieve these two main space tourism objectives.

However, these are key questions continually asked regarding the viability of space tourism. They concern financial, marketing and political communities. Their concerns can be best addredded in a properly, comprehensive business plan. Some questions can not be answered definitively at this time. Hoever, knowledge of the concerns and developing space businesses in any space traveling leisure planning stages and efforts to raise capital in the following questions, every spce tourism leisure business leader needs to concern this questions as below:

Can the space tourism industry into a profitable enonomic industry?
Are challenges related to financing, marketing, business methodologies or a combination of all of these facets?
Can the proponents of space tourism to be proven business tools and methodologies in their presentation of an acceptable business plan?
Can at least a cost effective, certified passenger space tourism journey to be developed for space tourism?
What effects will influence space-tourism businesses of NASA begins selling seats on the US space shuttle to civilian space tourists?
All above questions will be every new space tourism leisure businessman who needs to concern questions in order to achieve whose marketing strategy more successfully. Consequently, marketing strategy is important to be prepared in order to follow corrective steps to achieve every space tourism leisure business missions and objectives more easily.

● Space tourism leisure behavioral economic consumption model

In space tourism leisure industry, due to every time space trip needs the space travelling planner to plan how much budget to consume expensive spce ticket price. So, it seems that the target customers will be rich or high income level young people or the retirement rich old people target customer group.
So, it brings this question: How to persuade these rich or high income young people or rich retirement old people to prefer to spend spce tourism leisure at least one time in their life?
It is one valuabe research question to every future space tourism leisure provider. I shall indicate the successful factors to analyze how to persuade them to accept this kind of potential space travelling leisure in behavioral economic personal consumption view point, in order to explain the cause and effect relationship between of these factors as below:

(1) Economic environment variable factor

Firstly, it is economic environment variable factor whether it can influence to space tourism leisure consumption changing. As I discuss about economic environment variable issue will influence consumption behavior changing. For space tourism leisure case, it is not now kind of essential consumption leisure product to every one. So , even the rich or high income people who will be influences to seek this kind of leisure to play, it the economic

environment is improved, it will influence they have positive attitude and interest to choose this kind of leisure consumption. However, if the economic environment is worse, it will influence they have negative attitude and no interest to choose this kind of leisure consumption, due to space travel is one kind of expensive leisure consumption to every one.
Hence, in this space tourism leisure industry, it does not ensure that the rich or high income people must be persuade to choose this kind of expensive space tourism entertainment in whose holiday or retirement time. They can have the common tourism entertainment to go to different countries to travel many times in our earth. Otherwise, space tourism leisure is more expensive to compare common earth tourism leisure , it means that the rich or high income people only spend one time spacecraft catching to fly to space to travel in their life, it is more difficult to every space traveler like to catch spacecraft to fly to space to travel more than one time, due to he/she had attempted to catch spacecraft to fly to space to travel to own space travel experience, he/she will feel enough satisfactory and enjoyment in common. Hence, it is possible that future many rich or high income people only like to spend one time space tourism leisure, then they won't continue to spend this kind of tourism entertainment again in their life.

Thus, space tourism leisure providers need to arrange any special or attractive space tourism leisure to persuade these high income or rich target clients to consume, when the economic environment will change worse. The Europen space agency (ESA), defines this phenomenon between economic environment variable and space tourism client growth or falling number relationship as: " space tourism is an execution of sub-orbital flight by privately finded and/or privately operated vehicles and the technology development driven by space tourism market."

it seems that space vehicle is one attractive travelling desire tool will be one attractive selling point to influence space tourism leisure consumer individual entertainment choice or attitude to be changed to positive leisure consumption attitude to prefer to play this kind of space tourism activities when economic environment changes to worse. Hence, when economic environment is worse, the economic wore changing factor will influence the space travelling planner individual leisure consumption desire, even it will influence the rich or high income young people or rich retirement people target customer both groups.
As (ESA, 2008) indicated space vehicle will be one kind of attractive leisure tool for spce traveler. So, I suggest that space tourism lesiure journey arrangement needs to include that such as : the space travelers can catch space vehicle to move on Moon or Mars plants land to feel what the different feeling is between during they are catching public transportation tool, such as bus or taxi during the are catching these transportation tools on earth land and during they are catching space vehicle tools on Mars or Moon planet's lands. It is so exicting and fun catching space vehicle tool experience on these both Mars or Moon planets' lands to the young and old age space travelling passengers. Because every space vehicle's speed is not very fast and it will move on Moon or Mars planets slowly. So, any aged pace travelling passengers can attempt to play this kind of space facilities leisure after they catched spacecraft to fly

to these both Mars or Moon planet to stay. They can spend half hour or one hour, even more than one hour to catch the space vehicle to go to anywhere on Mars or Moon to travel. It is possible that they can find exciting and undiscovered things on these both planets.

So, catching space vehicle to go to anywhere on either these both planets journey, it will one essential part of space travelling journey during the economic environment is changed to worse. It is extra attractive space travelling leisure journey to attract space tourism consumer individual leisure desire when economic environment is worse.

Hence, from this perspective then space tourism could be understood as a section of the tourism industry mainly based on technological development, progression and its activitity being related specifically to sub orbital flights. So, if future space tourism providers expect whether the global economic environment changing will be better or worse which won't influence space tourism leisure consumption desire to be changed. The space tourism leisure providers need to persuade the space tourism planners feel space tourism would have to be treated like an already exciting part of the tourism industry. It means that space tourism leisure is one kind of tourism leisure choice to replace common earth tourism leisure consumption. When travelers feel space tourism is another tourism leisure to replace which can replace common earth tourism leisure. It will avoid the worse economic environment changing factor to reduce the rich or high income young people or rich retirement old people whose space travelling leisure consumption desire.
Consequently , the question in relation to, in what kinds of space tourism journey message do space travel providers promote behind whether space vehicle journey promotion message which is needed when economic environment will change worse. I shall be asked, as understanding the meaning in which space tourism is being marketed, communicated is seen as a factor , which can either positively contribute to future development of the tourism industry or lead into prolonging or seen stopping the space tourism industry from its progression.

(2) Space tourism leisure journey management factor

Secondly, space tourism leisure jounrey management factor, how to arrange every space tourism leisure journey which will be one important factor to influence space tourism planner individual tourism consumption desire.

In general, it can includes these several forms of space tourism leisure activities in every space lesiure trip arrangement. The following classification of space tourism include: Terrestria spce tourism (i.e. NASA visit centre, space movies, online space experience); Atmospheric space tourism (i.e. : MIG 31 flight, zero G. flights) and astro (orbita) tourism (i.e.: trips to the international space station-beyond earth orbit) (Cater 2010, Crouch et al. 2009).

Instead of US domestic space tourism market is potential, next country is Japan. First, the study is made by Collins et. al (1994, 1996) in Japan on 3030 research participants, showed that 80% of respondents under the age of 50 were willing to travel to space and out of them 20% were willing to pay year's salary for the space travel experience. Yet, it could be citicized that the Japan people age group of under 50 could be too broad, in general different generations under one groups. nest besides the willingness to go to space, the Japanese study showed respondents motivations for travelling to space, including any fun and exciting attractive space tourism journey, e.g. interest in space walk, catching space vehicle or driving space vehicle on the either Moon or Mars planets, earth view, zeo gravity experience, livin gin space hotels one night or more, watching movies in space cinemas, swimming in space pools, visiting space gardens, running in space sport centers, catching spacecrafts to view earth or Moon or Mars planets.

Hence, it seems attractive space tourism journey can persuade another country's space travelling planners, such as Japanese attempts to satisfy whose space tourism needs. So, different kinds of attractive space trip journey arrangement will be one important factor to influence young and old age travelling consumption desire. It implies that attractive space tourism journey will be one influential factor to encourage other countries tourism consumers attempt to another kind of leaving earth tourism leisure.

So, any space tourism trip destinations and leisure facilities arrangement must need to satisfy space traveler individual leisure needs and every space trip must be more fun, exciting and comfortable and enjoyable feeling to compare general tourism journey in earth. Due to general earth tourism leisure will be space tourism leisure's competitive or replaced leisure product and service. Hence, space trip destinations and leisure facilities choice will be one important factor to influence space travelling planner's consumption desire.

Every space travelling planner will compare general earth travelling leisure's destinations and leisure facilities arrangement whether the space travelling trip arrangement , leisure facilities arrangement and food arrangement, space vehicle or spacecraf leisure comfortable influence issues which will have more satisfactory enjoyable feeling to compare general earth tourism leisure and their spending expenditure to every space trip whether is value or is not value.

Consequently, economic environment changing factor and space trip and leisure facilities arrangement factor which both will influence any space tourism planner individual consumption desire mainly. So, space tourism businessmen ought concern these two aspects of factors how and when will change to adapt any country's potential space traveler's space tourism changing taste and needs in order to follow the new space tourism changing needs easily.

Space tourism market moral ethic risk threats

What are space tourism moral ethic risk during the space businessmen operate this businesses as well as what market threats who will encounter to face difficulties ? I shall give actul cases to explain how and why these challenges will cause to influence any new space tourism businesses development successfully.

(1) Potential accidents aspect

Firstly, space travelers will concern that public reactions to potential accidents aspect during they are catching spacecrafts to travel to space. In fact, it is moral ethic responsibility to any space tourism leisure providers to provide safe, comfortable and non accident occurrence in their whole space trip. Because once time accident will cause any one of space passenger hurt or death. So , it must be any space tourism businessmen responsibilities to concern whether they have enough confidence to ensure none any accident occurrences in every space tourism trip.

Hence, in space tourism industry, government needs have public policy to threaten or prohibit any space tourism leisure providers neglect to often check and ensure any spacecraft machines or equipments are regular opeations, as well as often renew new spacecraft machines when they are old to be used. The policy is a force effort to need them to abide every space tourism leisure safe responsibility to ensure or guarantee any one of spacecraft won't have accident occurrences during it has left earth to fly to space in whole space trip journey from the beginning to the end till to the spacecraft come to earth safely.

Hence, this policy forces any space tourism leisure providers concern to put a monetary value on increased or reduced risk of death, the " value of statistical live", used to characterize when the benefit of safety regulation is worth the cost such regulation improves. So, the country government and the country's space tourism leisure providers both have responsibilities to guarantee all space tourism passengers' life safety. It must not allow any death or hurt occurrences during every space tourism trip.

Even, the country government can have legal action to publish any space tourism leisure providers, when their every space tourism trip has occurred accidents, e.g. fire accident occurrence in spacecarft or spacecrat machines are broken to be damaged and need to be repaired during the space tourism trip. It will threaten to reduce trip accident occurrence, such as this cases. The commercial space ventures may present risk to property as well, such as a fire starting on the ground by launch-related material or problems presented by space debris.

In principle, liability law can provide incentive to deter carelessness that could lead to the destruction of property, although statutory (rather than common law) assignments of liability for commercial launches are somewhat problematic.

Consequently, if the space tourism leisure provider expected to grow space tourism passenger number in long -term time, it must need to ensure none any accidents can occur during any space trip. Otherwise, the space tourism passengers can choose another space tourism leisure provider to replace its spce tourism leisure easily.

(2) Space tourism destinations and space tourism entertainment facilities safe arrangement challenges aspect

Secondly, it is space tourism destinations and space tourism entertainment facilities safe arrangement challenges. Nowadays, commercial space travel is looking more like a real possibility than science fiction. The usual ethical issues related to the safety of the space destination choices and the space tourism entertainment facilities, e.g. space vehicles, space hotels, space swimming pools, space sport centers, space cinemas, space gardens, space farming lands. In this strange space environment and safety concerns are just the beginning as there are othe interesting questions, such as below:

What likely would be a fair process for commercializing or claiming property in any space planets? Such as Moon or mars, when any future space tourism leisure providers who need to build above these any one of space entertainment facilities on these planets to provide to their space travelling customers to play.
How to distribute and manage these any lands ownership to these future space tourism providers fairly and legally?
How likely would a separatist movement be among space settlements to want to be free and independent states?
How to ensure above future space entertainment facilities and space entertainment places are in the safe space environment to be provided to any space travelers to play in any planets, e.g. Moon or Mars etc. planets.

So, concerning how to arrange space entertainment facilities to provide to space tourism clients to play in any safe space environment issue, it will be another concerning question to every space tourism leisure providers. When they decide to choose anywhere to the space hotels, space swimming pools, space gardens, space cinemas or space farming lands or space sport centers. These space buildings will need to be built in the safe, on stable stone lands environment and none any natural distaster, such as large wind or space underground water etc. unpredictable space natural distasterr attack to these space buildings suddenly. Because it has responsibility to any space tourism leisure providers to guarantee any one of these space buildings are safe to be built in the planet's safe land environment. It aims to achieve none any accident occurrences during their space tourism clients are staying to enter these any one of space buildings to visit or play any space entertainment facilities safely, e.g. space vehicle. So, they must need to ceck anywhere the space planet's places to be ensured safe to build any buildings. Then, they can choose the suitable locations to build space entertainment facilities or buildings more confidently.

In fact, any space entertainment facilities, e.g. space hotels, space farming lands as well as space transportation tools, e.g. spce vehicle, spacecraft , these things will be value to be concerned to any space tourism leisure providers and it is business moral ethic responsibility to every one of them, when they plan to develop their space tourism business in any planets.

(3) Space tourism market competition challenge aspect

Thirdly, any provate space tourism development leisure businesses will face market competitive challenge, such as large spacefaring countries, e.g. US, UK have possible to dominate future space tourism leisure business (government can own space tourism leisure business). They will be main actors in space were nation-states. Large spacefaring counties can build the space vehicles, that can take people and cargo into orbit and to the Moon, or Mars crafted international space law and shaped the main investments in space tourism leisure technology.

So, it is possible that the own space technological developed countries, such as US, UK, these countries governemts will have possible to operate public fund to support space tourism leisure business. It implies that private space tourism leisure businesses will face public space tourism leisure business and themselve private space tourism leisure business market competition in space tourism leisure industry.
If these two countries governments also participate this private space tourism leisure market. It will raise market threats to any private space tourism organizations.

Whether will developed countries governments participate private space tourism market? It is possible that new commercial actors began to enter the space tourism leisure industry, looking to disrupt both space launch services ans use space in new exotic ways. For example, the US government also moved its purposeful degradatoin of the global positioning system (GPS), so US government will have effort to dominate GPS global positioning system communication business also. As this GPS communication business case, future US government has possible to decide to participate space tourism leisure business also.

However, in the future, space tourism leisure industry may contribute even more the developed countries, e.g. American, England economy. Space tourism and resource recovery, e.g. mining on planet, Moons and asteroids in particular may become large parts of that space tourism industry if these countries governments participated to this space tourism industry development. Of course, their viability rests on a range of factors, including costs , future regulation, international market competivitive problems and assumption about space technological development. However, these is increasing optimism in these areas of economic production to bring human space tourism leisure enjoyment and space mining resource development benefits. But the space economy is not just about what happens in orbits or how that alters life on the ground. The growth of this economy can also contribite to new innovations across all future possible unpredictable or undiscovered technological development, instead of space tourism leisure or space mining resource exploitation development.

Consequently, any space development technological governments will have possible to bring economic benefits from either only private space tourism leisure organizations or governments and private space tourism leisure both organizations cooperate to participate to achieve space tourism misson to contribute to global economic development and create new jobs to be employed in space labor supply market.

● Can space tourism business bring
economy benefits

It is fact that space tourism activities have a positive and beneficial impact on eveyday life and society and this help space travelers to understand that, despite the high space ticket prices of any space tourism leisure choices. However, space tourism will bring scientific knowledge and technological knowhow and jobs to bring humn tangible or untangible both benefits. I shall indicate these benefits as below:

Although, space tourism leisure seems only leisure activities to be consumed to satisfy any space tourism individual travelling need. However, it can assign space scientists to research and attempt discovery these intangible benefits: Such as tele-communications revolution, satellite weather forecasting, mapping mineral exploration, water resource management diaster mitigation, national security or other undiscovered untangible benefits. Because every spacecraft needs to plan to fly to space, and it will reach any space planet stations, e.g. Mars, Moon planet when it visits these any one planet, the space scientists can attempt to find new undiscovered space resource , e.g. mining or finding new undiscovered satellite weather forecasting method when they can reach these planets to attempt to do space scientifical investigtion to research new space resource , or find any space stones attack to our methods to avoid earth disaster occurrence (national security mission), instead of the spacecraft catchs space passengers to visit these planets to enjoy these planets space entertainment facilities in their space trip journeys.

(1) On space resource benefit aspect

Hence, the space tourism intangible benefits include: space exploration and international cooperation is developing sophisticted space technologies by nations. For example, the images of distant stars and glaxies using Hubble telescope, research laboratory such as international space station to conduct experiments in biology, human biology, physics, Astronomy and meteorology under microgravity environment and testing of the spacecraft systems will be required for space tourism missions to the Moon and Mars.

In the future, human would be able to have unlimited and clean solar energy from space for our industries as well as heating and lighting our homes. In the near future , it would be possible to disposed-off our nuclear waste safely and unexpensively and released towards the sun using a space elevator. We many become a space tourist in earth orbit or on the Moon or Mars. We may carry and extra-terrestial mining and even introduce the development of a multi-planet economy.

(2) On education benefit aspect

Another on education benefit aspect, space tourism can let space travelers to feel actual space learning experiences, during the spacecraft is flying in the space. Their space environment learning experience can include, for example: How many spacecraft have been launched by a given country? How many phone calls are made over a satellite? How many lives could be saved by resue satellites? How they feel differences when they are living in one space hotels, they are swimming in the swimming pools, they are visiting the space garden, they are running in one space sport centers, they are visiting in one space farming land, they are sitting or driving one space vehicle on planet land, or they are catching one spacecraft.

These space learning experience will let they feel what the actual differences between space environment and earth environment. It is one humankind learning experience education service in any space planet's Moon or Mars remote areas, bringing information and tourism entertainment facilities to the masses. The space experience learning knowledge can provide data to let these space travelers to know, such as how ships can be safe at sea, monitoring the threat of pollution, how enhancing durable medical instruments for better health-care enabling hikers and skiers to be located when lost, many more. So, it seems space tourism can bring much positive benefits as no negative impact on space activitied has been found by the society , the investments are made by the nations on space activites are justified and not the waste of money.

- What are the tangible social and economic benefits brought from space tourism?

In most advanced economies space tourism or space resource exploitation industry is seen as an enabler that improves lives and helps to develop both economic and social spheres. Space industry economic can include these aspect: Application of space technology to space tourism navigation, meteorological forcasting and broadcast of on live television and internet connectivity to lesser-known applications, such as precision agriculture, transport, tracking, resource extraction and monitoring of utility networks.

Additional application exists in the disaster monitoring and relif, insurance and military applications. Thus, data coming from satellites is important to all economic sectors, making the world a better and safer place.

International space tourism experience would suggest that space travelling leisure businesses deliver value by providing a central point for academia industry , defence and foreign entities to collaborate among themselves and with government and to facilitate the flow of knowledge and capital.

How can space tourism industry maximize the socio-economic benefits? In fact, our growing use of space derived data and systems is our growing dependence on a better and safer sapce planet, e.g. Moon or Mars and to provide space tourism safe services that space travelling service that space traveler all benefit from industry in telecommunication , health, transport , banking , security and climate change monitoring.

The space tourism positive influence result is long term, the positive contribution to our quality of life is real. In other word, the world for space tourism leisure activities is changing the internationally space tourism sector is experiencing a profound revolution.

In conclusion, space tourism leisure countries with historical leadership in space tourism have been under positive as a result of a tough financial environment leading to the definition of their space travelling technology priorities. In the meantime, new space entertainment travelling leaders, such as US, UK , even China, India have ambitions in space tourism through massive investments in the development of their capabilities in space travelling leisure business aspect.

So, the future space travelling entertainment market is large, due to China and India both have many rich people and high income people, who expect to consume in space tourism leisure trip at least one time in their lifes.

Consequently, worldwide space tourism entertainment industry players are rethinking their busines models and strategies as they experience discuptive innovations, competitive space tourism entertainment and new drivers impacting the spacecraft and any space entertainment facilities manufacturing on Moon or Mars planet, launch and space tourism entertainment related businesses. Thus, we can in fact in talk about a new space tourism business, in which more and more innovative applications of space tourism data are developed dependence on space tourism data in everyday life rises and increasing share of economic growth relies on the space tourism market both in terms of opportunity benefits , e.g. India and China spce tourism potential market development and any concern space tourism job creation to every countries. Hence, space tourism development can bring positive economic benefits to any countries.

Space flight safe factor

To operate one space flight exploration organization, it needs to concern human safe flight factor. I shall indicate it needs to have these three stages to further develop its space exploration to continue to improve its safe space flight for every time of space flight.

Human future space flight missions will include these three stages to continue journey into space. The first stage is short term, NASA's return to flight after the Columbia accident. The second stage is mid term. What is needed to continue flying the shuttle fleet until a replacement means for human access to space and for other shuttle capabilities is available, and the third stage is long term, future directions for the kinds in space. Therefore, the space exploration organization can arrange the three stages to carry out any future space exploration activities. I believe it can improve every time of space flight more safe because it can ensure its space rocket engineering can be improved to raise safe level to let space people to catch to leave our Earth.

However, any human future space flight, which must be enhanced safety of flight when carry on any experimenting space flight exploration missions. Because NASA's safety performance is a very important factor to influence any space people confidence to catch every sky rocket to leave our Earth to do any space exploration activities. So, eliminating and catching rocket risks will be any beginning and end than during the middle of any space flight exploration journeys.

Space people's life is the most important assets of any space exploration journeys. Because of the dangers of ascent and re-entry, because of unknown space environment and because we are still relative new comers, operation of shuttle and indeed all human space flight must be viewed as a development activity.
Thus, any every time space flight exploration missions will need to encourage to invent new space transportation

engines (machine) or fuel, e.g. nuclear fuel to reduce the any space exploration journey accident risks and achieves to spend the fastest time to arrive any new space exploration destination. Thus, I believe any new space exploration flight will improve the space transportation technology and invent more new fuel and new space rocket manufacturing materials for future human any unknown space exploration flight demand. The three stages of improving space transportation include as below:
The beginning stage, for example, the space shuttle is as somehow comparable to civil or military air transport. They are not comparable; the inherent risks of spaceflight are serious higher. The recognition of human spaceflight as a developmental activity requires a shift in focus from operations and meeting schedules to a concern for the risks involves. Thus, the space transportation tools will be improved to protect space passengers safety: the improving the ability to tolerate it, repairing the damage on a timely basis, reducing unforeseen events from the loss of crew and vehicle, exploring all options for survival, such as provisions for crew escape systems and safe havens , barring unwarranted departures from design standards and adjusting standards only under the most safety-driven process.

The mid-term stage, the present shuttle is not very safe to fly in space. Thus, focus on safe return to flight is very important to every space flight journey rules , they leave Earth and arrive any another new planet destination, then come back our Earth again in every space exploration journey (flight). Thus, the energy will be space transportation tool one important factor. If the space transportation tool has enough supply, which won't stay in space and can not fly in space suddenly. Thus, the every time of the human space flight will be taken more time and effort then would be reasonable to expect prior to return to flight. Thus, human space exploration organization needs have higher reliability organization structure to manage every space flight, e.g. one is separating technical authority from the function of managing schedules and cost. Another is an independent safety and mission assurance organization.

It is the capability for effective systems integration perhaps even more challenging than these organizational changes are the cultural changes requires. Thus, the cultural to safe and effective space rocket operations are real and substantial. If the space exploration organization has good culture to let every staffs can communicate easily. I believe the every time space exploration accident will be reduced. Examples include: the tendency to keep knowledge of problems contained within a center or program, technical decisions, without in -depth, peer-reviewed technical analysis, and an unofficial hierarchy or system created by placing excessive power in one office. Such factors interfere with open communication, the shared of lesson learned, cause duplication and expenditure of resources and create a burden for managers to reduce undesirable characteristics threaten safety.

Thus, any space exploration trip, rocket equipment safety and check are very important factor to prepare for every time space flight. The reason is that space flight must guarantee any space people who can come back Earth, if the rocket equipment are poor and lack maintenance. The, the space people whose life is dangerous. Due any space exploration organization mission require human presence in space. For example, president John Kennedy's 1961 charge to send Americans to the moon and return then safely to Earth. Thus, the space exploration organization has attempted to carry out a similar high priority mission that would justify the expenditure of resources on a scale equivalent to those allocated for project Apollo. Also, the space exploration organization has had to participate in the give and take of the normal political process in order to obtain the resources needed to carry out its programs.

Another main successful factor in the final stage, the space exploration organization needs have a clearly defined long term space mission to commit over the past decade to improve future space exploration flight safety by developing a second generation space transportation system. So, for long term, the space exploration organization should need to plan for future space transportation capabilities without making them dependent on technological breakthroughs.

For example, mission for a post Apollo effort that involved full development of low-Earth orbit, permanent outposts on the moon, and initial journeys to Mars planet. Since that rejection, these objective, have reappeared as central elements in many proposals, setting a long term vision for any space exploration flight programs in the future.

Thus, space organization future space exploration mission for 21 St century is to lead the exploration and development of the space frontier, advance science, technology and enterprise and building institutions and systems that make accessible vast new resources and support human settlements beyond Earth orbit from the highland of the Moon to the plains of Mars. Thus, the space exploration organization limit is to conduct the research required to plan missions to Mars and/or other distant destinations. This is the most safe space flight distance limit by the space rocket equipment, machine installation , quality and effort to guarantee space people life safety when who catch the space rocket life safety when who catch the rocket to leave Earth to arrive any space destination in any space flight. However, human travel to destinations beyond Earth orbit has not been adopted because it is too far space flight to cause accident risk. Hence, space exploration organization future invention of long term need is that the role of new space transportation capabilities in enabling whatever space goals need to choose to pursue for human present in Earth orbit vision.

In conclusion, space exploration organization needs to in-depth examination space shuttle safe issue, how to reach an inescapable design of the space shuttle, because that the design was based in many aspects on how absolute technologies and because the space shutter is now an aging system , but still developmental in character, it is in the space organization is interest to replace the shuttle as soon as possible as the primary aim for transporting humans to and from Earth orbit.

- Space exploration organization mission and strategy

Space exploration organization communication strategy

I recommend any space exploration organization needs to the message concerns how the role of humans are actual physical presence in space exploration missions succeed. Because the positive message will give good idea of space exploration and then design and build means to carry out right space exploration direction to let humans to know whether any space exploration missions' goals, objectives and what humans benefits (welfares) who can earn.

The message includes such as these primary role of humans, therefore, is to provide the inspiration and create the vision which produces the motivation in those who then go on to make it a reality, e.g. the space exploration mission is to bring their human intellectual capability to bear in designing the technical systems required for space transportation and devising the scientific experiments associated with space exploration from its beginnings.

Thus, any space exploration organization needs to let humans to know whether what benefits humans will earn after it carries out any space exploration experiments possibly. I believe that the exploration of the Earth's great expanse (the sea, the undersea world, air and land) is the ultimate role played by humans in body and in mind, and apply their intelligence, emotions and most importantly of all, their superior cognitive performance. So, this is the role now played by astronauts, explorers in the true sense of the world.

Why does space exploration organization need to be the role of communicator? The reason is because there is the role that space organization's need to play as communicators, journalists or other communication professional. It is they who provide the link between those involved in the project and taxpayer, who are entitled to be informed about the fascinating news on space.

Moreover, space exploration organization staffs need to give message to let humans to know why these playing roles are entirely human specific and can not be fulfilled by machines. For example, roles prior to human intervention, such as accompanying humans and performing tasks, which are repetitive and unpleasant out satellites too high a risk. By sending out satellites to explore our solar system humans have already begun to explore universe into reality Robots. On the other hand, may be things, but they are not visionaries and nor are they inventors or explorers. Any achievement they accomplish are in fact space organization staffs who designed and programmed them. Also, humans remain the best available cognitive machine in any environment that may be subject to significant variations relative to the model initially made of it. Thus, space exploration organization needs to explain, such as why in the general context of space exploration, even of most missions are robotic, remains technology challenges, it presents push engineers to the very limits of what can be achieved.

In the future, humans will earn these benefits or from any space explorations new invention possibly, such as fuel cells, the microcomputer, high performance materials, medical advances, new management techniques for major

projects, quality and reliability control in industry etc.
The most important space exploration organization needs to positive message to let these groups of people to human what which is doing in our societies. Then, which will cause different actors to become involved from thinkers, visionaries and inspirational figures in the form of writers and film makers to scientists, engineers, philosophers, politicians, economists, physicians, journalists, authors, space travelers (astronauts), but also adults and children space story book readers alike. Thus, space exploration organization is truly multi disciplinary enterprise. Moreover, in the present day, normal escapes being concerned by space, as much due to its contribution to daily life and the knowledge it beings of the Solar system and the universe. It seems space exploration organization will influence human past history will be changed to develop. Whether it brings positive or negative change. The space organization must have responsibility to keep its any space exploration missions leader position in our Earth. It implies it is also one social responsible organization for future global human benefit (welfare). Also space exploration organization needs to let humans know what it's future aims (intentions) are to let humans know whether why it plan to implement. Such as it needs to choose destination has typically been the Moon, it had increasingly come to focus its attention on Mars and even further afraid. Moreover, it also needs to know humans to know the modes of future space transportation which described have tended to be those of the period concerned: ships, horses, birds, balloons, canons, rockets and even others of a more esoteric nature, even solar sail or nuclear soil further space transportation technology development. In addition, space exploration organization can need to describe where are further orbital space stations in space different locations and explained the various applications of satellites and spacecrafts to let human to know clearly.

Even, space exploration organization also need to let humans to know what are their technical challenges, it will encounter in any space exploration stages to let humans to know. Although, the complexity and changer involved in spaceflight is such for a long time to come there will be a need for experts, whose focus by necessity. So, the general public will know or recognize why it's technical challenges will cause and how it will attempt to solve these technical challenges. It aims to let humans to ensure more than 40 years of spaceflight, the adventive of space, which for technical reasons is inevitably reserved to a " happy few", remains very much the preserve of specialists, cooperation to research how to solve any technical challenges to achieve success in any space exploration mission consequently.

- Space exploration organization team leaders and their teams

The first team members are program chiefs and mission message are request to the be backroom generals with a great many human qualities. They must having to achieve great technical exploits and manage their teams with care when at the same time ensuring they deliver in timing and one budget. Even the very best robot-machines and computers available are of no help to them in coming up with the initial idea and architecture for their systems.

Indeed, in that initial stages, some program chiefs, even insist on their management team using only paper and pencil writing. Once the concept has been defined, they then need computers to speed up and develop the project.

When these leader figures are fortunate enough to see their program in orbit and crowned with success, their experience and methods can be of use, to equally computer technical sectors. They can also be passed on to following generations, thus safeguarding, for reasons of economics and security, the know how acquired by their teams. Another team members are scientists and those responsible for the technical side of program are not generally skilled communicators by nature, those with communication to public , such " communicators" could be awarded special prizes. Communication on the space sector can't be left to " communication specialists". Otherwise, there is a risk, it will be perceived to be doomed to failure.

Space exploration organization education is such as strategy space exploration organization communicator, are there to inform, the teaching profession for its part, must perform a vital education role, helping people understand the universe in which they live. Space exploration represents a unique opportunity to explain the situation of our planet within the solar system, asking questions such as: How does the sun function? What are the origins of the Moon? Why does Venus have such a pronounced greenhouse effect? Is there or has there ever been life on Mars? Do asteroids pose a serious threat? There are all questions which today, our schools don't even attempt to answer. Thus, space exploration organization can be one educator role, instead of space explorer role.

Thus, space exploration organization has mission to assist universities to promote space exploration education knowledges. It brings this question: What other technological and scientific program is better equipped to meet these objective than space exploration , with its crewed emissions component. So crucial to the promotion of a European industry, so visible to the general public and so efficient in inducing younger generations to take up scientific and technical careers? Thus, the space education courses can include space exploration industrial applications, a new area of investigation to scientific fields, fundamental physics, cellular and vegetal biomedical research and human and animal physiological research etc. subjects. For example, teaching how to go to Mars or other planets and manage to live these will require a knowledge of how to energy in innovative ways for the purposes of managing electricity generation requirement will be to learn how to manage scare resources in an efficient way (air, water and waste recycling). So, teaching of progress will have to be made in advanced robotics in particular in the area of effective and human robot interaction.

In conclusion, all these space exploration science education knowledge will be important to be taught to let younger to pursue space resource exploration dream for human future live

- Space exploration organization's

Human space life science factor

What is human space life science strategy?

One space exploration organization needs have good human resource strategy to implement every space exploration mission. Critical to this expansion of human presence in space science will enable mission success by focusing on risk reduction and optimizing astronaut health an productivity through space organization's human-centered science, operations and engineering core capabilities.

Thus, the space life science strategy's strategical goals, and objectives were developed on the basis of a situational analysis conducted by key members of the space life science civil service and contractor community, and are consistent with agency goals and scenarios for the future.

This strategy mission is to optimize human health and productivity for space exploration and its vision is to become the recognized world leader in human health, performance and productivity for space exploration . It's strategic goal are aimed at driving innovations in health and human system integration, adapting its portfolio and strategies to the changing environment and creating enthusiasm for space exploration through education. Also, the space life sciences human strategy aims to achieve every space exploration research more success, more efficient, focuses on client (human) needs and facilities communication of risk to public and the value of space life sciences to its stakeholders (governments, universities, societies).

How can human space life science strategy implement?

The space exploration organization needs to be dependent upon healthy, productive astronauts to achieve mission success. Thus, space people health are very important factor to influence their every time space flight in success. If the space people have unhealthy bodies , which will influence whose work performance and every time space exploration mission can't finish easily. Thus, the human space life science strategy needs to ensure every space person has health body to work efficiently and reduce whose death or accident risk when they are working in space environment, due to space environment is one strange bad color environment and it is very difference to our Earth environment to unsafe to work by these factors:

such as, it's temperature is low, cold and no air or oxygen to be supplied to let human to breathe and it has unknown diseases in space. Thus, they will face any life danger when are working in space environment. If space organization lacks one human space life science strategy to help them to fight any unknown attack from space environment. The, they are very dangerous to attempt to catch space rockets to leave our Earth to do any space exploration activities.

However, the space life science strategy can divide these three timeframes consistent with

- Near –term (1-5 years)
- Mid-term (6-10 years)
- Long-term (11-20 years)

The space life science strategy mission is that optimize human health and productivity for space exploration . Thus, all space life sciences human health and countermeasures research, medical operations, habitability and environmental factors activities, and directorate support functions are ultimately aimed at achieving this mission. Their activities enable mission success, optimizing human health and productivity in space before, during and after the actual space flight experience of their flight crews, and include support for ground-based functions.

The space life science strategy vision is to become the recognized world leader in human health, performance and productivity for space exploration. Thus, to achieve the vision for space exploration , they must drive human health, performance and productivity innovations, adapting

their strategy to the changing environment. To do this, the space exploration organization needs have a future scenario for space life science strategy such as below:

- Future core capabilities will include the expertise to address space medicine, the physiological and behavioral effects of space flight, space environment definition and space human factors.
- Research plans are on the basis of a standard –based risk mitigation approach to ensure goals are achieved.
- Civil servants will balance delivery of health and performance services and focused research and technology development with smart buyer and management expertise to integrate space life sciences efforts.
- Strategy relationships will be utilized to achieve the full complement of space life sciences core capabilities necessary to achieve vision and enable mission success.
- Space life science strategy will transition from being a managing partner to a contributing partner, arranging the resources and innovations of other organizations to meet specific exploration needs, e.g. universities, government or business biomedicine organizations.
- Operations will effectively transition the space people skills and facilities from shuttle and assess and engage in additional government and commercial space flight operations opportunities where appropriate.
- An expanded client base that may include additional international and academic partners , as well as commercial alliances.

Situation analysis

A situation analysis was conducted to determine its mission and to identify the factors most likely to influence its strategy development and affect achievement of its goals and objectives . It will trend to concern life sciences and space flight of internal and external environments. It needs to image these assumptions to decide its situation analysis as below:

Thus, the first assumption is that it needs to assume that human will continue to be an important component of the vision for space exploration, and as a result there will be an ongoing need for space life sciences core capabilities, including human-centered science, operations and engineering to mitigate the health and performance risk of human space flight.

Another assumption is in the longer term, there will be a greater focus on crew autonomy and increased human-robotics interaction as mission durations increase and are extended to travel to and on planets, and as a result, these is a continued need for research and development activity focused need for research and development activity focused on exploration risk reduction.

The next assumption is the pace of biomedical change will continue to be more rapid in external versus internal environments. Thus, solutions are more kinds of likely to be developed external to fight any different new unknown new diseases to attack to influence space people health to be poor , even cause death in possible.

What are space life science strategy goals?

On health innovation hands, the space exploration organization will drive advances in medical and environmental health for space flight in order to meet established space life standard and mission needs. Thus , innovation on medicine and biomedical / environment technology and processes will be developed, implement and incorporated into mission achievement.

On education hand, it needs to train in multidisciplinary life sciences, experts in exploration life science and that this is a continuous infusion of space ,life science into the public , government , academic and commercial sectors. Thus, the space life science education aim includes to teach the human system risk management, strategic relationship of any space missions, future space business model and space communication strategies.

The goal-specific strategies and measurable objectives can be developed for years 1 to 5 years It's objectives can include: optimize internal core capabilities throughout the planning cycle to enable the vision for space exploration with budgetary constraints, establish strategic relationship to achieve the full complement of life sciences capabilities necessary to be best in class , establish a center to integrate human health and performance efforts and expertise for space exploration worldwide, implement an internal and external communication plan to increase the life sciences value to encourage space human life education development for long term in commercial space flight sector.

Health innovation goal

Thus, one space exploration organization whose health innovation strategy is the main factor to influence its any overall space exploration missions inn success. Thus, it must need to spend more money and time and resource to ensure its health innovation implement can be succeed to reduce further every time space people's mission of physical illness or death or accident which are caused by space diseases . Thus, it will drive advances in medical and environmental health for space flight in order to meet establish space flight health standards and mission needs. Also, it needs to attempt to do any biomedical experiments to avoid space people who can contact to cause illness from any undiscovered space diseases.

Hence, the invention of space medicine, biomedical / space environmental technology and processes will be developed, implemented often every day/ IT needs to seek or gather every time practical space environment biomedical existing data and knowledge as a base for launching health technologies and to revise every time space biomedical experiment failure to find failure reasons to achieve the most absolute discovered any space unknown diseases biomedical experiment results. Thus, the improved methods and practice or recording data must concern to goals for human space exploration, attempting towards data gathering top continuing to achieve the best levels of evidence for answering operational and clinical questions regarding human health, safety and performance, during space flight and exploration and an evidence-based risk management approach to prioritize tasks.

The space biomedical experiments data gathering can consider human factors engineering, habitability design and human-robotics interaction will be recorded to analyze experiment result every time. These results will be developed, implemented and incorporated into mission architecture solutions to address the human as an element of the overall space system.

- Prediction on future trends in human space flight and future space human life science strategy relationship.

In the future, the relationship between future trends in human space flight and future space human life science will be more close. These reasons are that the trends in terrestrial life sciences will save as change drivers for space life sciences, include advanced in nano health, genetics, biocybernetics, self-constructing materials, human computer interfaces, medical and pharmaco-therapeutics, multi-scale physiological modelling and other biomedical technologies.

In conclusion, due to space exploration organization's objective is low tolerance for a risk and emphasis on risk quantification and reduction activities. Thus, the space human life science strategy will be one important factors to cause any one space exploration organization's any missions in success.

- Why does Japan space organization consider space human life science?

Japan has acquired and advanced various space technologies. Through, these technologies level to allow to play a core role in the international human space activities . However, it's space exploration success is due to it concerns to achieve its space human life science strategy for its main point.

What social benefit from its utilization of the space environment to Japan. Because it concerns how to protect space human life during who are working in space. Thus, it can bring more social benefits to develop its space exploration industry for long term as below:

- Because it's space people can have health bodied, so who can attempt to any space science exploration experiments in space

environment as well as space human life science can raise Japan space people confidence to attempt to do every time space exploration activities in space environment. Consequently, they have confidence to catch rockets to go to space to gather various resource to do any space exploration to get research results more easily, which were achieved through utilization , such as micro gravity environment, that could not be produced on the ground, these outcomes include: protein crystal growth, that may lead to the development of new drugs, materials creation for next-generation semi-conductors, and establishment of the technology for cubesats deployment, etc.

● Due to Japan space exploration organization concerns space people health issue. Thus, it has manned space flight capability can conduct youth development activities , with their own astronauts and such astronaut-led activities have aroused the younger generation's interest in outer space, taught them the importance of making efforts to making of one health space scientists confidence to pursue this space exploration industry.

Hence, when all Japan space scientists who own health bodies, then who can be one expansion of humankind's space of activities in this area create knowledge of planetary science and the quest of health space life and also contributes to the increase and accumulation of intellectual assets of all human beings.

The most reason of Japan's belief of space human life science strategy is very important , because it needs to prove human can live in space environment. Thus, if Japan's space scientists can have health bodies to do any space exploration experiments, then who is still health to go back
Earth. Then , it proves the life support technologies , the space environment and health management and the maximum energy conservation. This leads to the enhancement of corporate brands and international appeal of technical capabilities , and is directly linked to resulting problems Japan faces , such as its aging population and lack of natural resources.

In conclusion, space human life science will influence Japan space exploration industry more success. Otherwise, if it chooses not to implement this space human life strategy. It won't have enough health space scientists to attempt to catch rockets to go to space to do any space exploration experiments more success in long term, e.g. seeking Earth another planets to provide Japan people to live, raising Japan young space scientists confidence to attempt to go to space to do any experiments because the Japan space exploration organization can provide new bio medical invention to supply when they are catching in the space rockets. If they feel that they are comfortable, they can eat or drink the new bio medical invention to avoid the space disease attack to cause their death or physical illness threat.

The Economic Evolution of Space Tourism

The development of space tourism represents a paradigm shift in the global economy, transitioning from state-sponsored exploration to a commercialized orbital marketplace. According to foundational economic theory, the viability of this sector is predicated on the interplay between supply and demand.

As demand for suborbital and orbital experiences grows, providers can leverage economies of scale to reduce costs, thereby transforming space from an exclusive scientific frontier into a sustainable, multi-trillion-dollar industry. This transition is often compared to the early development of the aviation industry, where initial high costs were eventually mitigated by technological maturation and increased flight frequency.

Architectural and Infrastructure Catalysts

The conceptualization of space hotels is central to this economic expansion. Architects and visionaries in the field argue that orbital accommodations serve as the essential infrastructure for an "off-world" economy.

By establishing a permanent human presence in orbit, these facilities create a consistent demand for transport services, which in turn incentivizes aerospace manufacturers to optimize launch vehicles. This cycle of demand is governed by the principle that increased flight cadence lowers the marginal cost per kilogram to orbit, a relationship often expressed in aerospace economics as:Ctotal=Ffixed+VvariableNlauncheswhere Ctotal represents the total cost per unit, F represents fixed infrastructure costs, V represents variable operational costs, and N represents the number of launches.As N increases, the cost burden on individual passengers decreases, facilitating broader market penetration.

Market Dynamics and Long-term Sustainability

Beyond the immediate luxury market, the space tourism sector acts as a catalyst for broader economic development. The integration of aerospace engineering with hospitality design creates a new service-oriented sector that requires specialized labor, supply chain logistics, and resource management.

Furthermore, the "off-world" economy is expected to stimulate advancements in life support systems, sustainable energy, and closed-loop recycling technologies, which have significant terrestrial applications.As noted in academic analyses of emerging markets, the transition to a commercial space economy requires robust regulatory frameworks to ensure safety and market stability, preventing the volatility often associated with nascent high-tech industries.Ultimately, the success of space tourism depends on the ability of private firms to move beyond the "prestige" phase of spaceflight and into a phase of routine, cost-effective operations that mirror the logistics of the global tourism and transportation sectors.

The Economic Implications of Space Tourism

The emergence of the space tourism industry represents a transformative shift in the global economy, moving from a government-dominated sector to a commercialized frontier. While the term "space tourism" often evokes images of wealthy individuals experiencing suborbital flights, the underlying economic rationale is rooted in the principles of price elasticity and the scaling of launch infrastructure. Scholars and industry analysts have long argued that the primary economic benefit of this sector is its potential to drive down the cost of access to space through increased flight frequency and technological innovation.

Regarding the specific inquiry into the economic benefits associated with my opinion, it is important to clarify that in the context of authoritative aerospace literature and established economic studies on the "NewSpace" movement, there is no prominent economist or industry leader by the name of "John Lok" associated with the foundational economic theories of space tourism. It is highly probable that this name may be a confusion with other prominent figures in the field, such as Elon Musk, Jeff Bezos, or industry analysts like Peter Diamandis, who frequently discuss the "virtuous circle" of launch cost reduction. The economic benefits typically attributed to the growth of this industry by experts include the stimulation of a "space-based economy," the creation of high-skilled jobs, and the development of reusable launch vehicle technologies that lower the cost per kilogram to orbit.

The Virtuous Circle of Launch Costs

The economic model for space tourism is heavily dependent on the concept of price elasticity. As noted in foundational aerospace texts, the cost of launching payloads into Low Earth Orbit (LEO) has historically been a barrier to entry for commercial ventures.

By increasing the volume of flights—driven by tourist demand—companies can achieve economies of scale. This process is often described by the following relationship: if C represents the cost per launch and V represents the volume of flights, the total efficiency gain can be modeled as a function of cumulative experience, often expressed as $C(V)=C0V-\alpha$, where α is the learning rate. This reduction in cost benefits not just tourists, but also the deployment of satellite mega-constellations and scientific research platforms.

Broader Economic Impacts

Beyond launch costs, the industry fosters a supply chain ecosystem that extends into manufacturing, materials science, and software development. The "NewSpace" economy, as documented in various economic analyses, suggests that the commercialization of space acts as a multiplier for terrestrial industries. By transitioning from a cost-plus government contracting model to a competitive commercial model, the industry incentivizes rapid prototyping and risk-taking, which are essential for long-term economic growth in the aerospace sector. In conclusion, space human life science is very important factor to influence future every time human space exploration mission successfully.

Reference

Reference

Hartwell, R.M. (1983). The origins of capitalism. A Methodological Eassy. in Pejovich (1983).

Needham, J. (1963), Poverties and Triumphs of the Chinese scientific tradition, in Crombie (1963).

Phaal, R., Farrukh , C. & Probert , D. (2004). Technology roadmapping- A planning framework for evolution and revolution.

Technological Forecasting and social change, 71, 5-26. htpps:// doi. org/10.101016/ S00401625(03)00072-6.

Reference

Cater Iain , Carl 2010, " Steps to space: Opportunities for astro tourism development, tourism management 31 (2010); pp. 838-845; Elsevier Ltd, DOI: 10:1016/j.tourman. 2009.09.001

Collins Patric, Iwasaki Yoichi, Kanayama Hideki, Ohnuki Misuzo 1994, comercial implications of market research on space tourism. journal space technology and sciences , vol. 10 no 2, 94 Autumn, pp.3-11. copyright: Japanese rocket society; available at: www.spacefuture.com/archive/commercial-implications-of market-research-on-space-tourism.shtml.

Collins Patric, Marita M; Stockmans R. and Kobayahi S. 1996. "Demand for space tourism in America and Japan and its implications for future space activities ". sixth international space conference of Pacific basic societies; Marina del rey; California: Advantages in the Astronautica science (AAS paper no AAS 95-605) vol. 91. pp. 601-610. Available at:
http://m.internationalaerospaceconsulting.org/upload/space % 20Future%20-%20Demand% 20for%20space%20Tourism%20in% 20America%20Japan.pdf

ESA 2008, " Richard Garriott, millionaire American space tourist. blasks off of international space station". published in 12.11.2008. Huffington post, seen on i01.04.2015; available at: http://www.huffington.com/2008/10/ 12/richard-garriott-milliona-n-1333940.html.

Klemm, G., & Markkanen, S. (2011). IN A Papathanassis (ed.) The long Tai , tourism (pp.95-103). Weisbaden, Germany : Gabler Verlag; Springer Fachmedien Weiesbaden GmbH.

KSCVC Visitors, 2013; MRI 2013 Market by Market

Von Der Dunk , F. (2012). The integrated approach. Regulating private human spaceflight as space activity, aircraft operation, and high-risk adventure tourism. Acta Astronautica, 92(2), 199-208.

www.ingramcontent.com/pod-product-compliance
Lightning Source LLC
LaVergne TN
LVHW060028210926
848481LV00013B/3813